CW01022942

The Life & Times of

PATRICK COMERFORD O.S.A.
(1586-1652)

Counter-Reformation Bishop
of Waterford and Lismore
1629-1652

MICHAEL G. OLDEN

© Michael G. Olden

Published by Michael G. Olden
Printed by Intacta Print, Waterford.

All rights reserved. No part of this publication may be reproduced or transmitted in any form or by any means, electronic or mechanical, including photocopy, recording or any information storage and retrieval system, without permission in writing from the publisher.

ISBN: 978-0-9573882-0-8

Cover photography by Terry Murphy, Waterford.
Front: Roman Catholic Cathedral, Waterford.
Back: Church of Ireland Cathedral, Waterford.
Design: Intacta Print, Waterford.

For the late Professor F.X. Martin O.S.A.
in fulfilment of a promise

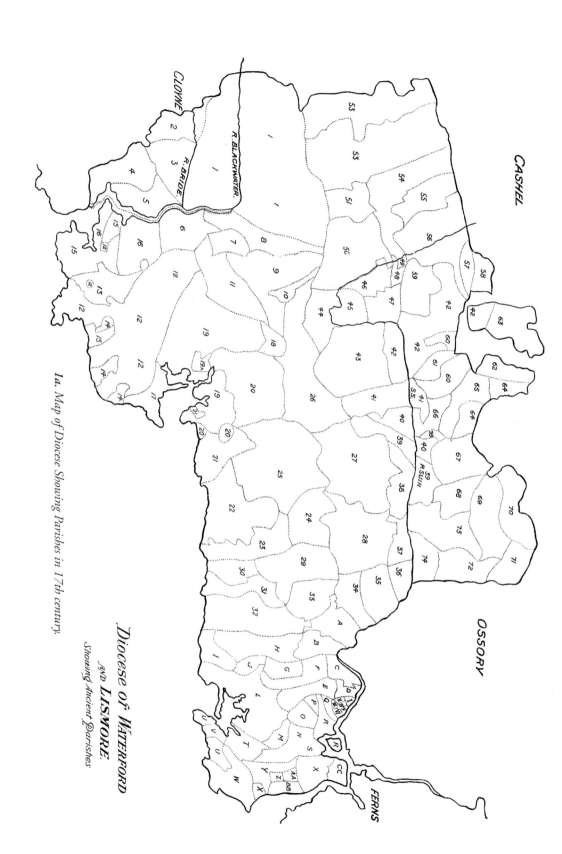

CLOYNE

CASHEL

OSSORY

FERNS

R. BLACKWATER

R. BRIDE

R. SUIR

Diocese of Waterford
and Lismore.
Showing Ancient Parishes

1a. Map of Diocese Showing Parishes in 17th century.

INDEX TO MAP.

DIOCESE OF LISMORE.

DIOCESE OF WATERFORD.

Contents

Map and Illustrations

List of Abbreviations

Anal. Hib   *Analecta Hibernica, including the reports of the Irish Manuscripts Commission* (Dublin 1930 -)

APF   *Archivio della Sacra Congregazione di Propaganda Fide*

Archiv. Hib.   *Archivium Hibernicum or Irish Historical Records* (Catholic Record Society of Ireland, Maynooth, 1912 -)

AV   *Archivio Vaticano*

BV   *Biblioteca Vaticana*

Collect. Hib.   *Collectanea Hibernica: Sources for Irish History* (Dublin, 1958)

Comment. Rinucc. Richard O'Ferrall and Robert O'Connell, *Commentarius Rinuccinianus, de sedis apostolicae legatione ad foederatos Hiberniae Catholicos per annos 1645-9*, ed., Rev. Stanislaus Kavanagh (I.M.C., 6 vols., Dublin, 1932-49)

Corish, Ir. Catholicism Patrick J. Corish (ed.), *A History of Irish Catholicism* (26 fascicles, Dublin and Melbourne, 1967 -)

Father Luke Wadding *Father Luke Wadding: Commemorative Volume,* ed. Franciscan Fathers, Dun Mhuire, Killiney (Dublin, 1957)

Gilbert, Ir. Confed. J.T. Gilbert (ed.), *History of the Irish Confederation and the War in Ireland 1641-3.....* (7 vols., Dublin, 1882-91)

Hist. Studies   *Historical Studies: Papers read before the Irish Conference of Historians* (I-VII, London 1958-69; VIII, Dublin, 1971, IX, Belfast, 1974)

I.E.R.   *Irish Ecclesiastical Record* (171 vols., Dublin, 1864-1968)

I.H.S.   *Irish Historical Studies: The joint journal of the Irish Historical Society and the Ulster Society of Irish Historical Studies* (Dublin, 1938 -)

Ir. Cath. Hist. Comm. *Proc.*	*Proceedings of the Irish Catholic Historical Committee* (Dublin, 1955 -)
I.M.C.	Irish Manuscripts Commission, Dublin
I.T.Q.	*Irish Theological* Quarterly (17 vols., Dublin, (1906-22) Maynooth, 1951 -)
F.L.K.	Franciscan Library Killiney
Lettere	*Lettere della Sacra Congregazione di Propaganda Fide*
Lynch, *De Praesulibus Hib*	John Lynch, *De Praesulibus Hiberniae potissimis* *Catholicae religionis in Hibernia, serendae, propagandae,* *et conservandae authoribus,* ed. J. F. O'Doherty (I.M.C., 2 vols., Dublin, 1944)
N.H.I., iii	T. W. Moody, F. X. Martin, F. J. Byrne (eds.), *A new History of Ireland, vol. iii, Early Modern Ireland,* *1534-1691,* (Oxford, 1976)
Irish Statutes	*The Statutes at large passed in the Parliaments held in Ireland* *from the third year of Edward II, 1320, to the twenty-sixth* *year of George III a.d. 1786* (20 vols., Dublin, 1786-1801)
S.O.C.G.	*Scritture Originali Riferite nelle Congregazioni Generali di* *Propaganda Fide*
Spicil. Ossor.	*Spicilegium Ossoriense: being a collection of original letters* *and papers illustrative of the history of the Irish Church* *from the Reformation to the year 1800,* ed. P. F. Moran (3 vols., Dublin, 1874-84)
Wadding Papers	*Wadding Papers, 1614-38,* ed. Brendan Jennings (I.M.C., Dublin, 1953)
Waterford Arch. Soc. Jn.	*Journal of the Waterford and South-East of Ireland* *Archaeological Society* (19 vols., Waterford, 1984-1920)

Note on Dates

During the period 1582-1752 the old style of dating which followed the Julian Calendar (named after Julius Caesar) was still followed in England and Ireland. This was ten days behind the new style, or Gregorian Calendar which had been introduced by Pope Gregory XIII in 1582 and which was followed by most countries in Europe, including the Papal States. As well as the ten day difference, the beginning of the year in the old style was Lady Day (25 March) but in the new style it was 1 January.

Bishop Comerford and many others when writing to Rome used the old style of dating. In any of his letters which were dated between 1 January and 25 March he always adds 'stylo veteri' to his date. This was important because the year would be different in both styles. For example, 8 January 1629 old style is 18 January 1630 new style; 24 February 1629 old style is 6 March 1630 new style. In such cases I give both dating styles, one in parenthesis. In 1752 the Julian Calendar of old style dating disappears completely.

Preface and Acknowledgments

The seventeenth century is complex. For Ireland it was particularly complex. In his introduction to his very fine overview of the century: 'Seventeenth Century Ireland – Making Ireland Modern', Raymond Gillespie makes use of a quotation from another outstanding contemporary historian, British Professor John Morrill, which is weighty and apt: "Whether we attempt to view the British problem (in the early modern period) as an example of the development of 'composite monarchies' or as an agent of the colonial expansion of the Atlantic seaboard powers, Ireland is a special case. It just will not fit in to any of the established patterns".

My attempt in this work, through the examination of the life and work of one seventeenth century Irishman, is to shed some light, whatever the wattage, on a special aspect of the special scene that is Ireland of that period. I have chosen an Irish Catholic bishop, not the most distinguished bishop of his time, but still significant. Over the years he has become my friend, and the scene of his labours and efforts, the diocese of Waterford and Lismore, is the part of Ireland which cradled me. I believe that a broadly biographical approach may illustrate the complexity of the Irish situation and may also provide the scope and structure which permit asides and relevant digressions which may prove necessary and helpful.

Patrick Comerford was a member of a newly established, post reformation, Catholic hierarchy in Ireland. It was a hierarchy composed, by and large, of well chosen intelligent members, all schooled in the universities of Europe, all speaking several languages, all gripped by a special urgency to create a new church for the future. Only a few members of that hierarchy have been given the attention they deserve. I offer the present contribution as a further instalment which may lighten the load of a future historian and be an encouragement to others to build up the general story of that interesting group of seventeenth century bishops.

The activity and progress of contemporary Irish church affairs was strongly influenced by the attitude of the government and administration; many church problems of the period can be understood only by a consideration of that attitude. The early life of Patrick Comerford must receive some attention because it affords an opportunity to discuss, in some manner, the background and training of an Irish counter-reformation priest. It also provides an uncontrived opportunity to form a view as to the progress, or lack of it, which was made by the counter-reformation in Ireland prior to Comerford's appointment as bishop in 1629.

In the light of the available documents, I attempt to sketch his efforts as bishop to reorganise a diocese which had been deprived for well over half a century of the ministrations of a bishop, and the problems which attended his task. Understandably, it is with the problems that one becomes mainly and inevitably involved. In a certain and real sense it had to be through the problems that growth and retardation, success and failure, make their presence felt. The reports submitted to Rome from Ireland deal far more frequently with complaints and grievances than with heartening accounts of progress and achievements. There were internal problems within the changing church itself, created, in the main, by the attempt of a new bishop to draw into the new centralised system, envisaged by the Council of Trent, the regular clergy, who for so long had been endowed with missionary permits and privileges. There were tensions too within the hierarchy itself, such as the serious disagreements between the Metropolitans and Suffragans. There were many external problems also, some arising from the suspicion and intolerance of the state, others from the deprivations of ecclesiastical property, and from the encroachments of the established church.

The involvement of Rome was very significant. It is hardly too sweeping to say that the counter-reformation in Ireland was, from first to last, a Rome-directed movement. One has to examine the significant contribution made by the Congregation of the Propagation of the Faith, *Propaganda* (founded 1622) towards the establishment of rules and decrees for the right governing of the Irish Church.

A very special source for this study has had to be the archives of *Propaganda*. Of particular importance have been the *Scritture Originali Riferite nelle Congregazioni Generali*, which contain many reports on the Irish mission of the time. The chaotic arrangement of the volumes of these *Scritture* for the first forty-seven years of Propaganda's existence makes it quite difficult to trace relevant material. One can never complacently declare that no important document has escaped one's notice. Fruitful though this service is, it is undeniably true that some reports and letters from Ireland to Rome never reached their destination at all. Bishop Comerford frequently complains to Luke Wadding that the latter, who lived in Rome, obviously was not receiving many of the letters sent to him. Letters, which seem to have taken from two to six months to travel from Ireland to Rome, were usually sent with casual travellers, through the Low Countries, Paris or the Iberian region. There was constant danger that they would be lost en route, or their progress halted by a change of plan on the part of their carrier. Sometimes the same letter was sent with several different travellers in the hope that at least one copy would eventually reach Rome. And sometimes in such cases the impossible occurred, and all the copies reached their destinations. I have come across three versions of the same letter in the archives from Bishop Comerford, two written in Latin and one in Portuguese. However, the remarkably thankful fact is that so much correspondence did succeed in finding its way to Rome; without it the historian of this period of Irish church history would indeed be impoverished. I have consulted every volume of the *Scritture* in which I had reason to believe there might be relevant material. One can only hope that one has been fortunate in not missing really important matter.

I have consulted the first twenty-one volumes of the *Acta* of Propaganda which cover the period up to 1652. The *Acta*, which are really the recorded decisions taken at the regular and special meetings of the Congregation of Propaganda, are very valuable in any study of Rome's attitude and contribution to the Irish church of the time.

The *Lettere della Sacra Congregazione* for this period proved disappointing; the references to letters sent to Ireland are relatively few. Only one volume of *Scritture Riferite Dei Congressi, Irlanda*, covers the period 1622-1668, and proved of little help. The *Acta* and *Scritture* of any of the Particular Congregations for Irish affairs at this time are found, not separately, but amongst the *Acta* and *Scritture* of the General Congregation.

The Irish matter in the various Vatican archive collections where one might hope to find information on this period, such as the Barberini and Borghese Mss. and the *Nunziatura di Fiandra* and the *Relationes Status* submitted to the Congregation of the Council, have been published. Except for the last which were of serious value, they did not prove directly helpful.

Useful information, often incidental and never in great quantity, was drawn from other Roman archives, namely those of the Augustinian and Jesuit general houses and the Irish college. A most important Roman collection, though now housed in the Franciscan archives Killiney, Dublin are the Wadding Papers, some already published. The process of transferring much of this archival material to University College Dublin is taking place – where I am sure it will be housed under optimum conditions. The Wadding Papers, published and unpublished, include the very large correspondence received by Luke Wadding from Irish bishops and others. Fortunately for the present study, Patrick Comerford, a kinsman and close confidant of Wadding, corresponded more frequently with Wadding than most. His letters are frequently of that intimate personal type, often colourful, even acerbic, which convey mood, and sometimes bias, as well as information to the historian.

In studying the counter-reformation period in Ireland the lack of source material here at home is a great disappointment. Time and again tantalizing problems would be solved if one could only have recourse to diocesan or parochial registers, or to the correspondence received from Rome and elsewhere by individuals, especially bishops and religious superiors. The very dearth of such documentary records tells us much while, at the same time, denying us the detailed information which we would so wish to possess.

In examining the role of a bishop in the 1640's it is indeed good fortune that so much expert study and publication has been undertaken, especially in recent times, by first class scholars. Few periods of Irish history have been so well served by such excellent research.

I owe a large debt of gratitude to many who have helped me prepare this study; to friends and colleagues, to archivists in Ireland and abroad, to the librarians in the National Library, Dublin, Marsh's Library, Dublin, Franciscan Fathers in Killiney, Augustinian Fathers in Ballyboden, Cistercians in Mount Mellary, Director and staff of Waterford Museum of Treasures.

I was fortunate to have been helped by good and able friends in arranging the illustrations, which I feel are very necessary in a work of this kind. I appreciate the work of Annette Toms who had the unenviable task of preparing the typescript.

Finally, I wish to record my appreciation of the kindness of Bishop William Lee of Waterford and Lismore for providing me with conducive conditions for study and for graciously making light my administrative and pastoral responsibilities in order that I could engage in my studies.

Michael G. Olden

Chapter One

OF A STRONG WATERFORD FAMILY

In common with many Irishmen of his time, and especially Irish churchmen, the subject of this story takes in a wide geographical canvas. Patrick Comerford was a citizen of the city of Waterford, born in 1586, died in 1652 in the city of Nantes, France. His life was cast in many different places, for longer or shorter periods. Outside of Ireland he spent time in Bordeaux, France, in Lisbon and Coimbra, Portugal, in the islands of the Azores in Mid Atlantic, in North Africa, in Spain, in the Spanish Netherlands, in Rome. His lifespan of sixty-six years marked perhaps the most distinguished of all European periods in the history of Ireland. Irishmen, priests and lay, were to be found all over Europe, students and professors in the great continental university centres. His own hometown, Waterford, was particularly distinguished for the presence of so many brilliant citizens who were celebrated throughout the continent.

His lifespan was in exciting times also. It was exciting for him to be exposed in centres such as Coimbra, Louvain, Rome where the new theology of the counter-reformation was being taught by outstanding scholars such as the great Suarez, and where the combative pastoral practice, arising from the Council of Trent, was presented to aspirants to the priesthood as the route to follow when they returned to their native country. As bishop of Waterford and Lismore 1629-52 Comerford became a member of an Irish hierarchy which was very distinguished. The members of that hierarchy built up a catholic church in the country which was refreshingly different in outlook from its predecessor of reformation times. Throughout the 1640's he, with his fellow bishops, spearheaded exciting movements in the political arena. They were actively involved in the Confederation of Kilkenny with all the complex hopes and disappointments which were associated with it. When Patrick Comerford left Waterford for the continent of Europe for the first time in 1603, Queen Elizabeth I had just died. When he left Ireland, from the fort of Duncannon, for the last time – in 1650 – Oliver Cromwell had just departed from Ireland after a hectic campaign. Much had happened to Ireland and to the Irish church in the exciting period between these two departures.

As well as situating him broadly in time and place it is necessary also to register him in terms of his caste or class. His family was an Old English family, prominent in a city that had Viking ancestry but, with the Anglo-Norman invasion of the twelfth century, became the second city of the island, noted for trade and wealth and a port that sent its ships not just to the great centres of the west and south west of the English coast, but also to the ports of France, Portugal and Spain as well.

The term Old English is applied to the descendants of those Normans or, more correctly, Anglo-Normans, who began to settle in Ireland after their first arrival in Bannow Bay and Baginbun on the Wexford coast in the twelfth century. The other racial terms which are

1

applied to the inhabitants of Ireland in Patrick Comerford's time are Old Irish and New English.[1] The Old Irish, descendants of the pre invasion Irish, whose language was the native Irish, and had their own social patterns with their chieftain and clans and distinctive culture, dwelt largely in rural Ireland. The third racial group is designated New English, the descendants of those who had come to Ireland long after the invasions and who were largely the beneficiaries of the various plantations and who received lands available after the dissolution of the monasteries in the 1530's and 1540's. The New English enjoyed much land in Munster and, indeed, throughout the whole country. One of their outstanding success stories was Richard Boyle, the first Earl of Cork, who acquired by various means large tracts of land in the valley of the River Blackwater and whose main seat was the Castle of Lismore which had in medieval times been the residence of the bishop of Lismore.[2] Boyle's sons, especially Lord Broghill, Earl of Orrery, were to acquire still more land as part of the Cromwellian settlement in the 1650's.

The Old English, so long established in Ireland, were landed people of enormous status in the country. Their chief representatives were the great earls of Desmond, Ormond and Kildare. They generally lived harmoniously with the Old Irish but they had a healthy distrust of the New English and its entrepreneur mentality and attitude. The Old English were catholic and largely remained so throughout the reformation period. Their language was English but the majority could understand Irish also. The palesmen and the large bulk of inhabitants of the premier towns such as Waterford, Wexford, Cork, Limerick, Galway, and Clonmel were loyal to queen or king and pope and also viewed themselves as good citizens of the land which they had inhabited for centuries. The built-in tensions created by such disparate loyalties was to create in the Old English of Ireland a severe and complicated strain as the sixteenth century gave way to the seventeenth.

The citizens of the large towns such as Waterford were a special section of the Old English class.[3] The majority were not landed people but they were connected through blood and marriage with substantial people of the land. Their particular source of wealth lay in trading and industry and especially in lucrative export activity. In Waterford the Comerfords were highly placed amongst the Old English families. They occupied a leading place among the families such as Rice, Lincoln, Sherlock, Lombard, Walsh, Strange, Wyse, Butler, Aylward, Dobbyn, Wadding, White, Morgan, Power, Madan, Corr. Over the centuries they had occupied important official roles in the city administration. Fulke Comerford was Mayor in 1448, Philip in 1570, Nicholas in 1586. Philip Comerford was Bailiff in 1558 and 1567, Nicholas in 1570, Patrick in 1572, 1573, 1574. Bailiffs were replaced by Sheriffs in 1575. Patrick Comerford

---

[1] An exciting and comprehensive treatment of the Gaelic and Old English elements in Irish society is to be found in Bernadette Cunningham, *The World of Geoffrey Keating, History, Myth and Religion in Seventeenth-century Ireland.* (Dublin, 2000)

[2] Canny N, *The Upstart Earl: a study of the Social and Mental World of Richard Boyle, first Earl of Cork, 1566-1643* (Cambridge, 1982)

[3] Clarke, Aidan *The Old English in Ireland, 1625-42* (London, 1966)

was Sheriff in 1577, Nicholas in 1575 and 1581, Edward in 1581, George in 1593, 1594, 1595, John in 1598.

No Comerford appears on such official lists after 1598. Nearly all the family names mentioned above disappear during the Cromwellian period and they never reappear. In their place on the official city lists by 1660 we find more evidently New English names such as Smith, Heavers, Lloyd, Mason, Newport. An old order had passed by the midpoint of the seventeenth century.

In the late sixteenth and early seventeenth centuries, when the Irish colleges were established in many parts of Europe, the name Comerford of Waterford occurs very frequently in the lists of students for the priesthood attending the colleges. As early as 1565 we find Nicholas Quemerforde, Waterfordiensis, Hibernus, Theologus, attending the University of Louvain, having previously graduated in Arts from Oxford. He was later to join the jesuits at Madrid in 1585.[4] He was possibly the first of thirty to forty Comerfords from Waterford who were to study in various colleges and universities in Europe during this period.

Robert Comerford, the father of Patrick, the future bishop of Waterford and Lismore, does not figure in the official lists of administrators of Waterford city. But we do learn from the great Parchment Book of Waterford that he, in 1599, was paying 7¼ d rent to the Corporation

> for the house wherein Edmond Keane dwelled and nowe Robert Quemeford dwelleth, next St. George is chapple in Mylke Street and he also pays 6d rent for the woodgarden of the same.[5]

Mylke Street, presumably the street where people purchased their milk, later in the eighteenth century was reduced to Milk Lane and later still it disappeared when Arundel Square was being enlarged in the nineteenth century. St George's chapel was one of the several chantry chapels erected by wealthy families in the complex of the cathedral of the Holy Trinity.

Robert Comerford was married to Anastasia White, one of the White family of Clonmel and Waterford, members of whom were prominent in both towns and from whom distinguished churchmen of the sixteenth and seventeenth centuries were descended.[6] Peter White, former dean of the diocese of Waterford and Lismore, conducted a renowned grammar school in

---

[4] Nicholas Comerford returned from Oxford to Waterford but was turned out of whatever preferments he had because he would not conform himself to the established religion, according to Anthony a Wood, quoted by Moran in his introduction to Peter Lombard's *'De Regno Hiberniae'* (Dublin 1868). He went to Louvain in 1565 and took his doctorate in theology there in 1576. He was again in Waterford in 1577, as is mentioned by Sir William Drury in a letter to Walsingham on 16 April of that year. Comerford left Ireland again and went to Madrid cf. Joseph P. Spelman, *'The Irish in Belgium',* *Irish Ecclesiastical Record* (1886), 642

[5] Byrne, Niall J (ed) *The Great Parchment Book of Waterford Liber Antiquiquissimus Civitatis Waterfordiae,* (Dublin, 2007), 195

[6] Power, Patrick, *Waterford and Lismore A Compendious History of the United Dioceses* (Cork, 1937), 1-53 gives a comprehensive account of the Catholic character of the diocese, particularly the city area, and of the prominent priests and bishops who were attached to the diocese.

Kilkenny which was attended by many famous pupils, including Peter Lombard of Waterford, future archbishop of Armagh who died in Rome in 1625, Richard Stanihurst, Dubliner, author and commentator on Ireland and religion, James White, vicar apostolic of Waterford and Lismore who was in charge of the diocese when Queen Elizabeth died in 1603 and who led the catholic people into the cathedral to celebrate when the news of her death arrived. It was he also who engaged in theological debate with the Lord Deputy, Mountjoy, who arrived outside Waterford with his troops to quell the ardour of the catholics in the city. There was Thomas White, S.J., founder of the Irish college in Salamanca in 1592 and who was involved also in the establishment of the Irish college in Seville in 1612 and Santiago in 1605. Thomas' brother Stephen, also a jesuit, was a renowned scholar in Europe, taught in Gras and Ingolstadt before returning to Ireland where he continued his historical researches and helped both the Four Masters and Seathrún Céitinn (Geoffrey Keating). He died in Galway in 1648.

Patrick Comerford had at least two brothers and three sisters. His brother, Philip, befriended him when he returned to Waterford as bishop in 1629. Another brother was captured by pirates, probably off the Irish coast in 1625 or 1626. In some of his letters and in other documents there are references to nephews, named Hackett, Giraldin[7] and Carew. An epitaph for his tomb in Nantes Cathedral was signed by two nephews: Patritius Hackett, Rector Ecclesiae S. Patritii Waterfordiensis and Nicolaus Geraldinus, nuper Vicecomes Waterfordiensis.[8] In common with many of the Old English families of Waterford, the Comerfords had many priest members in their family. Between 1590 and 1640 sixteen Comerfords became jesuits.

Patrick Comerford grew up in Waterford city. In 1600 when the population of Ireland, very difficult to estimate accurately, was probably about one million, Dublin probably had a little more than five thousand, Waterford and Cork probably had about 2,400 each.[9] Richard Stanihurst in his description of Ireland in 1577 writes of the city of Waterford as follows:

> properly builded and very well compact, somewhat close by reason of their thick buildings and narrow streets. The haven is passing good, by which the citizen through the increase of foreign traffic in short space attaign to abundance of wealth …. There belongeth more ships to the cities of Waterford and Wexford than to all Ireland besides.[10]

---

[7]   In the period under examination Geraldin was frequently used in Ireland in place of Fitzgerald.
      Fitzgerald was the family name of both the earls of Desmond and the earls of Kildare.
[8]   The lengthy epitaph and a eulogy in Latin may or may not have been placed in the tomb. They clearly
      were intended for that purpose. The epitaph is to be found in Moran, *Spicilegium Ossoriense*, vol. iii,
      89. The eulogy 'Umbra Proloquitur', spoken by the deceased from the shadow of death is to be
      found in *Brussells Bibiotheque Royale*, *Mss. II*, 2590, f. 222R
[9]   This estimate is based on Butlin, R. A., 'Land and the People c1600' *New History of Ireland,* iii, 159,
      and on Cullen, L. H. 'Economic Trends, 1660-91' ibid., 390.
[10] Stanihurst, Richard, 'A treatise containing a plain and perfect description of Ireland….Raphael
      Holinshed, *Chronicles (1807-8 ed.)*, vi, 21, 30

Fynes Moryson, writing somewhat later in 1617, states 'the houses of Dublin and Waterford are for the most part of timber, clay and plaster'.[11]

Waterford was prosperous due to its handsome port and the confluence in its harbour of three rivers, Suir, Nore and Barrow. Imports and exports were its stuff of life. Its extensive hinterland, enhanced by waterways, and, by the standards of the time, reasonable roadways, encouraged business and trade. Its exports to England, Wales and continental ports were largely of fish, pork, hides, leather, livestock and timber. Its imports were of essentials such as salt and coal and luxuries like wine and fine cloth. The city was protected by strong turreted walls, the oldest being the Viking encircling the little old Viking town, the more recent were the Norman walls surrounding the expanded medieval city.[12] As a substantial port town, Waterford looked to the continent and the English ports with greater interest than it had in its fellow towns in Ireland. Its communication and trading with Irish towns was done by water more usually than by land. In common with the other large Irish towns, Waterford was governed by a merchant oligarchy, composed of prominent families like the Comerfords. Between the prominent families there was much intermarriage; outsiders rarely entered into the picture. For example the two most influential Waterford churchmen of the period, both of whom spent much of their lives in Rome, Peter Lombard (1554-1625), archbishop of Armagh, and Luke Wadding (1588-1657) were first cousins and were also related to Patrick Comerford and to archbishop Thomas Walsh of Cashel, also a native of Waterford city (1580-1654)[13].

The citizens of Waterford cherished the many charters which had been granted to the city over the centuries. The first had been granted by King John in 1215. The most recent in

---

[11]   Fynes, Moryson, *An Itinerary………*, iii, 498
[12]   Howard, B Clarke (Ed.), *Irish Cities* (Cork, 1995) contains two excellent chapters on Watrerford and its development over the centuries: Terry Barry 'Like a little castle: Waterford in the Middle Ages' 191-203, Julian Walton 'From Urbs Intacta to Crystal City: Waterford 1495-1995' 204-217
[13]   Illustrative of the kinship between outstanding Waterford churchmen of the seventeenth century is a plaque erected in Waterford's Catholic Cathedral in 1919. It was erected, largely, due to the exertion of Canon Patrick Power, diocesan historian. It contains the names of only a few Waterford men but they are indeed noteworthy. Of special interest is the fact that they were all related to each other expect for one, Geoffrey Keating (Seathrún Céitinn), the priest historian, who came from the western end of the diocese. All, including Keating, are of Old English stock.
       Luke Wadding, O.F.M. (1588-1657) Historian and Theologian
       Peter Lombard (1554-1625) Archbishop of Armagh
       Patrick Comerford, O.S.A.(1586-1652) Bishop of Waterford
       James White, Vicar Apostolic of Waterford c.1693
       Michael Wadding, S.J. (1585-1645) Spiritual Writer
       Peter Wadding, S.J. (1583-1644) Chancellor of University of Prague
       Thomas Walsh, (1580-1654) Archbishop of Cashel
       Paul Sherlock, S.J. (1595-1646) Scripture Scholar
       Ambrose Wadding, S.J. (1583-1619), Theologian
       Geoffrey Keating, (1570-1650), Gaelic Scholar
       Luke Wadding, S.J. (1593-1650) Theologian
       Stephen White, S.J. (1575-1646) Historian
       Thomas White, S.J. (1556-1622) Founder of Salamanca
       Bonaventure Barron, O.F.M. (1620-1696) Theologian and Poet

our period was that of King Charles I in 1626. As was often the case with charters, this last was granted in return for money - £3000, a welcome donation to a monarch who was notoriously in need of money. The citizens valued their charters.[14] They also valued and esteemed the kings and queens who had granted them. Supporting the monarch especially in turbulent times was a valued hallmark of Waterford traditions. The first of the Tudors, Henry VII, gratefully acknowledged Waterford as one of the special places in Ireland where he could count on absolute loyalty. The citizens of Waterford had proved resolute in refusing to acknowledge the two pretenders, Lambert Simnel in 1487 and Perkin Warbeck in 1497. King Henry declared that the city deserved his deepest thanks: *Urbs Intacta Manet Waterford*. The motto has remained ever since irrespective of the reasons why it was uttered in the first instance. Many years later another Latin encomium was applied to Waterford, this time, it is thought by the Papal Nuncio Rinuccini, during the heady days of the Confederation of Kilkenny when the archbishop was solemnly welcomed to the city by the bishop, Patrick Comerford, and the civic rulers, and escorted to the cathedral. Rinuccini was reminded of the splendour of Rome and declared that Waterford was indeed a *Parva Roma*. In the seventeenth century, and particularly during the years of Patrick Comerford's episcopate, it could be said that the *Urbs Intacta* found itself in a somewhat uneasy relationship with the *Parva Roma* as Waterford city, county and diocese, had to deal with the complicated consequences of its loyalty to the King of England and its commitment to the Pope of Rome. In 1650, when Patrick Comerford had to go into exile to France where he was to die two years later, there was no longer a king of England and the lord protector, Oliver Cromwell, who replaced him, had set in train very speedily a course of action which closed the Roman catholic churches of Waterford and removed from the government of the city the staunch Old English catholic families such as the Comerfords, Waddings and Lombards. To borrow a couplet from the poet, John Oxenham:

> then came the wind and the driving rain, life was never the same again.

The introduction of the protestant reformation to Ireland in the sixteenth century naturally had deep significances for a city such as Waterford where English influence was traditionally strong and the actions of the crown were well respected. As the reign of Elizabeth advanced and increasing pressure to conform began to be applied, it became gradually and increasingly clear that a reluctant choice between crown and faith might be on the horizon and the indication was becoming more clear as to what that choice would have to be. However, for

---

[14] Walton, Julian, *The Royal Charters of Waterford* 39-52
The following give good, though differing overviews of the history of Waterford
Smith, Charles, *Ancient and Present State of Waterford*, 2nd Ed. (1774)
Ryland, R.H., *History, Topography and Antiquities of Waterford*, (1824)
Hansard, Joseph, *The History of the County and City of Waterford*, (1870)
Egan, P.M., *History, Guide and Directory of Waterford* (1894)
Downey, Edmond, *The Story of Waterford* (1914)

varying reasons, neither Elizabeth nor her three Stuart successors, James I, Charles I and Charles II, all protestants, were never in a position to grasp the nettle fully and make a complete issue of the religious question.   During the reign of James I (1603-25) the mayor and other officials of Waterford refused to take the oaths of supremacy and uniformity, as the law commanded. At the national level, pressure was applied unevenly and sporadically but there was never a clear outcome. On 4 July, 1605 a proclamation was issued commanding that 'Seminary priests and jesuits' leave Ireland by10 December 1605 and directing the laity to attend divine service in accordance with the law. On 13 July, 1611 this proclamation had to be reissued with continuing force against 'Seminary priests and jesuits'. The desired effect did not occur and even the hanging in Dublin of the aged bishop of Down and Connor, the franciscan Cornelius O'Devany in 1612, only reinforced determination on the part of catholics. Again, on 17 October 1617 a further proclamation ordering the banishment of all priests educated abroad was without effect. Some months later, 23 January 1618, an example was made of Waterford by the revocation of its charter as punishment for the continued election of recusants to high office in the city. Waterford remained without a charter until 1626. Near the end of the reign of James I, on 21 January 1624, yet another proclamation was issued ordering all catholic ecclesiastics to leave Ireland within forty days, but the proclamation had to be suspended one month later due largely to international repercussions. An even more stern proclamation was issued by lord deputy Falkland on 1 April 1629 forbidding the exercise in Ireland of any ecclesiastical jurisdiction deriving from Rome and ordering the dissolution of all religious houses on pain of confiscation. Immediately after the proclamation, Falkland was summoned out of Ireland. There was a serious attempt to enforce the 1629 proclamation but its effects were very temporary and, after a period of 'lying low' the catholic clergy felt free to continue at lease a guarded ministry, particularly in Dublin.[15]

In 1617 the lord deputy, Sir Oliver St. John, demanded the surrender of Waterford's charter, the guarantee of so many privileges and immunities. The response said a lot. The charter was quietly surrendered and the usual strong protestation of loyalty to the king was made on behalf of the city. The lord deputy dolefully remarked that none of the citizens of any consequence would ever make pretence of conforming in order to save their charter. He even suggested that the only solution for such a dilemma was to send over from England new inhabitants to rule the city. In fact the mayor and corporation of Bristol were contacted and sounded out as to their reaction if the city of Waterford was offered to them. The response to the hypothesis was a clear and understandable negative.

Reports were made from time to time concerning the open practice of the catholic faith in the city. One made around the time that Patrick Comerford was born is interestingly graphic. Its author was Marmaduke Middleton, the protestant bishop of Waterford and Lismore (1579-

---

[15] This period is very well treated in Clarke, Aidan, 'Plantation and the Catholic Question, 1603-23', New *History of Ireland*, vol. III, 187-232, and also 'Selling Royal Favours' 1624-32 Ibid, 233-42`

7

82). It is worthy of lengthy quote as it illustrates the ordinary, indeed the daily, practices of what Middleton calls 'the stiff-necked, stubborn, papistical and incorrigible people of the city of Waterford'.[16] Middleton states:

> Such is the miserable state of this wretched city, that all things are done contrary to the Sacred Word and blessed will of the Lord, and also her Majesty's most godly proceedings in causes spiritual – The Gospel of God utterly abhorred – The Church, in time of divine service, of all heads eschewed (nisi a paucis et id forma tantum). The Sacrament contemned and refused – Massing in every corner – No burial of the dead according to the Book of Common Prayer, but buried in their houses with dirges and after cast into the ground like dogs – Romerunners and Friars maintained amongst them. Public wearing of beads and praying upon the same – Worshipping of images and setting them openly in their street doors, with ornaments and deckings. Ringing of bells and praying for the dead, and dressing their graves divers times in the year with flower pots and wax candles. – No marriage agreeing with God's law and her Majesty's proceedings for either they marry in houses with masses, or else before two or three laymen without any minister taking of hands, and so they live as man and wife. - No punishment for this or any other sin. – The windows and walls of the churches full of images. – They will not deface them, and I dare not, for fear of a tumult. – None of the women do come either to service or sermons. – And to conclude, virtue is rejected and all vice embraced. This, Right Honourable, is the lamentable condition of this proud and haughty city of Waterford. – God convert their hearts.[17]

Marmaduke Middleton, an Englishman, was bishop of the established church in Waterford and Lismore. He was the first unambivalent church of Ireland bishop of the diocese. His two predecessors, Patrick Walsh (1551-78) and Nicholas Comyn (1519-51) lived in confusing times and showed confusion in their own episcopal lives. Middleton's tenure was short, only three years, after which he was transferred to Wales as bishop of St. David's where he had a controversial decade, ending in his deprivation from the see in 1592. He died a year later in 1593. As noted above, he understandably laments the refusal of the Roman catholics of Waterford to cooperate with the evangelizing efforts, and they were meagre, of himself and his clergy. But at least he had standing in the laws of the realm. He and his clergy had legal access to income which they might rightly consider inadequate and they had legal right to church buildings in which to conduct their religious services even though they might complain about the state of disrepair of these churches. In years before and for many years after Marmaduke Middleton's presence in Waterford, the Roman catholics had no bishop and few priests. Neither

---

[16] Brady, Maziere (ed), *State Papers concerning the Irish Church in the time of Queen Elizabeth,* 41
[17] Ibid, 39-40

had they any legal right of access to the church buildings in Waterford city and throughout the diocese. In the burial of their dead throughout the diocese, they had to secure the permission of the protestant ministers in order to open a plot in the cemetery and they had to pay the fee demanded for securing that permission.

In Waterford city, when Marmaduke Middleton was bishop and when young Patrick Comerford was born, there were six traditional parishes which contained churches, some in reasonable repair, others in serious disrepair. The cathedral of the Holy Trinity, commonly called Christchurch, St. Patrick's, St. Stephen's, St. Michael's, St. Peter's and St. Olave's, St. John's Within (the walls). These buildings and the graveyards attached to them were the legal property of the established church and its ministers. Throughout the rest of the diocese, from Killea in the east to the western boundary with the diocese of Cloyne and the northern boundary with Ossory and Cashel, there were one hundred and two parishes with their churches, sometimes more than one in a parish, all under the legal control of the established church.[18]

The church had held much property in early christian Ireland, in medieval Ireland, and in the period leading up to the reformation. In the diocese of Waterford and Lismore there had been old Celtic monastic foundations: in Ardmore (St. Declan), Ardfinnan (Árd N. Fhionáin – Height of St. Finnian, the leper), Clashmore (St. Mochua), Dair Inis and Molana (St. Molanfide), Lismore (St. Carthage or Mochuda), Mothel (SS Cuan and Brogán). These foundations had outreach or mission churches and centres through which the people were served long before medieval religious orders or secular parishes came into being after the eleventh century.[19]

In medieval times, with the arrival of recently established religious orders from the continent and England, new foundations of monks and friars and nuns began to make their appearance. In Waterford city, the benedictine priory of St. John the evangelist was established about 1190. It was under the protection of the benedictine priory in Bath, England. It was suppressed in 1536 and its property passed into lay hands, those of William Wyse of an influential Waterford family.

The cistercians had two foundations in the diocese: Inishlounaght, called *de Surio*, near Clonmel, founded in 1147 and initially colonized from Mellifont. It was suppressed in 1540. A much smaller foundation, Glanawydan or Glangrath in Monksland, in the parish of Kill near modern Bunmahon, was founded in 1170, but it did not last long and never had an abbot of its own but remained under the aegis of Inishlounaght. It had ceased by 1227.[20]

---

[18]   Power, Patrick, *Waterford and Lismore, a Compendious History of the United Dioceses*
[19]   Ibid, *The Place Names of Decies*
[20]   For religious houses in Ireland cf. Gwynn & Hadcock, *Medieval Religious Houses Ireland*. A thorough treatment of the cistercians is in Ó Conbhuibhe, Colum O.C.S.O *The Cistercian Abbeys of Tipperary*, also unpublished papers in Power Papers, Mount Melleray Abbey

The canons regular of St. Augustine had a significant presence in the diocese of Waterford and Lismore. There was Mothel, founded in 1140 and suppressed in 1540, Molana, founded in 1141 and suppressed 1541, Cahir, founded in 1200 and suppressed in 1540. In Waterford city there was St. Catherine's (site of present court house), founded in 1207 and suppressed in 1539.[21]

The dominican friars had a priory in Waterford city, St. Saviour's, later known as Blackfriars. It was founded in 1226 and suppressed in 1541. There was also probably a cell in Clonmel but it came much later in the 1640's and did not last long.[22]

The franciscan friars had three substantial foundations in the diocese: Waterford city, Greyfriars, founded in 1240 and suppressed in 1540, Clonmel, founded in 1269 and suppressed in 1540, Carrick-Beg, founded in 1336 and suppressed in 1540. There was a franciscan third order regular foundation, a community of lay people, single and married, in Ardfinnan. The date of its foundation is unknown but it was dissolved in 1542. The first and third Order of franciscans – again with several lay members, was set up in Curraheen, near Aglish in West Waterford. Little is known about it; it seems, for a time, to have been a home for the Youghal franciscans after their suppression and dissolution in the 1540's. There was a franciscan presence in Curraheen as late as 1731.[23]

The carmelites were not represented strongly in the diocese of Waterford and Lismore. There is vagueness and even uncertainly about a carmelite foundation in Clonmel. There are references to it and there is mention about its suppression in 1541 but there is no reliable knowledge as to its property. There is more certainty, but still vagueness, about a carmelite foundation in Ardfinnan. It was located about a mile from Ardfinnan, Our Lady's Abbey or Mainistir Mhuire, in the parish of Ballybacon. It is noted in the report on carmelites in Ireland which is published in Spicilegium Ossoriense. The heads and commoners of Clonmel, in a presentation made in 1537, state that the prior of this house was living in 'flagrant, continued and open immorality and that there was no divine service, though the office was endowed to the extent of a plowland'. There are still significant ruins of the church and of the lady chapel attached to it.[24]

The augustinian eremites (O.S.A.) , as distinct from the augustinian canons regular, had a priory in Dungarvan which was founded in 1290 and was suppressed in 1541. In the seventeenth century, the eremites established themselves in Waterford city on the site of St. Catherine's priory of the canons regular (present-day Courthouse) in 1629. They also, invoking Roman approval, laid claim to the abbey of Mothel which had also belonged in pre reformation

[21] Gwynn & Hadcock, op. cit, 197

[22] Flynn, Thomas O.P., *The Irish Dominicans 1586-1641*, 28-30

[23] Bhreathnach Edel, Macmahon Joseph O.F.M., McCafferty John (eds), *The Irish Franciscans 1534-1990*, 6, 321, 322, 323; Gwynn & Hadcock, op. cit., 243-4, 246, 260

[24] Gwynn & Handock, op. cit., 288-90

times to the canons regular. Patrick Comerford was to become a member of the Portuguese province of the augustinian eremites.[25]

In addition to the older religious orders which had been present in the diocese of Waterford and Lismore since medieval times there was an effective jesuit presence in the diocese. The presence increased as the seventeenth century progressed. The jesuits were present in Waterford city and in Clonmel where they engaged very much in teaching not just in the towns but in the outlying areas as well. We will return to the jesuit contribution in a later chapter when we deal with the relationship between bishop Comerford and the regular clergy in general.[26]

There is evidence of three convents or nunneries which existed in the diocese of Waterford and Lismore from medieval times, two of them surviving into the sixteenth century. It is very likely that there was a convent of St. Clare in Carrick-on-Suir which was founded in the late fourteenth century and was possibly one of three such franciscan convents in Ireland. The convent was suppressed in 1542. Another convent or hospice had been attached to the cistercian abbey of Inishlounaght almost from the beginning. But, in the course of his noted visitation of the Irish cistercian houses, Stephen of Lexington insisted, despite much opposition, that this convent be discontinued in 1228. The third convent in the diocese was founded in the fourteenth century by the Butler family, predecessors of the earl of Ormond, at Mollough on the river Suir near Newcastle. It was surrendered in 1540 by its last prioress, Joan Power. There had been an early Celtic nunnery in Mollough. The medieval convent is not believed to have been one of the continental type convents. Presumably, it was a descendant, with considerable remove, from the early Celtic convent.[27]

In the interest of completion and in order to present the religious heritage of Waterford and Lismore as bishop Marmaduke Middleton and young Patrick Comerford would have known it in the declining years of the sixteenth century, a brief treatment of remaining institutions and church property might be appropriate. The diocese possessed well above average remains of the crusading orders, the knights templar and knights hospitaller. The knights templar were first on the scene in the twelfth century. On their dissolution in 1308 their houses and considerable property were entrusted to the knights hospitaller.

The earliest foundation of knights templar dates from 1180 and was established at Crooke and Kilbarry on the River Suir adjacent to Waterford city, and much further west along the coastline at Rincrew, established also in 1180, on a hill overlooking the mouth of the River Blackwater near Youghal. On the suppression of the knights templar all three passed to the knights hospitaller who were assigned the responsibility of maintaining the suppressed templars for the rest of their lives. In the thirteenth century a preceptory of templars was established at

[25] Ibid., 299, 305
[26] McRedmond, Louis, *To the Greater Glory of God. A History of the Irish Jesuits*, 14-84
[27] Gwynn & Hadcock, op. cit., 310-11

Rathronan in South County Tipperary which was in the diocese of Waterford and Lismore. It also passed to the hospitallers in the early fourteenth century. In west Waterford at Bewley near Kilmolash there were remains of a small ruin from the fourteenth century which probably was a preceptory of the knights templar. More likely, because of the smallness of its size, it was a camera or small inn or resting place.[28]

The knights hospitaller, as well as inheriting the property and possession of the templars in the fourteenth century, had established three preceptories of their own: at Killure near Waterford city in 1212, at Crooke in 1314, at Kilbarry in 1314. There is no record of preceptors or members at Killure after 1348. In 1541, the properties of Crooke, Kilbarry and Killure were held by William Wyse of Waterford to whom reference has already been made in connection with the properties and church of St. John in Waterford city.

Hospitals and hospices were part of the religious and pastoral scene in the diocese of Waterford and Lismore in medieval times. At Carrick-on-Suir there was a hospital of St. John the Evangelist, under the rule of St. Thomas of Acon, founded c.1236, which lasted for at least a century and may will have been the hospital that was declared suppressed in 1536 after which it was given to Thomas Butler, 10th earl of Ormond in 1557.

In Clonmel a leper hospital was associated with St. Stephen's church. We read concerning it as late as 1510. In Dungarvan there was also a leper hospital, under the patronage of St, Brigid, but little is known about it. In the taxation list of 1302-06 we read of a 'hospital with vicarage' at Faithlegg in east Waterford and it is recorded that the knights hospitaller held tithes of the church at Faithlegg.[29] The canons regular of St. Augustine had a hospice at Molana near the mouth of the River Blackwater near Youghal. Lismore, with its ancient and venerable history, had in its monastic complex one of the earliest leper hospitals in Ireland. This healing christian presence may well have fitted in with the culdee spirituality which was a noted feature of the Celtic monastery of Lismore. The prior of Lismore leper hospital was acknowledged as having jurisdiction over all other leper houses in Ireland.[30]

Waterford city, at the close of the sixteenth century, had four hospitals or hospices: St. John the Evangelist which had been part of the early thirteenth century benedictine monastery, dependent on the monastery at Bath, England, St. Stephen's, a leper hospital, which was founded after 1185 and confirmed by King John to the poor of the city. It stood in St. Stephen's street. It was endowed by the Power family of Dunhill and had revenues from lands at Leperstown in the parish of Killea and from properties throughout the city. This hospital was not dissolved at the general suppression in the mid sixteenth century, the endowments being

---

[28] A thorough research has resulted in a fine study by Byrne, Niall, *The Irish Crusade, A History of the Knights Hospitaller, the Knights Templar and the Knights of Malta, in the South-East of Ireland* (Dublin, 2008)
also Gwynn & Hadcock, op. cit., 327-57
[29] Gwynn & Hadcock, op. cit., 310-11
[30] Ibid., 354

used later to maintain a public infirmary which, as late as 1746, had two homes for about forty sick people. This hospital went together with St. Stephen's church.[31] St. Mary Magdalen's chapel was outside the city walls and was associated with St. Stephen's hospital but was located in the area of St. John's Hill. Patrick Power suggests that the site of this hospital is that later occupied by the leper hospital, known in modern times as the County and City Infirmary[32] The latter hospital ceased to exist in 1987. Finally, there was the Waterford Hospital of the Holy Ghost. This was founded in 1544 in the suppressed franciscan friary at Greyfriars. It ranks as a foundation of King Henry VIII. In it were housed indigent people, usually females. In a new place, and under different administration, the Holy Ghost Home is still flourishing in Waterford city to this day.

We have been noting the property of one kind or another which, over the medieval and early modern centuries, had been connected with the diocese of Waterford and Lismore. Bishop Marmaduke Middleton and his protestant successor, as well as bishop Patrick Comerford, who was catholic bishop from 1629 till 1652, had a common complaint: they and their clergy suffered greatly from poverty. In the past, particularly up to the dissolution of the monasteries and friaries in the late 1530's and early 1540's, the church had as its inheritance vast lands, houses and other property. But, as time went on, most of the church property had passed into lay hands. Those lay hands, over the years, farmed the land, leased the property, and sometimes sold it to the best bidder, quite often to members of the New English section of society which was arriving in Ireland. The property was largely in the hands of protestants but not always so. Many of the Old English catholics also had made profitable purchases of former church lands from the descendents of those who had been granted the lands at the time of the dissolution of the monasteries. The hard fact was that by 1600 the erstwhile church property had been lost to the church, be that church protestant or catholic. What the leaders of both churches were left with was a people, a flock, on whose generosity they had to rely for revenue and maintenance. The protestants alone had legal rights to make demands on the people, on the small protestant population and also on the large, though often impoverished, catholic people. They also had legal rights and control over all places of worship and parish residences from the cathedral down to the smallest little country church or ruins of a church. The catholic leaders had no such rights. They might console themselves that they had a large and staunch flock, but its capacity to give them support was very small indeed. Both churches, protestant and catholic, had serious financial problems which caused them to experience friction with each other and also gave rise to internal troubles within their own clergy and laity.

---

[31] Power, Patrick, *History of Waterford and Lismore*, 334
[32] Id. 'Inquisition of 1661 regarding the Lazar or Leper House, *Waterford, Waterford Arch. Soc. Jn.*, vol i(1894-5) 115

Chapter Two

EARLY LIFE AND EDUCATION

Patrick Comerford was born in 1586 into the city and the civil and religious scene which we have attempted to describe. Waterford was the scene of his childhood and youth; the people, the churches, the streets of the city, would have been well known to him. From 1586 till 1603, Waterford city was his base and home. From 1603 till the early 1620's he was to live mainly on the continent of Europe, broadening his vision, learning new languages, becoming a theologian, a priest and a teacher. In the early 1620's he would return again to Ireland for a few years; then followed a shorter period in Spain and Rome where he was appointed and consecrated bishop of Waterford and Lismore. From 1629 till 1650 he never left his native land or, scarcely ever, his native diocese. In 1650 he sailed for St. Malo; two years later death came to him in Nantes on 10 March 1652.

The schooling of the children of the more affluent citizens of towns such as Waterford was clearly of a very high quality and standard. It had not been the intention of the authorities, in dissolving the monasteries and other religious houses, to leave Ireland without schools. Commissions on education were set up over the years which resulted in an education act passed by lord deputy Sydney's parliament in 1570 which laid down provision for the setting up of grammar schools throughout the country. Within a decade of this act, schools, which were officially recognised as protestant, were opened in towns such as Cork, Limerick and Waterford.[1] Difficulties were soon to arise because catholic pupils did not fit comfortably into what we would now refer to as the ethos of such schools. They, instructed no doubt by their families, would not have a problem recognising the queen in prayer and in other situations as sovereign, but they would not wish to acknowledge the sovereign as head of the church.

For a young boy like Patrick Comerford, schooling would have begun at an early age in one of several schools, sort of household schools, privately conducted in the city. Later, much later, such schools would have been termed Dame Schools; today we might call them kindergarten or pre-schools; their venue would have been a private house. The name, Mrs. Barden, is mentioned as the name of the lady who conducted the school to which Patrick Comerford was sent in Waterford. Luke Wadding, two years junior to Comerford, is said to have attended the same school. Perhaps it could also be said that Wadding's first cousin and also a relation of Comerford, the famous Peter Lombard, might have attended Mrs. Barden's school ten years previously. Barden was a well known name in Waterford but there is no verifiable contemporary evidence that a Mrs. Barden conducted such a school. There is a folk tradition in Waterford that she did. This may have its origin in J. A. O'Shea, O.F.M. *The Life of Father Luke Wadding*, published in Dublin in 1885. The reference in this book to Mrs.

---

[1] Hayes-McCoy, G.A., 'Tudor Conquest and Counter Reformation, 1571-1603, *N.H.I. vol. III*, 138-140

Barden's school was taken up by diocesan historian, Patrick Power, in a series of articles published in the Catholic Record of Waterford and Lismore under the title *Parva Roma* in 1914. He tells of Comerford and Wadding and Thomas Walsh, later archbishop of Cashel, learning at Mrs. Barden's academy 'to spell and count and to read from a horn-book'.[2] Accurate or not, such would, in general, have been the early schooling of privileged young catholics in the city of Waterford during the late sixteenth and early seventeenth centuries.

Luke Wadding in his writings does not refer to his early schooling but he does write of his native city with considerable sentiment many years later in the Annales Minorum.[3]

> My native town, which is called Port Lairge by the natives and Waterford by the English, while known to Ptolomy as Menapia, was founded, according to Camden, by Norwegian pirates; others by an Ostman named Sitaricus, about the year 155. It is situated in Munster and is remarkable for its unique position on the river Suir, for its commodious harbour, for its wealth and population and for its splendid buildings; but more so for the constancy with which its inhabitants have clung to Christian piety and to the Roman catholic religion. It is for the latter reason that it is dearer to me, and is held in greater honour, than on account of its being the place of my birth. In the many sufferings and grievous persecutions to which its inhabitants have been subjected, it has always remained firm in its attachment to the true religion, and therefore it deserves its motto 'Urbs Intacta Manens', because of its fidelity to God much more than because of its loyalty to temporal sovereigns. It is also most worthy of praise because of the intense devotion of its inhabitants to spiritual things; because of the all-embracing charity with which they receive pious strangers and suffer for the faith; because, living up to the maxim of Tertullian 'be ye more solicitous for the faith when in danger' – they watch over the purity of the faith with increasing vigilance and take the utmost pains to hand it down without stain to their children. Hence the city has been known by the name of 'Parva Roma' – 'Little Rome'. This small tribute of praise I owe to the place of my birth.

As we consider Patrick Comerford's youth in Waterford city, a youth he would have shared with young men like Luke Wadding, a quotation of Patrick Power in the articles mentioned above might be in order. It is imaginative but, at the same time, informative, as he deals with the unanswerable questions, and graphically suggests what life might have been like in the times of Wadding and Comerford and so many others. The picture, as painted by Power, has a value.

---

[2]   Power, Patrick, 'Parva Roma, Waterford of the early seventeenth century'; *The Catholic Record of Waterford and Lismore* II (Oct. 1914) 429

[3]   Wadding, Luke, *Annales Minorum* (2nd Ed.) Vol III, 45-6

Concerning the early years of the famous men enumerated we have, alas, only the most meagre account. What would we not give now for a diary lighting up with its intimate revelation the firesides around which the youths foregathered! How we should value their books of academic exercise or the familiar letters they wrote to one another, or to their parents, from Peter White's school at Kilkenny, or later, from Flemish colleges and Spanish convents. No early documents have unfortunately survived; grim persecution threw lengthened shadows over the land, and preservation of written documents was not easy, even if it were safe. We should like to know what recreations the youth engaged in and who were their intimate companions. Did they play bowls on the local green without the Close Gate, or fish for pike in Kilbarry on free days, or go bird-nesting by Kilcohan and Couse-Michael in spring, or bath at Gracedieu in summer! Probably they did all four, and probably they were more fanatically acquainted with 'the lovely green banks of Suir' than the average Waterford youth of today.[4]

Power is clearly drawing on the victorian period in which he himself grew up near the city of Waterford, but he paints a picture that probably had validity in the youthful days of Patrick Comerford.

When we leave the elementary school of Mrs. Barden (if it was Mrs. Barden!), we are on more firm ground. We know that there was in Waterford a classical school conducted by a catholic who was a man of renown, indeed of international renown. His name was John Flaghey (or Flahy or Flaghy). In the archives of the Irish college, Salamanca, we find the list of applicants who joined the college community from 1595 till 1619. Each applicant was obliged on entry to take three oaths: of obedience to the superiors; to observe all the college rules; promising to return after ordination to serve on the Irish mission. As well as the oaths each applicant also had to indicate the previous education which he had undergone. There are one hundred names on the list and, of these, sixteen mention the education they have received from John Flaghey of Waterford city.[5] Some declare that they have studied under Flaghey for four

---

[4]   Power, Patrick, op.cit., 399

[5]   O'Doherty, Denis, (ed) 'Students of the Irish College Salamanca (1595-1619), extracts from Los Archives del Real Colegio de San Patricio de Nobles Irlandeses, Salamanca; *Archiv. Hib* iii (1913) 1- 36

The sixteen names from the Salamanca list are:

Luke Vennet, Ferns,	1602		
Francis Grant, Waterford,	1602		
William White, Waterford,	1602	aged 19,	5 years with Flaghey
John Lombard, Waterford,	1602	aged 19,	5 years with Flaghey
Luke Wadding, Waterford,	1608	aged 16,	4 years with Flaghey
Thomas Wadding, Waterford,	1609	aged 15,	4 years with Flaghey
Thomas White, Compostella,	1609	aged 24,	2 years with Flaghey
Robert Walsh, a priest,	1609	aged 35,	5 years with Flaghey
Michael Browne, Cashel,	1609	?,	5 years with Flaghey
John Cormick, Waterford,	1609	aged 22,	7 years with Flaghey
Francis Braye, Lismore,	1609	aged 23	4 years with Flaghey

16

years, some for more than that. It is a remarkable commentary on Flaghey's reputation that in his school or house in Waterford he was able to bring his students to a point in the humanities where they could be accepted to study theology at the university of Salamanca. One student states that he studied logic under Flaghey. The youngest student on the list was Thomas Wadding of Waterford, aged fifteen years. The majority ranged from nineteen to twenty-four. Flaghey was clearly a highly respected teacher. It is very likely that other Irish colleges in Europe at the turn of the century were also receiving students who had been prepared in Waterford by John Flaghey.

Patrick Comerford does not appear on the Salamanca list. He never studied in Salamanca. But we know that he too, like so many others, had studied in Waterford under John Flaghey. Comerford's continued education was to take place in Bordeaux, Lisbon and the University of Coimbra. Flaghey's contribution to the education of Comerford was touchingly commemorated in an address presented by the students of the newly founded Irish College in Rome on the occasion of his consecration as bishop in 1629. This address which was published in book form is entitled *Coronatae Virtuti Reverendiss. D. Patriti Quemerfordi ex Sacro Eremit. D. Augustini Ordini Episcopi Waterfordiensis et Lismorensis Inaugurati Plausque Seminarii Hibernorum de Urbe, Roma, 1629.*[6]

In Flaghey's school, Latin and Greek would have been taught to an advanced level. English also would have been prominent in the course. One wonders if Irish would have featured? Probably not. The Old English of Waterford, the race to which Patrick Comerford, Luke Wadding, and so many others in Flaghey's school belonged, would have been much more interested in Latin, English, Greek and probably French than in Irish. The Irish language would have been the language spoken throughout County Waterford but it was little used, if at all, in the cities and large towns of Ireland with the exception of Galway. Probably Irish was understood in places like Waterford city and it may have been the language of some homes, but the majority of the citizens used English and, by 1600, nearly all correspondence especially of an official nature was in English. It is interesting that, in the many letters of bishop Comerford in Waterford to his great friend Luke Wadding in Rome, some are in Latin, some in Spanish, some in Portuguese, some in English, but none in Irish. Some of the letters are a mixture, perhaps Latin with paragraphs in Spanish or English but one never comes across a line of Irish in any of them. It is worth recording that, when Patrick Comerford left Waterford for the Irish College in Bordeaux in 1603, one of his companions was Geoffrey Keating, better known as

---

Dermot Hilan, Kildare,	1609	aged 20,	6 years with Flaghey
Robert Tue, Ossory,	1613	aged 19,	4 years with Flaghey
Matthew Sharpe,	1613	aged 19,	5 years with Flaghey
Richard Tobin, Limerick,	1617	aged 21,	6 years with Flaghey
Patrick Dobbin, Ossory,	1617	aged 23,	? years with Flaghey

[6] I have traced only two copies of this address, one in the National Library, Dublin, the other in the Franciscan Library, Killiney, Co. Dublin. The title in English might read: 'The praise of the Irish College, Rome, on the crowning with virtue of the Most Rev. D. Patrick Comerford of the Order of Eremites of St. Augustine as Bishop of Waterford and Lismore, Rome 1629'.

Seathrún Céitinn, from the north western part of the diocese of Waterford and Lismore. He became a diocesan priest and was later a subject of Patrick Comerford who was bishop of the diocese. Seathrún Céitinn, like Comerford, was of Old English stock but he loved all things Irish and wrote very significant treatises on Irish history and on spiritual and religious subjects. His most famous work, which is enormously significant as a history of Ireland both because of its content and because of the beautiful Irish in which it is composed, is Forus Feasa ar Eireann (a basis of knowledge about Ireland).[7]

When Comerford left John Flaghey's school, the Irish phase of his education was not yet finished. He had yet to attend the highly praised school of Fr. Peter White in Kilkenny. He was perhaps fifteen years of age and his stay with White would not have lasted more than two years. Peter White, known affectionately as 'the happy schoolmaster of Munster' was a native of Clonmel and a member of a highly regarded family. He was also a fellow of Oriel College, Oxford. Anastasia White, mother of Patrick Comerford, was also one of the White family. Peter was uncle to Thomas White who became a jesuit in Spain and was founder of the Irish college in Salamanca and was also involved in the Irish colleges of Seville and Santiago. Thomas' brother, Stephen White, also a jesuit, achieved a doctorate in theology from the University of Salamanca and went on to teach in the universities of Ingolstadt and later Dilingen in Germany. He returned to Ireland around 1630 and was friend to the Four Masters and to Seathrún Céitinn in their historical researches. He was also a scholar friend of archbishop Usher, protestant archbishop of Armagh. He died in Galway in 1648. Bishop Patrick Walsh of Waterford and Lismore (1551-78), who had conformed in the time of Elizabeth, was an ambivalent ecclesiastic, certainly not a protestant zealot. An example of his lack of zeal in the promotion of protestantism was his recommending for the office of dean of Waterford, Peter White a staunch catholic priest:

> I wish to commend to your honour (Lord Deputy Sydney) one Peter White…. a man very well learned, past degrees in schools, and of virtuous sober conversations.

Peter White was appointed dean in 1566; he remained a devout catholic and, after four years, he was deprived of the deanship. He left Waterford where he had been teaching in a school and, perhaps for reasons of safety, removed to Kilkenny. To his school in Kilkenny came catholic young men of Waterford and Clonmel and of other places. He had many outstanding students who were especially noted for their prowess in Latin – such as Peter Lombard, later catholic archbishop of Armagh, and Richard Stanihurst from Dublin who wrote of the school

> As from a Trojan horse issued men of distinguished learning – the Whites, Comerfords, Walshes, Waddings and Lombards.

---

[7] Cunningham, Bernadette, *The World of Geoffrey Keating*

In 1603 Patrick Comerford was to leave his school in Kilkenny to sail for the continent and become one of the first students in the Irish college at Bordeaux. 1603 was an eventful year for Ireland and for the city of Waterford. Early in April the news reached the city that Queen Elizabeth had died on 24 March. The news created a feeling of relief amongst the catholics of Ireland, especially in the cities and towns, that the harsh days for catholics were over and now, with a Stuart succeeding to the throne in the person of James I, son of Mary Queen of Scots and grandson of Elizabeth's first cousin, good times were surely coming.[8] Waterford, it can be said, led the way in celebrating the new state of affairs. The catholics of the city at once began a programme of assertion. Churches were formally repossessed, the mass was said at the altars once more; there were parades and public jubilation. But the government, in the person of lord deputy Mountjoy, who was in his final months in office, was not prepared to brook such action. In a celebrated march/tour of the provinces, he demanded that the catholics desist from such behaviour and especially return the church buildings to the protestants. His dealing with Waterford was singular. He and his men arrived at the city in May 1603. He was denied entry on the basis of immunities conferred by the four hundred year old charter. His riposte said it all:

he would destroy King John's charter with the sword of King James.

However, in the interest of peace, he agreed to debate some theological points with the leader of the catholics in the city, Fr. James White, vicar-apostolic. White, preceded by clergy, dominicans, in full choral dress, arrived at Mountjoy's camp in Grace Dieu outside the city. The debate was amiable and civilized – but a breakdown occurred concerning catholic teaching on temporal obedience and the papal claim to depose temporal rulers. Mountjoy insisted on submission. White's account of the affair is entitled 'The Irish Catholics after the death of Queen Elizabeth'. He is sensitive to the different dating system which obtained in Ireland and England as distinct from Rome: 'Her death, though it took place in England on the 24th March of 1603, was not known in Ireland until the 9th day of April of the following year (1604)'[9].

The effect in Waterford, White claims, was stunning and it took the catholics of Waterford quite a while to come to terms with the changes that should take place when such a long and difficult reign had ended. When the shock had been absorbed the people came to White's house and addressed him as their spiritual leader:

---

[8] King James' grandfather was James V of Scotland, son of Margaret who was sister of King Henry VIII.
[9] There is exciting drama in the various meetings between Mountjoy on Grace Dieu hill, west of Waterford city and Fr. James White, acting on behalf of the Catholic people of Waterford. The drama is worthy of recall, based as the account is, on a lengthy memorandum prepared by White for Pope Clement VIII. An English translation is in Egan, *Waterford*, 114-142

cf. also Clarke, Aidan, 'Plantation and the Catholic Question, 1603-23', *N.H.I.*, vol. III, 189

cf. also Cox, Sir Richard, *Hibernia Anglicana* vol. ii, part 2, 6 (London 1689-90) which gives an account of the contretemps between Mountjoy and White ; Cox marvels at the audacity of the friars who accompanied White and the cheek of one Dominican to take on Mountjoy in theological debate.

cf. Kew, Graham, *The Irish Sections of Fynes Moryson's Unpublished Itinerary* (I.M.C.), 53

The unjust and flagitious title by which the churches of God and of our fathers have been so long held by Calvinist, Lutheran, and atheistical ministers, has been to us the subject of frequent and most painful reflections. Now as these churches and all places of prayer (oratories) are the property of Catholics by hereditary right, we hereby request that you will reconcile them all by the solemn rights of the Catholic Church, and deliver them over to us, that in them we may profess the faith of God and of our fathers…. you are in this place the Vicar of the Pope and of the Apostolical See. We pray you, therefore, to accede without delay to this our most reasonable request: otherwise, we protest before God and his angels that we will send ambassadors to Rome to accuse you of being the sole cause why the exercise of the Catholic faith is not revived and established in this kingdom.

White, without delay, agreed to the request and on the 11th April he took peaceful possession of St. Patrick's church and 'purified it by public and solemn rite'. Then a solemn mass was celebrated in the church. This was greeted with hearty joy by the people but their requests went further: the cathedral church of the city must be purified and turned to catholic use. Led by White, the great church was entered, found to be in a deplorable state, cleaned and restored for several days by them all. Bells were then rung, sermons were given, solemn mass was celebrated and sacraments were administered. Later in the day

> James, son of the martyr Queen Mary, was proclaimed in the market place with the greatest solemnity.

Shortly after

> The mayor, magistrates and nobles and the whole body of the citizens proceeded to the Cathedral of the Blessed Trinity and, having taken their places according to their rank, the hymn of St. Ambrose, *Te Deum Laudamus*, was entoned and chanted by the choir as a thanksgiving.

The news of Waterford's repossession of the church spread and requests came pouring in for White to come to other places and purify their churches also. He said that he went to Clonmel, to St. Mary's church in Kilkenny, to the dominican church also in Kilkenny, to New Ross. He says in his report that the churches of Wexford were reconciled by the Rev. John Coppinger, the churches of Thomastown, Co. Kilkenny and Carrick-on-Suir by the Rev. Thomas Woodlock. Rev. William Nangle and Peter Strange reconciled the church of St. Mary's Dunkitt; Rev. Thomas Rachtur reconciled the metropolitan church of St. Patrick in Cashel and the grand church of the Holy Trinity in Fethard. Rev. Robert Miagh reconciled the cathedrals of Cork and Cloyne; and the Rev. Richard Arthur reconciled the cathedral and churches of the city of Limerick.

As a stern reaction to this widespread catholic upheaval originating from Waterford and Fr. James White, lord deputy Mountjoy, leading a strong army, arrived at the outskirts of Waterford on Low Sunday, 1 May 1604. Prayers and masses and a solemn procession was held in Waterford to invoke God's protection in the face of the Lord Deputy's arrival. Oaths were sworn and people publicly promised to die for their faith if necessity commanded it. The people deputed three leading citizens, Paul Sherlock, Paul Strange and Nicholas Wyse to meet with Mountjoy and invite him to enter the city but not to bring too many troops with him. Mountjoy, having crossed the Suir from Grannagh Castle to Grace Dieu, refused the request. It was then decided to send Fr. James White to meet with the lord deputy. To quote his own words :

> Having received the Lord Deputy's word for my own and my companion's security, through Richard Power, Baron of Curraghmore, Sheriff of the County and City of Waterford,....I proceeded from the Mansion House (*Domus Civica*) to the Cathedral, and taking down the crucifix from the high altar, carried it in my hands through the city, and thence proceeded to the camp, accompanied by Fr. Thomas Lombard (nephew of Archbishop Peter Lombard of Armagh and Rome) and other distinguished people. My companion, a cistercian, wore the religious dress of his order, his tonsure was also such as they wear: I was dressed in a long soutan, my square cap on my head, and a stole hanging over my shoulders.

White and his entourage were greeted by jeers when they arrived at the army camp. The lord deputy, who had his privy council with him, considered White to be guilty of treason for his opening the churches to the catholics. Mountjoy interrogated White on religious and political matters. There was much attention focussed on the crucifix which he was carrying. The soldiers jeered when Mountjoy referred to it as an idol. White countered by pointing to the cross of St. George which was so strongly displayed on the banners of the army. The eucharist was discussed, the cult of the saints, the adoration of statues. Even Machiavelli was invoked on the matter of taking up arms against one's king or one's lord. White refused to be drawn too deeply on this matter and declared that an army camp was no place for a reasoned discussion on such a delicate matter.

White returned to the city after a long interrogation but he was summoned back by Mountjoy later in the day. On his knees he pleaded for the free exercise of religion on the part of the citizens of Waterford. Mountjoy was conciliatory but could not act on behalf of the king in certain matters. He told White :

> that the king alone could grant liberty of conscience; that, without the royal consent, he (Mountjoy) could not promise anything of the kind; that, if the king consented, he would again restore the churches to us and defend us in the peaceful possession of them against our enemies. But that for the present, and until further orders, the king's

express wish was, that all things should continue in the same state in which they were on the death of the later queen (the murderess of his mother). But as he did not deem it expedient to coerce the conscience of any man in matters of religion, he would tolerate the exercise of the Catholic Worship for all, until his majesty issued contrary orders; he allowed priests to wear the clerical dress, and to celebrate mass in private houses, without being subjected to being molested as heretofore by the visits of bailiffs (*apparitoribus*) so long as the Catholics persevered in their loyalty and submission to the authority of the king.

On 3rd May Mountjoy entered Waterford and was given a declaration of the citizens' loyalty to the king. White, with some contentment, comments:

> This declaration was given to Sir Nicholas Walsh and to Mr. Gerald Comerford, second judge of the province of Munster, who both attested to us a second time on behalf of the Lord Deputy and in presence of the Mayor of Waterford, Robert Walsh, knight, that we had full liberty to celebrate Mass except in the churches, and to wear sacerdotal dress that became our profession and rank; that permission was repeated by the Lord Deputy a third time in his own mansion near the Cathedral Church of the Holy Trinity in presence of Thomas Cocles and Richard Boyle, two heretical officers.

All was well, according to White, for some time after the departure of Mountjoy. Divine worship was conducted, not in the churches, but in the private houses of the catholics. The soldiers who were left to keep law and order were well behaved and some even turned to the catholic church for spiritual aid. Some sermons by catholics were reported to military commanders who condemned them and leading religious figures such as White himself were watched carefully and were in constant danger of arrest. White was in serious trouble with a local, Richard Aylward, who, a pretended catholic, spared no effort to calumniate people like White to the authorities. Aylward succeeded in convincing the governor of the army, Sir Richard Morrison, that White was a traitor and should be dealt with severely. White was tried by Morrison in a semi-public arena but was acquitted. He was still accused by his enemies and plans were made to have him brought to Dublin for trial organised by Sir George Carey, then lord deputy.

The outcome was that White had to flee Waterford and he made his way to Bordeaux. From there, aided by Cardinal de Sourdis, archbishop of Bordeaux, he went to Rome where he penned the report which we have been examining. He concludes the report by assuring the Pope of the loyalty of the people of Waterford and, indeed, the people of Ireland to the Holy See. He addresses the Pope as 'illustrious Clement' and asks that he give all the support he can to the still suffering catholic people of Ireland.

So the status quo had to be restored. The excitement and disappointment and general upheaval may, perhaps, have been one of the final experiences of young Patrick Comerford before he left the city for the continent to begin his formal studies for the priesthood. He was bound for the wider world of Europe and a deeper appreciation of the counter-reformation within the catholic church.

Chapter Three

TO EUROPE AND THE COUNTER-REFORMATION

The Council of Trent which concluded in 1563, and which marks the codification of the catholic church's response to the reformation which was so dividing Europe, saw as crucial for this work, the presence of enlightened and committed bishops who would reorganise the church in every diocese in christendom. But bishops and priests and clearly defined territorial parishes in which well trained priests might reach out to the people, teach them with conviction and mediate God's love and concern to them through properly celebrated mass and sacraments, were not easy to find in the contemporary church[1].

The truth is that throughout Europe the majority of priests in the centuries before the reformation were poorly educated. This was particularly true of the secular clergy who worked in some kind of supervised way in the parishes of each diocese. Their training was quite haphazard and meagre. The monastic orders in their monasteries had provided some service of training for the aspirants to the secular priesthood, but, in the period before the reformation, the monastic orders were, by and large, in a declining state themselves. The mendicant orders had also done service in helping in the formation of secular priests. Perhaps, more importantly, the mendicants themselves had helped very much in towns and countryside, through preaching and catechising, to fulfil the need created by the inadequacy of the secular clergy.

Both monastic and mendicant groups had suffered enormously by the dissolution of the religious houses under Henry VIII in the 1530's and 1540's all over Ireland.

The usual preparation for priesthood, especially amongst the secular clergy, in the centuries before the reformation was more individual than organised or structured. Some, from the more wealthy sections of society, could cross the Irish sea and attend the great universities of Oxford and Cambridge where theological teaching was strong and where canon law, often the main key to preferment for clerics, could be studied. But there were little liturgical or pastoral aspects to these studies and the graduates were ill equipped to work effectively as priests in a parish. Anyway, most of them would not have envisaged parish life as their future.[2] More likely, they would hope and expect to find themselves after ordination in the curial service of the bishop of the diocese, managing ecclesiastical courts of law, relatively untouched by and concerned with the routine pastoral needs of the people. Their contacts would often have enabled them to obtain a benefice in the diocese which would be a financial support. The

---

[1] Corish, Patrick, 'An Irish Counter-reformation Bishop: John Roche, *I.T.Q.*, vol. XXV no. 2 (April 1958), 104-111

[2] Fitzpatrick, Elizabeth and Gillespie, Raymond, (eds) *The parish in medieval and early modern Ireland* (Dublin, 2006)

ordinary pastoral work associated with that benefice would be performed by a less educated cleric whom the privileged holder of the benefice would employ.[3]

The less privileged aspirant to the priesthood found that it was usually left to himself, perhaps, if he were fortunate, after attending the Latin school in his turn, such as John Flaghey's school in Waterford, to attach himself in a fairly unstructured way to a pastor in the area or to get acquainted with a monk or friar in a local religious house, in order to get the necessary practical knowledge required for priesthood. Sometimes, it would happen that a member of the staff of the cathedral or some other local church might be given some responsibility for instructing clerics and examining them after ordination. In effect, the majority of Irish clergy who could not go overseas to attend university received very little particularised preparation for clerical office. They were, by and large, unskilled in preaching and very deficient in theological knowledge. The vast majority of catholic clergy at the time of the reformation were in no position to enter into combat theologically with their counterparts in the established church. However, it must also be borne in mind that their protestant opponents were usually not well equipped in theological matters either.

The Council of Trent, taking a view of the entire church and the deficiency in the preparation of men for priesthood, directed, as a matter of supreme importance, that there be set up in each diocese or, in exceptionally difficult cases, in groups of dioceses, centres of formation or colleges which became known as seminaries. In many places throughout Europe such diocesan seminaries were set up in the decades after Trent. In many cases they were under the direction of members of the recently founded society of Jesus which was very much the spearhead of counter-reformation activity in the catholic church.

Jesuits were present in Ireland as early as 1542, very soon after the society was founded, but they could do little except send some depressing reports of the state of the church and people in the country. But David Wolfe, S.J., a Limerick man, who had been appointed papal nuncio by Rome to Ireland in 1560, might be considered the person who really began to alert Rome and churchmen in Ireland of the great need to educate priests properly in order that the counter-reformation be set in train effectively in the country.[4] It was clear, as noted by Wolfe, that the Irish dioceses could not even begin to consider creating seminaries in the country to prepare young men for priesthood. So, roughly speaking, from about 1560 on, a steady trickle of young men, especially though not entirely, from the towns such as Waterford, began to travel to Europe to be trained for the priesthood according to the new manner proposed by Trent. Some went in order to return as diocesan priests when their courses were ended. They would return as secular priests, but as secular priests with a difference, armed with a keen theological formation and a disciplined lifestyle which would alert the people to the dangers of the reformation and their special calling as members of the Roman catholic church, the true

---

3 Empey, Adrian, 'Irish Clergy in the high and late Middle Ages', Barnard, and Neely, W.G. (eds.) *The Clergy of the Church of Ireland 1000-2000*, 6-43

4 McRedmond, Louis, *To the Greater Glory of God, a history of the Irish Jesuits*, 17-28.

church of Christ. Many, in the course of their studies in Europe, joined religious orders. Of these, many came back to Ireland; others remained on the continent, sometimes in high academic posts or as pastoral workers in various countries. The trickle of 1560 began to grow as the second half of the sixteenth century advanced and, starting with Salamanca in Spain in 1592 and Donai in the Spanish Netherlands in 1594, Irish colleges, colleges specifically for the training of aspirants to the priesthood for Ireland, began to make their appearance in Europe.[5]

It was a powerful phenomenon on the Continent of Europe: so many Irish colleges, the majority to cater for secular priests, but many also for religious orders: franciscans, capuchins, dominicans, augustinians, cistercians, jesuits, benedictines. Some became large establishments such as Salamanca (1592), Lisbon (1593), Bordeaux (1603), Paris (1605), Louvain (1624), Rome (1628); others remained small, sometimes more like hostels where young Irishmen stayed in order to study at a college or university nearby.[6] The Irish colleges on the continent of Europe began in the late sixteenth century and some foundations were still being made as late as 1680 when Nantes was established. Some came and went after a few years, others were to last for centuries – right up to the end of the eighteenth century when revolutionary times forced at least a temporary closure. The establishment of Maynooth in 1796 and other major seminaries in Ireland around the same time eased the pressure on the continental colleges and enabled candidates for the priesthood to be trained in the home country. The Irish presence is still to be found to this day in Rome, Paris, Louvain. It would seem that about fifty colleges in all were established. Of the fifty, twenty-three were for secular students, nine for Franciscans, four each for cistercians, capuchins, dominicans, one each for jesuits and benedictines. They were to be found in the Spanish Netherlands, France, Spain, Portugal, Italy, Holy Roman Empire, Poland.

Some Waterford priests, such as Patrick Comerford, have earned a special place in the history of the Irish colleges in Europe. As mentioned already, Fr. Thomas White of Clonmel was founder of the Irish college, Salamanca in 1592 and was involved also in the establishment of the Irish college in Santiago in 1605 and of the Irish College in Seville in 1612. Luke Wadding, O.F.M., perhaps the most famous of all the Irish émigrés, was the founder of two Irish colleges in Rome: St. Isidore's in 1625 for Franciscans and the Irish college in 1628 for students for the secular priesthood. It is of interest that Patrick Comerford was a close relative of both Thomas White and Luke Wadding.

During the quarter century 1590-1615 there are recorded the names of over five hundred priests trained in Salamanca, Douai, Bordeaux and Toulouse. It could safely be reckoned that about one thousand priests from Ireland were trained in all the colleges in that period. Their work in Ireland was of enormous value to the build-up of the Irish church, particularly in the 1620's and 1630's when every diocese had a bishop and priests who had been

---

[5] O'Boyle, J., *The Irish Colleges on the Continent*
     Silke, John, 'The Irish Abroad, 1534-1691' *N.H.I.*, vol. iii, 587-633
[6] Morrissey, Thomas, 'The Irish student diaspora in the 16th century and the early years of the Irish College at Salamanca, *Recusant History*, XIV (1977-8) 242-60

trained on the continent of Europe. Through them, the spirit of the counter-reformation established itself in the Irish church.

Patrick Comerford left Waterford for Bordeaux in 1603. He was one of a considerable number of young men who had been gathered together in Munster by a Cork priest, Dermot O'Callaghan McCarthy.[7] McCarthy's intention was that these young men would form the nucleus and beginning of an Irish college in Bordeaux where the archbishop, Cardinal de Sourdis, had shown willingness to help with finances for the project. Amongst the students was Patrick Comerford. A report submitted to Lord Carew, president of Munster, by a spy named James Tobin in 1617 shows that, between 1603 and 1617, two hundred and fifteen Irish students passed through the Irish college at Bordeaux. Heading the list are Patrick Comerford, future bishop of Waterford and Lismore and Robert Barry, future bishop of Cork and Cloyne (1647-62). Both were to labour in adjoining dioceses in Ireland throughout the 1640's, and both were later to share the same burial vault in the Cathedral at Nantes; Comerford in 1652, Barry in 1662.

Comerford's stay at Bordeaux was very short but, despite that fact, a contemporary writer, John Lynch, remarks that he distinguished himself particularly in literature and languages.[8] Of the twenty-seven Waterford students named in James Tobin's list, the most prominent, perhaps, is that of Geoffrey Keating (Seathrún Céitinn), whom we have met before and who was to pursue in Ireland a scholarly life of great significance. He is styled Pere Geoffrey Keating D.D. He probably was a priest already in 1603 and may have, as Bernadette Cunningham suggests, studied for his doctorate in divinity at the University of Rheims.[9]

According to Lynch, Comerford fell ill during his first year in Bordeaux and had to return to Ireland. We have no other evidence about this interlude in his student life except that supplied by John Lynch. Again, following Lynch, we learn that he recuperated quickly in Waterford and sailed again to the continent, not to Bordeaux this time but to Lisbon where he was to enter the Irish college founded in that city in 1593 by Fr. John Howling S.J. from Wexford. When Comerford arrived in Lisbon, the Irish college was under the control of the jesuits. His cousin, Stephen White, had been one of its most brilliant students. Perhaps it was the White connection which attracted Comerford to Lisbon. In Lisbon, Comerford studied his formal philosophy course and, according to John Lynch, he graduated with high merit. On the completion of his philosophy course he followed the example of his friend and cousin, Luke

---

[7] Walsh, T.J., 'The Irish College at Bordeaux', *Journal of the Cork Historical and Archaeological Society*, L11 (1947) 10-25
Brady, John, 'The Irish Colleges in Europe and the Counter-reformation', *Ir. Cath. Hist. Comm. Proc.*, 1957
O'Boyle, J., *The Irish Colleges on the Continent*

[8] Lynch, John, *'De Praesulibus Hiberniae Potissimiss Catholicae Religionis in Hibernia Serendae, & Propagandae, et Conservandae Authoribus'* Ed. F.J. O'Doherty, 2 vols, I.M.C. (Dublin) 1944. Memoir of Comerford in vol. ii, 216
John Lynch became Archdeacon of Tuam. In the late 1650's, he translated into Latin Keating's 'Forus Feasa ar Eirinn'

[9] Cunningham, Bernadette, *The World of Geoffrey Keating*, 27

Wadding, and entered the religious life. He joined the order of the eremites of St. Augustine (O.S.A.). He would have known little about the augustinian eremites from his earlier days in Waterford. Their only house in the diocese of Waterford and Lismore had been in Dungarvan and that had been suppressed in the time of Henry VIII. It is of interest that four Waterford city students, contemporary in age, joined the augustinian eremites in the Iberian Peninsula: Richard Wadding, Richard Strange, Dermot McGrath and Patrick Comerford. Richard Strange (1581-1639) and Dermot McGrath (1586-1629) joined the Spanish province while Patrick Comerford and Richard Wadding joined the Portuguese province. All four had distinguished academic and subsequent careers in the order. Dermot McGrath had been a student of Peter White's school in Kilkenny. He then studied in Salamanca and was awarded a doctorate in divinity. He returned to Ireland around 1612 and settled in the Dungarvan area near where the eremites once had their friary. He was provincial of the newly created Irish province in 1623, and in 1625 he was appointed vicar apostolic of Elphin. Like McGrath, Richard Strange studied at Salamanca where he also received a doctorate in divinity. He became vicar general of the entire order from 1617 until 1620 and was based in Rome. He later became provincial in Ireland. It was he who founded a house of the eremites in Waterford city in 1629 on the site of the old abbey of the canons regular of St. Augustine.

Richard Wadding was professed two days after Patrick Comerford, on 19 September 1610. He also was a cousin of Luke Wadding and became professor of theology in Coimbra, Portugal. It seems that he never returned to Ireland.

Patrick Comerford, who, as was the custom of the augustinian eremites, took a religious name: Patrick ab Angelis, Patrick of the Angels, was professed on 17 September 1610.[10] The Portuguese province, which became independent of the Spanish province in 1482, had established houses in the Canary Islands (La Laguna) in 1505, and much later in the Azores, way out in the Atlantic ocean. When Comerford's novitiate was completed, he was sent to teach rhetoric to Terceira on the island of Angra do Heroismo in the Azores archipelago. His stay there probably lasted one to two years. It must indeed have been a strange experience for the young Irishman to be a member of the augustinian mission so far from his native Ireland and from Portugal, his land of adoption.

On his return from the Azores, it seems he was ordained a priest though no record of his ordination has been traced. He was then sent to study theology at the famous university of Coimbra where Luke Wadding had also studied. Perhaps their period of study overlapped for a short time. Coimbra was an old and highly acclaimed university centre and it was well patronised by the augustinians. A renowned augustinian theologian was professor there, Fray Gil of the Presentation, whom Luke Wadding later coupled with the great Francisco Suarez as

---

[10] The entry of his profession reads:
Fr. Patricio des Anjos, filho de Roberto Comorton e Anastazia White,Hibernios, fez proficao a 17 de Setembra de 1610. cf. 'Carlos Alonso O.S.A., Las Professiones Religiosas en La Provincia de Portugal Durante el Perioda 1513-1631', *Analecta Augustiniana*, vol. 48 (1985), 366

the outstanding theologians under whom he himself studied.[11] Wadding left Coimbra in 1613 but Comerford would have remained for several more years. In Coronatae Virtuti of 1629 we are told that Comerford, while still a student of theology at Coimbra, was a 'Negotiationum Socius' (Adviser) to his Portuguese provincial and was also adviser concerning the augustinian mission to the Azores.

According to John Lynch, Comerford, on completion of his theological studies in Coimbra, was appointed to teach not in Portugal but in Brussels. Lynch records that his time in Brussels was not of long duration. He had barely settled into his teaching duties when he was summoned to the general chapter of the augustinian eremites which was held in 1620. He was summoned, not as a representative of the Portuguese province, but of the Irish province. From this chapter he was sent back to Ireland to work on the Irish mission. This general chapter in Rome was the first general chapter at which the Irish augustinian eremites were given the status of a province. Previous to this, Ireland was not a province but formed a vicariate or 'limit' of the English augustinian province. The first Irish provincial who was sent back from this chapter to Ireland was Patrem Magistrum Nicolaum a Sancto Patricio. This newly elected provincial of Ireland was Dermot McGrath whom we have mentioned earlier. He can be termed the restorer of the augustinian eremites in Ireland. We mentioned that he had gone from Spain to Ireland in 1613. He seems to have been the only augustinian in Munster and he laboured largely around Dungarvan.[12] From this general chapter the appointment of Patrick Comerford was an unusual one. He was sent back to Ireland to help build up the augustinian eremites in the country but also as administrator of the monastery of Kells in the diocese of Ossory. Kells had been one of the major foundations, not of the eremites, but of the canons regular of St. Augustine who seem to have died out completely since the dissolution of the sixteenth century. The appointment of Comerford to this post had been approved by pope Paul V.[13]

Perhaps the appointment by the general chapter of Patrick Comerford to be prior *in commendam* of the abbey of Kells may be linked to the fact that Comerford had roots in County Kilkenny. Cousins of his had held some of the lands which had belonged to the abbey before

[11] Wadding Luke, *Annales Minorum*, a.d. an. 1530 no 27. Francisco Suarez (1548-1617) was one of the foremost Catholic theologians in Europe. Born at Grenada in southern Spain, he joined the jesuits at Salamanca in 1564. He taught in many centres of learning: Avila, Segovia, Rome, Alcala, Salamanca and Coimbra from 1597-1616. His written works, nearly all in Latin, run to twenty-six volumes.

[12] Perhaps Dermot McGrath, alias Nicolaus a Sancto Patricio, was a descendant of the McGrath family of Sleady Castle in the parish of Modeligo in west Waterford. The McGraths of Sleady had been patrons of the early medieval augustinian friary in Dungarvan. The tombstone of one of the McGrath chieftains, Donald, who died in 1400, can still be seen in the ruined church of Abbeyside, under the north window.

[13] The text of the appointment is in Augustinian general archives, Rome cf. Martin, F.X. and de Meyer: *Archiv. Hib* (1956) 129: *Tales litteras patentas dedimus Fratri Patricio ab Angelis ut infra, videlicet....Magister Fr. Fulgentius a Monte Giorgio venerabli et nobis in christo etc. Cum te de litteris et de religione nostra optime meritum esse fideli relatione perceperimus, spciali favore te prosequi volentes harum vi et serie litterarum nostrique officii auctoritate facultaten tibi damus, ut suspicias et exerceas administrationem Monasterii Kellensis Ordinis Canonicorum Regularium S.P.N. Auguistini in Diocesi Osorien. In Hibernia sub obedientia provinciali dictae provinciae ea forma qua Summus Dominus Paulus divina providentia papa v in suo placui te ad praefatam administrationem promovere dignabitur. Datum Romae...*(Dd 62, ff. 45V – 46R)

the dissolution. Kells had been one of the great abbeys of medieval Ireland, founded in 1193 by Lord Geoffrey Fitz Robert, baron of Kenlis in Ossory. Over the centuries it had amassed vast possessions in counties Kilkenny, Cork and Limerick.[14]

On his way to Ireland for the general chapter, Comerford visited Florence where there was a very strong augustinian presence. According to Lynch[15], and also according to the Processus Datariae which was drawn up at the time of Comerford's nomination as bishop of Waterford and Lismore, he either visited or attended for some time the *Academia della Crusca*, which was a noted place of learning, and he obtained a higher degree in theology, perhaps a doctorate or masters.[16] It was not uncommon in the seventeenth century for a person to gain a high degree from a university in which he may not have studied provided he could assure the professors of his learning and have references as to his character, experience and intelligence. In an epitaph prepared for his tomb many years later his nephews Patrick Hackett and Nicholas Geraldin declared that he received the doctorate in theology at Louvain (*Laurea doctorali me decoravit Louvaniensis Universitas*). This may be a conjecture on their part because of Comerford's time of teaching in Brussels.[17]

[14] Carrigan, William, *History and Antiquities of the Diocese of Ossory*, vol. iv, 64, 65
[15] Lynch, John, op. cit., vol.II, 116
[16] *Processus Datariae* vol. 8 ff. 21R-39R: attestation of Fr. Eugene Callanan of Killaloe; attestation of Hieronymus de Ghettis, prior general of the Eremites of St. Augustine, *Fr. Luke Wadding Commemorative Volume*, 551-4
[17] A copy of this epitaph by his nephews is in *Bibliotheque Royale, Brussels* ms. 11, 2590, f 222R

Chapter Four

IN IRELAND AGAIN
Prior of Kells 1620-27
Bishop of Waterford 1629-1652

Earlier we have mentioned the uneven position of the catholic church in Ireland between the death of Queen Elizabeth in 1603 and the coming of Oliver Cromwell in 1649. The law did not tolerate the catholics but, for many reasons, there was *de facto* toleration. There were harsh periods when proclamations against the catholic church were issued and the law against catholics was strongly enforced. We noted that such harsh periods occurred in 1605, 1611, 1613, 1624, 1629, 1653. But there were periods of *de facto* peace when catholics and their church received a chance to grow strong.

Patrick Comerford returned to his native land after an absence of nearly two decades. The years of his absence marked the bulk of the reign of James I who succeeded Elizabeth in 1603 and who died in 1625. During the reign of James, the son of Mary Queen of Scots and great grandson of Margaret, the sister of Henry VIII, there was a breathing space in Ireland from war which had so bedevilled the country during the reign of Queen Elizabeth.[1] With that breathing space, there came sizeable economic prosperity and a fairly even toleration towards catholics. James had chosen, as his motto '*Beati Pacifici*', 'Blessed are the Peacemakers' and he did endeavour throughout his reign of nearly quarter of a century to rule his three kingdoms of England, Scotland and Ireland in a peaceful manner. James was a complex man, idiosyncratic in manner but intellectual and religious. One achievement of which he was rightly proud was the translation of the bible into good English. He initiated it in 1604 by having chosen a well selected group of scholars and churchmen who completed their task by 1611. It was a masterly achievement.[2]

James was baptised a catholic but reared a protestant and his instinct undoubtedly was to have Ireland a protestant nation. But he was not attracted to unduly coercive means. Together with some of his advisers and, despite the attitude of others, he sought to travel the peaceful road of evangelisation rather than coercion. The pattern during his reign was usually a *de facto* toleration of the catholic religion but a clear message that the lawful religion for Ireland was protestantism. There was to be no question of catholics repossessing churches or religious houses which had been taken from them in the sixteenth century. There were periodic edicts

---

[1]   Olden, Michael, 'Kinsale to Benburb – a valuable breathing space in Irish History', *Léachtaí Cholm Cille* (Maynooth, (1971)
[2]   Nicolson, Adam, *Power and Glory, Jacobean England the making of the King James Biible* – an excellent account of the project

issued which banned 'catholic priests and Jesuits' from operating in Ireland. There was even execution of priests, the most notable being that of the aged bishop of Down and Conor, Cornelius O'Devaney, in February 1612. But there still was tolerance, not uninterrupted tolerance, but a tolerance positively encouraged by James I and by his successor Charles I. It was encouraged for varying reasons tied in with some conviction as to the best method of converting the Irish to protestantism and also with an eye to political considerations in England and on the continent.

When Patrick Comerford returned to Ireland in 1620, he would have detected an increased prosperity. There had been no war since the treaty of Mellifont had ended the Nine Years War in 1603. Nor was there to be war again until October 1641 when Sir Phelim O'Neill led the Ulster rebellion. Peace created the conditions for prosperity, on the land, in the towns, and especially in the port towns like Waterford where exports increased on a large scale; cattle and sheep to England, wool and cloth, timber staves for barrel making. Fishing was improving and salted herrings and other fish were loaded on ships for export to continental Europe.

John Lynch tells us that Patrick Comerford did not live in Kells, probably for the good reason that there was no accommodation for him. Kells was a ruined monastery and, being its prior had a symbolic value in that it pointed to hopefully better times ahead, but it would have meant little or nothing as a means of remuneration.[3] Comerford probably travelled out from Waterford and met the people of the district, said mass in their homes and administered the sacraments. As well as whatever limited ministry Comerford would have performed in Kells, John Lynch tells us that he spent much of his time in Waterford city giving missions and generally helping in the parishes of the city. His efforts were obviously noted and admired because, within a few years, the clergy of Waterford were sending petitions to Rome that he be appointed their bishop.

There is one valuable monument to Comerford's work during these years after his return. It takes the form of a lengthy polemical book written in reply to protestant attacks on the catholic church. It is entitled 'The Inquisition of a Sermon' and it was printed and published many years later when a printing press had been established in Waterford during the days of the Confederation of Kilkenny. The book constitutes an unsparing reply to a sermon delivered and later printed by Robert Daborne, protestant chancellor of the cathedral of Waterford in February 1617.[4] The first and shorter part of the work is devoted to a discussion as to the justice or otherwise whereby Waterford was deprived of its charter in 1617 because of the solid adherence

---

[3] Carrigan, Willian, op.cit., vol. IV, 56-71
[4] The full title of Comerford's work reads: '*The Inquisition of a Sermon preached in the Cathedrall Church of the city of Waterford, in February 1617, by Robert Daborne, Chancellor of the said Cathedrall etc.* ...... Printed at Waterford by Thomas Bourke. 1644
Daborne, Robert, *A Sermon Preached in the Cathedrall Church of the Cittie of Waterford*, (London, H. Gosson, 1618)

of its mayor and officials to the catholic faith. Daborne had declared that, of the different sets of juries set up to decide whether the charter be withdrawn or not, all agreed it should be withdrawn. Comerford denies the truth of this assertion and says that only one jury, and that one packed by people specially chosen by the government, found the city guilty and deserving of this punishment. Another jury, made up of the merchants of the city, considered that the charter should not be withdrawn.[5] Comerford, in many parts of the book, shows great regard for the staunch catholic faith of his native city and directs attention to the outstanding ecclesiastics whom Waterford had in recent times given to the church. The greater part of the book, twenty-one chapters, is devoted to doctrinal matters. Daborne's objections and arguments in the field of doctrine are refuted, sometimes mercilessly. Against the reformers, strong emphasis is placed on the papacy as the real authority within the church. The pope's position vis-à-vis the temporal ruler is set out and his authority to punish and even depose is vindicated. Problems in history such as the dispute between the emperor Henry IV and the pope, the dealings of the pope with king Henry VIII, and the excommunication of queen Elizabeth, are dealt with and the Pope's position and actions are defended. Calvinism and Lutheranism are examined; their antagonism towards each other and their weaknesses and contradictions are outlined. Comerford places strong emphasis on the distinction between the catholic priest and the minister of the established religion, and the lack of any priestly character in the latter is stressed. Running through the work is the evident anxiety on the part of Comerford to keep the faithful on their guard lest they be deceived by the ministers of the established church and forget the essential differences between their own catholic religion and that of the protestants. It is strong counter-reformation stuff and the style of writing is confident and confrontational. He talks of the 'pulpit-babble' of Daborne and the 'ugly monsters of errors, falsehoods, and slanderous calumnies lurking under the masks of counterfeit sincerity and of a pretended true gospel'. In Comerford's text, one finds the savage invective and biting sarcasm which later on, when he is bishop, reappears in some of his letters, especially to Wadding in Rome. The devastating manner in which the character of Daborne himself is summed up illustrates well the quality of Comerford's invective:

> After diligent search, I was informed that Master Dabourne was formerly a stage-play-maker in London, and that thriving ill with that hungry faculty, he fell in debt, for which being narrowly pursued by the Officers of Justice, he made a cunning escape, and never rested nor thought himself safe, until in Ireland he had the ocean betwixt him and his Creditors: Heere he was a long time after an indigent fashion; but when all his shiftes fayled him and all his grins, and crackes could not prevaille, he betooke

---

[5]   Ibid., 18ff

himself to the Sacred Ministry, wherein within few days, he was dub'd a Preacher of the Word, and soon after exalted to the Chancellorship of the Cathedrall of Waterford.[6]

At the conclusion of the book Comerford gives a detailed index or alphabetical table of contents showing the many topics covered in the two hundred and fifty-five pages.

For at least five years Comerford laboured between Waterford and Kells, defending the faith against heretical opponents and helping the catholics to deepen it in their own lives. In 1625, or, at the latest, 1626 a tragic family event occurred which forced him to leave Ireland once more. He was not to see Waterford again until 1629 when he returned as bishop of Waterford and Lismore. The tragic event was the capture at sea of one of his brothers who was probably engaged in commerce between Ireland and one of the continental countries.[7] It was an act of piracy, perhaps from Turkish or Algerian attackers. His brother was brought as a slave to north Africa. This was not an uncommon occurrence at the time. Indeed the Irish themselves were considered to be adept at piracy. In the sixteenth century there had been severe rivalry between seamen of Waterford and Cork, many of them pirates. With growing prosperity, trade developed and the seas around the south east of Ireland were busy with large and small ships and galleys. Piracy and smuggling were frequent. It was urged that galleys should be built and sent over to Ireland to keep the seacoasts from the O'Malleys and other rebels. These live by robbing poor fishermen and others that pass in small vessels.[8] In the parliament of 1612 it was decreed that every effort should be made to eliminate piracy off the coasts of Ireland.[9]

From north Africa it seems a demand for the ransom of Comerford's brother reached Waterford. Friends and family persuaded Patrick to set out for north Africa and seek to ransom his brother. So, having gathered an immense amount of money, including five hundred pounds from the unfortunate man's family of young sons, Comerford left Ireland for Spain.[10] He was successful in his mission, probably through the aid of the Trinitarian Order. He retrieved his brother from his captors but the success was quickly undone by the death of the liberated man almost immediately after landing on Spanish soil.[11]

On the death of his brother, Comerford did not return to Ireland but left Spain on 15 March 1622 for Rome to transact some business for his order in Ireland.[12] The next two years

---

[6] Ibid., 10. A little further on Comerford comments savagely on Mr. Daborne's 'vast and orbicular constitution of his monstrous big –paunch', a comment hardly relevant to theological argument!
[7] Lynch, John, op. cit., 116
[8] Calendar of State Papers relating to Ireland, 1601-03, 258
[9] Comerford to Wadding, 22 Nov. 1629, *Wadding Papers*, 320
Meehan, C.P, *The Rise and Fall of the Irish Franciscan Monasteries*, 421
[10] Comerford to Wadding, Antwerp, 19 July 1629, *Wadding Papers*, 299
[11] Lynch, John, loc. cit.
[12] Archbishop Thomas Walsh of Cashel to Wadding, Madrid, 14 March 1627, *Wadding Papers*, 243
Same to Same, Madrid, 13 April 1627, Ibid. 248

of Comerford's life were to be spent in Rome. He probably stayed with the augustinian eremites in their generalate in the city. He definitely met a lot with his cousin Luke Wadding in his newly founded college of St. Isidore's. When he finally left to return to Ireland, he was to do so as bishop of Waterford and Lismore. While in Rome, much of his time was spent in an effort to get restored to the augustinian eremites in Ireland the very wide missionary faculties which they once held but which had recently been revoked or seriously restricted by order of Pope Urban VIII. Comerford made a strong appeal to the Congregation of Propaganda Fide which promised to consider his request.[13] There is an undoubted irony in this request of Comerford's; later, as bishop of Waterford and Lismore, he was strongly to oppose the granting of wide faculties to the religious orders. At any rate, Propaganda decided to refuse his request because it felt that the increase of priests in Ireland in recent years had rendered missionary faculties unnecessary. To favour one particular group or order such as the augustinians would only fuel discord in the country.[14]

Although Comerford's request to Propaganda had not succeeded in 1627, he remained on in Rome. One reason for his prolonged stay was probably the pursuit of a request to the father general of the augustinian eremites for a maximum grant of faculties and concessions which he, Comerford, could put to good use in Waterford and Kells.[15] Another reason, and one of greater moment, must have begun to occupy his mind: he was being strongly suggested as bishop of Waterford and Lismore.

The diocese of Waterford and Lismore had been without a catholic bishop since Patrick Walsh died in 1578. Walsh had been appointed in 1551 and, although he was not deposed during the reign of Queen Mary, there can be little doubt that he was schismatical. He was by no means energetic in his ministry but, at least, he did not harass the catholic flock. It can be said that, effectively, from reformation times until 1629, the catholic diocese had no bishop. As had occurred in many other dioceses, Waterford and Lismore was placed under the jurisdiction of vicars apostolic. These were priests, not bishops, but in non sacramental matters they could act as bishops in the organisation of the diocese. There were three vicars apostolic in charge of the diocese since the death of Patrick Walsh: John White (1568-1600), James White (1600-1613), Thomas Walsh (1613-1626), later archbishop of Cashel. It was not until the first decade of the seventeenth century had passed that the question of appointing a bishop to the diocese was discussed. A priest named Derby Carty had been proposed for the see around 1615 but the

Walsh may have helped Comerford in the ransom effort. He had contacts with the Trinitarian Order and may even have been a member of the Order himself. Walsh's brother was a member of the Theatine Order and worked in Spain. The Theatines were founded in 1524 by John Peter Caraffa, bishop of Chieti (Theate), later Pope Paul IV, and were dedicated in a special way to the training of priests.

[13] APF, SOCG, 294, f. 96RV

[14] APF, Acta, 4, 28 August 1627, f. 279v no. 21

[15] Petitions to this effect from Comerford are in *Augustinian General Archives, Rome, Regestum Vmi Hieronymi de Ghettis ab anno 1627 ad an.1629* 188, 190

clergy were not in favour of his being appointed.[16] In 1617, Nicholas Fagan, cistercian abbot of Inishlounaght, near Clonmel, seems to have been strongly suggested as a candidate, and the likelihood that he would be appointed seemed strong, but Fagan died before the proposed appointment could take effect. According to Gams, Fagan was actually appointed but died before consecration. Gauchat makes no mention of him or of his appointment.[17]

In 1619 Luke Wadding, the eminent Waterford franciscan residing in Rome was suggested for Waterford and Lismore by the exiled archbishop of Tuam, the franciscan Florence Conry (Flaithrí Ó Maoil Chonaire), and also by the exiled earl of Tyrconnell, Hugh O'Donnell.[18] But it is very likely that Wadding who, like his cousin Peter Lombard, archbishop of Armagh but always resident in Rome, was too valuable an adviser on Irish and other matters to be allowed return to Ireland as a bishop. There is also the strong likelihood that Wadding as a person was averse to ecclesiastical preferment. We know that, many years later, he was not at all pleased when the Confederation of Kilkenny petitioned that he be made a cardinal.

At a meeting, more correctly a synod of the province of Armagh, held in Drogheda on 16 October 1626, it was recommended that the Waterford franciscan, Thomas Strange, be appointed bishop of Waterford and Lismore. The decrees or minutes of this synod are not extant but report of the recommendation reached archbishop Thomas Walsh of Cashel who was in Madrid. Walsh wrote to Wadding on 13 April 1627 objecting to the recommendation which, he says, had been made without his being consulted as metropolitan. He claims in the letter that the Waterford and Lismore clergy had written to him declaring that they did not want Strange as their bishop.[19] In fact a month before writing to Wadding on this matter, Walsh had met Comerford in Spain when Comerford was dealing with his brother's capture, death and burial. Walsh gave Comerford a strong recommendation to carry to Rome that he, Comerford, should be given the appointment to Waterford and Lismore.[20] So the lobbying for Comerford was taking place in Ireland but, more importantly, on the continent, in Spain and in Rome itself. It is reasonable to assume that Comerford himself, who was a relative of both Walsh and Wadding, had some involvement in preparing the way for his own eventual appointment.

But Comerford had strong support at home in Ireland also. He appears to have been the candidate most desired by the clergy of Waterford and Lismore. Many postulations came from Ireland to Rome that he be appointed:[21] Time and time again in later years Comerford was to

[16]   David Rothe, bishop of Ossory, to Peter Lombard, Archbishop of Armagh, 18 Decemer 1615, *Wadding Papers*, 5
[17]   Gams, *Series Episioporum Ecclesiae Catholicae*, (Ratisbon, 1823), 228
[18]   Conry to Cardinal Protector of Ireland, Fabrizio Veralo, Louvain, 10 Oct. 1619, *Wadding Papers*, 21 O'Donnell to same, Louvain, 7 Oct. 1619, Ibid, 20
[19]   Walsh to Wadding, Madrid, 13 April 1627, *Wadding Papers*, 248
[20]   Walsh to John Roche, Bishop of Ferns, Madrid, 14 March 627, Ibid., 244
[21]   Walsh to Wadding, Madrid, 20 February 1628, Ibid., 258;
       Comerford to Eugene Callanan, Rector of Irish College, Rome, 21 June 1629, Ibid., 293

protest that he himself had not asked to be made a bishop, as his enemies suggest, but that the clergy left no doubt that he was their candidate.[22] About this time also Comerford was suggested as bishop for the diocese of Derry but the earl of Tyrconnell, Hugh O'Donnell, objected, not for any personal reasons, but because Comerford was from the south of Ireland and would, therefore, not be acceptable to the clergy and people of the north.[23]

Apropos the appointment of 'outsiders' to an Irish bishoprick in the early seventeenth century Tadhg Ó hAnnracháin presents the problem well in a passage which deserves full quotation:

> To a very large extent, the episcopate were dependent on the local laity, particularly their own kinsfolk for the ordinary means of subsistence. For this reason, it was an enormous benefit to a bishop to be appointed to his native diocese as this vastly increased the likelihood that he could find accommodation in a secure network of friends and relations. The Bishop of Waterford (Comerford), for instance, habitually lived with his brother; the Bishop of Ossory (Rothe) alternated between his brother's house and that of his cousin, Viscount Montgarrett; and the archbishop of Dublin (Fleming), son of the baron of Slane, resided with kin and friends on the edge of his diocese. A bishop who was not native to his See, however, and dependent on the kindness of strangers, could encounter very severe financial problems. Moreover, the lack of a local network rendered a prelate far more vulnerable to other difficulties. Opposition was frequently expressed at the intrusion of outsiders into ecclesiastical positions. When this was added to the common resentment of a bishop's reforming activities, the result could be a backlash of antipathy which rendered it impossible for a bishop to function effectively. It was this lethal cocktail of financial insecurity and fear of the priests whom they had been sent to govern which led both the bishop of Raphoe, John O'Callanan, and the bishop of Kilmore, Eugene MacSweeney, to petition Rome to be transferred to the vacant diocese of Derry. It is not unlikely that Thomas Walsh's financial difficulties in Cashel were related to the fact that he himself was a native of Waterford and not of his diocese.[24]

Patrick Comerford in Waterford was to experience some of the difficulties mentioned in the above passage. He probably could have added another: the difficulties which a regular priest

---

[22] Comerford to Wadding, 22 Nov. 1629, Ibid., 322;
   William Browne (alias Comerford) to Wadding, Nov. 1632, Ibid., 616
[23] O'Donnell to Rome, 18 Nov. 1628, *Burke Papers*, Mount Melleray Abbey – a transcript of an original letter in the archives of the Irish College, Paris
[24] Ó h Annracháin, Tadhg, *Catholic Reformation in Ireland the Mission of Rinnucini 1645-1649*, 45-6

would experience in administering a diocese (such as Waterford and Lismore) where there would be serious disagreement and even conflict between the secular and regular clergy.

Comerford's relationship and friendship with Luke Wadding who had, well before 1629, replaced archbishop Peter Lombard, who died in 1625, as the outstanding Irish ecclesiastic in Rome, was undoubtedly a factor in his appointment as bishop. He may well have stayed with Wadding for much of his long sojourn in Rome. It is clear from his many letters afterwards to Wadding that he was on intimate terms of friendship with the staff and students of St. Isidore's.[25] It is of interest that in one important venture he seems to have collaborated with Wadding who, with the financial and other help of cardinal Ludovico Ludovisi, founded the Irish college Rome which opened on 1 January 1629. One of the foundation documents of the college, dealing with rules and regulations to be observed in the college, is signed by two people: Luke Wadding himself and Fr. Partitius ab Angelis alias Quemfordus.[26]

On 4 January 1629 Urban VIII chose Patrick Comerford to be bishop of Waterford and Lismore and commissioned the process of enquiry be set up to examine the candidate and the see. On 16 and 17 January this process of enquiry was conducted and the witnesses requested were: Anthony Hickey, an Irish franciscan; Eugene Callanan, priest of the diocese of Killaloe and rector of the recently opened Irish college, Rome, Hieronymus de Ghettis, prior-general of the eremites of St. Augustine. Also consulted was the attestation made in Madrid in 1627 by archbishop Thomas Walsh of Cashel which had been brought to Rome by Comerford himself.[27]

Comerford was preconised on 29 January 1629 and was formally appointed on 12 February 1629. In the bull of appointment he is allowed retain his priorship of the monastery of Kells and also the vicar-generalship of the canons regular of St. Augustine in Ireland for two years.[28]

On Sunday 18 March 1629 Patrick Comerford was consecrated bishop of Waterford and Lismore in the church of San Silvestro al Quirinale by cardinal Guido Bentivoglio, assisted as

---

[25] E.g. William Browne (Comerford) to Wadding, 18 January 1630 (8 January 1629 O.S.), *Wadding Papers*, 336

[26] Institutiones Domus Hibernorum de Urbe ab Ill.mo et R.mo D.mo Card. le Ludovisio S.R.E. Vice-Cancellario, ac Protectore, fundatae primo die anni MDCXXVIII (1628), Cleary, Gregory, *Father Luke Wadding and St. Isidore's College, Rome*, 195-202

[27] Av, Processus Datariae, 8, ff,21R-39R, *Father Luke Wadding Commemorative Volume*, 551-4
This was the usual procedure followed by the apostolic datary in the appointment of bishops. Anthony Hickey was an Irish Franciscan who had taught theology in Louvain before moving to Rome. We find him witnessing in many instances of enquiry concerning Irish bishops. He seems to have been well regarded as a friend of Luke Wadding. *The Processus Datariae* is also recorded in the archives of the Congregation of the Consistory: vol. 20, ff,. 202R-218V
The Processus in relation to Comerford, as translated by Fr. Giblin is given *in toto* in Appendix 7 of this work.

[28] BV, Mss. Barberini Latini, 2869, f. 16RV, 2933, f. CLIV (RV), ff. CLV (V)-CLVI(R), Giblin, Cathaldus (ed.), *Archiv. Hib.*, XVIII (1955), 79, 85

co-consecrators by bishops Consalvo Doranti and Benedicto Vais.[29] Cardinal Bentivoglio (1579-1644), of a wealthy and famous Bolognese family, had been nuncio in Brussels from 1605 till 1615 and in Paris from 1616 till 1621 when Pope Paul V made him a cardinal in Curia. For over twenty years in this post his secretary, or 'Irish Chaplain' as he called him, was John Roche who was bishop of Ferns from 1623 till 1636. Roche was very close to and friendly with Bentivoglio and may have spoken of Comerford to him over the years. There is clearly a gesture of friendship in the fact that Bentivoglio chose to consecrate Comerford and to do so in his own titular church of San Silversto al Quirinale. In subsequent years, in letters from Waterford to Wadding, bishop Comerford frequently sends special greetings to two cardinals: Bentivoglio and Ludovisi, protector of Ireland.

The consecration of a new bishop of Waterford and Lismore was marked in a special way by the students of the infant Irish College (there were just six students in the college at its beginning). They celebrated the occasion with a lengthy congratulatory address that was later published in book form. Its title is *Coronatae Virtuti*[30] and it is an excellent example of the Latinity in use by young Irish scholars on the continent in the seventeenth century. There are extant many laudatory addresses, versus, poems and epigrams in elegant Latin from Irish pens of the period. Benignus Millett mentions *Coronatae Virtuti* thus:

> The publication of specially composed verses, sometimes in highly stylised form on broadsheets and in booklets was an accepted usage in academic and court circles for important occasions. Irish clerical professors and students in various European centres of learning frequently contributed. Perhaps the best example is the skilfully wrought *Coronatae Virtuti* composed by the Irish in Rome in 1629 on the occasion of the episcopal ordination of the augustinian Patrick Comerford of Waterford. In the ranks of the priest-exiles there were at least a dozen minor poets whose elegies, acrostic poems, and religious verses still survive[31]

The final wish in the book is touching, coming from young exiles who would soon themselves be taking their place as ministers of the gospel in a difficult and troubled mission:

---

[29] Brady, R. M., The Episcopal Succession in Ireland, Scotland and Ireland, a.d. 1400-1875, vol. 11, 70
cf. Bull of appointment in Acta Camerarii Sacri Collegii S.R.E. Cardinalium 16, f. 282; cf. Gauchat, *Hierarchia Catholica*, IV, 360

[30] The full title is: *Coronatae Virtuti Reverendiss. D.Patritii Quemerfordi ex Sacro Eremit. D. Augustini Ordini Episcopi Waterfordiensis & Lismorensis Inaugurati Plausus Seminarii Hibernorum de Urbe*, Roma, 1629

[31] Millett, Benignus, 'Irish literature in Latin, 1559-1700, *N.H.I.* vol. III, 581
A copy of this address is in the Franciscan Library, Killiney and another in the National Library of Ireland.

Redi ad populares, quos reges, ad ecclesiam, quam eriges, adferes patriae laetitiam, urbi solatium, politico ordini felicitatem, sacro securitatem, adferes rebus afflictis levamen, lubentibus fulcimentum, delapsis restaurationem, languidis vigorem, squallentibus ornatum, tenebricosis nitorem, turbatis tranquillitatem, incompositis ordinem, laxioribus disciplinam, Catholicis spem, haereticis terrorem, bonis omnibus incrementum.[32]

The book, including four appendices, has sixty-four pages. The early part and the last part are chiefly rhetorical and replete with classical allusions. Mention is made of his family and the strong grounding he received in the faith. There is a narrative of his schooling where John Flahey is honoured, of his joining the augustinians in Lisbon, his time in the Azores, the city of Waterford and the other main towns of the diocese: Clonmel, Carrick-on-Suir, Dungarvan, Tallow. The outstanding families of Waterford city are praised: Walshes, Waddings, Sherlocks, Cuffes, Leonards, Woodlocks, Whites. Illustrious men of Waterford are chosen for special mention: Peter Lombard, archbishop of Armagh; Thomas Walsh, archbishop of Cashel; Thomas Strange, franciscan; Andrew Wise of the order of Jerusalem.

In Appendix I there is a list of some Waterford men at present teaching philosophy and theology: Peter Comerford in Louvain, Richard Wadding O.S.A. in Coimbra, John Walsh in Spain. Then there is a list of prominent franciscans and jesuits given: franciscan Thomas Strange of Santander, Martin Walsh of Naples and Rome, Luke Wadding the most eminent of them all. The jesuits mentioned are Luke Wadding of Compostella, Valladolid and Dilingen, William Morgan of Compostella and Palestrina, Stephen Marty of Salamanca and Valladolid, Patrick Sherlock of Compostella, Thomas Comerford of Spain, Richard Walsh of Salamanca, Ambrose Wadding of Dilingen. The whole book is a clever exercise in Latin prose and verse and it is also a nostalgic witness to the pride which the students in Rome had in their native land and how inspired they were by the continental sweep of some of the priests who had gone before them.

Patrick Comerford probably left Rome for Ireland in late May or early June 1629. We know that he was in Louvain by 21 June. The first evidence of his arrival in Ireland was his attendance at an important meeting of some Munster and Leinster bishops in Kilkenny 24-27 August 1629. His long journey from Rome is punctuated by letters from him mainly to Luke

---

[32] They tell him to
return to the people over whom he will reign, to the church which he will build up, to bring joy to the fatherland, to bring solace to the city, happiness to the political order, security to the sacred, comfort to those afflicted, support to those who are falling, restoration to those who have lapsed, vigour to those who are weary, beauty to those who are squalid, brightness to those who are gloomy, tranquillity to those who are troubled, order where there is disorder, discipline where these is laxity, hope to catholics, terror to heretics, and an increase of all things good.

Wadding and Eugene Callanan in Rome. These letters are pessimistic and rather unenthusiastic about the task that lay ahead for him in Ireland.[33] His poverty, some sad experiences involving Irishmen whom he seems to have met on his journey, and disturbing reports from his diocese, all tended to depress one who, in so far as we can judge from this and later correspondence, had a natural proclivity to pessimism. He writes that his poverty had been somewhat alleviated by money kindly given to him by cardinal Borromeo in Milan. He was also befriended while in Belgium by the archduchess Isabella of Spain who helped him obtain a pontifical and some other necessary books, and also to dress himself in secular attire which would be necessary in Ireland. Comerford considered that 1629 was not a happy year in which to be returning to Ireland. The harvest had been very bad and many people were on the verge of starvation. Many had fled the country in an effort to find work and food on the continent. Comerford, on his journey, had either met some of these unfortunates or had heard accounts of their behaviour. He speaks harshly of them in his letter of 19 July to Wadding:

> In oure countrie there was some dert of corne and mortalitie of cattle, wherefor our
> countriemen agmine facto rushed into England to begg and being trust out of England
> they flocked over to France and hether, to our greater disgrace; the base rogues could
> very well stay at home and feed upon fish and herbs and some butter and milk, which
> was not altogether so scarce. By little and little this idle sluggish rabblement doth
> leave Ireland to English, Scotts, and other nations, which one thinkes is a particular
> providence of God, because our owne Irish are not worthie to inhabit so mellifluous a
> countrie, *la verdadura tierra de cucana*[34]

Ironically, Comerford's views will change somewhat when he has lived a few months in this 'mellifluous countrie'.

---

[33] Comerford to Eugene Callanan, rector of Irish College Rome, Louvain, 21 June 1629, *Wadding Papers*, 293-4;
Same to Wadding, Antwerp, 19 July 1629, Ibid, 297-300.

[34] Ibid., 298
For a succinct account of the miserable harvest of 1629 cf. Dunlop, *Ireland under the Commonwealth*, i, ci

Chapter Five

A COUNTER REFORMATION BISHOP ARRIVES IN WATERFORD

The diocese of Waterford and Lismore to which Patrick Comerford returned in 1629 had not had a catholic bishop for a long time. The last appointment had been Patrick Walsh who became bishop by royal mandate in 1551. His career is an interesting example of episcopal diplomacy. He had at least two sons, one of whom, Nicholas, had been educated at Cambridge and became chancellor of St. Patrick's cathedral, Dublin. He had helped in the printing of the first Irish translation of the New Testament. Nicholas was made protestant bishop of Ossory in 1577. Patrick Walsh seems to have been catholic during the period of the Marian restoration. No record of Walsh's actual reconciliation with Rome exists. It seems possible that he procured a papal bull appointing him bishop of the diocese very early in the reign of Queen Mary. Fr. Thomas Strange, a Waterford man like Walsh, guardian of the franciscan friary in Dublin, in a letter to Luke Wadding in 1629 stated that

> Fr. Walsh, Lord bishop of Waterford, showed him in private an authentic copy of the bull[1]

Cardinal Pole, cousin of Queen Mary and papal legate to England with a mandate also to enquire into Irish affairs, did not question the orthodoxy or canonical position of Walsh.

However, the accession of Queen Elizabeth caused a rethink on the part of bishop Walsh. There is ample evidence that he was among the number of bishops who took the Oath of Supremacy, if not also that of Uniformity, while attending the Dublin parliament of 1560. The Crown clearly had confidence in Walsh and he was placed on several important royal commissions during the reign of Elizabeth.

Walsh was a conformist. David Wolfe, S.J. in his report on Ireland relegates Walsh to the category of state bishops in 1574. The likelihood is that Patrick Walsh went with whatever prevailing political wind that was blowing. Whether, at any particular time, he was schismatic or heretic or papist is impossible to say. He probably did not enforce the new religion with any zest or zeal. In 1566 he resigned the deanship of Waterford but he did a strange thing in rather daringly recommending that the most zealous catholic priest of the diocese, Peter White, be appointed to the vacancy.[2]

---

[1] Thomas Strange to Wadding, Dublin, 29 Nov. 1629 *Wadding Papers*, 319
[2] This was the Peter White who set up a school in Waterford and later in Kilkenny. Patrick Comerford and other prominent young people from Waterford attended White's school.

Patrick Comerford was, in 1629, returning to a diocese which had not experienced the services or attention of a bishop for nearly three quarters of a century; and he was a new kind of bishop for his diocese, a man trained in the ways of the counter-reformation, deeply convinced of the importance of the diocese and the central role of command which was to belong to the bishop alone.

The Irish catholic church had suffered very seriously throughout the latter half of the sixteenth century, the century of the reformation, when Henry VIII split with Rome, the century when protestantism was introduced to Ireland, when the monasteries and religious houses were dissolved and their property and other assets were largely granted to lay people. Many of these people were what is termed New English, such as Richard Boyle, great earl of Cork, who were to be found in increasing numbers in Ireland. Many episcopal sees were granted to men who had conformed to the new religion, some of whom had changed their allegiance from Rome to the crown.

The parish system in each diocese was taken over by adherents of the new religion. Tithes had to be paid to them by the people, the majority of whom were catholics, for the upkeep of the protestant ministers, bishops and local pastors. Many of the ministers had come over from England to the parishes, especially to the most prosperous of them. There were also catholic priests who, externally at least, had conformed to protestantism.

The reformation was a European affair and the catholic church had to address the reformation, the reasons which provoked it and the remedies, many of them crying out for implementation which were needed to establish the church on a firm and confident footing. From Rome's viewpoint much policy, called counter reformation policy, was determined for the entire church by the Council of Trent.

The council of Trent met for three lengthy sessions: 1545-47, 1551-52, 1562-63. It was not until the last session that Ireland was properly represented: by the bishops of Achonry, Ross and Raphoe.[3] Patrick Corish puts it well and accurately when he writes:

> In all its reforms, the Council of Trent had one overriding preoccupation – to ensure, in so far as legislature could ensure it, that the whole elaborate system of the church's pastoral ministry should be purged of the abuses which in the past had seemed to divert to almost any end except its true one of seeing that the consolations of religion were brought to the Christian people.[4]

---

[3] Theiner, A., *Alta S.C. Tridentinis*, ii, 53, 136, 228
  O'Sullivan-Beare, P., *Historiae Catholicae Iberniae Compendium*, I, 10
  cf. Trent, Sess. I, C. 8; XXIII, C. I, r, 9, 15, XXV, C.11 (all *de Reformatione*)
[4] Corish, P., 'An Irish Counter-Reformation Bishop: John Roche, I.T.Q. (Vol XXV, No. 2) April 1958, 105

The council had to attempt in the strongest of terms to sweep away the abuses which had made reformation so necessary. The council was the catholic church's supreme attempt to engineer strict reform from within in answer to the protestant reformation which had exposed the abuses of the past but, of itself, had created divisions of an enduring and indelicate nature in christendom.

Trent placed at the heart of its renewal and reform the bishop and his diocese. Abuses and exceptions and exemptions of the past, either in the selection or in the appointment of bishops, had to be swept away. Every care would have to be taken in future to appoint worthy men who would be the key vehicles of ensuring tridentine reform to every part of the church. The bishop emerges from Trent as the single and central source of jurisdiction within his diocese. He himself was to be answerable in a detailed and immediate way to Rome which had to reorganise itself to provide him with the encouragement and, if necessary, the guidance and correction that would be needed in ensuring proper pastoral care for the people of his diocese.

The bishop and his diocese were central. The parish and its pastor were to be the carefully and properly structured channel though which pastoral care, preaching and teaching, administration of the sacraments, provision of proper churches and schools, were to be provided for the faithful. It was absolutely crucial that the pastors, parish priests and their assistants, in the future would be properly trained and disciplined for their central role in dispensing God's grace to the faithful. This requirement meant that the training and preparation for priesthood should receive maximum attention in every diocese. That attention was to be ensured primarily by the establishment in every diocese, where possible, of colleges or seminaries or training centres, under the watchful and protective guidance of the bishop and staffed by excellent and well trained priests. What came to be known as the counter-reformation seminary was a very special outcome of the council of Trent. Without it the many other reforms proposed by the council would not have been possible. We have noted already (p.25-27) the proliferation of such seminaries in many European countries for the training of future priests of Ireland. Given the legal situation in Ireland in the late sixteenth and throughout much of the seventeenth centuries, the establishment of such seminaries in Ireland itself could not be contemplated.

Another outcome of the council of Trent which was to present many problems in Ireland (and even more so in England) was the position of the regular clergy. Monks such as the cistercians and canons regular of St. Augustine, and friars such as the franciscans, dominicans, eremites of St. Augustine, were to be found in pre-reformation Ireland. Many continued to exercise ministry, albeit often a covert ministry, after the dissolution of the monasteries in the 1530's and 1540's. Their method of training had to be revamped also and this could only take place on the continent of Europe. So we find students for the various religious orders side by side with students for the diocesan priesthood in seminaries in Spain, Portugal, France and Belgium and also in their own special centres of formation and study. When, as the seventeenth century got under way, we find these newly trained regulars returning to Ireland and joining with their senior monks and friars who had remained on in the country, difficulties were to arise with considerable frequency when bishops, new kinds of bishops, came to be appointed in the second quarter of the seventeenth century. There had been very few bishops in Ireland in the early years of the seventeenth century. This had meant that the regular clergy were not impeded in wide jurisdictional activity which they had exercised in matters like the administration of the sacraments, funerals, marriages, receiving maintenance and financial help from those of the faithful who could supply it. Differences, some serious, some even scandalous, were to occur between the secular clergy, answerable to the new kind of bishop and the regular clergy, still legatees of wide missionary faculties which had been given by Rome during the difficult years after the reformation.

In line with the thinking of the council of Trent, Rome had also to look to itself in the matter of reorganisation. As in the past, each country had a cardinal in curia assigned to it as protector. The protector was, to some extent, an honorific matter but he could be very necessary as a personal contact with the Pope and as an important adviser in appointments, particularly of bishops to Irish dioceses. The cardinal protectors of Ireland in the early seventeenth century were: Girolamo Mattei (1594-1603), Pompeo Arrigoni (1605-1616), Fabrizio Veralo (1616-1624), Ludovico Ludovisi (1624-1632), Antonio Barberini (1633-1645). It was becoming increasingly clear, as the seventeenth century progressed, that, while Ireland, unlike England, was not technically a mission country, because of its complex character, it had many features of a mission situation. Thus, when the new Congregation de Propaganda Fide was set up in 1622, much of the affairs of Ireland were dealt with by this congregation. The cardinal prefects of Propaganda were: Antonius Maria Sauli (1622), Ludovico Ludovisi (1622-1632), Antonius Barberini (1632-1671). For the period being discussed in this work, the secretary of Propaganda had much practical influence at a very high Roman level; Franciscus Ingoli (1622-1649), Dionysius Massari (1649-1664).

Patrick Comerford arrived in Waterford in 1629. He was a new kind of bishop, a product of the counter-reformation training which the council of Trent had encouraged. For a long time Rome had not been appointing bishops to Ireland because it felt that the Irish scene, akin to the scene in England, was not stable enough to allow the tridentine vision of reform centering on the bishop, his priests and his diocese, to be implemented. For quite a period, sometimes going back to the mid 1550's, many Irish dioceses had no catholic bishop. Rome had always tried to make appointments to the four archdioceses, Armagh, Dublin, Cashel and Tuam. As the 1600's got under way there was a fear that, as in England, the Irish hierarchy might cease to be. Irish influences in Rome itself were particularly fearful. Particularly strong pressure came from the Waterford man, Peter Lombard, who was appointed archbishop of Armagh but remained resident in Rome, never returning to Ireland. He was a strong adviser to the papacy on Irish matters. He saw value in King James' attitude of granting *de facto* tolerance to catholics in Ireland, while at the same time encouraging a gradual conversion of the Irish people to protestantism. Lombard died in 1625 and it was after his death that the Roman authorities systematically began to implement the building up of the Irish hierarchy which he, Lombard, had advocated. The exiled earls of Tyrone and Tirconnell were also encouraging the appointment of bishops to Ireland but their concern chiefly was with the northern dioceses and especially with the archdiocese of Armagh.

In 1600 the Irish hierarchy consisted of four archbishops and one other bishop. Only one was resident in Ireland: archbishop David Kearney of Cashel. Many dioceses, including Waterford and Lismore, had vicars apostolic who were appointed by Rome. In some cases, the metropolitan of the province, instead of applying to Rome for a vicar apostolic in one of the suffragan sees, might himself appoint a vicar general to govern the see. This happened in the case of Waterford and Lismore. Thomas Walsh was priest of the diocese and had been vicar apostolic of Waterford and Lismore. When he became archbishop of Cashel in 1626 he appointed one of the Waterford priests, Laurence Lea, as vicar general. Lea was in that position when Patrick Comerford arrived as bishop.

The situation in England was somewhat similar but serious differences were present. At the reformation all the dioceses and their cathedrals were taken over by the rulers of protestantism. Rome divided the country, not into dioceses, but into districts. There was only one vicar apostolic or arch priest who had episcopal orders, Richard Smith, titular bishop of Chalcedon who was appointed in 1625 and who had an uneasy regime until he finally decided to leave England in 1631. From 1631 till the 1680's there was no catholic bishop at all in England. England was very definitely seen by Rome as mission territory. So it was to remain in law until 1850 when the hierarchy was restored under Nicholas Wiseman, Spanish born but of Waterford parents. He was educated in his early years in Waterford before going to Rome where he was to spend many years. Wiseman, who became a cardinal in 1850, was the first archbishop of Westminster.

What might be termed the steady restoration of the Irish hierarchy could be said to have begun with the appointment of Kilkenny man, David Rothe, as bishop of Ossory in 1620. Rothe was vicar general of Armagh, deputising for Peter Lombard. He was looked on by many, including Patrick Comerford, as the leader of the Irish bishops through the 1620's and 1630's. To illustrate the change in the Irish church after the appointment of David Rothe, the following list surely emphasises the point:

1620	David Rothe	to	Ossory
1622	Thomas Dease	to	Meath
1623	Richard Arthur	to	Limerick
	Maurice O'Hurley	to	Emily
	William Tirry	to	Cork and Cloyne
	Thomas Fleming O.F.M.	to	Dublin

1624	John Roche	to	Ferns
1625	Patrick Hanratty	to	Dromore
1626	*Hugh O'Reilly	to	Kilmore
	HughMcCaughwell O.F.M.	to	Armagh (died 1626)
	John O'Cullenan	to	Raphoe
	Boethius MacEgan O.F.M.	to	Elphin
	Thomas Walsh	to	Cashel
1628	*Hugh O'Reilly	to	Armagh
1629	Patrick Comerford O.S.A.	to	Waterford and Lismore
1630	Roch MacGeoghan O.P.	to	Kildare
	Malachy Queely	to	Tuam
	John O'Moloney	to	Killaloe
	Bonaventure Magennis	to	Down and Connor
	Eugene MacSweeney	to	Kilmore
1642	John Bourke (de Burgo)	to	Clonfert
1643	Richard O'Connell	to	Ardfert and Aghadoe
	Edward O'Dempsey O.P.	to	Leighlin
	Heber Macmahon	to	Clogher
1645	Nicholas French	to	Ferns
	Edward O'Dwyer	to	Limerick
	Francis Kirwan	to	Killala
1647	Andrew Lynch	to	Kilfenora
1648	Patrick Plunkett O. Cist.	to	Ardagh
	Anthony MacGeoghegan	to	Clonmacnois
	Oliver Darcy O.P.	to	Dromore
	Terence O'Brien O.P.	to	Emly
	Boethius Egan O.F.M.	to	Ross
	Walter Lynch O.P.	to	Clonfert
	Robert Barry	to	Cork and Cloyne
	Hugh Bourke	to	Kilmacduagh

*Hugh McCaughwell O.F.M. died in 1626, the year in which he was appointed to Armagh. Hugh O'Reilly was transferred from Kilmore to Armagh in 1628.

These bishops were indeed, by and large, a remarkable group of men and, despite even the Cromwellian calamity at the mid point of the century their influence was destined to survive.[5]

---

[5] The nine appointments in 1648 were largely due to archbishop Rinuccini, the papal nuncio. He was to leave Ireland the following year.

Some of the bishops appointed 1629-1648 were of old English stock, some were of old Irish stock; also some were from the regular clergy, some from the diocesan or secular clergy.

As is clear from the name, the diocese of Waterford and Lismore was formerly two dioceses, one with its cathedral seat at Waterford, the other at Lismore. Indeed, for a brief period in the late twelfth and early thirteenth centuries, there was a third diocese also: Ardmore. It quickly became subsumed into Lismore. The dioceses of Waterford and Lismore were united in 1363 but they continued to hold separate chapters until the upheaval and almost the breakdown of catholic church organisations in the sixteenth century.[6] The diocese of Waterford and Lismore comprised, then as now, most of the present county Waterford as well as the major towns of south county Tipperary, with their surrounding countryside. Along the sea coast the diocese runs from Waterford city through Dungarvan and Ardmore to Youghal harbour. It is bounded on the west by the diocese of Cloyne, on the north by the archdiocese of Cashel, on the north east and east by the dioceses of Ossory and Ferns, both of which are in the metropolitan province of Dublin. The principal towns in the diocese of Waterford and Lismore in the seventeenth century were Waterford city, Clonmel, Dungarvan, Lismore, Carrick-on-Suir and Cahir.

As was mentioned earlier, the city of Waterford was traditionally royalist and had proven its loyalty to the crown many times over the centuries. Prior to Tudor times the rest of the diocese was little enough concerned with English rule. It lay largely under the leadership of two great Old English earls, Desmond and Ormond, whose frequent rivalry created much strife and havoc in the sixteenth century. Like their counterparts in the rest of Ireland, these earls administered feudal justice, each within his respective territory, and paid little more than nominal allegiance to their sovereign, the English monarch. Of more immediate relevance to the people of the area of the diocese of Waterford and Lismore were local lords such as the Powers of Dunhill and Curraghmnore in the east and the Fitzgeralds of Dromana, relatives of the earls of Dermond, whose major seat was Dromana in West Waterford. The area of the diocese in South Tipperary was largely controlled by the Butler or Ormond chiefs with bases in Carrick-on-Suir, Kilcash and Cahir. Also surviving were remnants of the old native great Irish families, O'Faoláins, McGraths, O'Kennedys. During the reign of Elizabeth these latter families were generally rendered submissive to the crown. Of the great Old English families Ormond was to become a most loyal follower of the crown and Desmond's power was largely destroyed forever with the suppression of the Desmond rebellion towards the end of the sixteenth century. The Plantation of Munster, which began in 1585, brought many new English into the area of the diocese of Waterford and Lismore. The best known of these were Sir Walter Raleigh with his seat at Youghal and much land in the Blackwater Valley and Sir Richard Boyle, the first earl of Cork, who was to acquire much of Raleigh's property and who had his main residence at the former episcopal castle at Lismore and also at Youghal.

---

[6] Power, P., *Waterford and Lismore A Compendious History of the United Dioceses, 11*

During the wars which marked the last ten years of Queen Elizabeth's reign, English officials, soldiers and adventurers engaged in the subjugation of much of the area of the diocese of Waterford and Lismore. During the reign of James I this trend continued. Many, in fact most, of the church buildings throughout the diocese were reduced to ruins during the Elizabethan period. Almost all the monasteries of the diocese had been dissolved during the Henrician period; the monks had, to a great extent, disbanded. Church property, which in some cases had been very extensive, had nearly always been leased to neighbouring landed people or became the property of the crown which leased it to new English applicants.

All of this meant that the catholic clergy, secular and religious, had to depend almost completely on the charity of their people and on whatever goodwill might be shown by those who had come into possession of church property. Despite the deprivations of property and the fairly continuous antagonisms towards catholic clergy, the number of priests in the diocese remained quite high. In 1610 it is recorded that there were at least thirty priests in Waterford city and sixteen in the country area. In addition to these secular priests, there were three cistercians, five franciscans, three jesuits and one augustine eremite.[7] Earlier still, in 1588, there is the visitation list of bishop Miler MacGrath. It is both confusing and sometimes grossly inaccurate; clearly papist clergy and new clergy of the established church were listed without discrimination; but the number of clergy is considerable.[8]

Despite the intermittent punishment for the faith during the reign of James I and the general attempt to make catholicism undesirable during that reign, the catholic church in Waterford and Lismore began to show obvious signs of benefit from the counter-reformation influences which were at work in the early 1600's. Signs of church reorganisation began to appear increasingly as the century went on. We read of a fairly large meeting or synod of clergy in Waterford city in 1607 under the presidency of the vicar apostolic, James White.[9] From 1610 on, the matter of the appointment of a bishop was being raised within the diocese of Waterford and Lismore. In 1617 Nicholas Fagan, abbot of the dissolved cistercian monastery of Inishlounaght near Clonmel, was being strongly suggested to Rome but his premature death prolonged the vacancy in the diocese for another twelve years.[10]

Patrick Comerford took up office in 1629. We learn something of the religious state of the diocese in the preceding year from a report submitted by the Jesuits who were living and working in the diocese, to their general, Mario Vitelleschi, in Rome. The report largely

[7] Trinity College Dublin, Mss. E3, 15 f. 37, a Report of Royal Officials on the state of the established church in the diocese of Waterford and Lismore, quoted in Power, P., 'Sundrie priests and friars', *Waterford Arch. Soc. Jn, XVI (1913)*, 127 ff.
[8] Power P., 'Bishop Miler Macgrath's Visitation of 1588', *Waterford and Lismore*, 351-6
[9] *Calendar of State Papers relating to Ireland (1606-1608)*, 117
[10] Lynch, John, *De Praesulibus Hiberniae*, ii, 115.
    In fact, Gams, *Series Episcoporum*, 228, lists Nicholas Fagan as having been provided to the See but as having died in 1617. Gams makes no mention of Patrick Walsh whom we discussed earlier.

concerns their own activity but it also has value in that it illustrates well the warm adherence of the people to the faith despite legal and other disadvantages. It comments too on the condition of some of the clergy in the diocese of Waterford and Lismore.[11] Concerning the city of Waterford the report says that, despite the fact that the catholics suffer a lot and are molested by protestants and government officials, their faith is to be seen in the way they provide support of many priests and religious. In vain do the heretics try to terrify the catholics by placing edicts and other proclamations on the doors of the churches. The jesuit fathers, continues the report, have organised a large sodality with great numbers enrolled, most of whom observe the rules well and attend monthly confession. Some conversions are reported and many unhappy marriages have been straightened out. Some time ago the fathers in Clonmel held a mission that was very successful: they went out into the country places to teach the people christian doctrine. In such places they reported that many of the parish clergy were ignorant and unable to teach the laity properly. In an attempt to remedy this situation the vicar general, according to the report, prescribed, *sub poena suspensionis*, that such priests learn by heart in short form the principal chapters of the Catechism and pass them on exactly as they have learned them.[12] The report describes the Holy Week ceremonies as being attended by large crowds. The great feasts such as Our Lady's Assumption were celebrated with fitting ceremony.

It seems correct to state that by 1629 the catholic church in Waterford and Lismore was becoming well organised, the devotional life of the people seemed strong, the number of priests, most of whom were by this stage continental trained, was considerable, though probably not yet fully adequate. One feels that, after the turmoil and uncertainty of the post reformation years, the decision in favour of remaining catholic, had been made by most people. It was for Patrick Comerford to manage the development and to give healthy impetus to proper pastoral activity which would secure the people in the faith. Problems lay ahead, many of them deep-seated, which would have to be tackled.

The diocese of Waterford and Lismore to which bishop Patrick Comerford came in 1629 was also the diocese of the established church. As in Ireland generally the picture here is not happy. As we have seen, the first conformed bishop, Patrick Walsh (1551-78) seems to have made little or no effort to propagate protestantism in the area. After him came Marmaduke Middleton (1578-82) who was involved in serious disputes with the mayor and citizens of Waterford and even with the protestant clergy themselves. Eventually the unhappy bishop had

---

[11] Jesuit general archives, Rome, *Anglia 41*, *Hiberniae Historia 1599-1692, Annuae Hiberniae Societatis Jesu Anni 1628*, 220-222

[12] It might be fair to assume that such priests in the country areas had been ordained in Ireland in the late Elizabethan period when any formal education would have been difficult or impossible. They would have been providing a service by administering the sacraments and celebrating the mass, but they would be quite unprepared for the task of preaching or educating the people.
Thomas Walsh was vicar-apostolic of Waterford and Lismore 1613-26 when he was appointed archbishop of Cashel. Presumably he then made Laurence Lea vicar general in 1626. Patrick Comerford renewed that appointment when he became bishop in 1629.

to resign his see and return to his native England where, in 1582, he became bishop of St. David's in Wales. Many charges and accusations were made against him there. He was deprived of his see in 1593 shortly before he died. On the departure of Middleton the see was granted *in commendam* by the crown to the established archbishop of Cashel, the infamous Miler McGrath. He remained in charge 1582-89. McGrath was to receive a second grant of the see *in commendam* on the death of Thomas Wetherhead, also known as Walley, an Englishman who was bishop of Waterford and Lismore 1589-92.

McGrath was a wily Fermanagh man, a former Franciscan priest, who had in the 1560's conformed to Protestantism and had rapaciously accumulated many important benefices, the most important of which was the archbishopric of Cashel. Sir John Davies, when attorney-general of Ireland, declared that McGrath held four bishoprics and seventy spiritualities! It was he who sold the episcopal estate and castle of Lismore to Sir Walter Raleigh who was to sell it subsequently to the first earl of Cork, Richard Boyle.[13] McGrath was detested by the people. The citizens of Waterford, protestant and catholic, made no effort to pretend courtesy to him on the occasion of his visitations to the city. In 1599 the Mayor and officials bluntly told him that they would have none of his kind among them. Very little taxes or tithes were paid to him and he was treated with open contempt. His real interest in religion, protestant or catholic, was probably very incidental and his main concern lay in the accumulation of wealth. However, he lived to a great age, said to be one hundred years, and he was buried on the Rock of Cashel in 1623.

In 1608 yet another Englishman, John Lancaster, was appointed by the crown as bishop of Waterford and Lismore. He ruled the diocese until his death in 1619. Poverty was a major preoccupation of Lancaster. In 1610 he is noted for holding the following benefices or preferments: prebendary of Carbally, prebendary of Outragh, treasurership of Lismore, prebendary of Tullaghorton, prebendary of Mora, prebendary of Donaghmore and Kiltegan, prebendary of Kilgobinet, prebendary of Kilrossanty, prebendary of Modeligo, vicarage of Ardmore, vicarage of Shanrahan and vicarage of Mothel. Clearly he can have been no way involved in direct pastoral care in these places, many of which were quite distant from Waterford city where he lived. Rennison is probably right when he suggests that the bishop's main reason for acquiring them for himself was that he could find no cleric or no suitable cleric to take them.[14]

In 1615 the commission set up by James I to enquire into the state of the protestant church in Ireland received a deposition by John Lancaster, junior, son of the bishop, and

---

[13]   Hansard, Joseph, *The History, Topography and Antiquities of the County and City of Waterford*, 372-404
[14]   Rennison, William, *Succession List of the Bishops, cathedral and parochial; clergy of the dioceses of Waterford and Lismore*. 62. The information as to the acquisitions made by Lancaster is also supplied by Rennison.

precentor of Waterford and also of Lismore as well as precentor of Disert and Kilmoleran and also vicar of Mothel. He declared in his deposition that the revenue which his father receives from the see of Waterford is not more than £60 per annum.[15] It had been reckoned that the episcopal temporalities of pre-reformation Waterford and Lismore had yielded well over a thousand pounds per annum, so it can be concluded how much of the property had passed into non-ecclesiastical hands.[16] Much property had passed into the hands of adventurers such as Richard Boyle, earl of Cork. Indeed Lancaster's successor as protestant bishop of Waterford and Lismore and a close relative of the earl of Cork, Michael Boyle (1619-35), complained strongly to London that the appropriation by the earl of Cork of almost all the lands of the see of Lismore meant that nearly every vicarage as well as the episcopal temporalities were held by him.[17]

According to the report of the Commission of 1615, the *Liber Regalis Visitationis*, the number of protestant ministers in the diocese was not large. In the diocese of Waterford the visitation returns only four preachers, of whom one is non-resident, and five reading ministers (who might conduct service but not preach). In the diocese of Lismore the return gives twelve preachers, of whom only seven are resident, and seventeen reading ministers. In the diocese of Lismore there is no schoolmaster; in Waterford there is one, the well known John Flahey whom we have met before in discussing the early education of Patrick Comerford. The comments regarding Flahy are interesting:

> There is in the city of Waterford kept by the citizens a publique schoolmaster in the city of Waterford, fflahy, who had great number of schollers resorting to his schoole. Upon our coming to Waterford we first sent for him, but could not get him to appear before us. We then required the Mayor and Sheriff of the city to bring him before us wth they answered they could not doe, by reason the said fflahy did fly out of the citty, a little before our coming. Whereupon we left a L[re] (letter) with the Lord President of that province under o[r] (our) hands, praying and requiring him in his Ma[ties] name to take order to suppresse him from the exercise of teaching and instruction of yought, for he traynes up shcollers to become seminaries beyond the seas and ill affected members, wth the L[d] President did undertake to perform.[18]

---

[15] This report is in the British Museum, Ms. 19, 836; it is printed in 'Documents illustrating the history of Waterford', *Waterford Arch. Soc. Jn.*, VIII (1902/3) 103-15

[16] *Calendar of State Papers Domestic* (1636-1637), 262

[17] Report printed in Coleman, J.,, 'The Earl of Cork's Appropriation of the Revenues of the See of Lismore and St. Mary's Collegiate Church, Youghal, *Waterford Arch. Soc. Jn.*,XI (1908) 230 ff. Bishop Michael Boyle's brother, Richard , was protestant archbishop of Tuam.

[18] Reeves Ms. 1066, Trinity College, Dublin

Bishop Michael Boyle died in 1635 and was succeeded by John Atherton from Somerset, England, He was a talented lawyer who determinedly attempted to recover for the established church the property and land which had been lost to the church since reformation times. He made many enemies who may perhaps have helped his downfall. He was charged with alleged sexual crimes with his proctor, John Childe. They were tried and executed in December 1640.[19]

The first record which we have of Bishop Comerford's presence in Ireland is his attendance at an important meeting of the Munster and Leinster bishops 24-27 August 1629.[20] According as the hierarchy grew in number such meetings became a special feature of Irish church life in the seventeenth century. It is not correct, as occasionally happens, to refer to all such meetings as synods. Concerning some of them, all we know is the bare fact that they took place. Concerning others, we read about them in reports sent from Ireland to Propaganda in Rome.[21] Some of the meetings drew up acts and legislation which were serious and synodical. These regular episcopal meetings, some diocesan, the majority provincial, a few even inter-provincial, became a clear feature of the counter-reformation in Ireland and, indeed, despite the later disruption of the Cromwellian period, a pattern of episcopal rule was created which was to outlive the seventeenth century. To a large extent, through the force created by such meetings, the catholic bishops were to emerge as the main agents of reform with strong jurisdiction over the clergy and their parishes. David Rothe, bishop of Ossory (1620-50) had been the effective leader of the Irish catholic church on his appointment as vicar-general of Armagh in 1610. He acted for Peter Lombard, the Waterford-born archbishop of Armagh who spent all his episcopal years in Rome until his death in 1625. During the period 1610 till 1625 David Rothe was the spearhead of many of these meetings of the bishops. He was to remain a strong moral force amongst the bishops throughout the 1630's and during the exciting times of the Confederation of Kilkenny in the 1640's.[22] He was friend of and strong influence on Patrick Comerford.

The meeting in Kilkenny in late August 1629 was held in bishop Rothe's residence but was presided over by archbishop Thomas Fleming O.F.M. of Dublin. Present at the meeting were: Thomas Walsh, archbishop of Cashel, John Roche, bishop of Ferns, Wiliam Tirry, bishop of Cork and Cloyne and Patrick Comerford, Bishop of Waterford and Lismore. It was Comerford's first episcopal meeting; it was also John Roche's first – even though he had been

---

[19] Norton, Victor, *The Life and Death of John Atherton*
Bernard, Nicholas, *The Penitent Death of a Woefull Sinner, or, the Penitent Death of John Atherton executed at Dublin the 5 of December 1640*
Clarke, Aidan, 'The Atherton File', *Decies* XI (1979) 45-55
[20] APF, SOCG, 294, f. 280 R
[21] The Roman Congregation for the Propagation of the faith or Congregatio de Propaganda Fide was founded in 1622, and the Irish church was placed under its supervision because of the missionary character of Ireland at the time. It is referred to by the abbreviated code name of Propaganda. Ireland (and Scotland and England) remained under Propaganda until 1908.
[22] A careful treatment and examination of these councils and synods is to be found in Forrestal, Alison, *Catholic Synods in Ireland 1608-1690*

consecrated bishop in 1627. It may also have been Thomas Walsh's first meeting as he had been in Spain for several years after his consecration as archbishop of Cashel in 1626.

We have referred earlier to bishop Comerford's journey home in the summer months of 1629.[23] Reports were reaching him while he was still on the continent of a disquieting change in the hitherto tolerating attitude of the government in Ireland towards catholics and their practice of their religion.[24] The reign of Charles I had opened benignly for the catholics. Charles was married to Henrietta Maria, daughter of Henry IV of France. An active and pronounced anti-catholic policy in Ireland would have caused strained relations with her native country. Of more particular concern to Charles was the fact that the war which had broken out against Spain in 1625 had gone very much against England and there was the ever present fear of a Spanish invasion of Ireland. The *de facto* toleration of catholics by the government in Ireland drew strong opposition from the leaders of the established church. Protestant bishops such as George Downham of Derry and James Ussher of Armagh and Malcolm Hamilton of Cashel accused the king of 'setting religion for sale' in the recent negotiations which had been taking place with catholic Old English leaders concerning the royal need for money to maintain and equip a proper army in Ireland. The outcome of protestant opposition was the transfer of the negotiations to the more private and sheltered scene of Oxford in England. Arising from these negotiations, in which Old English and more recent protestant settlers met prominent members of the English privy council, was the drawing up of 'His Majesty's instructions and graces', known colloquially as the 'Graces' which, in return for money to the tune of £40,000 per annum for three years, the crown would grant concessions to the Irish, protestant and catholic, in the area of land titles and toleration. It was all a bit hazy and the new English settlers gained much more from the negotiations than did the Old English catholics. Concessions were guardedly given in the matter of religion; the Oath of Supremacy, which was not removed, could be substituted by a simple oath of allegiance to the crown. Recusancy fines were not to be strongly enforced and, as regards land, the conditions of plantation were to be carefully regulated and compensation made for wrong done. A good deal of money was paid but the 'Graces' were never legalised and most of the promises made were never observed. Nevertheless, for much of his early reign king Charles could not in decency proceed against the catholics who formed the vast majority of those who contributed the promised sums.[25]

This is the backdrop to the toleration shown to catholics in the years leading up to 1629. The catholics took advantage of this toleration. Many churches were erected and crowds went openly to mass. Waterford was to benefit from this period of toleration by the restoration of its

---

[23] Supra. 41

[24] Comerford to Eugene Callanan, rector of the Irish college, Rome, Louvain, 21 June 1629, *Wadding Papers*, 295

[25] Clarke, Aidan, 'Selling Royal Favours, 1624-32' *N.H.I.*, vol. III, 235-8, *The Graces*, 1625-41

charter in 1626. The citizens immediately elected a catholic mayor, James Woodlock.[26] Throughout Munster the people of the major towns elected officials who were catholic and there was even witnessed the anomalous image of the mayor, the representative of his majesty, having the sword of the king carried before him to mass on Sundays. This state of affairs could not be allowed continue. Against his own better judgment, Sir Henry Cary, Viscount Falkland, Lord Deputy 1622-9, under special pressure of the privy council in England, had to act. On 1 April 1629 he issued a proclamation forbidding the exercise of ecclesiastical jurisdiction from Rome, and ordering catholic colleges and religious houses to be dissolved under pain of seizure.[27] In Dublin the proclamation was obeyed, at least for the time being. It was not so well observed throughout the country but it did have the effect of making people aware that toleration should not be taken for granted. It also fostered the fear that some more stringent measures might be taken by the government.

To Patrick Comerford, journeying to Ireland, the news of the changed attitude towards catholics was disquieting. Even more disturbing, perhaps, was news of serious dissensions within his own diocese of Waterford and Lismore.[28] In particular, he feared that he would have to face trouble with the cistercians in his diocese over the possession of the monastery at Mothel in the heart of county Waterford.[29] He writes to Eugene Callanan that he has received warnings that certain unsuitable individuals were trying to claim benefices in his diocese. He asks Callanan to do his best in Rome to prevent any grants of benefices in Waterford and Lismore which might be requested without his (Comerford's) consent.[30]

By August 1629, when Comerford had reached Ireland, the tension caused by Falkland's April proclamation seems to have subsided and meetings of clergy and other demonstrations of faith were occurring. Falkland himself had departed for England shortly after the proclamation in order to defend himself against many detractors. For the present the country was in the charge of an uneasy partnership of Richard Boyle, earl of Cork and Adam Loftus, Lord Justices. However, trouble was to break out again before 1629 was over.

With the general situation in Ireland in mind as well as the fear of upcoming trouble with the cistercians and perhaps with others, Patrick Comerford took his place at the meeting of bishops in Kilkenny in August 1629. One of the main matters discussed seems to have been the necessity, as laid down by Trent, of centering control and jurisdiction within the Irish church in the hands of the diocesan bishop. In all probability the basis for the discussions were regulations for the Irish church issued by the Holy Office in Rome in August 1626. A copy of

---

[26] Walton, Julian 'Agin the Government Sir Richard Aylward, Mayor 1592-93, 1605-6, 1607-7, 1616-17, McEneaney, Eamonn (ed.) *A History of Waterford and its Mayors*, 131-2

[27] *Calendar of State Papers relating to Ireland (1625-1633)*, 444 ff.

[28] Comerford to Wadding, Antwerp, 19 July 1629, *Wadding Papers*, 298.

[29] Same to Callanan, Louvain, 21 July 1629, ibid, 294.

[30] Ibid.

these regulations or decrees had recently been brought back from Rome by bishop John Roche who had only arrived in Ireland around the same time as bishop Comerford.[31] No copy of these regulations of the Holy Office has been found but it is clear that their main concern was the restriction of the extensive missionary faculties hitherto enjoyed by the regular clergy in Ireland.[32] Bishop Roche reported to Propaganda that many things were related at the meeting to their (the regulars') discredit and instances of their misconduct were recounted. Still the bishops agreed to proceed with much patience in their dealings with the regulars, awaiting better and more peaceful times when harmony would be more easily attainable. It was not the intention of the bishops to publish any decrees from the Kilkenny meeting. However, the regular clergy, concerning whom there was much discussion at the meeting, became suspicious and engaged in much comment and conjecture as to what decisions had been taken by the bishops.[33] The outcome of this was that Rome began to make enquiries and a report of the meeting and a copy of its decisions were sent by bishop Roche to Propaganda.[34]

The decrees are mainly concerned with establishing clearly the diocesan system and centralising the control in each diocese under the bishop. It was laid down that the tridentine legislation was to be observed in Ireland, except the decrees concerning marriage which required special promulgation, and also such regulations as clearly could not be applied in the peculiar conditions existing in Ireland. The bishop was to have control over all pastoral activity within his diocese; everyone, regular and secular, who had the care of souls in the diocese, was to be subject to the bishop's visitation. The hitherto wide faculties enjoyed by the regulars were declared restricted by the decree of the Holy Office of August 1626. It was the opinion of the bishops in Kilkenny that, because of the instability of religious conditions and the almost impossibility of practicing the communal life in Ireland, the religious orders could not be considered totally exempt. An attempt was made to prepare the way for an amicable solution to many problems which caused friction between the regular and secular clergy such as the right of burial (ins sepulturae) and funeral offerings (oblationes funerales). The final and sixteenth decree of the meeting expressed the wish that a similar meeting should be held every year or at least every two years. Bishop Roche concluded his report on the meeting to Propaganda with a simple sentence: 'Absoluto conventu recessimus ornnes ad suam quisue curam' – heartened and enlightened by mutual discussion and agreement, the bishops returned to their dioceses to

---

[31] Roche to Propaganda, 1 Dec. 1629, APF. SOCG, 204, f. 31 R
Same to same, 9 Feb. 1630, ibid., 132, f. 288RV
[32] An account of this Kilkenny meeting forms part of a report of bishop Roche to Propaganda on 1 December 1629, APF, SOCG, 294, ff. 312R– 319V
The acts of the meeting are in APF, SOCG, 294, ff. 269R-280R and are printed in Moran, *Archbishops of Dublin*, Vol I, 434-36
[33] Roche to cardinal Ludovisi, protector of Ireland, 20 July 1631, printed in Moran, *Spicil.. Ossor.,* I, 173
[34] Roche to Propaganda, 1 Dec. 1629, APF, SOCG 294, 312R – 319V

attempt to put into practice what might have seemed reasonable at the council table. A heavy task lay before them.[35]

And so Patrick Comerford left Kilkenny, a city he knew so well from his youthful days at Peter White's school and from his years as prior in commendam of the augustinian abbey of Kells which was only a few miles away. A few months later, after he had taken up office as bishop of Waterford and Lismore, he wrote to his friend and kinsman, Luke Wadding, with a heavy heart.[36]

> As for my relation of the state of the country, I may not extend my self very much therin, for I am not yet full seene in the carriages of many things; but this I can say, that it is the moisiest, the stormiest, the poorest, and most oppressed countrie that I saw since I left it until I returned. And it if were not for the same instinct of nature, dulcis amor patriae, with all my heart I would change with the houmbliest converso of your thrice happie college of St. Isidoro. As for tradinge, or stirring in mercantile affairs, which is nervus hujus regni, it is so much forgotten, that scarce a man doth know of what colour is the coine in this miserable island; the deart of the two last years, the universall sickness, the oppression of souldiers, besid other incumbrances have made Ireland to seem to be in verie deede te land of ire; at sea a merchant can not navegat two days, when he is taken either by a Hollander, or a Dunkerk, or a French pirate, or a hungrie Biscaner. The weather is soe rainie, and drousie continually, that it doth imprint, and indent in a mans heart a certaine saturn qualitie of heavinesse, sloughishness, lasiness and perpetual solute. Oure deputie[37] is gone for England, and in his steede doe govern the kingdome the lorde of Corck, and the lord chancelor[38]; what is theire minde, wee do not know yet, but if they will not expel us out of the kingdome, I know not what other punishment can they inflict upon us; for money, or meanes, they can not finde in any place of Ireland.

As he had done on his homeward journey from the continent, Comerford, in these early days in his diocese, stresses his personal poverty. He tells Wadding that, were it not for his brother Philip who gives him a bed at his residence in Waterford

> I know not where to blow in my nose.

He says that he does not receive much charity because people think he is a rich man; he is rich *'propter ius ad re*m' not *'propter ius in re'*. Any wealth which there was in the diocese has

---

[35] The acts themselves are in Moran, *Archbishops of Dublin*, Vol I, 434-6
[36] Comerford to Wadding, Waterford, 22 Nov. 1629, *Wadding Papers*, 320-5
[37] Viscount Falkland, Lord Deputy 1622-29
[38] Richard Boyle, earl of Cork and Adam Loftus, viscount of Ely O'Carroll and Lord Chancellor, governed Ireland until the appointment of Thomas Wentworth as Lord Deputy in 1622.

been appropriated by the protestants and whatever little falls to the catholics finds its way into the hands of the regular clergy.[39] We learn later, when controversy between the bishop and the regular clergy had broken out, from an opponent of the bishop why Comerford did not receive hospitality especially from the regulars:

> there are not two houses in the whole of the city where he (Comerford) is sure of a meal because the seculars themselves deplore his opposition to the regulars[40]

One of Comerford's first actions on arrival in Waterford as bishop was to visit the entire diocese; he found that the long vacancy had left it in a bad state. What struck him most forcibly in the course of his visitation was the great number of the old parish churches and spacious monasteries which had been reduced to ruins ' quae olim vomere predicationis, sacramentorum frequenti administratione, et Sanctus Ecciae Cath. ritibus exalta erant'. He reports to Propaganda that all the houses and oratories formerly used by the catholic clergy have been confiscated by the crown. The clergy are without houses and often have to go into hiding, the divine offices and sermons are forbidden under great penalties, and community life has been dissolved under the threat of severe punishment. No publicity is allowed in the performance of the functions of the catholic faith. In his visitation he visited all the parish priests and he administered the sacrament of confirmation to more than two thousand people, of whom many were sixty and seventy years of age and who never before in their lives have had the opportunity to meet a bishop and be consoled by his ministry. He reports that there are about forty secular priests in the diocese and that they are vigilant and attentive to their pastoral duties.[41] The regulars also, who number about thirty, he finds, on the whole zealous and a good example to the people. He is disturbed by the fact that the people in the outlying areas 'remotiores a civitatibus et oppidio' have not sufficient priests to attend to their pastoral needs. They have the

---

[39] Comerford to Wadding, 7 March 1630 (24 Feb. 1629 O.S.), Waterford., *Wadding Papers*, 345. In this letter Comerford gives his address as High Street, presumably where his brother lived. At this time High Street was perhaps the finest street in the city, the location of good business premises

[40] 'No tiene dos casa en toda esta ciadad donde le combidan a una comida, porque los mismos seglares sienten opposicion a Los Religioses' – Thomas Strange, guardian of the franciscan convent in Waterford to Wadding, Waterford, 10 Sept. 1631*Wadding Papers*, 580
Thomas Strange (Stronge) was a Waterford franciscan, a cousin of Wadding (and perhaps of Comerford). He began his franciscan life in Spain. Prior to that he had been a student of Douai and Louvain. He rose to high position in the Irish province and, for a while, he acted as agent for the Irish clergy in the English court. He was proposed for the bishoprick of Waterford and Lismore. He was falsely accused of heretical statements by secular priests in Dublin but.with Wadding's help, he cleared his name in Ireland and Rome. He was guardian of the franciscans in Waterford in 1629. He died in Waterford in 1645

[41] Comerford to Propaganda, 6 July 1630, APF, SOCF, 294 ff. 221R-222R; this report is printed in *Spicil. Ossor*. i, 165-9. Other reports, substantially the same as this one, submitted by Comerford to Rome in these early months of his episcopate, are in:
APF, SOCG, 132, f. 281R, 18 Jan 1630 (8 Jan. 1629 O.S.)
ibid., 132, f. 282R, 20 Jan. 1620 (10 Jan. 1629 O.S.)
ibid., 133, f. 281R, 20 June 1630

faith, but, being deprived of priests, they are a constant prey of the ministers of the established religion: 'Sitientes aquam salutis, esurientes panem verbum Dei, obsessi a lupis et ursis adversae professionis, vix inveniunt, qui vel fragmenta panis porrigat, vel calicem e profluente propinet'.[42]

In his early reports to Rome, Comerford states that, as part of a definite programme for reform, he convened a diocesan synod of priests at which statutes were drawn up for the proper organisation of the diocese. No copy of these statutes has been preserved but we can confidently assume that they were an application of the decisions taken by the bishops at the Kilkenny meeting held in the previous August. As a first move towards providing an efficient ministry for his flock Comerford appointed five more parish priests for the city of Waterford. He also, in those early days, assembled the regular clergy and informed them that the old missionary days were over and that Pope Urban VIII had withdrawn from them the extensive missionary faculties which they had previously held. In doing this, Comerford insists that he was only following the example of the rest of the bishops. But his announcement was by no means received peacefully. He says that the regulars immediately opposed him and resisted his attempts. They also encouraged the laity to join them in opposition to the bishop. He had thrown down the gauntlet to them and a bitter fight had begun. The regulars, Comerford claims, have been so audacious as to call in doubt the authority of the Holy Father himself to restrict the faculties which had been given to them. Thus, he sadly remarks, the very people who should be aiding the bishop to establish order and harmony are, in fact, stirring up dissension. They behave in an irreverent manner towards the bishop and towards other church dignitaries and they attempt to inculcate in the people a wish for a false democracy where the authority of the bishop would count for nothing. He suggests that the leaders of Propaganda in Rome and the superior-generals of the religious orders should write to each and every regular cleric in Ireland commanding them to obey the local ordinaries and to cease to stir up the people against them.[43] In his early reports to Rome he singles out the cistercians as the most troublesome of all the religious. Almost all the bishops, he claims, have trouble with them. They claim jurisdiction not merely over the remnants of their old monasteries but also over the parishes traditionally annexed to the monasteries, and they refuse to acknowledge the authority of the bishop over all the parishes in his diocese.[44]

In his early reports to Propaganda, Comerford touched on most of the difficulties which faced an Irish counter-reformation bishop in the first half of the seventeenth century. There was

---

[42]   APF, SOCG, 294, f. 221R, printed in Moran, op. cit, 165, 'thirsty for the water of salvation, hungering for the bread which is the word of God, attacked by the wolves and bears of a hostile profession, they can scarcely discover who it is who offers the fragments of bread or who holds forth the flowing chalice'

[43]   APF, SOCG, 194, f. 222R, Moran, op, cit., 168

[44]   Comerford to Propaganda, 18 Jan. 1630 (8 Jan. 1629 O.S.), AOF, SOCG, 132 f 181R

the general breakdown of diocesan discipline and organisation accentuated by wars and sporadic persecution following on the English break with Rome. There was the scarcity of well trained priests, especially in the rural areas, to attend to the people and counteract any proselytising activity which the ministers of the established church might engage in. There was the almost total lack of church buildings and religious houses. There was the extreme poverty of the church due to the appropriation of its land and property, which had sometimes over the years found its way into the hands of catholic lay people. And, particularly sadly from the point of view of the internal peace of the church, there was the beginning of scandalous friction with the regular clergy which would bring a host of other problems in its wake.

The year 1629 ended on an especially anxious note for the catholic church in Ireland following on a conflict which took place in Dublin on St. Stephen's day of that year. Falkland's proclamation against the catholics on 1 April 1629 had the temporary effect of halting the catholics in the open practice of the faith. But, with his departure for England shortly afterwards, they grew bolder again and began to resume open practice of their religion. This stirred up anger in the protestant leadership. Richard Boyle, earl of Cork, who shared the administration of Ireland with Loftus, Earl of Ely, decided to take action. He issued orders for the forcible suppression of some sixteen religious houses in Dublin and the arrest of a number of priests. On St. Stephen's day the protestant archbishop of Dublin, Lancelot Bulkeley, and the lord mayor of Dublin, sir Christopher Forster, raided the carmelite house in Cooke Street with the intention of suppressing it and imprisoning the priests. But the people came to the rescue of the friars, the invaders were forced to flee pursued by stone throwing catholics led by the widow Nugent of Winetavern Street.[45] Consequent on the event there was a stronger tendency on the part of the administration to a general enforcement of the anti-catholic laws not just in Dublin but throughout the country as well. In the city of Dublin, under the encouragement of Boyle, confiscations and burnings took place.[46]

Comerford deplored this state of affairs in a letter to Wadding and he expresses the opinion that the whole unhappy series of events was brought about by imprudent and defiant ostentation by the regular clergy.[47] We next meet with Comerford in these early months of his episcopate at a meeting of the Munster bishops in Limerick in January 1630 at which he was delegated by his fellow-bishops to make out a report to Rome on the state of the Irish church.[48]

---

[45] A detailed account of this event is given in the *Brevis Relatio* of Fr. Paul Brown, discalced Carmelite; cf. Glynn, Marcellus and Martin, F.X. (eds), 'The Brevis Relatio of the Irish Discalced Carmelites 1625-1670', *Archiv. Hib.* XXX (1962) 136-163

[46] Edwards, Robert Dudley, 'Church and State in the Ireland of Micheál ó Cléirigh 1626-41', Sylvester O'Brien (ed.) *Measera Mhichíl Úi Cléirigh*, 7 ff

[47] William Browne (Patrick Comerford) to Wadding, Waterford, 26 August 1630, *Wadding Papers*, 404

[48] Same to Same, 6 March 1630 (24 Feb. 1620 O.S.), *Wadding Papers*, 344. We have no decrees or decisions of this meeting but from it did come a petition to Propaganda to have Richard Connell appointed bishop of Ardfert and Aghadoe. He had been vicar-apostolic of that diocese since 1611. However, Connell was not appointed bishop until 1641. The petition was sent in a letter of the

Probably arising from the discussions at this meeting an interesting petition was sent to Rome, signed by Comerford and some of the Munster and Leinster bishops. It deals with the contemporary English catholic church. The bishops ask that Rome would increase the number of bishops in the country. They express anxiety concerning the situation in England and are aware that they themselves have much in common with the one vicar apostolic in England, the only bishop in that country, Richard Smith, bishop of Chalcedon. The Irish bishops remind Propaganda that, if Ireland had been left without bishops as England has been, the survival of the catholic faith in the country would not be at all guaranteed. They consider that in England things are improving and it would be greatly helpful if the number of bishops were increased, perhaps to three.[49]

It is true that the Irish and English scenes were in fact quite different. The situation in Ireland, where the reformation had not had at all the same opportunity to develop, facilitated the build-up of the hierarchy in the early decades of the seventeenth century. But it is also true that the internal problems of the English church were sufficiently similar to those in Ireland as to be a source of disquiet to the Irish bishops. Above all, the Irish bishops clearly were following the clashes between bishop Smith and the regular clergy. They cannot have failed to read some of the literature which emerged in England from those clashes. The settlement of the English controversy which was proposed by Rome in the form of the bull *Brittania* was decidedly in favour of the regular clergy and, with the departure of bishop Smith, England was left without any bishop at all for fifty years and, of course, the establishment of a new and full hierarchical structure did not take place until 1850.[50] The bull Brittania must undoubtedly have shaken Comerford and the other Irish bishops and can only have had the effect of sharpening their determination to make their own control of the Irish church more secure lest a similar fate be imposed upon them. The decade 1630-40 saw their programme being put into effect with sound success. The transition from mission to church was to prove quite different in both countries, Ireland and England.

---

archbishops of Cashel and Tuam and the bishops of Munster to Propaganda 20 January 1629 (O.S.), APF, SOCG, 14, f. 43R

Possibly at this Limerick meeting also the decision was taken to appoint Michael Cantwell, a Waterford priest who had left the jesuits, agent of the Munster and Leinster bishops in Rome, to succeed Eugene Callanan, rector of the Irish college, Rome, who had recently died. Cantwell was to prove a failure as agent especially because of the part he played in the serious disputes between the regular and secular clergy in the early 1630's.cf William Browne (Patrick Comerford) to Wadding, Waterford, 7 March 1630 (24 Feb. 1629 O.S.), *Wadding Papers*, 346.

Archbishop Thomas Walsh to Wadding, 17 Nov. 1631, ibid, 613

[49]   Archbishop of Cashel and bishops of Ossory, Ferns, Waterford and Lismore to Propaganda, APF, SOCG, 6 Feb. 1630, 132, f. 274R

Another letter to the same effect in *Wadding Papers*, 426-7

[50]   Bossy, John, *The English Catholic Community 1570-1850*

Burton, Edwin H., *The Life and Times of Bishop Challoner* (1691-1781), Vol. 1, 216-20

Chapter Six

BISHOP COMERFORD AND THE REGULAR CLERGY

(1) General Observations

The archives in Rome, particularly in the recently founded Congregation of the Faith, Propaganda, are the principal source of information on the health or otherwise of the catholic church in Ireland in the time of Patrick Comerford's episcopate, the third and fourth decades of the seventeenth century. It is understandable, but still curious, that the reports and letters from the counter-reformation bishops such as Patrick Comerford to Propaganda tend, in general, to be severely ecclesiastical and do not present any detailed analysis of the complicated political situation in Ireland. Comerford himself who, especially in his letters to Luke Wadding, is the most personal and indeed acidic of the correspondents from Ireland, makes little detailed comment on matters such as Thomas Wentworth, Lord Deputy 1633-40, and the complexity of his religious attitude, his *de facto* toleration of catholic practice despite his indifference and even hostility towards the catholic faith. Neither does Comerford institute comparisons between the Irish and English situations.

His correspondence is largely confined to the tasks, trials and tribulations which confront him in his efforts to be an effective counter-reformation bishop, and the successes and failures which are his lot as he tries to execute the tridentine reform in his diocese. His concern is mainly with the internal difficulties of the church, with the problem of attempting to arrive at an accommodation with the regular clergy in his diocese, with the injustice of the poverty which besets his diocese, with the tensions within the Irish church between the metropolitans and their suffragans.

The friction between the regular and secular clergy was very serious within the Irish church, particularly in the first half of the seventeenth century. To try to place this Irish struggle in perspective it is necessary to bear in mind that it forms part of a general uneasiness throughout the catholic world of the time, resulting from the attempted implementation of the reform decrees of the Council of Trent. But the Irish situation was special and was certainly not the one envisaged by Trent when it drew up its programme of reform. The peculiarity of the Irish situation made the solution of the conflict between regular and secular clergy most difficult and, in some aspects, impossible. In Ireland it was not just a matter of restoring the jurisdiction of the episcopate and of centralising control under the bishop, it was almost a matter of restoring the episcopate itself. This restoration had to take place in a country which, though solidly catholic in the faith of its people, was ruled by an heretical government which legally proscribed catholicism and, when it did not persecute, barely tolerated the church.

We have noted in Chapter 5 that in its reform decrees the main aims of the Council of Trent were to ensure that the pastoral ministry of the church would function properly, unimpeded by abuses, and effectively provide the people with the consolations of religion. Privileges would have to be swept aside, no matter by whom they were held, and abuses in all departments of the church would have to be eradicated. Trent, in its reform decrees, greatly increased the authority of the diocesan bishop. The diocese was the consecrated unit of pastoral ministration and the bishop's control in it was to be complete and effective. The pastoral work of the church was to be discharged by the bishop through his priests, particularly those constituted by him as parish priests. Other non-diocesan priests were to perform pastoral work subject to the permission and liable to the visitation and inspection of the diocesan ordinary. Like the bishop himself in his diocese the parish priest was bound to residence in his parish. The people of his parish were considered to be his responsibility and their salvation was to be his prime concern. The privileges, so common in the past, whereby non-diocesan priests attended to pastoral ministry independently of the local ordinary were swept away by Trent in its attempt to bring order and control into the diocesan system.

The reform decrees of Trent could not come into operation anywhere overnight. On the continent of Europe their implementation was impeded by the religious quarrels of the late sixteenth century and was particularly disturbed by the Thirty Years' War of the seventeenth century (1618-48). In Ireland the position was very complex. Due to the chaotic state of the country in the latter half of the reign of Elizabeth normal diocesan organisation had been impossible. The diocesan system did not break down as it did in England but it could have done and indeed we might say that it very nearly did. In fact in 1618 there was no bishop resident in Ireland. There were four metropolitans alive but all were on the continent of Europe: David Kearney, archbishop of Cashel, had left Ireland in 1618 and did not return. He died near Bordeaux in 1625; Eugene Matthews, archbishop of Dublin, left Ireland after 1614 and died in Rome in 1621; Peter Lombard ,appointed archbishop of Armagh in 1601, never returned to Ireland after his consecration. He died in Italy in 1625; Florence Conroy, O.F.M. was appointed archbishop of Tuam in 1608 and never returned to Ireland after his consecration.

These metropolitans appointed priests to cater for their archdioceses and also for some of their suffragan dioceses. These priests were sometimes vicars general or, if appointed by Rome, vicars apostolic. They were not bishops but they had quasi-episcopal jurisdiction over their diocese. It was not until the appointment of David Rothe to Ossory in 1620 that Rome had moved into a decision that, unlike the situation in England, there should in Ireland be a full restoration of a catholic hierarchy. As we saw in Chapter 5, the Irish hierarchy from 1620 on was pretty speedily re-established.

The new bishops appointed in the 1620's, 1630's and 1640's were a mixture: some were of old Gaelic stock, others were of Old English stock; within each stock some were chosen from the ranks of the secular clergy, some from the ranks of the regular clergy. Donal Cregan, who has made several perceptive studies of the whole period 1600-1650, enumerates that in that period nineteen bishops were of Gaelic stock, eighteen were of Old English stock, seven were Franciscan, one (Patrick Comerford) was an augustinian.[1] From the appointment of Rothe on, the episcopal appointments made a great change in the Irish church. A major influence in determining Rome to embark on the course of episcopal appointments to Ireland was archbishop Peter Lombard of Armagh who spent all his episcopal life *in curia* in Rome but wrote much to encourage the Pope in this regard. Lombard was also emphatic in advising that the catholic church should cooperate with the *de facto* toleration of catholics which was a feature in Ireland during the reign of James I (and , indeed, after Lombard's death in 1625, during the reign of Charles I). Lombard would not have agreed with the insistence of the nuncio Rinuccini in the 1640's that catholics should make clamant demands that Ireland should be legally accepted as a catholic country with all the supports and status of an established church.[2]

These bishops, who were appointed in the 1620's, '30's and '40's, had all received their training in the Irish continental seminaries of Spain, Portugal, the Low Countries and France. They had, in their student days, come into serious contact with the spirit of Trent. It was only to be expected that for them the reorganisation of the Irish church could only be along tridentine lines and the position of the bishop in his diocese could only be that envisaged in the reform of Trent. Patrick Corish has summed it up well:

> Naturally these bishops, themselves the fruit of a counter-reformation training, took the tridentine reformed episcopate as their model, and set about reorganising the religious life of their catholic people along the lines laid down by the Council, in place of the basically missionary regime under which the counter-reformation had worked in Ireland in the reign of Elizabeth. By contrast, England, where the bulk of the people had been lost to catholicism, and where the episcopal succession had been completely interrupted, remained a missionary country. In the pontificate of Gregory XV (1621-3) an attempt was made to provide England with a bishop, but the conditions there were heavily. against its success, and the experiment quickly ended in failure. The Irish bishops had problems very similar to those of their English colleagues in their attempts to turn a missionary regime into a diocesan one, but conditions in Ireland were so much more favourable that they succeeded where he failed.[3]

---

[1] Cregan Donal, 'The Social and Cultural Background of a Counter-reformation Episcopate', Cosgrave and McCarthy (eds), *Studies in Irish History presented to R. Dudley Edwards*, 85-117

[2] Cf. Lombard, Peter, *De Regno Hiberniae Sanctorum Insula Commentarius*, Louvain, 1634 ed. P.F. Moran (Dublin, 1868);
Byrne, M. J. (ed.), 'The Irish War of Defence 1598-1600' extracts from the *De Hibernia Insula Commentarius of Peter Lombard….*
Silke, J. J. 'Later Relations between Primate Peter Lombard and Hugh O'Neill', *I.T.Q.* XXII (1955) 15-30
Idem, Primate Lombard and James I', ibid. 124-50

[3] Corish, Patrick, 'An Irish Counter-Reformation Bishop: John Roche' *I.T.Q.* XXX (April 1958) 109.

The Irish church was fortunate in that these counter-reformation bishops in the early to mid-seventeenth century were, generally speaking, an outstanding body of men who brought strong energy and zeal to the task which they had to perform. But to replace a missionary regime with a centralised diocesan system could never be easy. In Ireland there were many obstacles. One of the serious difficulties was the position and attitudes of the regular clergy. One scholar, treating of the bishops in the 1640's writes, not surely without some humour:

> They (the bishops) were universally seminary trained, largely resident in their dioceses and their appointments to bishoprics were for the most part on the basis of religious rather than political criteria. Not surprisingly, therefore, they proved a very zealous body of pastors. Eugene MacSweeny, the bishop of Kilmore, apparently over-indulged in whiskey; Thomas Fleming, the archbishop of Dublin, probably laid himself open to accusations of gluttony due to his excessive corpulence; while John O'Moloney, the bishop of Killaloe, created antagonism because of his avarice and arrogance. However, this not particularly damning list seems to have represented the height of the hierarchy's scandalous excesses[4]

Ever since the dissolution of the monastic houses and friaries during the period of Henry VIII the regular clergy in Ireland had led a precarious existence. With the almost total destruction of all churches and religious houses during the Elizabethan wars their insecurity was further increased. But, despite the deprivation of churches and property they had, though in much reduced numbers, remained on in the country and they had been closely identified with the beginnings of the counter-reformation movement in Ireland from the arrival of the jesuit, David Wolfe, in 1650. From that time until, say, 1614, when a more organised programme began to be adopted, the counter-reformation in Ireland was a missionary one and the regular clergy played a significant part in it.[5] A missionary situation calls for missionary faculties and privileges and these the Irish regulars possessed in abundance: faculties and privileges which were used to advantage in the difficult Elizabethan period. That these faculties were extensive is clear from lists preserved in Propaganda archives as well as in the jesuit generalate archives in Rome and the franciscan archives in Ireland.[6]

---

[4]   Ó hAnnracháin, Tadgh, 'Lost in Rinuccini's shadow; the Irish clergy 1645-9', Mícheál ó Siochrú (ed.) *Kingdoms in Crisis – Ireland in the 1640's*; 177
[5]   Corish, Patrick, 'The Reorganization of the Irish Church, 1603-41' *Proceedings of the Irish Catholic Historical Committee, 1957*, 14
[6]   These lists are substantially the same and presumably were presented either directly or by written communication to the principal religious superiors in Ireland. The copy in the archives of Propaganda represents a grant made to the dominican order; APF, SOCG, 298, ff. 314R-316R. The jesuit grant is contained in jesuit general archives, Rome ,*Hiberniae Cathologi Antiqui*, 1611-1644, ff. 96V – 97V. The franciscan grant is in franciscan archives, Killiney, and has been published by Brendan Jennings in *Archiv. Hib.* XII (1945), 73-75
That the regulars set great value on such grants of faculties is clear from the fact of their publication in one of the most controversial books of the period; they are quoted by the author to prove the

These lists represent grants made in 1612 – only a few years before the hierarchy in Ireland began to increase in numbers and be properly re-established. The faculty grants range over a wide field: they apply to such matters as absolution from apostasy and heresy, dispensation from marriage impediments, absolution from all censures even those contained in the *Coena Domini* (bull of 1568 concerning censures reserved to the pope himself), the granting of permission to lay catholics to hold ecclesiastical property, the administration of all sacraments except Holy Orders and Confirmation, the granting of indulgences, the freedom to say mass in most places and at irregular times. Even a summary glance at such faculties shows the wide freedom from any local jurisdiction which the regular clergy in Ireland enjoyed and also the latitude that was given them by Rome in the exercise of their pastoral ministry. According as the counter-reformation hierarchy began to assume control in the Irish church, an attempt was bound to be made to curtail these extensive faculties; a clash between the regular and secular clergy was inevitable.

It would not be fair judgement for the historian to assess the position of the regular clergy in Ireland in the seventeenth century in terms merely of obstacles to the introduction of tridentine law and order into the Irish church. That they were a special element in a situation, the chaotic nature of which rendered such an introduction difficult, is true. But it would indeed be an unfair estimation of the regulars to consider their opposition to the bishops as merely a struggle for privilege or gain without any responsibility towards the progress of the Irish mission. In unbroken continuity since the reformation, the regular clergy had been in close touch with the people, and the people obviously looked to them with special confidence. The catholic life of pre-reformation Ireland had revolved to an unusual degree around the very many monasteries and friaries throughout the country. The close bond between the regulars and the people did not die with the reformation; the traditional nexus was still strong when the seventeenth century arrived. The number of parishes impropriate to monasteries and friaries had been high and it was only to be expected that, even after the dissolution of the religious houses, the people would still look to the regulars as their pastors. In many places and situations it was to the regulars that the people would look for the administration of the sacraments. In the cemeteries attached to their ruined churches many people would still wish to be buried. It should be borne in mind that in many cases the regulars in continuing to administer the *sacramenta parochialia* and indeed also to claim the *ius sepulturae* (right of burial) must often have been responding to the wishes, expressed or presumed, of the faithful. Any tendency to censure their activity as mere self assertion or desire for gain does not take into account the whole story.

---

independence of the regular clergy in administering the *sacramenta parochialia*: Edmundus Ursulanus (pseud.) (Francis Matthews O.F.M.), *Examen Iuridicum Censurae Facultatis Theologiae Parisiensis; et Eiusdem Civitatis Archiepiscopi Latae Quasdam Propositiones Regularibus Hiberniae Falso Impositas*, (Frankfurt, 1631) 131 ff

The clashes which arose from the attempt of the bishops, also men of zeal, to bring the regular clergy into line with a centralised diocesan system, were inevitable. These clashes were often aggravated and sharpened by the personalities on both sides. This seems certainly to have been the case in the diocese of Waterford and Lismore where the intransigence and inflexibility of the bishop did not make for easy relations with the regular clergy. In examining the contemporary reports made to Rome one has to keep in mind that they are largely concerned with the contentious and the unusual and the likelihood of exaggeration and hasty judgment cannot be ruled out. The really important and heartening fact concerning this period is that, despite serious clashes, the catholic church in Ireland was obviously making progress during these years of the seventeenth century, a progress which to a fair extent is poorly documented but which is certainly due to the regular no less than to the secular clergy. An interesting indication of the general zeal of the regular clergy is the fact that between 1600 and 1650 a sizeable number of bishops were chosen from their ranks.

An aggravating element in the situation was the intense poverty of the catholic church in Ireland in the late sixteenth and early seventeenth centuries. The religious had largely lost their monasteries and churches, the secular clergy had lost their benefices. The only support left to both was that which was given by the people. Hence, apart altogether from any delicate jurisdictional questions, it was of vital economic importance to decide which section of the clergy should have most dealings with the people. From the reports and complaints submitted by both the regular and secular clergy to Propaganda it comes across that the economic consideration was indeed very prominent in their thinking. These reports and complaints largely concern matters such as offerings from the people at special occasions and also the right to quest alms at funerals and wakes. The economic aspect of the matter was very acutely felt at the local parochial level.

In the first of the really important synods, that of the Dublin province but held in Kilkenny in 1614, presided over by archbishop Matthews of Dublin, there was much consideration shown to the regulars, and their significant co-operation with the local ordinaries, such as vicars apostolic and vicars general, was acknowledged. The ordinaries were encouraged to receive the regulars amongst the diocesan clergy and to consult with religious superiors concerning matters of pastoral importance. Also the synod wished that the regulars be allowed to use their faculties and privileges but – a foretaste of future restrictive intentions – in so far as they do not interfere with the prerogatives of the local ordinaries – 'quatenus locorum ordinariis non repugnant aut praeiudicant' [7]

The synod concluded the section on regulars with a warning that contentious cases are to be judged only by the ordinary, and the regulars are not to interfere in them by invoking any

---

[7]   The decrees of this synod are printed in Moran, *History of the Catholic Archbishops of Dublin*, Vol I, 441-63; decree *'De Regularibus'*, 458

privileges or faculties they may possess.[8] Four years later the synod of Armagh in 1618, held also in Kilkenny and presided over by David Rothe, who was vicar general of Armagh, appointed by the Rome-based archbishop, Peter Lombard, repeated verbatim this decree on the regular clergy. The regulars were being warned to be careful in their use of privileges.[9]

After 1618 the conflict between the secular and regular clergy grew increasingly pronounced. In a report sent in April 1613 by Guido Bentivoglio, nuncio in Brussels, to Rome it is declared, obviously on the information of the nuncio's Irish secretary, John Roche, later to become bishop of Ferns, that there were no conflicts between the secular and regular clergy in Ireland.[10] Some years later the same John Roche, now bishop of Ferns, has a less happy story to relate: in a report to Rome in 1625 he complains about contentious members of the regular clergy and of trouble-making cistercians and of conflicts between them and the secular clergy.[11]

A year earlier in September 1624, at a meeting of three of the Leinster and Munster bishops in Kilkenny, much stronger words were being used in connection with the conflict between the secular and regular clergy.[12] It was declared that the main object of the meeting was to restore harmony amongst the clergy and so permit progress in the building up of the Irish church. It decreed that regulars were not to act on obscure or doubtful privileges or on any privileges that were prejudicial to the local ordinaries. They were to refrain from giving dispensations in matrimonial matters or in regard to the holding by lay catholics of ecclesiastical property. They were not to cause any public commotion or attract government attention. There was to be restraint and avoidance of scandal in their sermons and conversations with the laity. Novices were not to be received in large numbers and all religious were to be properly trained before being permitted to operate on the Irish mission. The meeting in Kilkenny, above all, appealed for co-operation and harmony, and it stressed the necessity of a properly organised diocesan system for the welfare of the Irish church.

It is clear that, as the years went by, a progressive disquiet concerning the behaviour and attitude of the regulars was being expressed by the bishops and other ordinaries in the Irish dioceses. Reports were being regularly sent to the recently (1622) founded Propaganda Congregation listing complaints against the regulars and their refusal to co-operate with the bishops and other ordinaries.[13] In 1626 Propaganda made a special study of the situation and decided to enquire from the archbishop of Armagh, Hugh MacCaghwell, who was in Rome and

---

[8]   Ibid., 458
[9]   APF, SOCG, 294, ff. 51V – 52R, printed in Moran, op. cit., 430-1.
[10] AV, Fondo Borghese, Serie 1, vol. 269-72, f. 91V, printed in *Archiv Hib.* iii (1914), 302
[11] The original version of Roche's report is in Biblioteca Casanatense, Rome, Ms. 2410. I refer here to a printed version in Corish, 'Two Reports on the Catholic Church in Ireland in the early seventeenth century', *Archiv. Hib.*, XXII (1959) 149 ff
[12] This meeting, called by those who took part a *Consultatio Unitiva*, was attended by the bishops of Ossory, Cork & Cloyne, Limerick, Emly, the vicars general of Cashel, Waterford & Lismore (Laurence Lea), the vicars-apostolic of Ardfert & Aghadoe, Ross, Killaloe. A report of its decisions is in APF, SOCG, 294, ff. 46R – 49V, also in *Wadding Papers*, 83-8
[13] APF, SOCG, 294, f. 118RV;
       Ibid. ff. 355R - 357R

had just been consecrated, concerning possible remedies.[14] MacCaghwell replied in August and the congregation, having examined his suggestions, made a strong appeal for harmony and peace both to the Irish archbishops and to the fathers-general of the different religious orders in Rome.[15]

Probably arising from Propaganda's interest and efforts in the matter, a set of regulations withdrawing, to an extensive degree, the missionary faculties of the regular clergy in Ireland was drawn up, not by Propaganda, but by the Holy Office in whose competence such action lay. This withdrawal of faculties occurred in August 1626, the same month in which MacCaghwell reported to Propaganda.[16] We have no exact copy of these regulations but it is very likely that they are incorporated in the decisions taken by the bishops of Munster and Leinster at their meeting in Kilkenny 24-27 August 1629. We have previously noted that this was the first episcopal meeting attended by bishops Roche of Ferns and Comerford of Waterford and Lismore.[17] It is certain that bishop Roche had a copy of the Holy Office regulations and that he brought the copy back to Ireland in 1629.[18] The bishops at Kilkenny stressed that the regulars have no right to hold pastoral office and, if they do so in Ireland, it is only because of the special difficulties of the situation. In the exercise of such office they must be subject to the jurisdiction of the bishops. It was declared that the missionary faculties, formerly enjoyed by the regulars, had been withdrawn by Pope Urban VIII (1623-44). The withdrawal was stated to apply to religious prelates (such as cistercian abbots) as well as to ordinary priests and monks. The houses in which the regulars lived in contemporary Ireland were declared not to be exempt in the full meaning of the word.

We have noted in an earlier context, quoting Comerford's experience, that the reaction of the regular clergy to the episcopal meeting in Kilkenny in August 1629, was not at all favourable. The regulars were not fully convinced that their faculties had been withdrawn. The conflict was to intensify and continue for a number of years to come. It was to be 1635 before full agreement was reached between the bishops and the regular clergy. In the years after 1629 the individual bishops, such as Comerford, sought to establish firmly their jurisdiction and they inevitably were to cut across the privileges of the regular clergy. The friction was greater in

---

[14] APF, ALTD, 4, 18 July 1626, f. 97R., No. 11

[15] MacCaughwell, also called 'MacAingill' and 'Hugo Cavellus' archbishop of Armagh, a brilliant franciscan was born in Downpatrick and became a very prominent scholar in Louvain. He was well known in Rome where he co-operated with Wadding in the foundation of St. Isidore's. He had been definitor-general of the franciscans in Rome. He sent his suggestions to Propaganda on 13 August – APF, SOCG, 13 Aug. 1626, 294, ff. 129R – 121V. Propaganda wrote to the Irish archbishops on 21 Aug. 1626 – APF, Lettere, 1, f. 180R. MacCaughwell died unexpectedly in Rome the following month, Sept. 1626. His successor to Armagh was the bishop of Kilmore, Hugh O'Reilly, who was translated in 1628

[16] There is reference to these regulations in a document drawn up by the bishop of Ossory in 1631 entitled 'Cautio Ecclesiastica' and sent to Propaganda: APF, SOCG, 140, f. 336R.
The bishop of Ferns, John Roche, petitioned for a copy of these regulations from Propaganda, APF, SOCG, Acta, 16 April 1627, f. 205R. No. 7

[17] Text of the decisions of this meeting in APF, SOCG, 294, ff. 279R – 280R, printed in Moran, op. cit. vol. 1, 434-6

[18] APF, Acta, 4, 16 April 1627, f. 205R, No. 7

some dioceses than in others: it was severe in dioceses such as Cork and Ross, Ferns, and Waterford and Lismore. It might be said to have been most aggravated in Waterford and Lismore. The fact that the bishop himself was a member of the regular clergy, an augustinian eremite, made his behaviour towards them appear poisonous and disloyal to the regular clergy.

(2) Particular Controversies

The regular clergy in Ireland considered bishop Comerford to be one of their greatest opponents amongst the bishops.[19] Their difficulties with him were all the more surprising to them because he had been a distinguished member of the eremites of St. Augustine and he also had been given responsibility for the affairs of the canons regular of St. Augustine in Ireland. From the general tone of his letters to Propaganda and to others in Rome, especially to Luke Wadding, there were clearly many differences of opinion between him and the regular clergy, especially in the early years of his episcopate. Dedicated member of the regular clergy he may have been in earlier years, but now, after his elevation to the status of bishop, he was emphatically committed to the programme of establishing tridentine reform in his diocese even if this commitment was to cause hostility between him and the regulars.

On his return to Ireland in 1629, Comerford's first serious instance of disagreement was with the cistercians and their possession or appropriation of the abbey of Mothel located in the modern parish of Clonea and Rathgormack. As was the case with most of the early Irish monasteries and, more so, of the medieval monasteries, Mothel is situated in a beautifully scenic area of county Waterford. It nestles near the Comeragh mountains, is surrounded by fertile land, and flowing very near it is a lovely small river, the Clodagh. In the early Celtic church it was a monastic foundation associated with two saints, Cuan and Brogán. To this day an annual pattern is held in July near the holy well and primitive ruins of the early Celtic church. The successor to that early church was a handsome medieval abbey of the canons regular of St. Augustine which was established about 1140 and continued to be endowed over the centuries by the Power (de la Poer) family who were the Norman chieftains in this area, the heart of county Waterford. The abbey of Mothel was dissolved by the surrender of its last abbot, Edmond Power, on 7 April 1540. As sometimes occurred in dissolution situations the same Edmond Power was, within a few years, named the farmer of Mothel. The medieval abbey had possession of very extensive lands and it had impropriate to it the parishes of Mothel, Rathgormack and Ballylaneen, to which the abbot had been entitled to appoint parish priests.

On his journey back to Ireland from Rome Comerford had been alerted that the cistercians were going to cause trouble over the possession of Mothel[20] Very likely he consulted on the matter with his fellow-bishops at their meeting in Kilkenny in August 1629. Armed with their advice he raised the matter with the cistercians on his return to Waterford.[21] His adversary was John Madan, a cistercian abbot and well-known Waterford ecclesiastic whom Comerford himself had singled out some ten years previously as shedding lustre on his native

---

19 Thomas Strange to Wadding, Waterford, 10 Sept. 1631, *Wadding Papers*, 579
20 Comerford to Eugene Callanan, Louvain, 21 June 1629, *Wadding Papers*, 294
21 Same to Propaganda, 18 Jan. 1630 (9Jan. 1629 O.S.), APF, SOCG, 132, f .281R
   William Browne (Comerford) to Wadding, 18 Jan. 1620 (8 Jan. 1629 O.S.), *Wadding Papers*, 335-6

city.[22] For several years before Comerford became bishop, John Madan, perhaps aided by documents received from Rome and perhaps supported by the archbishop of Dublin, Thomas Fleming O.F.M., had declared himself abbot of Mothel and had installed some small number of fellow cistercians into residence of a kind in the ruined abbey. In his reports and letters to Rome concerning Mothel, Comerford keeps repeating that Mothel had been a medieval abbey, never of the cistercians, but of the canons regular of St. Augustine. The only substantial abbey which the cistercians ever held in the diocese of Waterford and Lismore was Inishlounaght (de Surio) near Clonmel. When Mothel was dissolved in 1540 it was formally listed as Mothel Abbey O.S.A.[23] Some ten years, perhaps, before Comerford became bishop the abbey, or what remained of it, was re-occupied not by the canons regular, but by the cistercians. Certainly in 1621, as a witness to the settlement of a controversy in the archdiocese of Cashel, between the cistercian abbot of Holy Cross, Luke Archer, and a secular priest, David Hennessy, Madan signs himself Fr. Thomas (alias) John Madan, *elect. Ab. De Mothalibus*[24] We know also that, on Trinity Sunday 1625, archbishop Fleming of Dublin solemnly performed the blessing of John Madan as abbot of Mothel in St. John's Church, Waterford. On the same occasion he also blessed two other cistercian abbots: Lawrence Fitzharris of Inishlounaght and Christian Barnwell of St. Mary's Abbey, Dublin.[25]

Shortly after taking up office bishop Comerford confronted Madan and challenged him. The bishop denied him any right over what had always been an Augustinian abbey. Comerford reports that there were two arms to his challenge of Madan: one, Madan's action was a violation of the bishop's jurisdiction as ordinary of the diocese over the appointments to parishes in the diocese; secondly, as lawful vicar general of the canons regular of St. Augustine in Ireland, Comerford insisted that the decisions as to who should occupy the abbey of Mothel lay with him. The cistercians never had any right to be involved. Madan, however, asserted that Mothel was listed as one of the Irish abbeys belonging to the cistercians and that he himself had received an apostolic letter appointing him as its abbot. Moreover, Madan claimed that he had

---

[22] cf. *The Inquisition of a Sermon*, 170
     Comerford deals in detail with the Mothel affair in letters to Wadding and in reports to Propaganda.
     Comerford to Wadding, 22 Nov. 1629, *Wadding Papers*, 322-4
     same to same, 18 Jan. 1630 (8 Jan, 1629 O.S.) ibid., 335-6
     same to same, 6 March 1630 (24 Feb. 1629 O.S.) , ibid., 345
     same to Propaganda, 18 Jan. 1630 (8 Jan. 1629 O.S.) AP, SOCG, 132, f. 281R
     same to same, 6 July 1630, APF, SOCG, 294, ff. 221R-222R
[23] White, Newport, *Extents of Irish Monastic Possessions 1540-1541*, (I.M.C.), 331-2
[24] Renehan, Laurence, *Collections of Irish Church History*, ed. by D. McCarthy vol. i, 270
[25] Power, Patrick, 'The Priory Church and Hospital of St. John the Evangelist Waterford', *Waterford Arch. Soc. Jn.*, II (1894) 95;
     APF, SOCG, 3 April 1627, 130, f. 3R. – a report by Fra Patricio di S. Giacomo, a discalced carmelite, who was visiting Waterford, which says that the priests of Waterford and Lismore would wish to have John Madan as their bishop and have sent his name with some others to Rome. In this report Madan is described as 'excellente theologo, bon praedicatore, et exemplare in vita et moribus, super omnes coetaneos suos in genere suo'

received the abbey with the full permission of Laurence Lea who, as vicar general, was in charge of the diocese prior to Comerford's appointment as bishop.[26]

In a strong letter to Wadding, Comerford makes his case against Madan's position. When in Rome he had done much historical research on the matter; clearly he had been anticipating trouble. An apostolic notary had checked out the matter and clearly proved that all the record books in the *Dataria* and *Cancellaria* in Rome declare that Mothel was always an augustinian house. Comerford told Madan that Luke Wadding himself can vouch for the fact. With an ill-tempered and personal touch he declares to Wadding that the entry of Mothel on a cistercian list is no great wonder when one considers the notoriously acquisitive activity of the cistercians in Ireland and the pains they have taken to usurp other monasteries in the dioceses of Ferns and Cork and Cloyne.[27] As regards the permission granted by Laurence Lea, who has since died, Comerford holds that Madan is not releasing the whole story. Before granting his permission Lea had insisted that Madan sign a formal statement to the effect that he would immediately surrender the abbey to anyone who, at a future date, might lay just claim to it. Indeed, according to Comerford, Lea admitted afterwards that, if he had been sure at the time that the abbey had never been cistercian, he would not have allowed Madan's claim to it at all.[28]

But, despite Comerford's remonstrations, Madan remained unchanged and he continued to defend himself on the grounds that he had been appointed by Rome. This early experience by Comerford of Roman appointees created in him a strong antipathy to any interference on the part of Rome in the provision to Irish benefices or offices without consultation with the local ordinaries involved. Several times he expressed himself on the matter in later reports to Propaganda.[29] In the matter of Madan's presumed appointment to Mothel, Comerford states that the bull of provision must have been surreptitious because he himself had been assured by the official in Rome that, in the curial registers, Mothel was definitely not cistercian.[30] Madan remained unmoved. He refused to attend the synod which the bishop called shortly after his return to the diocese. Nor would he allow a monk whom he had placed in charge of the parishes annexed to the abbey to attend the synod or to obey the bishop or receive him on his visitation. In the face of this open disregard for his authority Comerford made a strong appeal

---

[26] This information emerges from an attestation and profession of faith signed by Madan in Waterford on 20 August 1626 and witnessed by Laurence Lea and other secular and regular priests of Waterford, printed in *Wadding Papers*, 229-230. The other signatories are: Fr. James Madan, guardian of the Waterford franciscan convent, Fr. Richard Strange, definitor of the augustinian eremites, Fr. Nicholas Comerford, canon or precentor of the Cathedral of the Holy Trinity, Waterford, Fr. Thomas Strange, definitor of the Irish franciscan province

[27] Comerford to Wadding, 22 Nov. 1629, *Wadding Papers*, 323-4

[28] Ibid.

[29] Comerford to Propaganda, 16 Oct. 1632, printed in Moran, Spicil. Ossor., vol. II, 81 ff.;
Same to same, 14 Feb. 1633 (4 Feb 1632 O.S.),
APF, SOCG, 134, f. 238 RV.

[30] Same to same, 18 Jan 1630 (8 Jan. 1629 O.S.),
APF, SOCG, 132, f. 281R. From this letter it is clear that, before he left Rome for Ireland, bishop Comerford had armed himself with the necessary historical and legal information to overthrow Madan's claim to Mothel.

to Propaganda and stated that, in his opinion, only a censure by the Holy Father himself would silence Madan. Comerford requested that the case be placed for solution in the hands of either the archbishop of Cashel or the bishop of Ferns.[31]

Tensions within the Irish church were not unconnected with tensions within the Roman curia. Propaganda was not established until 1622 and it was to take quite a number of years before it could be seen to be fully in charge of its designated territories, which included Ireland. Old habits die hard and curial agencies such as the Datary and the Holy Office and the Secretariat of Briefs were slow to forego powers which they had possessed for a long time. The Irish bishops clearly detected a certain inclination of favour in both the Datary and the Holy Office towards the regular clergy. The bishops viewed the new congregation, Propaganda, as their ally and defender.

In the Mothel case Propaganda, realising the intensely local nature of the problem, played for time by requesting that the surreptitious bull, by which Comerford alleged Madan had got possession of Mothel, should be forwarded to the congregation in Rome, so that a properly informed decision could be taken. Perhaps, also, Propaganda was engaging in a curial detective operation which could establish a trail to a Roman source of unhealthy and illicit interference.[32]

In the meantime Comerford announced that, in the interest of harmony, he had agreed to let the matter lie for a period of six years. His attitude, however, remains firm and he takes the opportunity, in a letter to Wadding, to criticise severely the activity of the cistercians in Ireland. They have many monasteries throughout the land and still they insist on intruding themselves into abbeys and property which rightfully belong to other orders. He refers to 'Paul Ragged' who holds four abbeys *in commendam*. Why can he not give Madan one of his abbeys and so avoid the disgraceful conduct which is taking place in the diocese of Waterford and Lismore?[33] He asks Wadding to reinforce his own reports to Propaganda by explaining the whole case of Mothel to Francesco Ingoli, secretary of Propaganda. In fact, Ingoli and the other officials of Propaganda were well informed concerning cistercian activity in Ireland through complaints coming from many Irish bishops. The accusations are usually similar to those made by Comerford: the performance of the pastoral ministry in parishes without any reference to the

---

[31] Ibid.
[32] APF, Acta, 7, 5 Aug. 1630, f. 116R, No. 48
      APF, Lettere, 10, 16 Aug. 1630, f. 84V
[33] Comerford to Wadding, 22 Nov. 1629, Wadding Papers, 320-5
      Paul Ragget or Ragged (Ragesius) was an able but controversial cistercian. He became abbot of St. Mary's abbey in Dublin city. According to Thomas Walsh, archbishop of Cashel. Ragget had let it be known that he himself had been nominated archbishop of Cashel but his name was withdrawn in favour of Walsh because of Spanish influence
      Thomas Walsh to John Roche, bishop of Ferns, Madrid, 14 March 1627, *Wadding Papers*, 243-6

local ordinary and, in general, the claiming of complete exemption from the jurisdiction of the bishops.[34]

Of significant alarm and disappointment to Comerford was the manner in which the regular clergy in general supported Madan in his struggle with the bishop. In a clearly depressed state he informs Wadding that, led by the franciscan Thomas Strange, a malicious and calumnious campaign was being directed against himself. So widespread was the campaign that the archbishop of Dublin, Thomas Fleming, himself a regular, wrote a letter of advice to the bishop of Waterford and Lismore, clearly showing, according to Comerford, that he believed much of the calumny that was being spread. It was Comerford's opinion that it would be more fitting for the archbishop of Dublin to keep his own house in order than to be interfering in the affairs of Waterford and Lismore.[35] With a touch of asperity he calls to Wadding's mind the advice which he (Wadding) imparted to regular bishops in the past:

> I heard you oft times speak the manner of government wee regular bishops ought to keep in our dioceses, and made an observation of your good meaning: let everie bodie answer for his own acts.[36]

Despite the angry stubbornness of both parties in the Mothel controversy, the dispute remarkably came rather swiftly to an amicable conclusion. It seems to have happened, perhaps facilitated by a mediator whom one would suspect to have been a fellow-townsman of them both, archbishop Thomas Walsh of Cashel, by a coming together of the two parties. Both Comerford and Madan appear to have admitted guilt and hastiness in judging the other. Madan agreed to withdraw his monk from the parishes in question and promised not to interfere with the bishop's jurisdiction any more.[37] For the next decade correspondence with Rome does not reveal any further disputes between the bishop of Waterford and Lismore and the cistercians. However, scars probably remained. Later on, with the temporary recovery of some ecclesiastical property in Ireland following on the rebellion of 1641, relations between Comerford and the cistercians became strained once again. This time the dispute concerned the possession or repossession of the church of St. John the Evangelist in the city of Waterford. This later dispute can only be properly appreciated in the context of the rebellion and the Confederation of Kilkenny. We will look at it later.

---

[34] APF, Acta, 7, 22 Nov. 1639, f. 108R, No. 42;
Ibid., 8, 23 Aug. 1632, f. 107R, No. 24;
Ibid., 10, 1 Sept. 1635, f. 308R
Bishop Roche of Ferns issues a very strong condemnation of cistercian acquisitiveness and greed to enjoy jurisdiction with little sense of responsibility: 'Ma nostril cisterciensi vogliono essere tutti abbati senza conventi, senza monahi, senza disciplina regolare, tutti vogliono esser capi, nessuno vuol esser braccio ne piede. Et questa disordine vien fomentato assai dalla dataria Romana, che da bulle d'abbati a quanti le demandano'. APF, SOCG, 15 Nov. 1634, 105, f. 479V
[35] William Browne (Comerford) to Wadding, 18 Jan. 1630 (8 Jan. 1629 O.S.), *Wadding Papers*, 335-6
[36] Ibid., 336
[37] William Browne (Comerford) to Wadding, 6 March 1630 (24 Feb. 1629 O.S.) *Wadding Papers*, 345

Beginning with his painful experience of Madan's stubborn opposition to his authority, we could say that Comerford, even though he was a distinguished religious order man himself, as bishop got off to a bad start with the regular clergy. Early events seem to have set him on a suspicious and even hostile course in his dealings with the regulars; it was a course which sometimes expressed itself in unreasonable behaviour. He had the unpleasant experience of having to deal in his early months with a much more scandalous situation than that created by John Madan. One of Comerford's early actions on taking up office as bishop was to appoint a priest named Walter Travers as parish priest of St. John's Grange (part of modern Powerstown and Lisronagh parish), on the northern boundary of the diocese, near Clonmel. This appointment was resented by a certain Edmund Everard who claimed that the parish historically belonged to the order of St. John of Jerusalem. He himself, Everard asserted, was the only member of that order left in Ireland, and so the parish was rightfully his.[38] Furthermore, Everard declared that, before Comerford had been appointed bishop, the archbishop of Cashel had acknowledged his claim and had recognised him as a member of the order of St. John. For his part, Comerford informed Wadding that Everard was a man of ill repute. He had been a student in Lisbon when Comerford and Wadding were there. Later he had returned to Ireland and married, but subsequently had deserted his wife and had become a priest. The bishop denied that the archbishop of Cashel could, with any validity, have accepted him as a member of the order of St. John of Jerusalem because the superior general of that order had, many years previously, decreed that, in view of the total lack of property belonging to the order in these countries, no-one from England, Scotland or Ireland should be received into the order. In any case, according to Comerford, it was reliably said that, when archbishop Walsh had gone from Rome to Spain in 1626, he expressed regret that he ever had anything to do with Everard and that he sent word revoking any authority he had given him. At any rate, Everard approached the newly appointed parish priest and ordered him to perform no pastoral duties in the parish of St. John's Grange.[39] Travers ignored the order and, on the following Sunday, went to the church to say mass for a large congregation. In the congregation was Everard who, in Comerford's words, scandalously

> lept on and snacht away from the altar the chalice, the patena, oste, velum,, and all, and gave them to his horssboy who stoode at the doore with a good gelding and upon the spur carried all to Fidert;[40] and Edmund spoke many wordes in derogation of my callinge and place, and said he did not esteem me more than the same parish priest[41]

---

[38] Comerford reports on this affair in a letter to Wadding, 22 Nov. 1629, *Wadding Papers*, 324-5; also to Propaganda, 18 Jan. 1630 (8 Jan. 1629 O.S.), APF, SOCG, 132, f. 281R
[39] The church in question is called St. John's, but the area or parish in which the church is located is called Baptistgrange
[40] Fethard, a borough town in south Tipperary within the archdiocese of Cashel
[41] Comerford to Wadding, 22 Nov. 1629, *Wadding Papers*, 324

The account of this singularly scandalous incident was received with alarm by several of the other bishops. In commenting on the event in a letter to Wadding, bishop Roche of Ferns took the opportunity to touch on the unusually difficult obstacles which were impeding Comerford in the ruling of his diocese:

> Your friend Comerford of Waterford is an honest man, and if any should report ye contrary to you, suspend to believe any whit then well of him. He has entered into a charge wher every body did what it pleased him hitherto, and now yt ye good man would faine goeve a forme or face to ye confused administration which was heretofore, he endureth much contradiction from such as ought to assist him; and I am sorry that I must depose of our F. Strong (Strange) yt he is a party against him, and generally held in this land to be ye maine stickler against ordinary jurisdiction, and yet himself affecteth ye charge of ordinary beyond many others, as is said of him. I doubt not but yt you have heard how Waterford is vexed by cistercians and a pretended chaplain of Malta, in all which F. Th. Strong has his oare. Use your owne discretion in advertising him how yt is not well donne....[42]

We hear no more of this incident but it can be assumed that the hostile public opinion aroused by his actions prevented Everard from asserting himself again. Whatever support he had formerly received from Strange and other regular clergy surely was withdrawn when the lengths to which he was prepared to go became evident. However, there remains an element of riddle attached to the Everard incident. The order of St. John of Jerusalem, of which he claimed to be a member, was not a military order, such as the templars and hospitallers, although it is sometimes thought to have been. The order in question is not to be confused with the military order of knights (hospitallers) of St. John of Jerusalem. It was a connection of the *Fratres Cruciferi* (crutched friars in England); it had not many houses in Ireland. Its main centre was the priory and hospital of St. John the Baptist outside the New Gate in Dublin which was founded about 1188. This priory was dissolved in 1539. The Dublin priory had considerable possessions in Dublin, Meath, Carlow, Louth, Cork and Tipperary. The possessions in county Tipperary are of interest in the context of the Everard incident. The Irish name for the area known in south Tipperary and in the diocese of Waterford and Lismore is Achfad where there was a sizable grange connected with the order of St. John of Jerusalem. It had a castle, fifty-one acres and twelve cottages which had been leased in 1541 to the countess of Desmond.[43] Everard probably was a member of the order and, as such, made a claim on the grange with the small parish church nearby. It is possible that he may have invoked a family connection also: the last prior and the one who surrendered the Dublin priory in 1539 was Sir Thomas Everard. The

---

[42] J. R. Turner (John Roche) to Wadding, Jan. (?) 1630, *Wadding Papers*, 332-3
[43] Brooks, E. St. J., *Reg. Hosp. St. John B. Dublin*, v-vii
Gwynn & Hadcock, *Medieval Religious Houses Ireland*, 212

Everards were a strong landed family in South Tipperary. The reference to the archbishop of Cashel, whom he said had given him permission to claim Baptistgrange or Achfad, fits in somewhat with the possibility that archbishop Thomas Walsh, a close relative of Luke Wadding, may himself have been a member or, at least, an associate of the order of St. John of Jerusalem. In a list of names of Irish ecclesiastics suggested for promotion to the episcopacy and dated 1626 we find an entry: Dominus Thomas Walsheus, sacerdos ordinis Sti Johannis Jerosolemitani, anglo-hybernus, in civitate Waterfordiensis diocesis Lismorensis et Waterfordiensis, provinciae Casseliensis natus, et in Hispania educatus.[44] This list is in the Wadding Papers and was very likely drawn up by Wadding himself. Whatever his shortcomings in personal and priestly behaviour, Everard may have had some reasons to fasten on Baptistgrange as a possession to which he conceivably had some rights.

For Comerford the Everard incident must have further confirmed him in lack of sympathy with the general behaviour of the regular clergy in Ireland. This lack of sympathy could at times express itself in unreasonable behaviour on his own part. An example of such lack of reasonableness might be found in his disagreement with the jesuits in Waterford city concerning the possession of the church of St. Peter.

Before we look at the cause of the Waterford disagreement between the bishop and the jesuits some general remarks on the jesuit mission in counter-reformation Ireland might be helpful as a backdrop. The jesuits were indeed a fine productive force in the contemporary church in Ireland. They were quintessentially a counter-reformation order and, unlike the well established religious orders, they were new to the Irish scene, coming 'without baggage' from the past, as one might say. A few years after their foundation and, while their founder St. Ignatius Loyola was still alive, they appeared in Ireland as part of a world-wide out-reach to save and spread the church after the reformation. The first jesuit appearance in the persons of Fathers Paschase Broet and Alfonso Salmeron was premature and unsuccessful. They came in 1542 and remained only a few months. They departed quite unimpressed, and even depressed, at the state of the country.[45]

---

[44] *Wadding Papers*, 174-6

[45] Much of the account of the jesuit presence and work in Ireland in the later sixteenth and the first half of the seventeenth century comes from *Memorials of the Irish Province S.J.* Sundry memories, letters, obituaries, historical essays etc., a number of them duplicated, have been bound under the above title. There are various authors, most of them anonymous. It was privately printed at various dates between 1899 and 1914. The volume includes the following sections:
Short memoirs of the early Irish Jesuits who worked in Ireland down to the year 1840 by Jospeph McDonnell S.J.
'A short History of the Irish Province S.J.' Part 1
'Memorials of the Irish Province S.J.' Vol. i, no. 2
'Memorials of the Irish Province S.J.' Vol. I, nos. 3-7
cf. also McRedmond, Louis, *To the Greater Glory of God, a History of the Irish Jesuits*, 1-84
also Hogan, Edmond (ed)., *Ibernia Ignatiana: seu Ibernorum societatis Jesu Patrum monumenta collecta, vol. I (1540-1607)*. No further volume(s) published

Two decades later a more forceful and effective visitation occurred – in 1561 – conducted by Fr. David Wolfe, a native of Limerick, who had joined the jesuits in Italy. He came armed with considerable papal authority and bore the title Nuncio Apostolic. His mission was of importance especially because his reports to the authorities in Rome were very revealing. He it was who began to encourage young men to travel to the continent in order to be trained as priests in the new counter-reformation seminaries that had been recently founded. The hope was that these young men would return to Ireland and become an effective counter-reformation force in the country. Wolfe operated mainly in the Munster towns where he set up schools. He supplied Rome with names of priests who would make suitable bishops in Ireland. He sent some to Rome to be consecrated bishops, among whom were O'Herlihy of Ross, MacCongail of Raphoe and O'Hart of Achonry. These three returned from Rome via Trent where they attended the final session of the great Council. Wolfe was jailed in 1567, later escaped to Spain in 1572. But he had sown good seed. After him jesuits began to arrive in Ireland. In fact the government developed a fear, paranoia, concerning the jesuit presence in the country. In various proclamations against catholics in the late sixteenth and early seventeenth centuries jesuits are usually singled out for special mention as seriously dangerous. As the seventeenth century came in the number of known jesuits in Ireland began to grow; we know of six in 1604, eighteen in 1609, forty-two in 1626. Especially after 1626 and, under the guidance of a celebrated superior, Robert Nugent, the jesuits in Ireland grew in influence, particularly educational influence, as the seventeenth century progressed. Nugent had colleges established in many of the towns such as Dublin, Drogheda and Waterford. By 1640 the jesuits had thirteen residences, mostly in Leinster and Munster. Of course, they became very involved also in some of the Irish colleges on the continent, which involvement gave them serious influence over the future Irish priests. They were, through the will of Cardinal Ludovisi and much to the disappointment of Luke Wadding, given charge of the Irish college in Rome in 1635. The founder of the Irish college in Salamanca was a jesuit from Clonmel, Thomas White; he was also involved in the Irish college in Santiago and in the one in Seville. Many young men from Waterford, related to Luke Wadding, Patrick Comerford, Thomas Walsh and others, joined the jesuits on the continent and some of them became very distinguished academics in colleges and universities throughout Europe.

Wolfe had not always received strong support and encouragement from the Irish bishops in the 1560's and early 1570's. Their attitude is understandable. They were confused enough by reformation pressures; some were unsure as to their own status theologically and juridically. An outsider from a recently founded religious order, who had been sent from Rome to be their adviser and even to be suggesting candidates for bishoprics, was not always very acceptable to some of them. But the jesuits themselves in general became much admired by the people particularly through their retreats and missions in the towns and also in the country areas. As time went on, they were accorded sincere respect from the bishops, especially from the new style of bishops appointed after 1620. They seem to have been quite removed from most of the regular-secular conflicts in the first half of the seventeenth century. During the years of the Confederation of Kilkenny, the jesuits seriously sought to avoid running counter to the bishops and, in so far as they could, to the nuncio Rinuccini.

The jesuits had rented residence in Waterford and Clonmel from the first decade of the seventeenth century. A father Thomas Wise, surely a native of Waterford, was working in Waterford city from 1604 till his death in 1628. In 1613 he was joined by Father John Lombard, in 1615 by father Thomas Rafter, in 1616 by Fr. Edmund Cleere, in 1617 by Father Thomas Comerford (a relative of bishop Comerford) and father Pierse Strange. In 1630 they were invited by the mayor, William Dobbyn, to establish in the city a college or large grammar school. It had many classrooms and a library.

In Clonmel we know the names of three jesuits, but there may have been more, in the early seventeenth century: Nicholas Lainich who died in 1625, Andrew Mulroney who died in 1631, Andrew Sall who later went to Waterford where he was professed in 1654. In both towns the jesuit communities engaged in full pastoral work and also went out into the country areas to administer the sacraments and catechise the people whose knowledge of the faith was often very meagre.

The jesuits' record in the diocese of Waterford and Lismore was commendable. Like the other religious orders they had received the full grant of faculties from pope Paul V in 1612. It does seem clear from their reports that they seriously attempted to exercise these faculties subject to the control of the ordinaries. That would indeed have been the way of the counter-reformation to which the jesuits in a very special manner were committed.[46]

In their early years in the city of Waterford, the jesuits had no church but it was their claim that on 3 April 1609 pope Paul V granted them the church of St. Peter which was in ruins at the time.[47] The execution of the pope's bull was entrusted to the bishop of Waterford and Lismore but, as the see was vacant at the time, the execution did not take place. The jesuits asserted that on 3 January 1629 pope Urban VIII committed the execution to Comerford, the bishop-elect of Waterford and Lismore who was in Rome at the time. The jesuit Report says that, on his return to Ireland as bishop, Comerford delayed in performing this task on the grounds that he had too many other difficult problems to face at the time. Now, sometime in the middle 1630's, the Report claims that matters have improved and the grant of the church should be made to them. But the bishop, shifting his ground, claimed that the Pope had not been informed before he made the grant that the church of St. Peter was the title and property pertaining to the office of archdeacon of the cathedral of Waterford. Hence the grant was not

---

46 cf. Report in jesuit general archives, Rome, Anglia 41, *Hiberniae Historia 1599-1692*, 221
47 Information on this dispute is largely drawn from a report (undated) made to Rome by the jesuits. A copy is contained in the archives of the Irish college, Rome and is printed in Moran, *Spicil. Ossor.*, I, 300-02. The jesuits had charge of the Irish college from 1635 which might explain the presence in the college archives of the report. It might (only might) be a pointer to a date after 1635

valid and Comerford said that he felt under no obligation to have it executed. He declared that, although the church is small and the offerings from the parish are very little, the archdeacon has no other source of income. The jesuits did not agree that the pope's concession was invalidated because there was no mention in the grant that the church pertained to the office of archdeacon. It had been clearly granted to the jesuits as a parish church. In any case they declare that the church or parish are of no financial value at all. According to their report the present archdeacon swears that he does not receive any money from the parish which is made up of about thirty poor families.

The bishop refused to be moved despite the fact that the entire city and the magistrates asked him to accede to the legitimate request of the jesuits. The archdeacon himself, according to the Report, was quite prepared to hand over the church to the society. The jesuits asked Rome to declare that the pope's concession would still have been made even if he had known that the church pertained to the office of the archdeacon. If necessary, the few parishioners in the parish could be joined to one of the four or five neighbouring parishes in the city. It was the opinion of the Report that the office of archdeacon should be suppressed in contemporary Ireland as it carried no revenue and there was no question of a place in choir or even a place where a chapter could meet. An archdeacon's duties in the Ireland of the time, the jesuits declared, were merely to assist the bishop at ceremonies. There were, they felt, too many of such poor miserable archdeacons in the country!

Comerford does not appear to have raised this controversy in his report to Propaganda. Possibly he felt that his attitude would neither appear convincing nor be pleasing to the Roman authorities. There seems to be no trace of the matter in the archives of Propaganda. But we do know that the case was referred, perhaps by Comerford himself, to the papal nuncio Rinuccini during his time in Ireland (1645-9).[48] The nuncio deputed archbishop Walsh of Cashel to look into the affair and decide in favour of one of the parties. In 1648 the archbishop reported to the nuncio that he failed completely to persuade Comerford to grant the church to the jesuits and had been forced to declare against him. He consequently handed over St. Peter's to the jesuits. The archbishop suggested that the nuncio should transfer the title of archdeacon to another church or to some chapel of the Cathedral.[49] The jesuits immediately proceeded to build up the walls of the old ruined church. It was roofless so, as a temporary measure to guard against rain, they placed a large sail across from one wall to the other. They thus gave some dignity to the building.[50]

The jesuits had only a short-lived possession of St. Peter's church. They ministered in and from the church during the plague which swept through the city and countryside in 1650.

---

[48] It is of interest that in the instructions given to Rinuccini by Rome he was directed to arrange that a church in Waterford be given to the jesuits: *Commentarius Rinuccinianus*, XXXV-LI

[49] Archbishop of Cashel to Rinuccini, Waterford, 29 May 1648, *Comment. Rinucc.*, iii, 317 ff.

[50] Power, P., 'Random Gleanings in Diocesan History', *Catholic Record of Waterford and Lismore*, IV (Aug. 1916) 107-10. It should be remembered that at this time in the 1640's the catholics had taken possession from the established church of many churches in the country, including cathedrals

With the fall of the city to General Ireton on 6 August 1650, catholic life in Waterford was completely disrupted. Both bishop Comerford and the jesuits were rendered helpless. For Comerford the two years of life left to him were spent in illness and in exile. Of the jesuits we know that two members of the community, James Walshe and George Dillon died of the plague. A third, Gregory Dowdall, left Waterford to go to New Ross. A few, perhaps Edmond Cleere and Andrew Sall, may have gone into hiding.[51] The Cromwellian decade descended on Waterford city and on the diocese of Waterford and Lismore. The bishop emerges from the controversy over St. Peter's as being obstinate and unreasonable. St. Peter's church itself probably resumed its status as a lifeless ruin. No trace of it can be seen in our time.

---

[51] Report in jesuit general archives, Rome, Anglia 41, *Hiberniae Historia*, 1599-1692, 336V - 342V

(3) The Sorbonne Propositions

Of the many religious orders which had been established in the diocese of Waterford and Lismore before the suppression of the monasteries and religious houses in the time of Henry VIII it would seem that only three, the cistercians, franciscans and dominicans were to a fair extent still organised and leading, in some fashion, the common life during the episcopate of Patrick Comerford. A fourth, a post-reformation arrival, the jesuits, can be added.[52] The franciscans and jesuits had houses in Clonmel and Waterford, the Dominicans had a house in Waterford city, and the cistercians, having relinquished their claim to Mothel, had only the ruined abbey of Inishlounaght (de Surio) on the banks of the river Suir near Clonmel. With all three, cistercians, franciscans, jesuits, Patrick Comerford crossed swords: we have noted the nature of his disagreement with the cistercians and the jesuits, both concerning the possession of churches and the right to conduct pastoral ministry in parishes over which the bishop claimed complete competence. His quarrel with the third group, the franciscans, was a more bitter, more sustained and more personal one. They, being the most numerous of the regulars in his diocese, as they were in Ireland generally seem, in a special way, to have become identified in Comerford's mind with the whole regular position. He claims that from the franciscans he received most criticism and defiance. Their provincial who was guardian of Dublin (1626-29) and of Waterford throughout much of the 1630's, was a Waterford man, a school-fellow of Comerford, but now his greatest opponent, Thomas Strange. Many considered him to be the defeated candidate for the bishoprick of Waterford and Lismore, as indeed, could also be said of Comerford's other serious opponent, John Madan, the cistercian. Strange and his fellow franciscans were the most deeply involved in one very sharp series of clashes between the regular and secular clergy. What were known as the Sorbonne Propositions and the bishop of Waterford and Lismore's stand in the controversy surrounding the propositions were to cause deep and personal resentment.

On his return to Ireland Comerford several times tells Wadding (who was a close friend of both Comerford and Strange) that the franciscans were the greatest trouble-makers in his diocese and indeed throughout the rest of Ireland as well.[53] He singles out Thomas Strange who, at this time 1630, '31, was guardian of the franciscan house in Waterford, for special judgement:

---

[52] The two augustinian orders, eremites who formerly had a friary in Dungarvan (Abbeyside) and the canons regular of St. Augustine who had been established in Cahir, Molana, Mothel and St. Catherine's, Waterford city, do not appear to have been organised at this period at all.
cf. Power, P., *Waterford and Lismore*, 56, who says that, according to the testimony of John Brennan, bishop of Waterford and Lismore (1671-93), some few eremites continued to live together, not in Abbeyside where their foundation used be, but in nearby Dungarvan

[53] Comerford to Wadding, 18 Jan. 1630 (8 Jan. 1629 O.S.), *Wadding Papers*, 334; same to same, Nov. 1631, ibid., 515

it is well known that one turbulent head did stir most discorde, controversie, and inimitie in all places to which he came in this kingdom, the report that goes of him doth paine me, and if God of his mercie do not stop certaine courses, it be feared that the same turbulent fellow shall undoe himself and others, and be a great disgrace to many, he is the ringleader of all the malice and wrate wrought against me; he is the setter on of others; but I trust in God and his protection.[54]

Led by Strange, the franciscans considered Comerford's strong opposition to the regular clergy an example of monstrous ingratitude for all they had done for him. According to the bishop, in their insensitive calumniation of him they declared that he had quickly forgotten how prominent they had been in petitioning that he be made a bishop and how it was through the efforts of their most illustrious member in Rome, Luke Wadding, the appointment of Comerford to Waterford and Lismore had eventually been made.

This allegation proved very hurtful to Comerford, especially any suggestion of ingratitude on his part towards his closest friend and dear cousin, Wadding. He protested heatedly to Wadding that he had never sought a postulation for the episcopacy from any man and, in fact , the secular clergy of Waterford and Lismore and the archbishop of Cashel had also postulated that he be appointed. Surely, he asked Wadding, he had some personal merits to recommend him, besides having to depend entirely on the petition of the franciscans.[55]   This sense of rejection, which was noticeable immediately on his return to his diocese, his feeling especially that the regular clergy, and, in particular, the franciscans, resented his being made bishop when better men, such as Strange and perhaps Madan, had been passed over, may account for much of Comerford's personal hostility to them. However, Comerford's suspicion on this matter does not seem to be as well founded as his letters would indicate. Contemporary letters from the regulars, particularly from Strange himself, do not demonstrate resentment at Comerford's appointment as bishop but rather show annoyance at his subsequent behaviour. It has to be understandable that the franciscans and other regular clergy would have expected sympathy and understanding from a regular bishop such as Comerford. Men like the franciscan, Thomas Fleming, archbishop of Dublin, had not forgotten their fellow regulars on being raised to the episcopacy.[56]   Fleming is held up as a model with whom Comerford is contrasted unfavourably.[57] There is no doubt that, prior to his appointment as bishop, Comerford's record as a regular priest in Ireland had been inspiring. His appreciation of the central role of the regular clergy in the Irish mission is well represented in a letter written by him to Propaganda in 1627 requesting that their former missionary faculties should be restored to his own order of

---

[54] Same to same, 18 Jan. 1630 (8 Jan.1624 O.S.), ibid., 334-5
[55] Ibid.
[56] Aspects of the relationship between archbishop Fleming and trouble-making secular priests in Dublin and his support for the franciscans are well described in Thomas O'Connor, *Irish Jansenists*, 130 - 48
[57] Thomas Strange to Francis Matthews O.F.M., Waterford 24 Nov. 1630, *Wadding Papers*, 441

augustinian eremites, even though they were few in number in Ireland.[58] It is of interest to note how differently he views the situation when he has become bishop. No longer for him is the Irish situation to be considered in terms of the individual activity of any particular priest or religious order; rather, will real and lasting progress be recorded only if all the various elements in the Irish church be co-ordinated properly and, very importantly, be organised under an efficient episcopate.

Becoming a bishop has changed many a man. It is undoubtedly true that bishop Comerford was convinced of the necessity of centralised episcopal control in the Irish church but his attitude to the regular clergy can hardly be entirely attributed to this conviction. Perhaps some weakness in his own character may also have played a part in determining this attitude, an attitude that was sometimes unreasonable and even bitter. This change in one from whom they had reason to hope for much was bound to sadden the regular clergy. Thomas Strange bitterly complains to Wadding that

Our Patrick is altogether opposed to the regulars, all orders alike complain of him[59]

There are traitorous hints in the Comerford depicted in the letters of Strange.

In making any judgment, perhaps we should keep in mind that Thomas Strange was a defeated candidate for the episcopacy though, in fairness to him, he does not reveal resentment on this account in his letters to Wadding. It was Strange who led the early opposition to the bishop on the occasion of his clash with John Madan over the cistercian occupation of the abbey of Mothel. There is mention of a reconciliation between Comerford and Strange on the occasion of Madan's submission to the bishop in March 1630. But the good relationship was not destined to last very long. Within a year they were quarrelling again.[60] This fresh quarrel occurred in connection with Comerford's stand in the controversy over what are known as the Sorbonne Propositions.

The trouble began in Dublin. In the archdiocese there was a circle or coterie of secular priests, working in Dublin but natives of the neighbouring diocese of Meath. This group revolved around an ex capuchin, Luke Rochford, who conducted a grammar school in Bridge Street in the parish of St. Audeon. Prominent amongst the circle in this discussion group were three secular priests: Paul Harris, Patrick Cahill and Peter Cadell, all of the Meath diocese. Cahill ministered in the parish of Donnybrook, Cadell ministered in Swords, Paul Harris was of English birth, his real name was Paul Green. He had been educated in the English college, Seville, and ordained for ministry in the English mission. But he came to Ireland as chaplain to

---

[58] Comerford to Propaganda, 1627, APF, SOCG, 294, f. 96RV.

[59] Strange to Wadding, Waterford, 30 May 1631, *Wadding Papers*, 525

[60] Comerford writes in happy mood to Wadding on 8 March 1630 (28 Feb. 1629 O.S.), 'El padre fray Thomas Strang me pidio perdon, y me prometio de so parte, y de la parte de sus hermanos buena correspondencia, y que no se desmandarian en hablar mal de mi', *Wadding Papers*, 345
But the following year Strange writes to Wadding, again complaining about Comerford's attitude to the regulars: 'Nuestra Patricio es todo opuesto a reglares', ibid, 525

the Luttrell family which had strong Meath connections. Harris was highly intelligent and seemed to thrive on controversy, particularly involving the regular clergy.

In 1627 there was a heated disagreement between Luke Rochford and Thomas Strange (whom we have met many times already) who was at the time guardian of the franciscans in Dublin. The disagreement centred on the right to preside at the burial of a wealthy Dublin merchant, Thomas Plunkett. Strange won the tussle even though the funeral mass and service was conducted in the chapel attached to Rochford's school in Bridge Street. Retaliating action against Strange occurred, at the instigation of Rochford's circle, when accusations were made that Strange, in a sermon in Dublin, had claimed that the regular clergy were in a far higher place in the church hierarchy than the secular clergy. Harris penned a well publicized letter in connection with the claim made by Strange. The letter was rather cynically signed Philadelphus (brotherly love).[61] Strange replied and signed his letter Philalethes (lover of truth). Harris then published a pamphlet: Fasciculum Florum in Horto Thomas Strange Collectorum.[62]   This was an insulting anti-regular piece of propaganda. It, like Harris' letters, was distributed throughout Dublin and, indeed further afield. It angered the franciscan archbishop of Dublin who, supporting Strange, forbade any further distribution of the writings of Harris. Harris and his supporters now strengthened their case against Strange and the regulars by expanding their accusations into propositions which eventually amounted to eleven which, it was claimed, were taught or professed by the regular clergy in Ireland. Some of the propositions were indubitably heterodox which, in accordance with practice of the time, justified their being referred for judgment to intellectual centres such as the Sorbonne in Paris and the University of Louvain, hence the name Sorbonne Propositions. Perhaps this move would not have reached very far but two other causes of war came to be associated with the propositions. One was an account of the acrimonious clashes in England between Richard Smith, bishop of Chalcedon, and the regular clergy; the other was a dispute between archbishop Fleming of Dublin and Patrick Cahill over the latter's obtaining from the Roman Datary in 1629 an appointment to St. Michael's parish in Dublin. The three items of controversy were somehow seen as a package or cocktail, heavily indicative of misbehaviour on the part of the regulars on either side of the Irish Sea. The outcome of it all was that the eleven propositions and the related matters were referred to the Sorbonne. Some prominent Irish clerics in Paris – no friends of the regulars - made arrangements for the presentation of the material to the Sorbonne. The actual presentation to the theological faculty of the Sorbonne was facilitated in a special way by the testimonies of relatively influential Irish clerics who were in the city, particularly James Fallon, vicar general of Achonry, Terence Coughlan, vicar apostolic of Clonmacnois, Michael Cantwell, a priest of Waterford and Lismore, an ex Jesuit, who had recently been appointed agent of the Munster bishops in Rome and was on his way to take up residence in that City.

---

[61]   O'Connor, Thomas, *Irish Jansenists*, 153-4;
        Moran, P.F. *History of the Catholic Archbishop of Dublin*, vol. I, 376-9
[62]   'A bunch of flowers collected in the garden of Thomas Strange'

In a letter to Wadding, Thomas Strange said that the 'gentlemen of Paris' decided to associate the Irish propositions with the Smith controversy in England.[63] The faculty of theology referred the propositions to about twelve doctors of theology for investigation. Irish priests then resident in Paris were interviewed. The propositions and accompanying opinion were formally presented to the faculty of theology in December 1630. The Sorbonne faculty and some French bishops who had also been consulted censured the propositions. The censure, as translated into English, by Paul Harris, was published in April 1631 by the English college at Douai and it was widely distributed throughout Europe. Its title was "Censurs of certaine propositions, partly brought out of Ireland, partly drawne out of two English bookes".[64]

The propositions and their censure caused much grief and difficulty to the regulars of Ireland. Some of the propositions made extravagant claims for the regular clergy, such as the assertion that religious superiors possess a greater dignity than bishops; others were blatant falsehoods such as the one which held that the pope could not recall the privileges that had been granted to the regular clergy.

We give here the eleven propositions as they were presented to the Sorbonne faculty. They are in the exact form in which they were presented to pope Urban VIII, perhaps by Luke Wadding; *Wadding Papers*, 510, 11.

Propositiones undecim quas falso dixit Patricius Cahill passim in Hibernia a regularibus doceri, et curavit a Parisiensibus condemnari in odium regularium:

1. Hierachia ecllesiastica constat ex pontifice cardinalibus, archiepiscopis,, et regularibus.
2. Sacerdotes sunt meri saeculares.
3. Regulares sunt veri et soli curati sive pastores.
4. Regulares possunt ministrare omnia sacramenta, etiam invito parocho.
5. Parochiani non tenentur in propria parochia communicare in paschate.
6. Solis regularibus competit vocari patres.
7. Ecclesiasticae hierarchiae pars prudentior selectiorque sunt regulares
8. Superiores regularium digniores sunt episcopis; siquidem dignitas pastoris petenda est conditione sui gregis, quemadmodum opilio dignior est subulco.
9. Securius et salubrious est peccata regularibus quam pastoribus confiteri.
10. In partibus haereticorum non tenetur populus christianus necessarium sustentationem suo parocho subministrare, quia bona ecclesiastica ab haereticis possidentur.
11. Privilegia regularium non potest papa revocare.[65]

---

[63] Strange to Wadding, Waterford, 10 Sept. 1631, FLK, Ms. D. 11, ff. 427-30
[64] The original censures were published in Paris with the title: *Censura Propositionum Quarundam, cum ex Hibernia Delatarum, tum ex Duobus Libris Anglico sermo conscriptis....exceptarum*
[65] 1. The Ecclesiastical hierarchy consists of pope, cardinals, archbishops and regulars.

A month after the Sorbonne condemned the propositions pope Urban VIII in a brief entitled 'Brittania' strongly came down on the side of the regulars in their quarrels with bishop Richard Smith in England. Smith was deeply hurt by the papal decision and shortly afterwards he left for France and never returned to England. For many years afterwards the English church had no bishop. Smith corresponded with bishop David Rothe of Ossory and we have noted already that several of the Irish bishops, including Comerford, had pleaded with Rome to support Smith in his differences with the regulars.

The Irish bishops were disturbed by the bull 'Brittania'; perhaps if things came to a formal showdown in Rome between them and the regulars, Rome might look in a similarly benign manner on the regulars. Fallon, vicar general of Achonry, who had supported Cahill and Harris in the preparation of the propositions in Paris and who strongly opposed the regulars, wrote to Wadding in 1631 to the effect that bishop Comerford of Waterford and Lismore and bishop Roche of Ferns seem to have believed that the Sorbonne propositions were in fact being taught by the regulars in Ireland:

> the bishops of Ferns and Waterforde writeth that they (the regulars) continue as yet in such scandalous manner and the bishop of Waterforde writes that if ther be noe correction soone, ther will be a new Schisme[66]

It is likely that Wadding would have been supportive of the regulars in this whole matter and that he would not have approved of Fallon's contribution to the controversy.

The regulars counter-attacked after the Sorbonne censure of the propositions. A sharp and bitter reply was published in the form of a book with the title 'Examen Iuridicum censurae facultatis theologiae Parisiensis' written by an Irish franciscan, Francis Matthew, under the pseudonym Edmundus Ursulanus.[67] This book was a savage attack on the Irish hierarchy and the secular clergy in Ireland. It was described by Comerford as a

---

2. Priests are merely seculars.
3. Regulars are truly and only carers and pastors.
4. Regulars can administer all sacraments even if the parish priest does not wish it.
5. Parishioners are not bound to make their Easter communion in their own parishes.
6. Only the regulars can be called fathers.
7. The more prudent and select part of the ecclesiastical hierarchy are the regulars.
8. The superiors of the regulars have more dignity than bishops; such as the dignity of the shepherd depends on the condition of his flock so the shepherd is superior to the swineherd.
9. It is safer and more beneficial to confess sins to the regulars rather than to the pastors.
10. In countries dominated by heretics, Christians are not obliged to provide material support to the parish clergy, because ecclesiastical property is in the hands of heretics.
11. The pope cannot revoke the privileges of the regular clergy.

[66] Fallon to Wadding, Paris 1631, *Wadding Papers*, 468
[67] This work was published at Frankfurt in late 1631. Matthews is also referred to as O'Mahony. As the Irish word for Mahony is 'Mathgamhain' which means a 'bear' the pseudonym 'Ursulanus' is

hellhacht pamflett with heapes of manifest lyes and calumnies cast upon the bishops of this kingdome[68]

Such accusing and attacking language as is contained in this book was bound to antagonise the bishops whom the author blames for the forwarding of the propositions to the Sorbonne. However, in fairness, the majority of the bishops gave clear written testimony that the regular clergy had been unjustly maligned and were not guilty of teaching what the propositions contained. Rome had been consulted on the matter, letters of complaint were sent by bishops and members of religious orders at the unrest and divisions in the Irish church arising from the Sorbonne propositions. Formal attestations were sent by the jesuits (10 May 1631), the cistercians (10 June 1631), the Dominicans (4 July 1631), the capuchins (6 July 1631), the carmelites (25 July 1631),the augustinian eremites (2 June 1631), the franciscans (1 May 1631), and by many individuals from various orders, all denying that the Sorbonne propositions were being taught by their members in Ireland.

Rome did what Rome often does and does well; it appealed for harmony and reconciliation.[69] It went further as the Irish scene became more angry and divided. Propaganda, through the nuncio in Flanders, commissioned the archbishops of Dublin and Tuam and the bishops of Kilmore and Kildare to conduct a formal enquiry into the whole affair and inform the holy see whether or not the propositions were taught by the regulars.[70]

This commission met during 1631 and, without too much delay, came to the anticipated conclusion that the propositions had never been taught by the regulars in Ireland and that they should be vindicated of the accusations made against them.[71] As mentioned above, many individual Irish bishops made their reports to Propaganda at the time the commission was doing its work. In many cases the regulars had canvassed their views and asked them to write to Rome on their behalf. However, four bishops: Ossory, Ferns, Cork and Cloyne, Waterford and Lismore proved uncooperative and became the subject of much angry complaints by the regulars.

These four bishops had all had serious difficulties with the regular clergy over the years. Their refusal now to testify that the regulars did not teach what was contained in the propositions probably indicates more an anti-regular mentality and general unwillingness to

---

explained. Comerford, taking into account the savage nature of the book, suggests that 'Ursulanus' comes from 'Ulciscor' ('avenge oneself on'), letter to Wadding, 1632, *Wadding Papers*, 619
[68] Same to same, 30 October 1631, ibid, 609
[69] Propaganda to the archbishop of Dublin, 18 August 1630, APF, Lettere, 10. f. 90R
Same to the four archbishops, 20 Sept. 1630, APF, Lettere, 10, f. 105R
[70] Letter of bishops of Ossory, Ferns, Cork and Cloyne, to Propaganda, Nov. 1631, APR, SOCG, 150 f. 326 RV
[71] Report of archbishops Fleming and Queally and of the bishop of Kilmore on the propositions, Athlone, 4 Sept. 1631, *Wadding Papers*, 571-3. The bishop of Kildare made his report to the nuncio at Brussels, 3 Sept. 1631, ibid, 574-6

accommodate their wishes than a solid belief that the accusations were true. David Rothe of Ossory was the acknowledged leader of this small group; he was the longest reigning bishop in the country and, more than any other bishop, he had witnessed the division between secular and regular clergy grow steadily since about 1614. He appears to have been of the definite opinion that the regulars were the real trouble makers in the affair. For him and his three colleagues the most unforgiveable aspect was not the accusations regarding the propositions but the savage attack on the bishops particularly that expressed in the book of Edmundus Ursulanus.[72] All four asserted that the submission and condemnation of the propositions was unfair; they never, in writing to Propaganda or Fr. Wadding, claim that the regulars did in fact teach what was contained in the propositions. But neither were they prepared to give a written testimony as to their innocence. Their suggestion was rather that investigations into the whole matter should cease and that silence should be imposed on both sides.[73] There may have been an element of self-protection in their suggestions to Rome. They may have feared that a thorough investigation might portray themselves in a somewhat unfavourable light and a misinterpretation might be placed on an action which they had performed. Patrick Cahill of Dublin was preparing to travel to Rome via Paris to plead his case against his archbishop, Thomas Fleming. He approached some of the bishops including Rothe of Ossory and Roche of Ferns and possibly also Comerford, for a written testimony as to his good character and credibility. The testimonies of Rothe and Roche are available and are carefully worded. They state specifically that the authors in no way intend to prejudice the case pending in Rome between archbishops Fleming and Cahill. They simply state that Cahill was an upright man who had done fruitful work for souls.[74] In the light of Cahill's subsequent conduct in Paris in favour of submitting the propositions to the Sorbonne they would understandably prefer not to be associated with him in any reports that might be submitted to the Roman authorities.

In a bitterly strong letter to Wadding in the autumn of 1631 Thomas Strange recounts how, having obtained testimonies as to the innocence of the regulars from so many bishops he, as head of the Waterford franciscans, together with John Madan, the cistercian abbot who had trouble with Comerford over Mothel, Richard Strange, provincial of the augustinian eremites, Peter Strange, prior of the Waterford dominicans, and John Lombard, rector of the Waterford jesuits, approached Comerford and asked that he also might testify as to the innocence of the

---

[72] Letter of bishops of Ossory, Ferns, Cork and Cloyne, to Propaganda, Nov. 1631, APF, SOCG, 150, f. 326RV; William Browne (Comerford) to Wadding, Waterford, 30 Oct. 1631, *Wadding Papers*, 609

[73] Letter of bishops of Ossory, Ferns, Cork & Cloyne, to Propaganda, Nov. 1631, APF, SOCG, 150, f. 326V

[74] Testimony of David Rothe, bishop of Ossory, concerning his letter to Patrick Cahill, *Wadding Papers*, 452
A letter worded in the same manner was written by John Roche, bishop of Ferns, *Wadding Papers FLK*, D11, f.221
Thomas Strange in a letter to Wadding, 30 May 1631, states that Comerford also had written in Cahill's favour, *Wadding Papers*, 525.

regulars.[75] The bishop, according to Strange, was evasive and said that he would have to take eight days to investigate and consider the matter. Comerford then went and visited the regular clergy in the diocese and found none of them guilty of teaching what was contained in the propositions. But still he showed himself unwilling to grant them his testimony. Due to his obstinacy tempers became frayed. At a second meeting John Lombard told him

> that if there was the finger of God in the religious state....neither he, nor how many bishops soever might join with him, would suffice to destroy the work of God[76]

Finally, according to Strange, the bishop agreed to give his testimony on condition that the regulars would give him their testimony that neither he nor any other bishop in Ireland had interfered with the oratories or possessions of the regular clergy. Strange declares that they were prepared to give testimony that Comerford himself had not so interfered, but, not being fully aware of the situation in all the dioceses, they could not give a general testimony for the whole country. The bishops of Ossory and Ferns, Strange says, had stipulated the same condition because of internal problems in their own dioceses. Strange tells Wadding that Comerford's final refusal to vindicate the regulars in writing was really due to his fear of displeasing the bishop of Ossory. Rothe was an implacable opponent of the regulars and his influence on Comerford and on most of the Munster and Leinster bishops was considerable. Strange says that Rothe together with bishop William Tirry of Cork and Cloyne and Matthew Roche, vicar apostolic of Leighlin (brother of bishop John Roche of Ferns)

> have caused our Patrick to dance to their tune and have made him altogether such an adversary of the religious clergy as if he had never worn the habit, or as if he had been expelled from religion[77]

Comerford's version of his encounter with the delegation of regular clergy who came to him on this matter is different. He admits that the propositions were unfairly attributed to the regulars in Ireland. But he is not satisfied that each individual member of the regulars in Ireland is free of guilt. In fact, certain individual regulars in his own presence and hearing have defended three or four of the propositions; and he had been told by some of the bishops that it was some regulars from his own diocese who were the greatest proponents of the propositions.[78] Still he says that he told the deputation that he himself had no part in the drawing up of or the

---

[75] Strange to Wadding, 10 Sept. 1631, *Wadding Papers*, 569-83

[76] 'que si en el estado religioso estava el dedo de Dios ....que ni el ni quantos obispos se juntassen con el bastarian destruir la obra de Dios' ibid., 580

[77] He describes the affair in two pessimistic letters to Wadding: 30 Oct. 1631, *Wadding Papers*, 607-15 and Nov. 1631, ibid., 615-20

[78] It is quite possible that he has Thomas Strange O.F.M. in mind here as it was generally believed that it was Strange's sermons in Dublin which really marked the beginning of this particular secular-regular clash. cf. supra 130

submitting of the propositions for censure in Paris. He had objected to the generalised way in which they had been attributed to the regulars. Finally, he said that he refused to sign a testimony there and then because he was the youngest bishop in the province and could not be expected to take the lead in such a matter. The metropolitan, archbishop Walsh, happened to be in Waterford, his native city, at the time and Comerford tells Wadding that he referred the deputation to him. The regulars then went to see the metropolitan and, the news of the appointment of the commission of enquiry by the nuncio of Brussels having arrived, they returned no more to himself. Comerford claimed to Wadding that, in their interview with him, the regulars were very discourteous. He said he could not have acted other than he did because the deputation refused to withdraw some of the propositions and also because they continued to adhere to some of the calumnious statements which had been made against the bishops in the recent controversy.

One cannot with full confidence determine which of the two accounts, that of Comerford or that of Strange, gives the facts as they actually occurred; both are clearly emphasising their own side of the story. It does seem, however that Comerford was excessively intransigent in the whole affair. His implicit assertion of willingness to follow the metropolitan's line of action was not carried out, as the archbishop had testified to the innocence of the regulars. Strange undoubtedly had a point in declaring that Comerford chose to follow the bishop of Ossory and declined to take any action that might displease him. It cannot be doubted that Comerford sincerely believed that individual regulars were in fact teaching what was contained in the propositions and he was not sufficiently disposed to the regulars as a whole to give formal recognition that such individuals were the exception. It would seem that he felt that, be the accusations concerning the propositions true or false, the regular clergy needed a lesson and he was not prepared to detract from the efficacy of that lesson. Abstracting from the rights and wrongs of the Sorbonne affair, he took severe exception to the manner in which regulars were wont to rise up in arms at the slightest rebuke from a bishop and also the fact that often a single delinquent member of a religious order was defended by the whole order. He wrote to Wadding:

> ....if any selous or well meaninge man amonge us finde fault with any disorder committed by a regular, or complain of him to his immediat superiors, in steede of amendment or redresse the superior of that order, yea and all the orders will stand in defence of that transgressor, and hold it a pondoner (point d'honneur) to boulster and defend that transgressor against all men; and thus persons of sele and obligation to looke to the common good of the kingdome are deluded, and noe expectation given them of reformation[79]

---

[79] *Wadding Papers*, 608-9

Individual regulars take advantage of this tendency and do what they please knowing they will not be corrected. The result of all this, according to Comerford, is that the entire clerical order was falling into decay and the clergy were becoming more of a scandal than an example to the laity. Comerford asks Wadding to try to bring it about that the regulars who are causing most of the trouble be punished: 'projiciantur in mare ne tota navis periclitatur'[80]

The affair of the Sorbonne propositions undoubtedly represents an unjust attack on the regular clergy. The main responsibility has to be placed on the shoulders of a few embittered individuals, particularly secular priests such as Paul Harris, Patrick Cahill, Peter Cadell, who had grievances of their own against the franciscan archbishop of Dublin, Thomas Fleming. These and others made capital out of the general tension in the country between the regular and secular clergy. At the same time it would be an unfair judgment to say that the regulars emerge from the controversy blameless. There was the intemperate preaching of Thomas Strange and others which helped ignite the flames of discord and division. And defensive methods like those of Edmundus Ursulanus and Paul Harris were excessive and highly imprudent in their negative references to some of the bishops. Judgment has to be passed against bishop Comerford's treatment of the regulars in the affair; and his defence of his actions was not convincing. If he believed, as he obviously did, that the regular clergy did not generally teach what was contained in the propositions he owed it to his conscience and to their reputations to grant the written attestation to that effect, qualifying it, if necessary, as the archbishop of Cashel had done.[81] That he could not bring himself to do this does not do him credit.

With the vindication of the regulars by the episcopal commission and the request for silence on all parties by Propaganda, the Sorbonne affair gradually died.[82] However, those bishops such as Comerford who had not co-operated with the regulars were noted and not easily forgiven. In Dublin Paul Harris continued to hurl insult in pamphlet after pamphlet at archbishop Fleming and the regular clergy. Again and again he recounts the controversy over the propositions and he severely castigates those bishops whom he considered to have played into the hands of the regular clergy. He particularly selects the 'regular bishops', bishops who had been members of religious orders, for excoriation. It is an interesting commentary on Comerford's reputation as a stern opponent of the regulars that Harris, in one of his best known publications, should single him out from all the regular bishops for praise:

> Patrick Comerford, bishop of Waterford, Augustin, which last is the only indifferent Friar Bishop unto the clergy, of all that ever yet were sent into this kingdome[83]

---

80 Ibid., 610, 'Let them be thrown into the sea lest the entire ship be destroyed'
81 Archbishop Walsh's attestation, Wadding Papers, 585, says that regulars did teach proposition no. 5 that parishioners are not bound to receive their Easter communion in their own parish.
82 Bishop Roche to Propaganda, 19 Nov. 1633, APF, SOCG, 294, f. 185R
83 Harris, Paul, 'Fratres sobrii estote 1 Pet. 5. 8. or An admonition to the Fryars of the kingdom of Ireland, to abandon such heretical doctrines as they daylie publish to the corruption of our holy faith, the ruin of our souls, and their own damnation which sleepeth not'. 1634, 67

Harris pursued his various cases, including a case against archbishop Fleming, through the Civil Courts, and it is very likely that he was funded to some degree by the government in doing so. Wentworth, the new Lord Deputy, heard both sides in the case which Harris took against Fleming in 1634. He dismissed both and more or less told both to behave themselves. Bishop John Roche, in reporting the matter to Propaganda declared that Wentworth's interest in the matter was

> not through any affection which he bears ourselves but because the laity are always more or less agitated by our dissensions[84]

Time tended to heal the conflicts and Harris was let alone to fulminate as he wished against the regulars. Few took any further notice of him.[85]

---

[84] Roche to Propaganda, 15 Nov. 1634, printed in *Spicil Ossor.*, I, 197-9
[85] Corish, 'An Irish Counter-Reformation Bishop: John Roche.', *I.T.Q.* XXVI (April 1959) 113

(4) Conclusions

We have been attempting in this chapter to examine some of the principal disagreements which bishop Comerford had with the regular clergy. Together with the bishops of Ossory, Ferns, Cork and Cloyne, he perhaps experienced the greatest difficulties with the regulars. Being a regular himself, he incurred more hostility for his anti-regular stand than any other bishop. Given the counter-reformation mindset of the bishops appointed to the Irish dioceses in these early years of the seventeenth century, it was to be expected that there would be tension between any bishop in Ireland and the regular clergy of his diocese. Still an easy or simple explanation of Comerford's hostility is difficult to explain. Conjecture must enter into the attempt.

There is no evidence to prove that Comerford ever had any rupture with his own order of the augustinian eremites. In fact the indications are very much to the contrary. During the two years in Rome before he became bishop his relations with the Roman superiors of his order seem to have been very happy. The superior general, Hieronymus de Ghettis, made a very strong attestation of Comerford's character, ability and dedication in the investigation conducted prior to his nomination as bishop. During his early years as bishop, when the crises involving the regular clergy were at their height, correspondence between Comerford and the Irish representative of the order at the General Chapter in Rome shows that the relations were still very good.[86]

In fairness to Comerford it should be borne in mind that his diocese was particularly disturbed by unduly independent behaviour on the part of the regular clergy. This can probably be explained by a consideration that, of all the larger dioceses in Munster province, Waterford and Lismore had been without a bishop for twice as long as the rest. For over fifty years there had been no proper centralised control. It must also be remembered that Comerford had a very difficult beginning to his episcopacy in Waterford and Lismore. The quarrel awaiting him on his arrival concerning the cistercian occupation of Mothel was hard on him; it was also hard on the regulars who were given cause to fear that worse was to come. Certainly their reaction was hostile as the bishop repeatedly describes. In the early months also the Everard affair and the sacrilegious behaviour in the church of Baptist Grange was very alarming to Comerford as it was indeed to all the Irish bishops. It was understandable that he should have set his face against such deplorable conduct and seek to rectify, once and for all, a situation in which such conduct was possible.

Perhaps Comerford's problem was more personal, more within himself. Perhaps the personal character and temperament of the man may have contributed considerably to the severity of his attitude towards the regular clergy. If one is judging properly from his letters, especially his highly personal letters to friends like Luke Wadding, Comerford was an

---

[86] Maurice Connell O.S.A. to William Poore (Comerford), Rome, 1 Nov. 1630, *Wadding Papers*, 431-3

extremely sensitive person with a strong tendency to be pessimistic about life in general. The word melancholic enters one's mind quite frequently as one reads his correspondence. In some of his letters, especially the deeply personal ones to Wadding, there is sometimes no relief at all from the gloom and misery and from the personal persecution which he claims to suffer from his calumniators, from those who misrepresent his actions, from the poverty of his conditions of living, even from the bad Irish climate! Sometimes one is tempted to consider that his accounts of the hardships and opposition which he suffers are magnified quite beyond the reality of the situation.

Comerford's sensitivity to opposition from the regulars, particularly from the franciscans, is particularly noticeable in the early period of his episcopate. Of special significance in determining his attitude may have been his conviction, voiced time and time again to Wadding, that the regulars, and in particular the franciscans, did not consider him the most suitable candidate for the episcopate, nor the means by which they may have felt he attained to it fair. Especially in the early months, severely playing on his mind was the consideration that the franciscans must resent the choice of himself, an augustinian eremite, as bishop over the head of their own more powerful order and especially over the head of their candidate, Thomas Strange, who had been recommended by so many bishops.[87] That there was some local disappointment at the choice of Comerford may be true, but, as has been remarked earlier, there seems to be no trace of it in the letters from Thomas Strange, even in the letters which are critical of Comerford. In dealing with the regulars Comerford does not seem to have been able to travel the road of gently winning over his opponents; his temperament seems to have determined that he would choose rather to travel the road of insistence and uncompromise with his friend, David Rothe of Ossory.

But when some calm developed after the affair of the Sorbonne propositions, and some years later in 1635 when Propaganda issued a set of decrees entitled *Decreta pro Recto Regimine Ecclesiarum Hiberniae*[88] which will be examined in a later chapter, relations between Comerford and the regulars improved very considerably. He can happily declare in a report to Propaganda in 1639 that most of the strife within the church in Ireland had ended.[89] There were occasional clashes with the regular clergy in the post 1640 period but it was in the 1630's, especially the early part of that decade, that the Irish church could be said to have come to terms with the new diocesan organisation stemming from the Council of Trent. The clashes which

---

[87] Strange had been recommended to Wadding for the bishoprick of Waterford and Lismore by the
      archbishop of Dublin, Thomas Fleming ,and by the archbishop of Cashel, Thomas Walsh:
      Thomas Fleming to Wadding, 26 Oct. 1626, *Wadding Papers*, 235;
      Thomas Walsh to Wadding, 13 April 1627, ibid., 248
      Wadding, it would seem, probably had a preference for Comerford. In the appointment of a bishop to
      his native diocese of Waterford and Lismore, Wadding's recommendation would surely have been all
      powerful in Rome
[88] 'Decrees for the Right Ruling of the Irish Churches'
[89] Relatio Status, printed by J. Hogan from the archives of the Congregation of the Council
      'Miscellanea Vaticano-Hibernica', *Archiv. Hib.* V(1016) 107-112

had taken place were hefty but they were inevitable to a degree. Once they had worked themselves out of the system, the tridentine organisation was henceforth to be accepted as the basic structure of the catholic church in Ireland.

Chapter Seven

THE PROBLEM OF ECCLESIASTICAL REVENUE

The church in pre-reformation Ireland, whether it was the church of the monastic foundations and the friaries or the church of the parishes and dioceses, had assets and some wealth. But it was a complex church and its assets and wealth were very complex indeed. Lay control of and involvement in monastic possessions and in parish structures had become widespread especially in the later Middle Ages.[1] Powerful monasteries frequently exercised control over many parishes. The parish system was not just a simple area where the people were under the spiritual care of a parish priest appointed by the bishop and subject to the bishop. It was a much looser situation. In fact, the bishop's control, either financial or pastoral, was often quite small. For example, in the diocese of Cloyne in the fifteenth century, it has been estimated that of one hundred and thirty churches with pastoral care, seventy-five were impropriate to monastic or collegiate churches and twenty-one were in lay patronage. The old medieval co-arb and erenagh families were also in the equation.[2]

With the dissolution of the monasteries in the 1530's and 1540's the situation worsened even further. The monastic lands were claimed by the crown itself or granted by the crown to individual owners. A similar fate befell the lands attached to the benefices which were the main support of the parishes and the secular clergy. The dissolution of the monasteries and the establishment of the state church meant that the catholic church was almost completely deprived of its property and church buildings. Legally, it had no right to possess anything, in fact it possessed very little. What little it possessed was mainly in the form of priests' houses, or in many cases only the use of houses for the priests. From this impoverishment of the catholic church it should not be concluded that the established or state church, which legally inherited the complex and pretty messy organisations and revenue sources which made up the pre-reformation Irish church, was in a handsome and wealthy state. It was not.

Falkland's proclamation of 1629 showed that quite a number of private houses were possessed by the religious orders.[3] The lease for such houses would have come from wealthy catholic patrons who befriended the orders. But from the almost total loss of property stemmed many problems and abuses within the catholic church itself. In particular it introduced into the controversy between the regular and secular clergy an economic factor which often caused intense disagreement and even bitterness at the local parochial level.

---

[1] Corish, Patrick., *The Catholic Community in the Seventeenth and Eighteenth Centuries*, 21-24
[2] Buckley, D., 'Diocesan organisation in Cloyne', *Irish Catholic Historical Committee Proc*eedings (1956), 8-11
[3] Edwards, R.D., 'Church and State, in the Ireland of Míchél Ó Cléirigh, 1626-41', S. O'Brien (ed.), *Measgra i gcuimhne Mhichíl Úi Cléirigh*

In the reports of most of the bishops to Propaganda the problems of ecclesiastical revenue are stressed. Due to the sameness of many of the reports the amount of specific local information is not great, but the frequency with which the matter is raised leaves no doubt that the question was a very vexed one in contemporary Ireland. The basic problem was the great poverty of the bishops and priests as a result of which there occurred frequent strife and rivalry over the right to command whatever few sources of revenue that existed. In addition there was the problem as to what mind and policy the Irish catholic church should have concerning the total recovery of or, at least, the partial compensation from the revenue of the church's former possessions, be they monastic or parochial. An added complication was the fact that a considerable amount of these possessions had found their way, through sale and re-sale, into the hands of the church's own catholic laity. The experience and remarks of the bishop of Waterford and Lismore sheds some light on this complicated situation.

The diocese of Waterford and Lismore was no exception to the general poverty-stricken condition of the Irish church. The bishop in his letters frequently stresses his own personal poverty and that of the diocese generally. He tells Wadding that he receives nothing from the former ecclesiastical property in the diocese, and the revenue which he gets from the abbey of Kells which, as vicar general of the canons regular of St. Augustine, he holds *in commendam*, is very slight.[4] He explains to Wadding that his inability, because of so many other duties, to visit Kells contributes to his slightness of revenue. There is no revenue from the ruined abbey of Kells or from its former possessions, but the person who held it *in commendam* would be entitled in a moral way to receive the contribution of the faithful in the area annexed to it. In this general regard he requests Wadding to procure for him from the Roman authorities (presumably from the Datary) the title to whatever little revenues attach to the monastery of Cahir in his own diocese of Waterford and Lismore. Cahir had also belonged to the canons regular of St. Augustine.[5]

True to his displeasure with the regulars Comerford tells Wadding that the regular clergy seemed to possess whatever little is available. As for himself, were it not for the help which he received from his own family in Waterford he would probably starve.[6] He has no residence and many of his letters are addressed 'e loco refugii nostri' while one letter comes from High Street, Waterford, where he apparently was staying with his brother.[7] In the seventeenth century High Street was one of the principal streets for business and residence in the city. In 1641 a house or houses in High Street were the official residence of the protestant dean and chapter. The old cathedral, then in the hands of the established church, stood nearby.

---

[4] William Browne (Comerford) to Wadding, 26 Aug. 1639, Wadding; 26 Aug. 1630, *Wadding Papers*, 405

[5] Ibid.

[6] Same to same, 6 March 1630 (24 Feb. 1629 O.S.), *Wadding Papers*, 345

[7] Ibid., 347

While the catholic church in the diocese of Waterford and Lismore was impoverished, the established church was little better. The condition of the latter in the diocese in 1630 was much the same as it had been since the reformation nearly a hundred years previously. In a report submitted to the archbishop of Canterbury in 1634 by bishop Michael Boyle, protestant bishop of Waterford and Lismore (1619-35) it is shown that much former church property in the diocese had been appropriated by adventurers from England, especially by the earl of Cork, Richard Boyle.[8] Bishop Michael Boyle was an Englishman and a relative of the earl of Cork. He declared that his predecessors, caring little for the good of the church, alienated most of what property had come down to them. The result was that, whereas the revenue from diocesan property should amount to about £1600.00 pr annum, he gets only about £100.00. In another report made in the same year it was declared that the earl of Cork had seized all the old manors from which revenue traditionally came to the clergy, also the vicarages which were meant to support the vicars choral of Lismore cathedral.[9] When Thomas Wentworth became Lord Deputy of Ireland in 1633 one of his well planned aims was the proper organisation of the established church in Ireland.[10] Through various schemes and stratagems he improved the financial condition of that church considerably. In 1637 an agreement was reached between the protestant bishop of Waterford and Lismore, John Atherton, and the earl of Cork whereby the latter consented to ensure certain lands and revenues to the church.[11]

Thomas Carte in *The Life of James Duke of Ormond*, 2nd ed. Vol. I, 68, gives an interesting and characteristic account of the protestant church in Ireland in the seventeenth century:

> The bishopricks themselves, though many in number, yet but of small revenue, having the greatest part of them been depauperated in the change of religion by absolute grants and long leases (made generally by the popish bishops that conformed) some of them not able to maintain a bishop, and no good benefice near them to be held in commendam. Several were by these means reduced to £50 a year, as Waterford, Kilfenora and others, and some to five marks as Cloyne and Kilmacduagh. And as scandalous livings naturally made scandalous ministers, the clergy of the established church were generally ignorant and unlearned, loose and irregular in their lives and conversations, negligent of their cures, and very careless of observing decency in divine worship, in a country where they were endangered on one hand by an infinite number of obstinate recusants (as almost all the old natives were) and on the other by a shoal of factions and irregular Puritans, brought by Sir Hugh Montgomery and other planters out of Scotland who kept up their Scottish discipline and way of worship,

8 *Calendar of State Papers relating to Ireland 1633-47*, 7 March 1634, 44-7
9 Ibid., 3 May 1634, 48-50
10 Clarke, Aidan, 'The Government of Wentworth', *N.H.I.*, vol. III, 157-8
11 *Calendar of State Papers relating to Ireland 1633-47*, 19 July 1637, 166-8

offered daily insults to the established Church-Government, and treated the rites of administering the Sacraments with insufferable contempt.

Until the year 1637 the established church of Waterford and Lismore, despite its strong legal standing, remained very poor. The improvement then effected was soon to be cancelled by Wentworth's fall from power in 1640 and the catholic dominance consequent on the rebellion of 1641.[12]

While the established church could take the earl of Cork and other adventurers to task, and attempt to retrieve from them former church possessions, there was little to be gained by bishop Comerford and the catholics acting in similar manner. However, as has been stated earlier, not all church property was in the hands of the heretics. One of the earliest observations which Comerford made after his arrival in his diocese was that catholic laity were in possession of quite an amount of church property.[13] By 1630 many decades had passed since most of its lands and possessions had been appropriated from the catholic church. It was only to be expected that catholics would, as time passed, come into possession of land that had been acquired by English adventurers. Some of these adventurers, who had been coming to Ireland since Elizabethan times, had become disappointed with the general conditions in Ireland. Some moved on to try their luck in the new colonised land across the Atlantic; a greater number decided to return to their own country. Before leaving Ireland such people disposed of their Irish possessions and it was usually immaterial to them whether the purchaser was a catholic or a protestant. Comerford himself tells Wadding that a lay cousin of his own had come into possession of much of the lands once attached to the Cahir abbey of the canons regular of St. Augustine.[14]

One of the questions which began to vex the catholic bishops in Ireland in the second quarter of the seventeenth century, as they strove to organise their church, was according to what right should such catholics retain these former church lands and other property or what obligation should they incur by virtue of such retention? The truth is that catholics, such as Comerford's cousin in Cahir, probably did not want to deal with such questions at all. If pursued on the matter they probably would invoke the dispensation granted by cardinal Reginald Pole, papal envoy to England, during the reign of queen Mary, enabling all those individuals and corporations who had received grants of ecclesiastical property from the government in the time of Henry VIII and Edward VI to retain what they had received.[15] This dispensation was given legal force in Ireland by the Irish parliament of 1557.[16] Most of the Irish catholics who held such property in the 1620's and 1630's had not received it by grant of the

---

[12] J. T. Ball, *The Reformed Church of Ireland*, p. 132-5
[13] Comerford to Propaganda, 6 July 1630, APF, SOCG, 294, f. 221V
[14] William Browne (Comerford) to Wadding, 26 Aug. 1630, *Wadding Papers*, 405
[15] Comerford to Wadding, 12 March 1631, ibid., 489.
[16] 3 & 4 P.&M., C 6, *The Statutes at large passed in the parliaments held in Ireland*, Vol. 1, 249 ff.

101

sovereign, but they had bought it from those who had, and so they felt in justice entitled to retain what they had bought.[17] This attitude, of course, went hard on the catholic clergy whose personal poverty was very serious; it also disabled them from attending to the repair of the ruined churches which were to be seen in every parish. The argument of some of their flock in favour of the retention of former church property had an unreasonable ring about it. In a letter to Propaganda in 1636 Comerford remarks that it was not just the possession of lands that was in question. Some catholics had even bought and were still buying from protestants the right to collect tithes and other ecclesiastical revenue from their fellow catholics.[18] This was a deplorable situation, and, in the past, Comerford had asked Wadding to use all his efforts to find a solution.[19]

According to Comerford there was a serious difference of opinion in Ireland as to whether Cardinal Pole's dispensation had any validity in Ireland. Some held, he remarks, that Pole's legatine power did not extend to Ireland at all. In the heat of controversy people are saying strange things: that Pole was suspected of false dealing and even schism, and that his dispensation in relation to church property was recalled as soon as Paul IV became pope in 1555. Comerford suggests that Wadding would provide a helpful service to the Irish church if he could trace the relevant documentation in the Vatican archives and clarify the situation once and for all.[20] As might be expected from Comerford, he accuses the regular clergy of using Pole's dispensation as a tactic to embarrass the bishops. The regulars, he declares, are advising lay people not merely to hold on to church property but to resist paying any compensation to the bishops. According to Comerford it was in the past customary for those catholics who held what used be church property to make some contribution from the revenue towards the upkeep of the clergy. In doing this, Comerford alleges, the lay people were simply following the *monitum* of cardinal Pole in his dispensation which was based on prescriptions of natural and ecclesiastical law. Over the years, he adds, such contributions were demanded by church regulations drawn up at national and provincial level.[21] This statement by Comerford to Propaganda is borne out by the faculty grants made by Rome to the regular clergy of Ireland as far back as 1612. They are informed that catholics who possess ecclesiastical property may continue in their possession provided that they agree to accept the judgment of the church concerning its restoration whenever that becomes possible. In the meantime, the regulars are advised that such people should be directed to give alms to those who possessed the property before the schism and they are always to remain mindful that the property really belongs to the church.[22] However, despite the custom and the regulations, Comerford regretfully informs

---

17 Comerford to Propaganda, 25 Jan. 1636, APF, SOCG, 140, f. 43V
18 Ibid.
19 Same to Wadding, 12 March 1631, Wadding papers, 480 ff, cf. also Nicholas Laffan (David Rothe) to Wadding, 20 July 1631, ibid., 554
20 Comerford to Wadding, 12 March 1631, ibid., 489
21 Same to Propaganda, 25 Jan. 1636, APF, SOCG, 140, f. 43V
22 Jesuit general archives, Rome, *Hiberniae Catalogi Antiqui 1611-44*, f. 97V

Propaganda that the catholic possessors of church property no longer made any compensation to the church.[23] It is clear that he considers the regular clergy largely responsible for the discontinuation of the custom of making compensation. As soon, he says, as the bishops and parochial clergy came to be properly organised in recent times and began to labour incessantly in watching over their flock, the possessors of ecclesiastical property began to declare obstinately that they were not bound to contribute to the support of the bishops or parish priests. In taking this stand the people claim that they are following the advice of unnanned 'Viri Docti', learned men who, Comerford ironically adds, 'Occultari caute cupiunt, dum mercedem pastoribus debitam ipsi, pro utili data opinione, recipiunt'[24] Comerford tells Propaganda that it would be of great value if the pope himself would declare that the opinions of these 'Viri Docti' are erroneous and that the laity who possess ecclesiastical property are bound to contribute each year towards the decent and fitting support of their bishops and parish priests.[25]

For his own part, Comerford expresses the opinion that, in these more peaceful days, the church should receive back at least that part of its property which has come into the hands of catholics, its own members. He is puzzled, he declares, that laymen, on the advice of clerics, can in conscience retain possession of church livings to which lately the pope has been making explicit appointments.[26] If a bishoprick is conferred upon a man 'cum iuribus et pertinentiis', or similarly in the case of a vicarage or parish, it must mean in the mind of the holy see that cardinal Pole's dispensation does not stand in contemporary Ireland.[27]

Apropos his own diocese Comerford tells Wadding that the people of Waterford

eat of church livings to a great extent.

They have come into possession of much church property and they make little or no attempt to recompense the church. They are notorious, he says, throughout all Ireland for this practice and, in his opinion, no good will come of it.[28] He personally has not received any retribution for all the property that should be his:

Since I came to this charge, I did not receive as much as a fardinge of any that hath church livings in it, in consideration of my charge[29]

---

[23] Comerford to Propaganda, 25 Jan. 1636, APF, SOCG, 140, f. 43V
[24] Ibid., *Viri Docti* = learned men
      'They hide themselves cautiously as they themselves, in reward for the useful opinion which they give, receive the donation which should have been given to the pastors'.
[25] Ibid.
[26] Here he clearly has in mind the recent appointments of Irish bishops which signifies Rome's intention to restore the hierarchy to Ireland
[27] Same to Wadding, 12 March 1631, *Wadding Papers*, 490
[28] William Browne (Comerford) to Wadding, 26 Aug. 1630, *Wadding Papers*, 405
[29] Same to same, 12 March 1631, Ibid., 489

Still he declares that he will keep an open mind on the whole matter, pending Wadding's investigations in Rome.[30]

Some other members of the hierarchy do not seem to have been as patient as Comerford appeared to be. Whereas, in some respects, the regular clergy were accused of using cardinal Pole's dispensation to release the laity from the obligation of making compensatory contributions to the hierarchy, some of the bishops themselves, notably Dease of Meath and Rothe of Ossory, were also invoking Pole's dispensation to deny the regular clergy right to their ancients monasteries and church livings.[31]

Undoubtedly, ambiguity surrounds Cardinal Pole and his position, especially in the matter of church property. It was a legal minefield and was never properly understood. Pole was a distinguished Englishman, of royal Plantagenet ancestry. He was made cardinal by pope Paul III in 1536; he had been, for a period, one of the presidents at the Council of Trent, and was frequently thought of as a future pope. When the catholic Mary Tudor became queen on the death of Edward VI in 1553, Pole was appointed by pope Julius III as papal legate to England to help the new sovereign in the restoration of England to Catholicism. He became the last catholic archbishop of Canterbury in 1557 and died on 17 November 1558, the same day as his cousin queen Mary. As papal legate, Pole confirmed lay possession of church property in England, property that had been confiscated during the reigns of Henry VIII and Edward VI. This applied to England only.[32] But, at the request of queen Mary and of her husband Philip of Spain, the pope, Paul IV, elevated the lordship of Ireland into a kingdom in June 1555 and subsequently appointed Cardinal Pole as legate to Ireland in July 1555.[33] Pole, as legate to Ireland, requested the Irish parliament to repeal all anti-papal legislation and to confirm in their possession people who had come into their lands through confiscation. Pole declared that such owners should bear in mind that their property was church property. He phrases it as follows in his request to the Irish parliament:

> being conscious of their own salvation (the proprietors) would at least ensure that from church goods, especially those parts that had been apportioned to provide livings for those ministering to the people, they would provide these pastors, persons and curates with sustenance in a way appropriate to their status in such a way that they might exercise the care of souls in a suitable fashion and sustain the burdens they thereby incurred.[34]

It was an appeal for generosity. Pole would have recognised that any more firm action on his part in the matter of confiscated property would have caused major disturbance. The Irish

---

[30] Ibid., 490
[31] Report (presumably by regular clergy) to Propaganda, undated, APF, SOCG, 132, f. 264R
[32] Dickens, A.G., *The English Reformation*, 361
[33] Hagan, J. (ed.) 'Miscellanea Vaticano-Hibernica, 1420-1631, *Archiv. Hib.*, IV (1915), 217
[34] *Comment. Rinucc.*, vol I, 112

parliament agreed to this appeal and to much else in June 1556.[35] Pole intended to make a visitation to Ireland but he never did. Pope Paul IV relieved him of his legatine authority in 1557. There was legal ambiguity about Pole's dispensation in Ireland and the matter remained unclear after his death and after the accession of queen Elizabeth in 1558.

The question of the occupation of church property by the laity was referred to Rome by many of the Irish bishops, including bishop Comerford. Rome decided that the matter should be studied by a particular congregation which had been set up by Propaganda in February 1633 to prepare a general set of reform decrees for the Irish church. This particular congregation, realising how delicate the problem was, did not wish to come to any immediate decision.[36] The suggestion it made in July 1633 was extremely general and showed its reluctance to aggravate a complex situation by anything other than general directives. It suggested that in the matter of recovering church property from heretics *per viam contractus* so much depended on the individual circumstances of each case that the only feasible option to pursue was to refer all the details from Ireland to Rome and await direction from there. As regards property possessed by catholics who defended themselves by invoking cardinal Pole's dispensation all the particular congregation was prepared to do was recommend that an enquiry be made in Rome into the nature and extent of Pole's faculties. Similarly, an enquiry should be made into the faculties which the missionaries in Ireland had received regarding the settling of disputes concerning the possession of church property by catholics.[37] This was very much a holding tactic which the particular congregation passed up to the general congregation of Propaganda.

The general congregation declined to make any decision on the matter of the possession of church property by catholics and it declared that no reply should be given for the present concerning the dispensation of cardinal Pole. Propaganda was obviously hoping that times would contribute to the settlement of the affair; the congregation clearly did not wish to be coerced into imposing a solution which was bound to be resented by one side or the other. In a rather complicated manner, the congregation declared that, when petitioned, permission could be given to catholic laity and clerics to recover, presumably by purchase, church property from heretics provided those who did so purchase subsequently were to restore it to its real owners (i.e. those who held the property before the schism of the sixteenth century) having, of course been justly compensated themselves for their expenses.[38] The secretary of Propaganda, Francesco Ingoli, himself made a separate comment on this matter in which he expressed the opinion that catholic laymen in possession of church property should make some contribution towards the upkeep of the church from the revenue they receive.[39] The above decision taken by the general congregation of Propaganda in November 1633 was incorporated into the set of

---

[35] *Irish Statutes*, vol i, 259-60
[36] APF, Acta, 11 July 1633, 8, f. 260R
[37] Ibid.
[38] APF, Acta, 15 Nov. 1633, 8, f. 323R
[39] APF, SOCG, 294, f. 330R

decrees drawn up for the right ruling of the Irish church and was officially noted in the minutes of a meeting held on 16 December 1633.[40] Two years later, in his comments on the decrees drawn up by Propaganda for the right ruling of the Irish church, Patrick Comerford seems to accept that no clear cut solution was possible to the problem of the catholic possession of church property, and he contents himself with taking on board the suggestion of Ingoli referred to above. He asks that the pope make it incumbent on such possessors to pay some annual sum towards the support of the clergy.[41]

The problem of the occupation or possession of church property, particularly by catholics, was never really solved by Rome or by the Irish hierarchy. There were too many vested interests and deeply held views to enable a fair and acceptable solution to be found. The problem did become somewhat less acute when the church recovered a share of its former possession from the non catholics in the few special years after the rebellion of 1641. But the problem of catholic possession of church land was to be raised several times at the Confederation of Kilkenny.

In the Irish church of the seventeenth century, deprived almost entirely of all its possessions, strong emphasis was bound to be placed on whatever other sources of revenue that were available. In fact such revenue came from scarcely any other source than the contributions of the faithful. Apart from any jurisdictional question, it mattered a great deal which priest or group of priests were entitled to minister to the people. Controversies were bound to arise on this matter, within the secular clergy itself between rival claimants to the same benefice, and, of course, between the secular and regular clergy, to determine who had the primary right to engage in pastoral activity in a particular area or on a particular occasion. Such controversies erupted in the diocese of Waterford and Lismore. In a letter to Propaganda in 1632 the bishop dealt with certain aspects of the situation.[42] He begins by describing the general situation of the catholic clergy in Ireland. Except in very few cases they have no churches and have no ecclesiastical property from which to derive income. Nearly always the sacraments have to be administered and mass has to be celebrated in the private houses of the people. The only support which the priest receives is that which is given by the people on the occasion of the administration of the sacraments. Comerford stresses that the term 'benefice' in contemporary Ireland means no more than the right to administer the sacraments and receive the offerings of the people in a specified area. But the bishop laments the fact that priests who have been given the right by the bishop are frequently not allowed the undisturbed possession of it, because strangers may turn up in the area with rescripts (nearly always from Rome) entitling them to named benefices, and they cause strife which is very disedifying to the faithful. The parishioners take it very badly that their faithful parish priest, often himself a native of the area and related by blood to them, who may have been serving them well for many years might be

---

[40] APF, Acta, 8, ff. 337R – 344V
[41] Comerford to Propaganda, 25 June 1636, APF, SOCG, 140, f.43V
[42] Same to same, 16 Oct. 1632, *Spicil. Ossor.*, vol I, 180-3

deprived by these newcomers of his right to minister amongst them. An appalling consequence of these rescripts is that many excellent priests cannot be persuaded to accept the care of souls in an area or parish lest they be suddenly expelled by a newcomer armed with a Roman rescript. By newcomer here Comerford very likely has in mind priests ordained abroad for Ireland '*ad titulum missionis*'[43] who return to Ireland legally unattached to any particular diocese. There is considerable complaint in letters to Propaganda from many of the Irish bishops concerning the ordination of individuals who have no recommendation from bishops or vicars-apostolic in Ireland. Sometimes the rectors of continental seminaries are blamed for promoting such people and supplying them with a rescript which permits them to be ordained by a bishop on the continent of Europe. In connection with this problem, and because of the non-existence in Ireland of benefices in the strict canonical sense, Comerford suggests that, for the proper control of parish administration, the local ordinaries in Ireland should have full authority to appoint parish priests *ad nutum amovibiles*.[44] He asks that the holy see approve of any appointments which he has already made to parishes and he hopes, as he has hoped before, that, as long as the present disorganised conditions continue, no rescript will be granted for benefices in the diocese of Waterford and Lismore without specific commendatory letters from him.[45]

Complaints were also reaching Propaganda from other bishops concerning the problem of revenue. Bishop John Roche of Ferns was clashing with the cistercians in his diocese who were seeking revenue for pastoral care of parishes which in the past were impropriate to monasteries such as Dunbrody and Tintern which were in his diocese. The archbishop of Dublin, Thomas Fleming O.F.M., complained concerning the indiscriminate granting of benefices to individual priests by the Datary in Rome.[46] Such rescripts as Fleming had in mind were being granted by the Datary, so Propaganda, having considered such complaints, decided to inform the Datary and the Secretariat of Briefs, which also dealt with such matters, that scandal and strife were being caused in the Irish church by the granting of benefices without the approbation of the Irish bishops. Propaganda requested that no such benefices should be granted without it (Propaganda) being consulted.[47] Comerford's recommendations that the appointment to benefices would be best regulated by placing it in the hands of the local ordinary by which he would be enabled to appoint parish priests *ad nutum amovibiles*, was studied by Propaganda but the decision was made not to accept the recommendation.[48] Propaganda felt that it was preferable to maintain the system incorporated in the general set of decrees recently

---

[43] 'With the right to minister as a missionary'
[44] 'Who may be removed at the will of the local ordinary'
[45] Ibid., 182. In another letter to Propaganda, 14 Feb. 1633 (4 Feb. 1632 O.S.) Comerford makes the same appeal, APF., SOCG, 134, f. 238R; and again in a letter written together with the other Munster suffragans, 30 Dec. 1633, APF, SOCG, 194, f. 276R
[46] Roche to Propaganda, 1 Dec. 1629, APF, SOCG, 294, ff. 313R - 314V
     Fleming to same, 4 May 1629, Ibid., 132, f. 283R
[47] APF, Acta, 16 Dec. 1633, 8, f. 340R
[48] Ibid., 11 July 1633, 8, f. 161R

(1633) drawn up for the right ruling of the Irish church whereby such appointments would be made in Rome but the Datary was to consult Propaganda before making them.[49]

It was only to be expected that the question of ecclesiastical revenue would provide yet another source of conflict between the regular and secular clergy. Comerford, writing to Rome in early 1633 on behalf of the Munster bishops, declares that the province of Munster and particularly his own diocese, was vexed by disputes over the question of precedence and revenue between the regulars and seculars.[50] He does not go into specifics but, from other reports to Rome we get a fair idea of what the situation was like. The methods allegedly used by the regulars in collecting alms caused much annoyance to the bishops and secular priests. The cistercians were accused of excessive use of relics. The dominicans were reported to have gone so far as to change their name to the more attractive or catchy one of 'Religiosi Beatae Virginis' in order to provide a further enticement to the people to contribute.[51] The regulars were quick to their own defence. According to them they were not the only ones who sought alms from the people. In contemporary Ireland all ecclesiastics were compelled to depend on alms, the seculars no less than the regulars.[52] Again the bishops resented the manner in which the regulars contrived to claim the right to administer the sacraments in the parishes and to receive the offerings made by the people on these occasions. In the Kilkenny meeting of August 1629, the first episcopal meeting which Patrick Comerford attended, this practice by the regulars was strongly opposed by the bishops. Propaganda kept insisting that in such matters the regulars must be subject to the local ordinaries.[53]

On this matter of 'pastoral competition' the problem which received most emphasis in the Propaganda documents was that of conducting the office and burial of the dead – the *ius sepulturae*, as it is generally called.[54] It had both canonical and economical aspects and proved to be a source of much bitter dissension between the regular and secular clergy. The basic

---

49   Ibid.
     This solution of Propaganda made in 1633 does not appear to have solved the problem of the granting of benefices by Rome. In 1635 complaints were still coming from Ireland that the Datary was continuing its practice of granting benefices often to unworthy people who have no recommendation from the local ordinary in Ireland. Propaganda was puzzled and was inclined to feel that there must be some exaggeration in the reports from Ireland. It claimed that provisions are not being made in Rome for appointment to benefices in Ireland except '*in forma dignum*' or with testimonial letters from ordinaries:
     APF, Acta, 30 July 1635, no, f. 288R., No. 50;
     Ibid., 1 Sept. 1635, 10, f. 307V, No. 7
50   Comerford to Propaganda, 14 Feb. 1633 (4 Feb. 1632 O.S.), APF, SOCG, 134, f. 238RV;
     An account of the controversy is given in a report to the nuncio at Brussels, 22 Aug. 1639, Wadding Papers, 393-404 also in a report to Propaganda, APF, SOCG, 14, ff. 170R – 181V.
51   APF, SOCG, 14, f. 164V
     Ibid., Acta, 11 July 1633, 8, ff. 262V – 263R
     cf. Flynn, Thomas, *The Irish Dominicans 1635 – 1641*, 252, 255
52   Report to the Nuncio at Brussels, 22 August 1630, *Wadding Papers*, 395
53   APF, SOCG, 294, f. 179RV
     Ibid. Acta, 16 March 1633, 8, f. 299R
54   This question of Ius Sepulturae (right of burial) receives strong mention in:
     William Tirry, bishop of Cork and Cloyne to Propaganda, APF, SOCG, 294, f. 280R
     Also from grievances listed in ibid., f. 307RV;
     also in APF, Acta, 5 Sept. 1630, 7 f. 124R, No. 31

difficulty was to decide whether, in particular circumstances, the regular or secular clergy should have precedence at the mass and office of the dead and at the subsequent funeral. The canonical, and indeed, liturgical matter of precedence had the economic implications that whoever took precedence also received the funeral offerings or the greater part of them. The funeral offerings or *quarta funeraria* were made up of the money given to the priest or priests who conducted the funeral. Traditionally in Ireland many of the cemeteries had been attached to the monastic foundations. Even after the dissolution of the religious houses at the time of the reformation, people still continued to bury their dead in the adjoining cemeteries. In normal circumstances there would have been no canonical problem in regard to such funerals. The remains of the dead person would have been brought to the monastery or priory church and from there be brought for burial in the cemetery. The funeral rites would have been conducted by the regular clergy to whom the church and cemetery belonged. But since the reformation most of the churches had become disused and ruinous, so the mass and office of the dead usually had to be conducted in the home of the deceased person. The regulars claimed the right to come to the house and conduct the mass and office there, and then remove the body to the cemetery. All of this would take place in two cases: one, if the person had chosen to die in the religious habit or, two, if the person was to be buried in the cemetery of the regulars. In either of these situations all the offerings made in connection with the funeral would belong to them.[55] The secular clergy contested such claims with considerable heat. They held that the private house of the deceased was a non-exempt place and, if a mass for the dead was to be celebrated there, the right to say it belonged to the parish clergy. The riposte of the regulars was that, were it not for the unhappy situation obtaining in Ireland, services for the dead would be taking place in their churches. It was unfair that the seculars should seek to turn the penal laws against the catholic religion to the exclusive disadvantage of the regular clergy. The seculars insisted that neither should the penal laws be used against them; the regular clergy had no right to go about setting up exempt places whenever they wished. Many local and disedifying quarrels took place in full view of the faithful at the time of funerals. Comerford tells Propaganda that Waterford and Lismore had more than its share of them. The greatest trouble-makers in this regard, he claims, are the franciscans, who tolerate no opposition. They claim precedence over the local parish priest and even over the vicar general or the dean of the cathedral if they happen, at the wish of the dead person, to be present at the funeral.[56]

The bishops in Kilkenny in 1629 had stated clearly that, at all funerals which take place within the confines of a parish, the regulars must give precedence to the local parish priest. However, in regard to the connected question of funeral offerings the bishops did not make any

---

[55] The custom of being buried in the habit of a religious order was widespread in contemporary Ireland. Many complaints come to Propaganda concerning attempts by regulars to induce people to be buried in the habit by guaranteeing them special rewards after death:
APF, SOCG, 14, f. 171R

[56] Comerford to Propaganda, 14 Feb. 1633 (4 Feb. 1632 O.S.), APF, SOCG, 134, f. 238V

general ruling but expressed the wish that each local ordinary would come to a just agreement with the regular clergy. In the case of Waterford and Lismore the regulations which Comerford established concerning funeral offerings did not please the regular clergy.[57] In times past the offerings used be made at the graveside. They were originally intended, in part at least, for the repair and maintenance of the church or monastery with which the cemetery was connected. Since the reformation, however, the protestant ministers used present themselves at the grave and demand the offerings on the grounds that, as they were the legally recognised religious ministers of the area, the renovation of the church was their responsibility and concern. As a result of this development, in order to avoid having to pay the protestants, the catholics developed a custom of having the offerings collected, not at the graveside, but on the way to the cemetery where the protestant ministers would have no jurisdiction. The custom also developed of dividing the offerings into three parts: one, for the monastery or church whenever in the future it might be possible to restore or renovate it; the second, for the priest or priests who were conducting the funeral; the third, for the poor. This arrangement, however, led to abuses. In the case of funerals conducted by regulars the parochial clergy tended to claim that, as the offerings were collected outside the cemetery, the regulars (like the protestants) had no right to them. Comerford and Bishop Tirry of Cork and Cloyne decided to make definite regulations on the matter: the offerings were still be to divided into three parts but one part was to go to the bishop, the second to the parish priest, and the third to the other priests, presumably to the regulars if they were conducting the funeral. This arrangement transferred what was formerly given towards the renovation of the monastery or church to the local parish priest. The result was, according to one report, that no attempt was being made to rebuild the ruined monasteries. The wealthy people, whose offerings might be large, no longer wished to be buried in the monastic cemeteries and chose instead to be buried near the parish church. In this way in the dioceses of Waterford and Lismore and Cork and Cloyne the funerals came more and more into the hands of the parish clergy.[58]

The controversy in Ireland over precedence and *ius sepulturae* must indeed have proved perplexing to the officials of Propaganda. It marked yet another instance in which the Irish situation did not correspond to what the officials would have considered a straight-forward changeover from a missionary regime to a diocesan one. It was not simply a matter of gradually bringing the regular clergy to accept the control of the hierarchy as Trent decreed. Due to the anti-catholic laws and the deprivation of property and churches, delicate and, in a real sense, insoluble problems concerning matters such as the nature and extent of exemption were bound to occur. In fact, Propaganda found it impossible to propose any satisfactory solution. In the decrees for the right ruling of the Irish church, drawn up in 1633, all that Propaganda felt able to do in this matter was to state the general law and declare that normally secular clergy preceded

---

[57] Report to the Nunco at Brussels, 22 August. 1630, *Wadding Papers*, 393-404
[58] Ibid., 399

regulars. As regards precedence at office for the dead, mass and funeral, it decreed that, when a person was to be buried from the church of the regular clergy, they, and not the seculars, should have charge of the funeral.[59] This proposed solution, of course, could not meet the Irish situation because the crux of the problem lay in the fact that the regulars usually had no churches and were compelled to attempt to constitute the private house of the deceased person into an exempt place for the purpose of the obsequies. Propaganda did come to realise that something more would have to be done. In 1635 we find it submitting the following *casus* to the Congregation of the Council (i.e. the congregation set up to interpret the decrees of the Council of Trent):

> In Hibernia ob prohibitionem exercitii Catholicae religionis accidit multoties, ut officium defunctorum, seu exequiae in domibus ipsorum defunctorum, qui habent vel eligunt sepulturam apud regulares peragentur, quaeritur an hoc casu praecedentia in officio seu exequiis celebrandis debeatur parochis an vero regularibus?[60]

The Congregation of the Council replied in favour of the parish priest but it declared the wish to examine the question in greater detail. Its final decision was given on 12 May 1635:

> Sacra congregatio cardinalium Concilii Tridentini interpretum secundum ea, quae proponuntur, censuit, in funeribus, quae extra ecclesias regularium inter fines parochialium fuerint, praecedentiam deberi parochis[61]

This solution came down strongly against the regular clergy. How it was put into effect at local level back in Ireland it is impossible to say. It probably was applied unevenly and depended on the personal relationship between the clergy involved. The problem would, in any case, have eased somewhat a few years later when both regulars and seculars came back into possession of many of their former churches and other property including cemeteries during the years of the Confederation of Kilkenny 1642-49. However, it is highly likely that the controversies concerning ecclesiastical revenue would not have endeared bishop Patrick Comerford to the regular clergy of his diocese or to many of their lay supporters and friends.

---

[59] APF, Acta, 16 Dec. 1633, 8, f. 344R

[60] "In Ireland because of the prohibition of the catholic religion it often happens that the office of the dead or the funeral rites for those who have died and who posses a grave or have chosen to be buried with the regular clergy are held in their own homes. The question is in such a case does precedence belong to the parish priest or to the regular clergy?"
APF, SOCG, 19 Jan. 1635, 14, f. 190R

[61] "The sacred congregation of cardinals for the interpretation of the Council of Trent has decided that in the case of funerals which take place outside the churches of regular clergy within the boundaries of parishes precedence should be given to the parish priest"
Ibid., 12 May 1635, i4, f. 191R

Chapter Eight

THE METROPOLITAN AND HIS SUFFRAGAN

The reorganisation of the Irish church in the first half of the seventeenth century was inevitably beset with serious difficulties. It marked a strong attempt to build up within the framework of a new centralised diocesan system a church almost totally lacking in possessions, legally unrecognised, and which had been unaccustomed for well over half a century to little in the way of central control or discipline. From without there was the ever present fear of the unpredictable or unexpected acts of political disapproval and, indeed, persecution. There was the meagre, indefinite and unreliable nature of the church's revenue which brought with it a host of delicate problems. Within the church itself there was the explainable friction generated between the secular clergy, standing usually for the new centralised control, and the regular clergy, adjusting themselves to the new system with difficulty, and conscious of indelicacy and ingratitude in the manner in which they were being drawn into that system. The main agents of this reorganisation, the bishops of the period 1618 till Cromwellian times, had indeed to prove themselves able and zealous in order to make it a success. It is a tribute to their ability and zeal that they were largely successful. Within a comparatively short time, mainly in the decade 1630-40, order was largely imposed and the hierarchical system, envisaged by the Council of Trent, was firmly established in Ireland.

It is ironical that within the hierarchy itself, so united in its aims and ideals, there should have been division and friction which must have made the task of reorganisation much more difficult and, to some extent, must have retarded the work of reform. This division particularly expressed itself in disagreement between the metropolitans and their suffragans. Patrick Comerford was seriously involved in perhaps the most pronounced of the divisions, that between the archbishop of Cashel and his suffragans in the province of Munster. Some treatment of this division is necessary as we attempt to understand properly the problems attached to the counter reformation in Ireland, particularly as they affected the bishop of Waterford and Lismore. In attempting to reconstruct the various aspects of the controversy some appreciation is gained of the complex religious situation in Ireland at the time and the inevitable tensions that occurred as the different jurisdictional elements in the Irish church became established and their limits became defined.

The tension between metropolitan and suffragan was probably most pronounced in the province of Cashel but it also existed in other provinces. In Dublin the archbishop, Thomas Fleming, had serious clashes with Matthew Roche, brother of bishop John Roche of Ferns, the vicar-apostolic of Leighlin, and was in a fairly permanent state of disagreement with David Rothe, bishop of Ossory. In the province of Tuam the archbishop, Malachy O'Queely, was in controversy with the warden of Galway, Andrew Lynch, and the bishop of Elphin, Boethius MacEgan.[1] In the province of Cashel there is no evidence of trouble between the metropolitan and the suffragans until the early 1630's for the very good reason that the archbishop of Cashel, though appointed in 1626, was abroad in Spain and in Rome until 1629.[2]

Thomas Walsh, archbishop of Cashel, was a native of the city of Waterford, born in 1588, a cousin of Thomas Strange O.F.M. and Luke Wadding and possibly also of Patrick Comerford. Comerford and Walsh grew up together in Waterford and attended the same schools both in Waterford and Kilkenny. In 1602 Walsh was a student in the Irish college in Salamanca.[3] They were friends, despite later differences and even open criticism of Walsh's behaviour by Comerford. Walsh had supported Comerford's appointment as bishop of Waterford and Lismore but it seems his first choice was his controversial cousin, the franciscan Thomas Strange.[4]

The first indication of trouble within the province of Cashel appears in a petition to Propaganda by bishop John O'Moloney of Killaloe in May 1631 that the archbishop of Cashel be asked to desist from attempting to conduct a visitation of the diocese of Killaloe. O'Moloney asserts that not only does the archbishop claim the right to conduct one visitation but says that he is entitled to do so every three years.[5] There may well have been personal antipathies between Walsh and O'Moloney for a considerable period. Certainly, at the time of O'Moloney's appointment to Killaloe, Walsh was not in favour of him but strongly proposed Malachy O'Queely, who was also a Killaloe priest. O'Moloney's appointment to Killaloe has a strange ring to it. The strong favourite for the episcopate with the majority of the Killaloe priests was O'Queely. O'Moloney had been living in Paris in 1630; in fact he had a house there where he conducted hospitality especially for Irish émigré priests and students.[6] Perhaps from that house there developed a campaign to have O'Moloney, not O'Queely, appointed to Killaloe. The case of both priests came before the Datary in Rome within a few days of each other, O'Queely on 5 April 1630 and O'Moloney on 15 April 1630. The attestation in favour of O'Queely by archbishop Walsh from Spain in 1626 is interesting and revealing.[7] He refers to

---

[1] Report on these controversies by archbishop Hugh O'Reilly of Armagh to Propaganda, 5 Aug. 1634, APF, SOCG, 105, ff. 469R – 470R
[2] Thomas Strange to Wadding, 5 Aug. 1628, *Wadding Papers*, 268
[3] He is described as a priest of the Order of St. John of Jerusalem. He had a brother a member of the Theatine order. Thomas Walsh returned from Spain to Ireland and ministered as a priest in his native diocese of Waterford and Lismore. He was vicar apostolic for many years cf. *Wadding Papers*, 175, 178.
[4] Walsh made, from Spain, an attestation in favour of Patrick Comerford for Waterford and Lismore, cf. Gibbin, Cathaldus, 'The Processus Patariae and the appointment of Irish Bishops in the seventeenth century', *Father Luke Wadding Commemorative Volume*, 553
[5] Reference to O'Moloney's statement is in a Brief of Pope Urgan VIII, 7 June 1631, *Wadding Papers*, 526-9
[6] O'Connor, Thomas, *Irish Jansenists*, 93, 160
[7] The file containing the discussion and decision on the appointment of O'Queely to Tuam is in Processus Datariae, vol. 9, ff. 130R – 144V, printed in Gibbin, Cathaldus, *Father Luke Wadding Commemorative Volume*, 557-60; the file containing the discussion and decision on O'Moloney's appointment to Killaloe is in ibid., vol. 9, ff. 147R - 164V

the fact that O'Queely had been vicar-apostolic of Killaloe and that he had carried out the duties connected with that office with great success, having reformed the clergy and the people much to the admiration of the catholics and non-catholics alike, so much so that the other prelates in Ireland have chosen him as an example in the work being done by themselves in their various dioceses. Walsh goes on to say that, by unanimous consent, the clergy and people of Killaloe have petitioned to have O'Queely appointed their bishop, as have prelates from the whole of Ireland. This sign of strong approval may be gathered from letters sent to the late archbishop of Armagh and primate of Ireland, Peter Lombard in Rome. Walsh went further than proposing O'Queely; he came out strongly against any other contenders. He insists that, should O'Queely not be appointed, it would be a cause of great scandal to the clergy of Killaloe and an offence to the people to give the see to another, as there is nobody among those others, who aspire to that office, equal in merits or in talents to O'Queely, or who would repair the damage which would be done by his non-appointment.

Rome was in a quandary. Clearly, O'Queely was very highly regarded in Ireland and in Killaloe. However, when the Datary met ten days later to discuss O'Moloney, it was faced with a strong array of support for him – from important sources. Hugh O'Neill, Earl of Tyrone, sent a letter from Brussels recommending him; before he died in Spain the archbishop of Tuam, Florence Conry, wrote in his favour, and the rector of the University of Paris, Lemaistre, paid strong compliments to his distinguished learning and character.[8]

The upshot was that Maurice O'Queely was promoted, not to Killaloe, but to the archbishopric of Tuam and John O'Moloney was appointed to Killaloe. The strongest support for O'Queely had come from people and clergy in Ireland. O'Moloney's net had been cast wider with little support from Killaloe. Clearly, in the appointment of O'Moloney, the pressure was strong and Rome, not for the first time, sought to please both sides.

In 1631 it appears that Walsh began to conduct a systematic visitation of all the dioceses in his province. By November of that year, he tells Wadding, he had visited Killaloe, Kilfenora, Limerick, Emily, Ardfert and Aghadoe. At the time of writing he was dealing with Cork and Cloyne.[9] As mentioned above, O'Moloney of Killaloe objected to this visitation. According to the archbishop, O'Moloney was not the only one to do so. The suffragans proceeded to resist with considerable determination this interference, as they viewed it, by the archbishop of Cashel. A lengthy complaint was submitted by them to Propaganda, and Patrick Comerford was deputed to reinforce it with a letter of his own.[10] The general claim of the suffragans was that Walsh, and other metropolitans also, were ignoring the rights and jurisdictions of the suffragans and were behaving in a manner contrary to the prescriptions of the Council of Trent. They claim also that the metropolitans were constituting courts of appeal

[8]   Giblin, Cathaldus, Loc. Cit.
[9]   Walsh to Wadding, Waterford, 17 Nov. 1631, *Wadding Papers*, 612
[10] Munster Suffragans to Propaganda, 30 Dec. 1632, APF, SOCG, 294, ff. 275R – 278R
      Comerford to same, 14 Feb. 1633 (4 Feb. 1632 O.S.), Ibid., 134, f. 238 RV

to try cases in which the suffragans' decisions should normally be final. The metropolitans were accepting all sorts of frivolous appeals, often based on the accusation that the full canonical solemnities were not being observed in the trials conducted by the suffragans. The suffragans were not denying that the trials which they conducted were not fully in accordance with the requirements of canon law. According to them, an open trial dare not be conducted in Ireland because of the danger of persecution by the civil authorities. All that the bishops are able to do in this regard is to go from place to place without notaries or other assessors. Controversies had to be judged in summary manner. But it sometimes happened, say the suffragans, that advocates and other curial officials, who were eager for money, when they detect some defect in the judicial process, persuade the defeated or losing party to appeal to the metropolitan. On being apprised of such defect the archbishop of Cashel insists that the trial by the suffragan, if still in progress, be suspended until he could examine the case and the method of procedure. The result is, the suffragans claim, that there is nothing but contempt shown towards their efforts to conduct trials and also to the decisions which they pronounce. Cases are dragged out interminably. The irony of it all is that a case is never ultimately determined in proper canonical manner by the metropolitan court. The metropolitans themselves, in all this matter, are the prey of subtle advocates who have scant regard for justice. Many litigants, when they experience the delays and expense involved in the metropolitan tribunals, decide to settle the matter between themselves or before an arbitrator. Many, in desperation, return from the court of the metropolitan to the *judex a quo* (the judge from whom the appeal to the metropolitan was taken).

In connection with this practice of the metropolitan of hearing appeals from the suffragans' courts is his claim to be entitled to make triennial visitation of the entire province.[11] The suffragans oppose such visitation very strongly. It is 'inutilis, moleste, periculosa et contraria dispositioni Concilii Tridentini'.[12] The suffragans are indignant. They are ruling their flock diligently and do not deserve such treatment from the metropolitan. Besides, they ask, what is there to visit? There are no chapters, no cathedrals, no parish churches, no benefices, no monasteries or hospitals, which would normally be the object of such a visitation. Furthermore, it is unfair to expect the laity, on whom devolves the duty of looking after the bishops and priests, who have no houses or means, to have to extend hospitality to an archbishop and his retinue as well. Indeed, the suffragans also declare, a visitation of the kind conducted by archbishop Walsh is very dangerous in contemporary Ireland. The laity are liable to confiscation of whatever property they have and to long imprisonment for harbouring ecclesiastics who derive their jurisdiction from the *Curia Romana*. The laity take risk enough

---

[11] Ibid.
[12] Munster suffragans to Propaganda, 30 Dec. 1632,
    Ibid. 294, f. 227R
    'It is useless, annoying, dangerous and contrary to the disposition of the Council of Trent'

in attending to their own bishop and clergy without having to cope with the dangerously ostentatious pomp and ceremony which sometimes attends the metropolitan visitation.

Before all other considerations, the suffragans claim that such visitation is contrary to the decrees of Trent. They insist, and they base their case on the answer received by the bishop of Killaloe to his complaint of May 1631, that the metropolitans have no right to conduct a visitation of the dioceses of their suffragans, except in accordance with Trent, session 24, Cap 3 – that is, for a known reason and with the approval of the provincial council.[13] The suffragans declare that this matter of visitation had been discussed at the provincial councils of Limerick (1629) and Fethard (1632) but in both cases the archbishop had failed to show the bishops why it was expedient that he should visit their dioceses. Still he has obstinately insisted on going ahead with the visitation. It was with great difficulty that they succeeded in persuading him at Fethard to desist until the suffragans had got the views of the holy see on the matter. It was the opinion of Comerford that, if the archbishop should resume his visitation before word arrived back from Rome, there would be intense strife in the province and great scandal would come of it.[14]

Walsh defended himself strongly in letters to Wadding and to Propaganda.[15] He contends that visitation was absolutely necessary due to the mismanagement of their affairs by several of his suffragans. He claims that many lay people and clergy were being oppressed by treatment they were receiving from the suffragans, especially in the dioceses of Killaloe and Cork and Cloyne. What other recourse is open to such people in a land so distant from Rome than to appeal to the metropolitan? According to Walsh, the main reason for the opposition of the suffragans to him is jealousy.

> I am opposed by all my suffragans, repining that any, and especially a Waterford (man), should have that eminency over them; but I gave them leave to say or thinck what they please, and doe proceed quietly *sine strepitu* in my visitation. …. They have nothing to oppose (but) the limitation of (the) Councell, which they would have me onely observe….. they nott able to observe any other decree of it[16]

Walsh claims to Propaganda that, in his dealings with the suffragans, they have shown him no respect or reverence. By their attitude they have made it clear that they are not prepared to bow to any superior who will restrain their excesses.[17] To the charge that he had disobeyed the prescriptions of the Council of Trent, Walsh simply replies that the decrees of that council had

---

[13] Brief of Pope Urban VIII concerning visitation by metropolitans in Ireland, 7 June 1631, *Wadding Papers*, 526-9
[14] Comerford to Propaganda, 14 Feb. 1633 (4 Feb. 1632 O.S.), APF, SOCG, 134, f. 238R
[15] Walsh to Wadding, Waterford, 17 Nov. 1631, *Wadding Papers*, 611-5;
Same to Propaganda, 30 May 1634, APF, SOCG, 134, f. 237RV
Same to same, 3 June 1634, Ibid., 134, f. 236RV
[16] Same to Wadding, 17 Nov. 1631, *Wadding Papers*, 612
[17] Same to Propaganda, 30 May 1634, APF, SOCG, 134, f. 237R

never been promulgated in the province of Munster. Hence the law to be followed in the matter of metropolitan visitation and in cases referred to the metropolitan court was the *Ius Commune* and the ancient practice of the church in Cashel. According to him, the decrees of Trent could not be enforced in Ireland because of the danger from the civil power. He, therefore, seeing that a secret introduction of the tridentine decrees might only cause scandal and division, never authorised or allowed the promulgation of the decrees and was waiting until such time as they could, in the right manner, be unanimously accepted by all.[18] The suffragans, on the other hand, contended that the decrees of Trent had been received in the province of Cashel as long as fifty years previously.[19] In actual fact there never was, nor could there be, a formal promulgation of the tridentine decrees in Ireland, but they had been accepted throughout the country for a long time. In the provincial synod of Dublin, which was held in Kilkenny in 1614, it was decreed that Trent should be accepted in general in Ireland but that, due to the difficulties of the times, the full execution of all its ordinances would have to be deferred to a more favourable time.[20] In the meeting of Munster and Leinster bishops, attended by archbishop Walsh in Kilkenny in August 1629, it was agreed that Trent should be accepted in all matters which did not require express and specific promulgation such as the decree concerning clandestine marriages, and which the present conditions in Ireland rendered impossible such as decrees concerning tonsure and clerical dress, and the establishment of diocesan seminaries.[21]

Walsh was not on safe ground when he declared that the old law still operated in his province and that Trent had no force because it had not been publicly and formally promulgated. When confronted with the declaration made at Kilkenny in 1629, Walsh described it as more a secret agreement than a promulgation. It was, according to him, more a preparation for a future time when the Council of Trent could be properly received rather than a sign of definite or explicit acceptance. It was his view that, because of the state of the country, no one could contemplate the introduction of tridentine law into contemporary Ireland. But in view of the fact that tridentine reform was the basis of all the reorganisation of the church then being attempted in Ireland, Walsh's position could not be considered tenable. Later on, in the decrees drawn up by Propaganda for the right ruling of the Irish churches (1633), the congregation emphasised that the tridentine law on provincial visitation was binding in Ireland: such visitation was to be conducted only with the consent of the provincial council. When such a

---

[18] Same top same, 3 June 1634, Ibid., 134, f. 236R
[19] Munster suffragans to Propaganda, 30 Dec. 1632, Ibid., 294, f. 277V
[20] Decretum de receptione Concilii Tridentini, printed in Moran, *History of the Catholic Archbishop of Dublin*, vol. i, 441
[21] This decree is in APF, SOCG, 294, f. 279R:
      'Concilii Tridentini ex deliberato consensus renovator receptor quoad omnia, quae non exquirunt expressam, et specificam promulgationem, quale est decretum de clandestinis matrimoniis, et prater ea quae presenti rerum, et temporum statui incompossibilis videri possunt in encyclical administratione, et oeconomia, qualia sunt decreta de tonsura et habitu clericali de praebenda theologali, de erectione seminarii et similia'

council could not be held, recourse was to be had to Rome, stating the reasons why visitation was considered necessary.[22]

This ruling by Propaganda did not solve the problem of metropolitan visitation in the province of Cashel because, subsequent to it, there broke out again the quarrel between archbishop Walsh and bishop John O'Moloney of Killaloe concerning another visitation of Killaloe by Walsh. In late 1633 or early 1634 O'Moloney was accused to Rome of conducting ostentatious and excessively expensive visitation of his own diocese and of imposing a heavy tax on his priests, with the penalty of being deprived of their benefices, such as they were, if they refused to pay.[23] O'Moloney succeeded quickly in convincing Rome of his innocence of the first charge.[24] But the second charge concerning the tax allegedly levied on priests continued to be brought against him, and, in connection with it, the archbishop of Cashel intervened. Walsh seems to have visited the diocese of Killaloe and received from some of the clergy who were hostile to the bishop a complaint which he sent to Rome in March 1635.[25] The matter developed into a heated controversy and the Propaganda archives contain numerous letters for and against O'Moloney from his own clergy of Killaloe.[26] Propaganda deputed the archbishop of Tuam, Malachy O'Queely, a native of Killaloe, to investigate the complaints against O'Moloney and the latter's relations with archbishop Walsh. The reply of O'Queely came late in 1635 and in it he reported that the bishop of Killaloe would not co-operate with him in his investigations and, in fact, showed himself generally disrespectful. It was the opinion of O'Queely that the archbishop of Cashel should be allowed conduct a visitation of Killaloe

> ...ubi sat multa, timeo, inveniet, quae maturam reformationem postulabunt, et quae potius expediret intra privates parietes cum honore sepelire, quam scriptis mandare aut ad urbem mittere[27]

Rome does not appear to have followed the advice of the archbishop of Tuam, and the controversy carried on for several more years. Comerford and the other Munster suffragans sent

---

[22] APF, Acta, 8, 16 Dec. 1633, f. 341V:
'Quo vero ad visitationem provinciarum, sacra congregatio censuit observandam dispositionem sacri Concilii Tridentini ubi concilia provincialia celebrari possunt; ubi vero non poterunt, archiepiscopus debere ad sedem apostolicam recurrere pro obtinenda facultate suas visitandi provincias, significatis causas ob quas necessaria sit eorum visitatio'

[23] Letter of some clergy of the diocese of Killaloe to Propaganda, 20 Jan. 1634, APF. SOCG, 77, f. 382R.
Letter of other clergy of Killaooe to same, 30 March 1635, Ibid., 135, f. 197R
APF, Acta, 10, 12 Nov. 1635, f. 331V, No. 1

[24] Ibid., Lettere, 24 Nov. 1635, 9, f. 72V

[25] APF, SOCG, 30 March 1635, 135, f. 197R

[26] Ibid., 20 May 1635, 77, f. 370R
Ibid., 1 June 1637, 139, ff. 156R – 257R
Ibid., 31 Aug. 1637, 140, f. 136RV

[27] Archbishop of Tuam to Propaganda, 11 Oct 1635, APF, SOCG, 140, f. 138V
"...where, I am afraid, he will find a great deal of matters which demand mature correction and which it would be better to have buried privately and with honour than committed to writing or sent to Rome"

a strong defence of O'Moloney to Propaganda in which they claim that the bishop had been seriously calumniated. They can vouch for his excellence and probity which they have witnessed often in their provincial councils. They declare that the scandal caused by the controversy is very serious; the adversaries of the faith have made great capital out of it. They ask Propaganda to declare O'Moloney to be an upright and zealous man.[28] Another letter reached Propaganda from the archbishop of Cashel asking that O'Moloney be condemned and heavily censured. In it he says that O'Moloney has ignored papal provisions to benefices in his diocese and has appointed many worthless men.[29]

Propaganda made another attempt to solve the problem. The bishop of Ossory, David Rothe, and the vicar general of Cloyne were appointed to judge the controversy and report to Rome.[30] In a letter to Propaganda in late 1637 bishop Rothe remarks that there are signs of reconciliation between Walsh and O'Moloney. In another letter in early 1639 he writes joyfully that, on the feast of the exaltation of the Holy Cross, 14 September 1638, a formal reconciliation took place in his presence. Both the archbishop and his suffragan, on bended knees, embraced each other and the long quarrel was over.[31] There must have been faults on both sides in this dispute. One is puzzled by the rather sinister hints made by Walsh as to the importance of secrecy when O'Queely was deputed to interview O'Moloney. There is a touch of mystery about certain aspects of O'Moloney's behaviour, even before his appointment as bishop. However, in his favour, account must be taken of the staunch support he received from his fellow suffragans. The main disagreement between archbishop Walsh and his suffragans focussed on his tendency to admit appeals too easily from the suffragans' courts to his own, and also on his claiming the general right to conduct visitation regularly in each of the dioceses of his province. As seen above, this latter disagreement came to a head in his lengthy conflict with the bishop of Killaloe who was supported in the matter by Comerford and the other suffragans. In general one forms the opinion from an examination of the sources that there was a fairly chronic inability on the part of Walsh and the suffragans to co-operate evenly with one another. This emerges from the tendency each part has to disparage each other in letters to Rome and from Walsh's slowness to consult and dialogue with the suffragans on matters which they claim were of importance for the province as a whole. It is likely that Walsh disagreed with both Comerford and Tirry of Cork and Cloyne concerning their treatment of the regular clergy in the affair of the Sorbonne propositions. Tirry claimed that the archbishop generally favoured the regulars in their disputes with the seculars.[32] In actual fact, although Walsh was by no means as unpopular with the regular clergy as were Comerford and Tirry, he was not completely *persona*

---

[28]   Munster suffragans to Propaganda, undated, APF, SOCG, 139, f. 268R

[29]   Walsh to Propaganda, undated, Ibid., 139, f. 269R

[30]   APF, Acta, 12, 16 June 1635, f. 103R No. 49;
       Ibid., Lettere, 28 June 1636, 9, f. 78V

[31]   Bishop Rothe to Propaganda, 28 Sept. 1637, APF, SOCG, 140, f. 134V
       Same to same, 24 Jan. 1639, Ibid., 139, f. 314R

[32]   Tirry to Propaganda, 4 March 1636, Ibid., 106, f. 37RV

grata with them either. Thomas Strange felt that Walsh also, like Comerford, was unduly influenced by David Rothe of Ossory.[33] Perhaps, as a fellow Waterford man, Walsh does not appear to have had a strong dislike of Comerford. It is interesting that in his letter to Wadding in November 1631 he does not mention Waterford and Lismore at all in listing the dioceses which he has visited or which he intends to visit. In that same letter he singles Tirry out as

> my greatest oppositor in this business[34]

An indication of Walsh's (and we may include the other three metropolitans also) judgment on the activity and contribution of their suffragans in the task of reorganising the contemporary Irish church is their belief that the number of bishops in Ireland could, with profit, be reduced. The archbishop of Cashel suggested to Propaganda that in the larger provinces, Cashel and Armagh, the metropolitan and three suffragans would be sufficient; in the smaller provinces, Dublin and Tuam, the metropolitan and two would be appropriate.[35] In this suggestion Walsh takes into account the economic argument. He says that some of the dioceses are very poor and it is too much to expect the laity to support so many bishops. In his own province he claims that Waterford and Lismore, Cork and Cloyne, Limerick and Killaloe are large dioceses, three of them with cities, which can afford to support their bishops. Hence it is, he says, that the bishops of these dioceses are not interested in the suggestion of reducing the number of bishops; nor are they prepared to discuss matters relating to the support of bishops. The problem does not arise for them; as long as they have enough themselves they do not worry.[36] But the archdiocese of Cashel itself and the dioceses of Emly and Kilfenora are very poor. Walsh recommends that Cashel and Emly should be joined together.[37] In their comments on the decrees drawn up by Propaganda in 1633 the four archbishops repeat the view of Walsh that three suffragans would be sufficient in the larger provinces and two in the smaller ones.[38] The Propaganda decrees had suggested that four suffragans in the larger provinces and three in the smaller seemed correct.[39] The only other members of the Irish hierarchy whose comments on the Propaganda decrees seem to be preserved in the Propaganda archives, perhaps the only others who in fact sent any comments to Rome, are bishop John Roche of Ferns and Patrick Comerford of Waterford and Lismore. Roche, adhering to a view which he had voiced before, was in agreement with the archbishops as to the need for a reduction in the number of

---

[33] Thomas Strange to Wadding, Waterford, 10 Sept. 1631, *Waterford Papers*, 580
[34] Walsh to Wadding, Waterford, 17 Nov. 1631, *Wadding Papers*, 611-15
[35] APF, Acta, 9, 16 March 1633, f. 206V
[36] Walsh's views are contained in Edmund Dwyer, agent of the archbishops of Tuam and Cashel in Rome, to Propaganda, undated, AF, SOCG, 294, f. 361R
[37] Francis Matthews O.F.M. to Wadding, Louvain 14 Nov. 1630, *Wadding Papers*, 436
      Walsh to same, Waterford, 17 Nov. 1631, Ibid. 613
[38] Four archbishops to Propaganda, 28 Nov. 1635, APF, SOCG, 140, f. 33R
[39] APF, Acta, 8, 16 Dec. 1633, f. 340V

suffragans.[40] But Comerford held very firmly against any proposed reduction. In his comments on the decrees, which he sent to Rome in early 1636, he suggests that four suffragans were needed in Cashel province. These, according to him, should be: Cork and Cloyne, Limerick, Waterford and Lismore, and Killaloe. He would agree that Emly and Kilfenora should be joined to Cashel and Limerick respectively; Ardfert and Ross could be left to vicars-apostolic.[41] Comerford admits that the people may be too heavily burdened by having so many bishops and that the episcopal dignity may suffer from the inability of the bishops to receive proper sustenance. At the same time, he is very much aware of the positive contribution of the bishops and of the necessity of keeping up a steady number of appointments. He stresses that it in only by the vigilance and authority of a bishop that both secular and regular clergy can be properly disciplined, the faith and obedience of the people confirmed, and many evils avoided. He says he has little regard for bishops who aspire to govern several dioceses together. In attempting to administer more than one diocese such bishops do not confer much benefit on the people. It is enough and more than enough, he claims, for one man to try to rule one diocese. When a man desires more territory he is faced with the prospect of long and wearying journeys and other great difficulties, all of which are more conducive to injuring the episcopal dignity than the want of proper sustenance.[42] It is of interest, and perhaps typical of the time in Ireland, that Comerford is so preoccupied with the matter of episcopal dignity.

Tension between archbishop Walsh and his suffragans was further aggravated by his apparent unwillingness to discuss matters of importance with them as frequently as they would wish in provincial council. This unwillingness was demonstrated clearly in his long delay in letting the suffragans see the draft of the decrees for the right ruling of the Irish churches which he had received from Rome. Drafts of these decrees, drawn up in Rome in 1633, were sent to the four archbishops to be communicated to their suffragans in order that all the Irish bishops could send their comments and suggestions to Propaganda.[43] They were sent to the archbishops in January 1635 but Comerford was of the belief that the archbishops made no attempt to communicate them to the suffragans. Bishop John Roche agreed with Comerford concerning the delay. Apart from their apparent inability to have a strong sense of solidarity with the suffragans which would prompt them to consult with them on such matters, it may have been that the archbishops were not too enthusiastic about the decrees, at least about some of them which ran counter to their own suggestions such as the one dealing with metropolitan visitation and the one dealing with the number of bishops requisite for Ireland. The archbishops made a joint set of comments on the decrees. Their comments were brief and curt which may indicate lack of enthusiasm. The comments from Roche and Comerford were more lengthy and detailed.

---

[40] Roche to Propaganda, 4 April 1635, APF, SOCG, 14, f. 134R
    Same to same, 1 Dec. 1629, Ibid., 294, f. 318R
[41] Comerford to Propaganda, 20 Jan. 1636, Ibid., 140, f. 44R
[42] Ibid.
[43] Propaganda to the four archbishops, 23 Jan. 1635, APF, Lettere, 9, f. 65R

A whole year went by before Comerford received a copy of the draft decrees from archbishop Walsh. He ironically remarks that the copy he received from Walsh contained less information than he had seen elsewhere.[44] Comerford tells Propaganda that he made some delay in offering his comments on the decrees because he had hoped that the archbishops would, as the congregation had suggested, convene the suffragans and have a general discussion with them. But recently, he says, he has heard that the archbishops met secretly and, having made their own comments on the decrees, decided not to call the suffragans together for a discussion. Perhaps, Comerford wryly adds, they considered such convocation to be

> periculosam, nimis laboriosum, et supervacaneum[45]

In one of his letters to Propaganda commenting on the decrees for the right ruling of the Irish churches Comerford remarks that archbishop Walsh has clashed with his suffragans concerning the places in which he holds provincial councils.[46] According to Comerford the metropolitan has proved very unreasonable and he insists on convening such councils sometimes in parts of the province which are in no way central or convenient, and at other times in dangerous areas where there is not a corner which is not inhabited by hostile people:

> quarum vix est angulus, in quo non habitat plures haeretici, ex quibus alii sunt magnates, alii equites, alii justiciarii, alii praesidiarii milites, alii ministri regii, et turba multa cleri protestantis et colonorum[47]

To hold a council in such places is dangerous both for the bishops themselves and for the laity in whose house the meetings have to be held. Comerford says that it is the contention of the suffragans that, in accordance with the sacred canons, in convening a council account should be taken of the inconvenience caused to some in attempting to reach the venue because of the long journey. Councils should be held in accessible places

> in loco non multum remoto

---

[44] Comerford to Propaganda, 25 Jan. 1636, APF, SOCG, 140, f. 43R;
Comerford probably has in mind here a copy of the decrees which bishop Roche of Ferns, having failed to receive any communication from his metropolitan, had received unofficially from one of his many contacts in Rome in March 1635.
The archbishops' comments on the decrees are in a letter to Propaganda, 28 Nov. 1635, APF, SOCG, 140, f. 33RV

[45] Comerford to Propaganda, 25 Jan. 1636, Ibid., 140, f. 43R.
The bishop of Cork and Cloyne also complains about this failure of the metopolitans to communicate with the suffragans concerning the draft decrees:
Tirry to Propaganda, 4 Mrch 1636, Ibid., 106, f. 37RV 'dangerous, too laborious and superfluous'

[46] Comerford to Propaganda, 25 Jan. 1636, Ibid., 140, f. 46R

[47] Ibid., He mentions ' nobles, knights, justices, military leaders, ministers of the kingdom, large crowds of protestant clergy and of colonists' It would appear that there must be some exaggeration at play here

Furthermore, they should not be held at disadvantageous times, such as in the winter when the journey is hazardous. The archdiocese of Cashel itself or any of the central dioceses in the province would be acceptable to all, if the metropolitan would agree. It may well be, he declares, that, remembering the opposition which Walsh encountered at the interprovincial council in Kilkenny in 1629 or the provincial council in Fethard in 1632, he is rather anxious to avoid such councils in the future. In convening them in remote places he was at least hopeful that his suffragans would not be present in full strength. There seems to be no record or mention of any further provincial councils in the province of Cashel.

The amount of complaints concerning controversies in the Irish church which was reaching Propaganda was indeed considerable, so the congregation contemplated sending some person to Ireland who would superintend the implementation of the 1633 decrees and who would advise as to the real state of affairs in the country. But, due to the dangers involved in having any official representative from the holy see in Ireland, the idea was dropped.[48]

However, it was clear to Propaganda that the intensely local and peculiar quarrels with which the Irish church was vexed could not possibly be solved from Rome. Ireland was special. Unlike the situation on the continent during the post-reformation period, Ireland was unique in that the majority of the people were catholic but the country was governed by an heretical king and administration. There might be *de facto* toleration of catholic clergy and people but the constant possibility of persecution created a tension and nervousness which bedevilled the possibility of a proper solution to many problems within the church. The absence of legal status or rights for the catholic church weakened the genuine efforts being made by Propaganda in Rome. In the end of the day the most that Propaganda could do was give broad directives and indicate the general law. Someone was needed on the spot to decide the rights and wrongs of individual conflicts. So, in 1635, it was suggested in Rome that the four archbishops be appointed apostolic delegates with the right to judge and settle controversies between bishops and regular clergy and between secular and regular clergy.[49] On 10 December 1635 this recommendation was accepted by the general congregation of Propaganda and then ratified by the pope.[50] The faculty was granted to the archbishops for two years. They were given the right to settle all disputes between clergy. If a settlement was proving impossible and the matter was serious they were to refer it to Rome and, pending Rome's reply, forbid the parties to make any innovation. If the controversy was between the archbishop and a bishop, the bishop on whom the parties should agree within fifteen days should be the apostolic delegate. If the parties could not agree on a bishop then the nearest bishop should perform the office unless he himself was an interested or involved party, in which case the oldest suffragan of the province should be the delegate. It was cumbersome and complex but Propaganda was doing its best for a scene which

---

48 APF, Acta, 8, 15 Nov. 1635, f. 325
49 APF., SOCG, 12 May 1635, 14, f. 130R
    Ibid., 14, f. 140R
50 APF, Acta, 10, 10 Dec 1635, ff. 361V – 362R

was not run-of-the-mill. The main aim was to get problems settled as far as possible within Ireland itself. It seemed to work well and reports reached Rome that the scheme had good results and was responsible to a considerable extent for the cessation of most clerical controversies in the late 1630's.[51] However, it would be very surprising and even miraculous if such a grant of jurisdiction to the metropolitans would appeal to the suffragan bishops. While Comerford is silent on the matter, his neighbour, Bishop Tirry of Cork and Cloyne, objected that the granting of such jurisdiction to the archbishops was imprudent because they had always shown themselves partial to the regular clergy.[52]

Like many of the other tensions in the Irish church at this period the conflict between the Munster suffragans and their metropolitan seems to have settled itself as 1640 drew near. By the time, September 1638, when Walsh and O'Moloney were reconciled there seems to have been reasonable harmony within the Munster hierarchy. Later in the 1640's there was division within the hierarchy regarding the censures imposed by the nuncio Rinuccini but the stance taken then by individual bishops does not appear to be related to the earlier division of the 1630's.

The serious disagreements between archbishop Walsh and his suffragans, of whom Patrick Comerford was probably the closest to him personally, enable us to see some of the difficulties which were built into the task of reorganising the Irish church along tridentine lines. The bishops, metropolitans and suffragans, were undoubtedly men of zeal, eager for the good of the church, but the task which they had to face was great and the conditions under which they had to work were complex and sometimes chaotic. Trent and its meetings and its decrees were a long way from Ireland geographically and in many other regards. The coal-face at which the re-established Irish hierarchy worked was not one envisaged by the fathers of the Council of Trent. It was inevitable that there would be jurisdictional and pastoral difficulties in bringing the fruits of Trent to Ireland. These difficulties were felt strongly even within the hierarchy itself.

---

[51] APF, SOCG, 140, f. 22R
[52] Bishop of Cork and Cloyne to Propaganda, 4 March 1636
Ibid., 106 f. 37RV

Chapter Nine

CO-OPERATING WITH ROME

1. Decreta Pro Recto Regimine Ecclesiarum Hiberniae[1]

From a study of the documentation available, particularly in Roman sources, we have been attempting to explore the counter-reformation reorganisation of the Irish church and the problems connected with it, drawing particularly on the activity of Patrick Comerford, bishop of Waterford and Lismore. We have been examining the aspects of that reorganisation which have come to light from documentation of the period 1630-40, a really special decade in seventeenth century Irish Catholicism. With the outbreak of the rebellion in 1641 Ireland, clerical and lay, became much engaged in the political and military question and especially in the constitutional experiment known as the Confederation of Kilkenny. In the years immediately after 1641 there is less attention focussed on the pastoral and more strictly religious questions and problems which had been such a feature of the preceding decade. With the communication to Ireland in 1635 of the decrees drawn up by Propaganda for the 'Right ruling of the Irish churches' there is a noticeable decline in reports of controversy to Propaganda.[2] The perceived assumption has to be that the situation had eased considerably and that the Irish church was settling down in its acceptance of the tridentine organisation. It seems appropriate, therefore, at this stage, before we look at the changed situation after 1641 and before we examine Patrick Comerford's part in that situation, to consider the constructive role which Rome played in the reorganisation of the Irish church and the co-operation which it received from the hierarchy, particularly, because of the interest of this study, from the bishop of Waterford and Lismore.

In the early part of our treatment we touched on the interest which Rome displayed in the religious situation in Ireland during Elizabethan times. With the sending of David Wolfe S.J. in 1560 the holy see began what might be termed an initial sponsoring of counter-reformation activity in Ireland. There was considerable religious confusion in the country. People and clergy, including bishops, were unsure about what was new and how radical it was. Beginning with Wolfe, Rome raised a red flag of warning and people began to reflect and discuss seriously what was happening. The excommunication of queen Elizabeth in 1570 was a stark reminder of the seriousness of the situation as Rome perceived it. There was strong Roman involvement in the setting up of the many Irish seminaries in Europe during the later sixteenth and early seventeenth centuries.

As time went on, perhaps most significant was Rome's growing ability to distinguish between England and Ireland in the matter of counter-reformation reorganisation. The

---

[1] Decrees for the Right Ruling of the Irish Churches, APF, Acta, 8, 16 Dec. 1633, ff. 337R – 344V
[2] These decrees are referred to in the Propaganda archives as '*Decreta pro recto regimine Ecclesiarum Hiberniae*'

hierarchy was not re-established in England and its establishment was not attempted for a long time to come. The bull Brittania of pope Urban VIII in 1631 settled for an acceptance that England was a missionary country and would remain so for the foreseeable future and would have to be treated as such by Rome. The realisation was growing in Rome that Ireland was different. As the initial unsureness waned the great majority of its people had made up their mind that Catholicism was to remain their faith and that is was quite different from the established religion, the protestant faith. A very strong influence in determining Rome's attitude to Ireland was an Irishman, indeed a Waterford city man, whose family was connected with prominent Waterford families such as the Waddings, the Comerfords, the Stranges. This was Peter Lombard.[3]   Lombard was born in Waterford in 1554, educated at Peter White's school, studied in Louvain where he was celebrated as a brilliant student. After ordination and further studies he was sent by Louvain University as an envoy to Rome, particularly on theological matters. He became a close friend with the exiled Earl of Tyrone, Hugh O'Neill who had settled in Rome with many of his followers who had left Ireland in 1607 in the flight of the Earls.[4] Quickly Lombard became the main adviser in Rome on Irish affairs. He was also from 1602 till 1607 the chief theologian to the congregation *de auxiliis* which was dealing with the Molinist//Thomist theological controversy on the nature of grace. So well was he regarded by the Vatican that in 1601 he was appointed archbishop of Armagh, primate of the Irish church. He never returned to Ireland but remained in Rome as chief adviser concerning the Irish church. In a long treatise 'De regno Hiberniae sanctorum insula commentarius' circulated in manuscript primarily to brief pope Clement VIII on Ireland's history and religious position, he influenced Vatican thinking about Ireland.[5] Lombard drew papal support and finance for several of the Irish colleges on the continent of Europe. He succeeded in getting papal approval for Irish students to be ordained *ad titulum missionis* on the nomination of the rector of their college without the need of a recommendation from any bishop in Ireland. This was meant to expedite the return of badly needed young priests to Ireland. It had the disadvantage of emphasising the missionary character of Ireland in the early seventeenth century. As a kind of corrective, Lombard lobbied in Rome for the appointment of a complete Irish hierarchy. He also encouraged a theological principle which would help Rome to understand how catholics in Ireland could accept a heretical monarch as their lawful sovereign. This was a breakthrough of considerable significance. It especially enabled the Old English in Ireland to justify their loyalty to the catholic faith as well as their loyalty to king James and later king Charles. It was

---

[3]   A well researched contribution on Lombard:
    Smith, David, 'Peter Lombard (1554-1625) Prelate, Politician, Pragmatist', *Decies* No. 56 (2000) 35-73
[4]   cf. *Turas na dTaoiseach as Éirinn from Rath Maoláin to Rome* (Tadhg Ó Cíanáin's contemporary narrative of the journey into exile of the Ulster chieftains and their followers, 1607-8 – the so called 'Flight of the Earls'), ed. By Nollaig Ó Muráile, incorporating work by Paul Walsh (+1941) and Tomás Ó Fiaich (+1990)
[5]   This treatise was published in book form in 1632, years after Lombard died. It was edited by P. F. Moran, Dublin in 1868.

to influence much thinking that took place in the Confederation of Kilkenny, long after Lombard had died. Lombard was also understanding and supportive of the attitude of King James of *de facto* toleration of catholics in Ireland. His influence in this regard created a mood which was helpful to newly appointed bishops, like Patrick Comerford, taking up episcopal duty in Ireland in the 1620's and 1630's. Lombard died in Rome in 1625.[6] Much later his attitude towards *de facto* toleration caused anguish to the papal nuncio Rinuccini who failed to understand how such a situation could ever be acceptable and who argued rather for the establishment in Ireland of a truly catholic state.

While Lombard in the early seventeenth century was using his influence in Rome, the reorganisation was taking place at the local level in Ireland. Synods, provincial and inter provincial, were an important feature of the work in Ireland. We know of many which were held such as Cashel provincial synods of 1606, 1612, 1614, 1630, 1632 but decrees from most of them are not extant. A provincial synod of Dublin province which was held in Kilkenny in 1614, presided over by archbishop David Matthews of Dublin who was then probably the only bishop in Ireland, is significant. Its first act was to profess loyalty to the holy see and to accept, in so far as was possible, all that had been laid down by the Council of Trent.[7] The same desire to co-operate with the holy see was expressed in the decrees of a synod of Armagh province held in 1618 in Drogheda under the presidency of David Rothe, vicar general of Armagh, and later bishop of Ossory (1620-50). With justification Patrick Corish styles David Rothe as the 'founding father' of the new episcopate which was about to be established in Ireland.[8] Rothe, a native of Kilkenny, had been a student at Douai, Spain and Rome. In Rome he became archbishop Peter Lombard's confidant. When he returned to Ireland in 1609 he was both vicar-apostolic of Ossory and Lombard's vicar-general and vice-primate of Armagh. We have already referred to Rothe as the dominant figure in the two meetings of the Munster and Leinster bishops, one in 1624, the other in 1629, the decrees of which have been preserved.[9] In the twenty or more synods and for meetings of bishops held in the years between 1614 and 1640 the principal aim of those who took part was to bring Ireland, in so far as it was possible, into conformity with the decrees of Trent and to establish tridentine order and organisation in the Irish church. We have seen earlier that Patrick Comerford attended the 1629 meeting in Kilkenny and there helped to draw up the regulations which he was to attempt to apply in his

---

[6] On archbishop Peter Lombard's influence cf. the following:
Silke, J. J. 'Later Relations between Primate Peter Lombard and Hugh O'Neill' I.T.Q. XXII (1955) 15-30;
-------- 'Primate Lombard and James I' Ibid., XXII (1955) 124-50;
-------- 'Hugh O'Neill, the Catholic question, and the papacy', I.E.R. civ (July - Dec. 1965) 65-59;
-------- 'The Irish abroad 1534-1691', N.H.I., vol. III, 596-98, 619-25

[7] The decrees of this synod are printed in Moran, History of the Catholic Archbishops of Dublin, vol I, 441-463

[8] Corish, P., *The Irish Catholic Experience*, 100-1

[9] Renehan, L., Collections on Irish Church History, Ed. Daniel McCarthy (Dublin, 1861-74), vol. 1, 149
For 1624 meeting
Moran, op.cit., vol. I, 434   For 1629 meeting

diocese in the years ahead.[10] The discussion at this meeting seems to have been largely based on a set of regulations issued by the Holy Office in August 1626 which represents perhaps the earliest formal attempt by Rome to provide a solution to the rather general confusion in the Irish church.[11]

In most of the sixteen decrees drawn up at this Kilkenny meeting of 1629 the bishops were occupied with rules for the guidance of the regular clergy and with efforts to develop proper harmonious relations between the regulars and the hierarchy. In the decrees we find many of the problems which were to vex Patrick Comerford and his fellow bishops for years to come. The subjection of the regulars to the bishops in all pastoral activity was stressed. It was also pointed out that the houses of religious, in so far as they existed at all in Ireland, could not be considered to have that sufficient stability which would entitle them to full exemption from diocesan control. Precedence was to be accorded to the parish priest in his parish. In matters such as funeral offerings it was recommended that each local ordinary should work out a reasonable arrangement with the regular clergy. The bishops at the meeting also dealt with other matters which were to worry the Irish church in later years. They stressed that caution should be observed in choosing suitable subjects for the priesthood and in giving recommendations to those going abroad for seminary training. Bishops were to respect each other also. Each bishop was to take care lest he would encroach on the jurisdiction of his neighbouring bishop. The metropolitans were reminded that they should be understanding and respectful in the matter of appeals from the suffragans' courts to their own. Attention was also given to the delicate question of ecclesiastical property; the dispensation enabling catholics to retain such property was declared to be reserved to the bishop alone.

In general, it is evident that at that meeting in Kilkenny, the Munster and Leinster bishops were seeking reform of their church in 1629. Their efforts were based on Roman suggestions taken in conjunction with their own experience and observations. But the decisions arrived at in Kilkenny were not put into effect without great difficulty, and then only with qualified success. We noted earlier how disappointed bishop Comerford was at the poor reception his early attempt to apply these decrees received, especially from the regular clergy.[12] In the years following 1629, as we have noted, the problems discussed at Kilkenny continued to torment the Irish church: clashes between the hierarchy and the regular clergy continued and even grew more acrimonious; the metropolitans and their suffragans did not, for quite a while, enjoy the hoped-for harmony with each other; former ecclesiastical property remained a very real problem. It was to prove necessary for Rome to intervene again, this time in a more thorough manner and, it would seem, with greater success. The congregation of Propaganda Fide was to be the main agent of this new intervention.

---

[10] Cf. Supra 84-5
[11] The decrees of this meeting are in APF, SOCG, 294, ff. 279R – 280R printed in Moran, cf, cit., 434-6
[12] Comerford to Propaganda, 6 July 1630, APF, SOCG, 294, f. 2221R

1. Benedictine Abbey of St. John's, Waterford. Established c.1190. Suppressed 1536.

2. Augustinian Abbey, Kells, Co. Kilkenny. Founded 1183. Suppressed 1540.

*3. Franciscan Friary Waterford (Greyfriars). Founded 1240. Suppressed 1540.
Statue of Luke Wadding O.F.M. (1588-1657).*

4. Dominican Friary Waterford (Blackfriars). Founded 1226. Suppressed 1541.

5. Christ Church Cathedral, Waterford in 17th century (Exterior).

6. Christ Church Cathedral, Waterford in 17th century (Interior).

7. *Letter of Bishop Comerford, Propaganda Archives 1629.*

8. *'Inquisition of a Sermon', Waterford 1617, 1644.*

9. *Courthouse Waterford, site of St. Catherine's Augustinian Abbey. Founded 1207. Suppressed 1539.*

10. Augustinian Priory O.S.A., Abbeyside, Dungarvan, Co. Waterford. Founded 1290. Suppressed 1541.

11. Augustinian Abbey, Mothel, Co. Waterford. Founded 1140. Suppressed 1540.

12. Archbishop Rinuccini, Papal Nuncio to Ireland 1645-1649.

13. 'Coronatae Virtuti', Rome 1629.

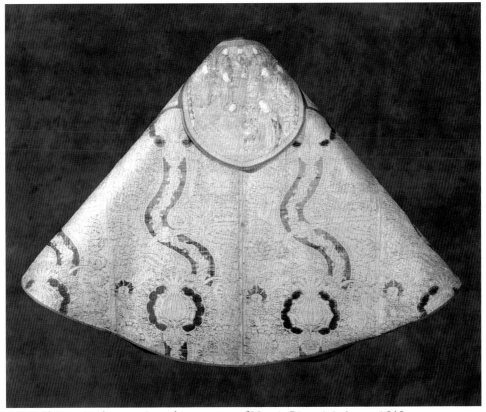

14. Gold Cope (15th century), used in reception of Nuncio Rinuccini, August 1646.

15. Irish College Paris - Founded 1605.

16. Irish College Salamanca - Founded 1592.

Since its foundation in 1622, Propaganda had been kept informed by reports mainly from bishops and prominent members of the religious orders. Of particular significance was a lengthy report on Ireland's background and on the contemporary religious situation by archbishop Eugene Matthews of Dublin, submitted to the congregation in the very first year of its existence. Matthews was then living in Rome and was to die there in the following year, 1623.[13] Of serious importance also was a report by John Roche, agent of the Irish bishops in Rome and later bishop of Ferns, sent to Propaganda in late 1625 or early 1626.[14]

From the beginning Propaganda cannot but have been intrigued by the Irish situation. In several aspects it was unique. Propaganda, founded to deal with missionary territories and missionary problems, undoubtedly saw in Ireland many missionary conditions verified. In 1622 the hierarchy was still very depleted with only one or two bishops in the country; the priests working in the country were conducting their ministry with missionary faculties and, as one would expect in a mission country, largely without churches or possessions. But, unlike a mission country, where neither people nor rules would be expected to be catholic, in Ireland the people were devotedly catholic and the government was professedly hostile. The restoration of the hierarchy in such a country was a far more delicate task than its establishment in a straight-forward mission country. By 1629 the hierarchy was well on the way to being built up again but propaganda could see that delicate problems of jurisdiction were continuously turning up, generally aggravated by the suspicions and hostile attitude of the government. To the extent to which Propaganda did not nor could not understand fully the complexities of the Irish scene did its attempt at a final and comprehensive solution, expressed in a special set of decrees in 1633, fail to meet the case fully. On many questions, particularly concerning the matter of precedence between secular and regular clergy, and the question of ecclesiastical property, the puzzled congregation could do little more than state the general law and hope that time would eliminate the obstacles to the application of that general law. However, it has to be said that, on the whole, Propaganda tackled the Irish question well and produced a sound set of decrees which made a very sizeable contribution towards the ordering of the Irish church in the late 1630's.

Since 1622 Propaganda had been studying and filing the reports from various persons and groups. The general congregation had set up a number of what are termed particular congregations to deal with Irish affairs and to report back to the general congregation for decisions. The first such particular congregation was set up on 8 January 1631 to examine proposals for the revision of parishes in the province of Tuam.[15] On 24 February 1633 a more

---

[13] Matthew's document is dated 4 Feb. 1623 and is entitled:
'Brevis informatio ad illmos. D.D. cardinales S. Congregationis Prop. Fidel de statu religionis in regno Hiberniae, et praesente ejus necessitate exhibita', cf. references in Moran *Archbishops of Dublin*, 288-93
Archbishop Matthews to Propaganda, APF, SOCG, 294
Ibid., Acta, 3, 20 Dec. 1622, f. 24V, No. 11

[14] Biblioteca Casanatense, Roma,, Ms. 2410, printed in Corish 'Two report on the Catholic Church in Ireland in the early seventeenth century', *Archiv. Hib.*, XXII (1959) 148-162

[15] APF, Acta, 7, 9 Jan. 1631, f. IV

significant particular congregation was set up to deal with the more general question of the reforming of the Irish church.[16] Under the presidency of Antonio Barberini, cardinal prefect of Propaganda, this congregation was composed of four curial officials: Paulutius, Torniellus, Oregius, Bocabella.[17] Throughout 1633 these officials met and considered the reports on a whole host of letters from bishops and clergy of Ireland concerning the state of the Irish church.[18] By March 1633 certain tentative decrees had been arrived at. These were further discussed, and, in August 1633, they were presented to the general congregation of Propaganda which decided to distribute them to the cardinals in Curia for further consideration.[19] At a meeting of the general congregation held on 15 November 1633 the cardinals, to whom the draft decrees had been referred, reported their agreement with the proposed decrees and added some amendments.[20] The minutes of the meeting of the general congregation of Propaganda on 16 December 1633 contain the fullest list of the decrees and it is stated that the Holy Father, having made some further amendments, approved them.[21]

Propaganda then in 1634 referred the decrees for comment and suggestion to the four Irish archbishops and also to a group of Irish ecclesiastics living in Rome, prominent among whom was Luke Wadding.[22] This group, which met in St. Isidore's College, probably had many meetings during 1634. At a meeting on 9 October 1634 it offered its comments to the general congregation of Propaganda.[23]

We have noted above that copies of the decrees were sent to the four archbishops of Ireland in early 1635. The archbishops did not promptly communicate them to their suffragans for comment. Nor did they call a meeting of the suffragans to discuss them. They themselves met and sent a short commentary on the decrees to Rome.[24] Consequently, as Comerford remarks, it was left to the suffragans to comment on the decrees individually and send their

---

[16] APF, Acta, 8, 195R
[17] Cardinal Antonio Barberini was nephew of pope Urban VIII and of cardinal Francesco Barberini and cardinal Carlo Lorenzo Magalotti. He was uncle of cardinal Francesco Barberini iuniore. He retained the prefecture of Propaganda from 1632 till his death in 1671. He held, among many offices, the Grand Priorship of the order of St. John of Jerusalem, which may account for the granting of the church of Baptist Grange to Edmund Everard, which we examined earlier.
[18] APF, Acta, 8, 16 March 1633, ff. 193R – 209V
Ibid., 11 July 1633, ff. 260R – 264R
[19] APF, Acta, 8, 13 Aug. 1633, f. 283R, No. 17
Amongst the specific suggestions from Irish bishops which were discussed was one from Comerford recommending that parish priests in Ireland be made *ad nutum amovibiles*; this suggestion was not accepted and it was decided that the better course was to ask the Datary not to nominate candidates to benefices in Ireland without consulting Propaganda: APF, Acta, 8, 11 July 1633, f. 261R
[20] APF, Acta, 8, ff. 323R – 325R, No. 20
[21] Ibid., ff. 337R – 344V
[22] Ibid., 10, 14 July 1634, f. 93R, No. 29
APF, SOCG, 14, ff. 138RV
APF, Acta, 10, 11 Oct. 1634, ff. 131R – 133R
[23] The suggestions of this group are in APF, Acta, 10, 11 Oct. 1634, ff. 131R – 133R. As a result a more concise and slightly altered draft of the two last sections of the decrees is found in the Minutes of Propaganda for 19 Jan. 1635, APF, Acta, 10, ff. 176R – 177V
[24] The four archbishops to Propaganda, 28 Nov. 1635, APF, SOCG, 140, f. 33R

comments to Propaganda.[25]   In fact it seems that the only bishops who sent their formal comments to Rome were Comerford himself and John Roche of Ferns.[26]   In order to appreciate Propaganda's efforts and achievement and also in order to get a view of Comerford's attitude to many of the questions involved, an examination of the set of decrees and the bishop's comments on them are necessary at this point.

The decrees are referred to by Propaganda as *Decreta pro recto regimine ecclesiarum Hiberniae* (Decrees for the right ruling of the Irish churches).   The plural 'Ecclesiarum' (Churches) is used to embrace the many aspects and sections of the Irish church. It obviously is not meant to include churches other than the catholic church.

The decrees are divided into seven main sections, only the last four of which were sent to the Irish bishops for comment. The first three sections concern the Roman Curia. We have noted already that the problems in Ireland also threw up problems and tensions within the curia in Rome. The recently formed Propaganda congregation had difficulty establishing itself firmly in the face of vested interests and jurisdiction enjoyed by long established bodies such as the Datary (dealt with grants and dispensations and benefices), the Secretariat of Briefs (dealt with administrative affairs on behalf of the pope), the Holy Office (guarded the teaching of the church), the Congregation of the Council (set up to be the authoritative interpreter of the Council of Trent).

The first set of decrees concerning the Roman sections was for the guidance of the cardinal protector of Ireland who, at this time, was also the prefect of the congregation of Propaganda Fide – Cardinal Antonio Barberini. This decree was mainly concerned with the appointment of bishops. In future, it stated, the commendation of a particular person by members of the Irish nobility was not to determine episcopal appointments in Ireland. This was clearly an attempt to curtail the influence of important Irish exiles such as the Earl of Tyrone, O'Neill, and the Earl of Tyrconnell, O'Donnell.[27]   It was rather the wish of Propaganda that the rectors of Irish seminaries and the superiors of religious orders should be asked for advice and recommendation in such matters.   The congregation also suggests that, in view of the complaints reaching Rome that the bishops who were members of the regular clergy were tending to favour their own regular clergy, for the future, as a practical rule, at least the Irish metropolitans should not be chosen from the regulars. This was a decree, the report of which when it reached Ireland, caused reaction from the four archbishops because it could be interpreted as an indirect judgement on the activity of the franciscan archbishop of Dublin, Thomas Fleming.[28] Of importance also in this section drawn up for the cardinal protector, was

---

[25] Comerford to Propaganda, 25 Jan. 1636, APF, SOCG, 140, ff. 44R – 45R
[26] Comerford's comments were sent to Propaganda, 20 Jan. 1636, APF, SOCG, 140, ff. 43RV – 46R.
   Roche's comments were sent, 4 April 1635, APF, SOCG, 14, ff. 133 ff.
[27] In the past Tyrone and Tyrconnell had exercised considerable influence. We noted earlier that
   Tyrconnell objected to the proposed appointment of Patrick Comerford to the See of Derry, APF,
   SOCG, 294, f. 410V
[28] APF, SOCG, 140, f. 42V

the congregation's judgement on the position of catholics who were in possession of ecclesiastical property. This has been examined elsewhere and we have noted that the congregation wished to leave them undisturbed for the present.[29]

The second set of decrees of this first section was drawn up for the guidance of the Holy Office and for a particular congregation which had been set up to provide a general revision of missionary faculties. This latter congregation had been established in March or April 1633 to review the missionary faculty question throughout the whole world; the Irish situation was part of its remit.[30] In this decree Propaganda asks the Holy Office to request the pope to restrict the faculties hitherto given to Irish bishops to their own dioceses and not to allow them to be validly exercised anymore in any other part of the three kingdoms of Great Britain. Formerly, although the Irish bishops were appointed to specific dioceses, the faculty grants they received had extra-diocesan application and range. The proposed restriction, now requested by Propaganda, sends out a signal that missionary conditions no longer obtain and the Irish bishops should exercise their jurisdiction in the normal manner.[31] Several decrees in this section deal with writings and sermons of the regular clergy against the hierarchy and seculars, and, in particular, with the book of Edmundus Ursulanus. The Holy Office is asked to condemn the book and to ensure that there be no further writing of this kind. In the final decree in this section, Propaganda asks that the particular congregation for reforming missionary faculties should take steps to avoid granting faculties to missionaries in Ireland which enable them to administer the parochial sacraments, because Ireland was at present being well supplied with priests and bishops. The exercise of such faculties would only cause hurt and trouble.

The third set of these early decrees concerns the Datary. They form an attempt on the part of Propaganda to prevent indiscriminate granting of dispensations to Irishmen who come to Rome without dimissorial letters or commendations from bishops, and who seek to be ordained priests. This was a problem about which Patrick Comerford had complained several times. From his *Retatio Status* of 1639, which will be dealt with later, it seems that he did not consider this decree of Propaganda very effective.[32] The congregation also seeks to prevent benefices being granted, as so many Irish bishops are claiming, by the Datary to Irishmen who were not recommended by their ordinaries. In future Propaganda wishes to be consulted by the Datary before any such grants are made. We mentioned in an early reference that this decision of Propaganda contained in this decree was preferred to the suggestion of Comerford that the ordinary in Ireland be given the right to grant the benefices himself.[33] The final decree aimed also at the Datary, asks that any appointments so far made by bishops in Ireland be ratified.

---

[29] APF, Acta, 8, 11 July 1633, f. 260R
[30] APF, Congregationi Particolari, Miscellanee Missioni, 10, ff. 155R – 157V
[31] The bishops had the privilege 'Utendi facultatibus in aliis vicinis regionibus sub dominio Regis magnae Brittaniae, according to faculty grants for Irish bishops contained in jesuit general archives, Rome, *Hiberniae Cathalogi Antiqui 1611-1644*, ff. 85
[32] Printed in 'Miscellanea Vaticano-Hibernica', *Archiv. Hib.* V (1916), 109
[33] Comerford to *Propaganda*, 16 Oct. 1632, *Spicil, Ossor.*, i, 182
APF, Acta, 11 July 1633, 8, f. 261R

This was something which Comerford had requested in one of his letters to Rome.[34] However, for the future, the decree states, such appointments are to be made by Rome, consideration being given to the recommendation of the Irish bishops.

The next four sets of decrees were sent to the bishops in Ireland for their comments. Comerford, as we noted earlier, sent back his comments in two letters : one which is a commentary proper, dated 20 January 1636; the other is a more general letter arising from an examination of the decrees, dated 26 January 1636.[35] He shows himself very enthusiastic for the decrees and considers them to be excellently and carefully drafted; they are an example of the solicitude and fraternal care with which the holy see regards Ireland.[36]

This fourth set of decrees and the first on which Comerford comments concerns the archbishops and bishops of Ireland. Propaganda, mindful of the complaints that there were too many bishops in Ireland, suggests that the episcopal dignity would be better preserved if the number of bishops was confined to a metropolitan and four suffragans in the two larger provinces (Armagh and Cashel) and a metropolitan and three suffragans in the two smaller ones (Dublin and Tuam). This number was greater than the archbishops or bishop Roche desired, but Comerford strongly agrees with it and, as was noted earlier, had stressed already the value of a good supply of bishops in Ireland and the danger of giving more than one diocese to one man.[37] At this point Comerford digresses from the subject of the decrees to condemn the indiscriminate granting of dignities and benefices in Ireland by the Roman curia. He has deplored this practice before. He says that the recipients of such grants are often quite unworthy and they cause quarrelling and scandal when they return to Ireland seeking to oust the priests who are faithfully serving there.

The decrees for the bishops continue with a dispensation relaxing the Irish bishops, because of their poverty and other difficult circumstances, from performing their *ad limina* visits personally for the next twenty-five years. Comerford agrees that this is the only possible thing to do while the present conditions remain. He also agrees fully with the next two decrees which insist that bishops, in visiting their dioceses, and archbishops, in visiting their provinces, should conduct themselves with respect and moderation and they should adhere diligently to the ordinances of the Council of Trent. Obviously Comerford would have special welcome for the decree concerning metropolitan visitation, although, as we noted earlier, the controversy, between archbishop Walsh and his suffragans continued in the province of Munster until the late 1630's. Comerford welcomed the next decree which states that in the matter of appeals to the metropolitan court the archbishop should be guided by the bull 'Archiepiscopalis Authoritas' of Clement VIII. He also registers agreement with the final decree in this section

---

[34] Comerford to Propaganda, 16 Oct. 1632, *Spicil. Ossor.* I, 182
[35] APF, SOCG, 140 ff. 435R – 46 R
[36] APF, SOCG, 25 Jan. 1636, 140, f. 43R
[37] APF, SOCG, 20 Jan. 1636, 140, f. 44R
Ibid., 25 Jan. 1636, 140, f. 43RV

which declares that Trent should be received throughout all Ireland, if at all possible, and that its prescriptions and those of Gregory XV regarding exemption should be observed by the regular clergy.

There follows at this point a single decree concerning vicars-apostolic in Ireland. As has been noted earlier, these had been appointed by Rome to many Irish dioceses during the Elizabethan period and also in the early seventeenth century.[38] They had been the subject of much complaint by the metropolitans who held that they were even more insubordinate than the bishops because they claimed that, not being suffragans in the normal sense, they were not subject in any way to the metropolitans but received their jurisdiction from Rome and were accountable only to Rome.[39] The decree here says that, if the reports concerning the excessive number of bishops are true, then there is no longer a need for vicars-apostolic. If a bishop has charge of more than one diocese he can himself appoint a personal vicar to rule one of them. Comerford does not comment on this decree but in the letter accompanying his comments, he repeats his preference that he would like to see a diocese properly ruled by a vicar-apostolic than half ruled by a bishop.[40]

With the next lengthy set of decrees, dealing with the regular clergy, Comerford is in full agreement although he has doubts if some of the decrees will be capable of application in contemporary Ireland. It appears obvious from these decrees concerning the regulars that Propaganda had been convinced by the reports of Comerford and many of the other bishops that a great deal of the tension in the Irish church was being caused by the misbehaviour of the regular clergy. It calls here for the cessation of all the abuses which are being attributed to them. In the matter of importunate begging by the regulars, their superior-generals are to be warned that, unless a reform takes place, the Irish bishops will be asked to take action. The congregation wants correction of an alleged tendency on the part of the regulars to direct their ministry in a special way to the more wealthy class, thus not attending so well to the poor. The regulars are exhorted to observe, where possible, the law of cloister and to conduct themselves with modesty and sobriety on all occasions. Much greater care must be taken in the reception and training of novices; novitiates must be properly organised and conducted. Once again the regulars are asked to refrain from making attacks on the hierarchy in their sermons. There is to be no preaching in a diocese without the permission of the local ordinary. Cistercians are singled out and warned to be careful and reverent in their questing for alms and to refrain from any abuses in connection with relics.

The decrees for the guidance of the regular clergy come down heavily on the side of the bishops in the matter of the administration of the parochial sacraments. Whether regular clergy are appointed to parishes by the bishops themselves, or conduct their ministry in parishes

---

[38] Jones, F. M., 'Canonical faculties on the Irish Mission in the reign of queen Elizabeth 1558-1603' *I.T.Q.*, XX (1953), 152-171

[39] APF, Acta, 4 March 1638, 12, f. 36V

[40] APF, SOCG, 140, f. 43R

annexed to their monastery, they must be subject to the bishop in accordance with the prescriptions of Trent and the constitution of Gregory XV. Even where the regulars have their mission directly from Rome and their faculties from the Holy Office the congregation asks that, in receiving such grants, they be obliged to respect episcopal and parochial rights. It is clear that these decrees would be welcomed by Comerford who had claimed to have had difficulty with the regulars on practically all the points raised. However, he confines his comments now to the indiscriminate reception of novices and the undisciplined manner in which they are being trained. It is his opinion that the regulars will be corrected in this matter only with difficulty. One senses, he states, no sign of piety or mortification or monastic discipline in the novitiates. People think they are behaving as good religious and are satisfying all their obligations if they merely wear the religious habit on a certain few days in the year. The rest of their time is spent wandering around the towns and countryside begging. He thinks that the pope should personally intervene to prohibit such behaviour. At this juncture Comerford takes the opportunity to deplore the practice of the Datary of granting indults so that Irish students may be ordained 'ad titulum missionis', without any recommendation from their ordinaries. The result of such action on the part of the Datary, according to Comerford, is that too many priests, unlearned and unzealous, are returning to Ireland and are wandering up and down the country attached to no diocese and subject to no bishop. They cause great scandal to the faithful:

> ....certe tot sacerdotes plerumque indocti, et immorigeri, turmatim repatriantes facient sibi invicem angustias, populum catholicum nimis gravabunt, clerum in vilipendium, et vituperium adducent, ac vagis suis et frequentibus discursibus de diocese in diocesim, de parochia in parochiam innumere scandala parient[41]

This matter of too many unattached priests drew comment from Comerford years previously also. In a letter to Wadding in 1631 he writes:

> However our countrie is soe furnished with clergymen that ere it be longe we are like to have one against every house, and beinge soe many in a poore beggarlie countrie, *facimus invicem angustias*, and the laytie begins to frowne at us; especially consideringe that most of our clergie are idle, contentinge themselves to say masse in the morninge, and untill midnight to continue either playinge or drinkinge or vagabondinge; and as moste of them are unlearned, they make a trade of beinge ecclesiasticalls, thereby to live idle, sitt amonge the best, goe well clad, and if I would

---

[41] APF, SOCG, 140, f. 44RV
"....certainly so many priests, frequently unlearned and unbiddable , returning to their country in squadrons, will crowd each other out and will weigh down the catholic people with burdens and will reduce the clergy to cheapness and shame, and with their wanderings and frequent running about from diocese to diocese, from parish to parish, will cause innumerable scandals"

say it, swager. A man can not sitt at table to a raffe of tripes but presentlie one or two clergie menn will come in; a mann can not visit a friend in towne or abroade but there he shall meet two or three clergiemen; and a lass, very few spend one hour in a twelvemonth to teache the Christian doctrine, or instruct yonge childer[42]

Comerford seems alone in this assertion that there were too many priests in Ireland. The problem with his friend, John Roche of Ferns, in 1635, was that there were too few. In fact, from Comerford's own *relatio status* in 1639, which we will examine shortly, he states that, while the number of priests in his diocese has grown, there is still plenty of work for all to do.[43] The explanation perhaps lies in the fact that Comerford was probably inveighing against the unattached priests. From the context of his letter to Wadding in 1631 one might be justified in concluding also that he has in mind mainly the regular clergy. He certainly at that time wrote to Wadding in a depressed mood at the height of the crisis over the Sorbonne propositions and we should probably allow for some exaggeration. All in all, it does not seem that the clerical situation in Ireland at the time was as bad as Comerford depicts.

The final set of the decrees of 1633 deals with both regular and secular clergy and is an attempt to regulate the conduct of both and to inspire harmony between them. Bishops and religious superiors are asked to take steps to ensure that their clergy do not refuse to administer the sacraments when money is not given. All the comments sent to Rome, those of bishop John Roche, the four archbishops and Comerford, react strongly to the implied accusation in this decree. Comerford states that such an accusation is the work of calumniators. The accusation, he feels, has it origin in a misrepresentation of a decree of some provincial councils which advocates that a sum of money should be paid to the parish priest, '*intuitu laboris in administratione sacramentorum*'. The parish priests, however, are commanded by the provincial councils never to refuse the sacraments to the poor if this money is not paid. Such payment is necessary as the parish priests have no other means of support.[44] Comerford here rather pointedly confines himself to defending the position of the parochial clergy; presumably, he is leaving it to the regulars to exonerate themselves. He agrees with the next two decrees which condemn the frequentation by priests of taverns and their engaging in feasts with heretics and women. Also condemned is the practice of holding elaborate celebrations on the occasion of the feasts of the patron saint of a parish or of a religious order. Here again, rather bluntly, he says that the superiors of the regular clergy ought to superintend the conduct of their own subjects in these matters.

At the end of its long set of decrees, Propaganda finally attempted to solve the problem of the *ius sepulturae*, the burial of the dead, probably the most intractable of all problems at the local level. The congregation had to content itself with laying down the general ruling that

---

[42] Comerford to Wadding, 30 Oct. 1631, *Wadding Papers*, 609
[43] Comerford to Propaganda, 20 Jan. 1636, APF, SOCG, 140, f. 44V
[44] Comerford to Propaganda, 20 Jan. 1636, APF, SOCG, 140, f. 44V

normally the secular clergy should precede the regulars. However, in accordance with Trent, when the remains of the deceased are brought to the church of the regulars the office of the dead and other services should be conducted by the regulars rather than by the parish clergy. Comerford, while not commenting directly on this, states that the crux of the whole problem surrounding *ius sepulturae* is the practice of the regular clergy of declaring the private house of the deceased an exempt place and equating it with a monastery for the purpose of precedence.[45] The congregation concludes its decrees by commanding the regular clergy to guard against attempting to entice people to be buried in their churches by special promises of eternal happiness. They are commanded to pay the *quarta canonica* in accordance with the prescriptions of Trent.

It has to be said that the *Decreta pro recto regimine eccclesiarum Hiberniae* represent a fine effort on the part of Propaganda to deal with the outstanding pastoral problems in the Irish church and to help create a climate where the work of the counter-reformation could be performed more effectively. It is evident from the decrees that the officials at Propaganda had taken careful note of the content of the many letters and reports which had reached them from Ireland since 1622. The *decreta* represent a very good attempt to deal with the problems which these letters and reports contained. The *decreta* endeavour to make a definitive break with the former missionary regime. Undoubtedly problems continued to exist in the Irish church: it has already been noted that the tensions between metropolitans and suffragans did not die out until well after the *decreta* were issued. Also, we still hear of trouble with the regular clergy in the late 1630's and in the 1640's. One very significant outcome of the *decreta* was the further establishment of Rome and, in particular, of Propaganda at the heart of the reform of the Irish church. The bishops emerge strengthened in their dioceses. The central role of Rome is emphasised, perhaps as never before, in the *decreta* and by the mood in which they were created. Much trouble was to descend on Ireland and the Irish church in what might be called the Cromwellian decade 1650-60. But, with the restoration, there was strong improvement; the hierarchy was quickly re-established; it was a hierarchy that had been given the sharpest focus in the *Decreta pro recto regimine eccclesiarum Hiberniae*.[46]

---

[45] It is possible that this question of precedence may not have figured in the copy of the decrees which Comerford received from the archbishop of Cashel because, on the recommendation of the commission which had met in St. Isidore's in Rome, it was referred by Propaganda to the Congregation of the Council for definitive ruling. Comerford refers to it here perhaps because he may have seen it in the draft which bishop Roche had been sent before the St. Isidore's commission held its meetings. Comerford comments on the question at the end of his letter of 20 Jan. 1636, APF, SOCG, 140, f. 45R

[46] Because of their real significance the *decreta* themselves are given in Appendix 1 of this work; the comments of bishop Comerford are in Appendix II, his accompanying letter is in Appendix III; the comments of the four archbishops are in Appendix IV.
The comments of bishop John Roche are dealt with in Corish, 'An Irish counter-formation bishop: John Roche', *I.T.Q.*, XXVI, No. 4 (1959), 317-21

2. Relatio Status of 1639

In the preceding section we have examined the co-operation between the new bishops, especially Patrick Comerford, and the holy see, and the active role of Propaganda in the progress of the church in Ireland in the early seventeenth century. The nexus between the bishops and Rome continued and created an increasing bond between the Irish church and the papacy. Right from his appointment as bishop, Comerford kept in close touch with Rome in two ways: one was by direct letters and reports to Propaganda and the second was by his correspondence with Luke Wadding, by far the most influential and esteemed Irishman in Rome. Comerford was probably the most frequent correspondent from Ireland to Wadding; his letters to Wadding are highly personal, and he makes no secret, in all his letters to his friend, of the mood out of which he writes and his deep antipathies to certain people and groups. As Wadding carefully filed Comerford's letters away in his study in St. Isidore's, he must have smiled knowingly as he pictured the mood of the bishop of Waterford when he was penning the different letters.

In his early years bishop Comerford wrote frequently to Propaganda, usually concerning some crisis or problem or persons who were injuring the Irish church.[47] After the transmission to Ireland in 1635 of the *Decreta pro recto regimine ecclesiarum Hiberniae*, it is understandable that, having sent his lengthy comments on the decrees, Comerford's correspondence with Propaganda might decrease somewhat. To the bishops the *decreta* must have shown that Propaganda was very well informed on the Irish scene and had done all it could for the present to provide a solution to many problems. In Comerford's early reports to Rome he gave a fairly detailed account of his diocese. In 1629, when he arrived as bishop, he records that the churches were in ruins and the people, especially in the rural areas, were deprived of priests to minister to them and to teach christian doctrine. He reported on his extensive visitation of the diocese and the administration of the Sacrament of Confirmation to thousands of people. A synod was convoked and synodal decrees were drawn up. Some new parish priests were appointed.

In 1639 he was ten years a bishop. In ordinary circumstances he should have been journeying to Rome to make his *ad limina* visit and to report on the state of his diocese. But the Decreta, as was noted, had dispensed the Irish bishops from going to Rome for the next twenty-five years. But they were expected to send to Rome a *Relatio Status* (Account of the state of the church). This Comerford did in 1639. The *Relatio Status* was sent, not to Propaganda, but to

---

[47] Comerford's principal earlier reports were:
18 Jan. 1630, APF, SOCG, 132, f. 281R
Same date, ibid., f. 283R
20 Jan. 1630, ibid., f. 282R
20 Jan. 1630, ibid., 204, ff. 221R – 222R
16 Oct. 1632, printed in Spicil Ossor., I, 180-83
14 Feb. 1633, APF, SOCG, 134, f. 238R

the Congregation of the Council[48] It was submitted to the Congregation *per procuratorem*, the procurator being Father Edmund O'Dwyer, a priest of the archdiocese of Cashel, friend of Luke Wadding. In 1634 O'Dwyer had been appointed representative or agent of many Irish bishops in Rome.. To observe the proper protocol O'Dwyer, on Comerford's behalf, visited the tombs of St Peter and of St Paul and formally presented the *Relatio Status* to the Congregation of the Council.[49]

When Comerford began to write his *Relatio Status* of 1639 he was writing from an Ireland and an Irish church that had changed considerably since his early episcopal years. Much change in Ireland in the 1630's was the work of Thomas Wentworth. Wentworth was appointed Lord Deputy of Ireland on 12 January 1632.[50] He was a man of considerable intelligence, a forceful character, energetic and vigorous. He could be politically tactical but often unsubtle and even superficial. From his previous work in various London departments of administration, sometimes dealing with matters relating to Ireland, he was knowledgeable about Ireland and well aware of its complexity. His outstanding characteristic undoubtedly was his absolute and undivided loyalty to his royal master, Charles I. From his previous years, as one of the close advisers to the king in England, he knew well the difficulties the monarch was having with the wealthy class in England and, in the matter of religion, with the puritans in England and Scotland. When appointed to Ireland it was Wentworth's resolve that Ireland should provide a steady revenue which would help solve many of the king's financial worries. The instinctive loyalty of the Irish to the Stuart monarchy would be harnessed to support the king, especially in matters of finance, in his constant struggle with the parliament in London.

There was much development in Ireland under Wentworth's rule. He fostered industry, especially that type of industry, such as linen making, which did not compete with English industry. Trade developed remarkably and the seas around Ireland were rid, to a large extent, of pirates. By various stratagems, rents to the crown were increased and the titles of much Irish land were declared to belong to the king. Great landowners, particularly new English landowners such as Richard Boyle, the great Earl of Cork, who had hitherto possessed their fortunes largely undisturbed, were now compelled to make hefty contributions to the exchequer. The result of Wentworth's Irish policy was that within a few years the king was benefitting well

---

[48] The *Relatio Status* is printed in Hagan, J., from the archives of the Congregation of the Council, 'Miscellanea Vaticano-Hibernica', *Archiv.Hib.*, V (1916) 107-112
[49] In 1645 O'Dwyer was appointed co-adjutor bishop to the very elderly bishop Arthur of Limerick.
[50] He was created earl of Strafford in 1640; he was executed in London on 12 May 1641. Of particular help in treating of his dealing with Ireland are:
Kearney, H. F.,　　*Strafford in Ireland 1633-41*
Wedgwood, C.V., *Thomas Wentworth, first Earl of Stafford 1593-1641: a Revaluation*;
Clarke, Aidan,　　'28 November 1634; a detail of Strafford's administration', *R.S.A.I. JN..*, XCIII (1973) 162-7
　　　　　　　　'The Government of Wentworth, 1632-40' and
　　　　　　　　'The Breakdown of Authority, 1640-41', *N.H.I.*, Vol. III, 243-269, 270-288
Ranger, T. O.,　　'Strafford in Ireland: a Revaluation', Aston, Trevor (ed.) *Crisis in Europe 1560-1660*, 271-293

from the country; the country in turn was enjoying a certain prosperity of its own from Wentworth's programmes.

His interest in Ireland was not deep or respectful. Fundamentally he saw the country as a useful support for the king who was running deeper and deeper into trouble in England. As time went on the different classes in Ireland, catholic and protestant, lost trust in Wentworth. His policies were to make him many enemies both in Ireland and England. He had no intention of allowing the Dublin parliament a free hand. His lack of respect for it and for its members became clearly evident as time went on. That same parliament was happy, at a later stage, to combine with the parliament in London in the overthrow and downfall of the earl of Strafford. Wentworth was a thorough and ruthless man who had no qualms in cutting through opposition to his plans. This aspect of his character was demonstrated in his critical courtship of the Old English class in the matter of the 'graces' of 1628 and the crown's failure to honour its side of the bargain. Later, when it suited him politically, Wentworth's attitude towards this class changed and he wrote them off as dangerous to the state and over-influenced by the jesuits and friars in their attachment to the papacy. He also came to dislike the new English planter class such as the earl of Cork, who were unscrupulous and selfish in their attitude to their land and rights. He also caused disturbance and fear in the Old Irish class mainly because of his planned attempt at what is called the Plantation of Connaught. Although the effort to acquire the land in that province was not very successful it created unease amongst the Old Irish and made them feel ever more insecure about their property.

Wentworth's regime in Ireland, which was to contribute to his personal downfall, did provide a fairly settled period for the catholic church, a period during which the church made considerable progress. In the matter of religion Wentworth found himself running into trouble on several fronts. He refused the proposal coming from many members of the established church to re-introduce and re-emphasise the recusancy fines which were a financial punishment on catholics for refusing to attend protestant services. Wentworth's refusal and objection was political, not religious. He had no liking or feeling for catholicism and he looked forward to the day when it would cease to be a feature of Irish life. But he considered that the re-enforcement of the recusancy fines would cause more trouble than it was worth at the present time. He was not prepared to complicate the political aims which he had by a strong move against catholics. To avoid provocation he let it be known that catholics could practice their religion without hindrance. He went further and restrained the ecclesiastical courts of the established church from proceeding against catholic baptisms, marriages and funerals. His attempt to keep peace with the catholics helped to alienate him from the members of the established church.

But Wentworth's innate sense of order and proper procedure prompted him to tackle many of the problems, especially financial, which beset the established church. Ever since the dissolution of the monasteries in the mid-sixteenth century church property and tithe income had become very complicated as to right of ownership and proper valuation. A great deal of such property was in the hands of lay people and families who, over the years, would have leased them from the crown itself. Also, church property was sometimes in the hands of the descendants of previous ministers of religion. The outcome of such legal confusion was that the protestant bishoprics in Wentworth's time had become seriously devalued financially and consequently proved unattractive to properly qualified clergy. Wentworth attempted seriously, and with considerable success, to solve many of the financial problems which were besetting the established church. In 1635 he agreed that royal impropriations of church property should be taken from the laymen who had come to possess them and be given to the established church on condition that an annual rent be paid to the crown by the church.[51] Title deeds in Ireland were very often insecure and unclear, especially where former church property was concerned. Old English and new English and some Old Irish landowners felt threatened by Wentworth's attitude in regard to land. As a result he made many Irish enemies who were not helpful to him when he was put on trial by the parliament in London in March 1641. His execution on Tower Hill on 12 May 1641 was not a serous cause of grief to many in Ireland. The great earl of Cork was unashamedly pleased.

But, as mentioned above the catholic church made progress during Wentworth's time. With religious practice relatively unimpeded and clergy left in a fair degree of freedom, the counter-reformation thrust of the church developed in the decade 1630-40. Catholic bishops in most dioceses began to acquire houses in which they lived and worked. Numbers of clergy continued to grow and the new clergy who had been trained on the continent were, by and large, well able for their ministerial work, the administration of the sacraments, preaching at mass, and teaching christian doctrine wherever a suitable place could be found. Religious orders operated fairly openly in the towns. Novitiates were even set up so that a young man could receive initial training and formation in his native country before being sent for final training for priesthood to places in Spain or France or the Low Countries or Rome.

But it must be said that all was not rosy for the catholic church during those years. Despite the quiet progress that was being made during Wentworth's time, the bishops and clergy had to move cautiously. An example was the bishops having to avoid the risk of attaching publicity to their provincial or diocesan meetings.[52] From Wentworth's own letters we read that archbishop Walsh of Cashel was forced to go into hiding in 1637 because the government, believing him to be in conspiracy with Spain, was determined to arrest him.[53] It is clear also that Wentworth's government, as a policy, lost no opportunity to encourage internal dissension within the catholic church. It proved a staunch supporter of trouble-makers like Paul Harris who embarrassed the catholic hierarchy.[54] Neither was Wentworth prepared to tolerate

[51] The revenue of the protestant diocese of Waterford and Lismore increased considerably as a result of Wentworth's policy. Wentworth particularly humiliated the earl of Cork and forced compensation from him for the church; also bishop Atherton was successful in reclaiming much church property.
[52] Edwards, R. D., 'Church and State in the Ireland of Mhicíl Úi Cléirigh, 1626-51, S. O. Brien (ed.), *Measgra i gchuimhne Mhicíl Úi Cléirigh*, 1-20
[53] Knowler, William (ed.) *Strafford's Letters*, I, 171, 187-9
[54] Bishop Roche to Propaganda, 15 Nov. 1634, *Spicil. Ossor.*, i, 198

such evident demonstrations of catholic vitality as the existence of catholic schools or the open exercising of episcopal jurisdiction. But, obstacles notwithstanding, the catholic church at this time in Ireland had reason to be relatively content that it was not formally persecuted and, provided it did not intrude unduly on to the public scene, it enjoyed a considerable degree of toleration.

It was from such an Ireland that Patrick Comerford sent his report to the Congregation of the Council in 1639. The report is quite long and informative. It is more informative than most of the contemporary *Relationes Stati* which, around this time, came to the Congregation from other Irish bishops. It has a special value when one contrasts its contents with the contents of letters and reports sent eight or ten years previously by Comerford himself to Propaganda. One can deduce fair progress in the diocese during those years. The *Relatio* also gives much information, immediate and local, concerning the treatment of catholics by the bishop and ministers of the established church.

The report is signed 'e loco nostri refugii', just as were many of the letters in the early years of Comerford's episcopacy, a fact which emphasises that Comerford was still the bishop of a church which did not enjoy much right under civil law, despite whatever measure of tolerance the government might think it wise to allow. He probably had the use of a house in Waterford city but the official episcopal residence was occupied by the bishop of the established church. In the report Comerford stresses that catholics have to be just as careful and cautious as they have ever been. The government was at heart unfavourable towards catholics and would tolerate no publicity or ostentation on the part of catholics. He reports that in his visitation of his diocese he is compelled to remain in hiding in the houses of his priests: 'Furtim incedere cogo ad tugaria parochorum'. Serious caution had to be observed in organising any meetings or public events. He says that he has experienced much difficulty in securing a sufficiently safe and remote house in which to hold diocesan synods, a number of which he has apparently convened. His visitations are occupied largely with the administration of the Sacrament of Confirmation and with the settling of disputes and quarrels and the correction of abuses. In exercising such jurisdiction, especially in legal matters, great care has to be observed because sometimes incorrigible and disobedient people will not hesitate to summon the bishop before the civil courts.

Church property, he claims, is in exactly the same situation as it was when first he became bishop. All the churches remain in the hands of the protestant clergy. The catholic bishop and priests are still compelled to depend for support on the benevolence of their relatives and friends. Comerford continues to be annoyed by the fact that lay catholics are still in possession of much church property. As he has frequently done in previous communications with Rome, now again he asks that such people be compelled to devote a certain part of their revenue towards the support of the bishop and his clergy. Otherwise, he says, let them be declared *mala fide* possessors, notwithstanding their appeal to supposed dispensations or statutes of parliament.

He reports that in all there are 170 churches in his diocese; there are 15 monasteries, some for men and some for women. There are 12 hospitals or houses where strangers may find rest. Of course, he adds, all the monasteries and most of the churches are still in ruins. The protestant clergy, who legally possess these buildings, have little interest in preserving them. All their interest and enthusiasm is expended on the collecting of money for themselves. As regards the number of catholic clergy, the diocese is much better supplied than it was in his early years as bishop. There are now 104 priests altogether in the diocese, 59 seculars and 45 regulars. In 1631 he had reported that there were 40 seculars and 30 regulars. The population of Ireland generally in the early seventeenth century is much discussed and disputed. One cannot be certain in this matter but one is inclined to go with Prof. Louis Cullen, a truly acknowledged expert in such matters, that the population of Ireland in 1600 was c.1.4 million rising remarkably rapidly to 2.1 million in 1641. Waterford city in 1600 had not less than 2,400, equal to Cork and smaller than Limerick, Galway and Dublin. A guess will have to do and I would suggest that the population of the diocese of Waterford and Lismore in 1639, when Comerford wrote his report, might have been between 40,000 and 50,000. If this is correct it would mean that the number of priests given in his report would be adequate to the needs of the faithful.[55]

Of the secular clergy now working in the diocese, he states that 45 are engaged in parish work; he commends them highly for their zeal. The remaining 14 seculars are chaplains in private houses of catholics. The other *relationes stati* of this period do not mention the fact of priests as chaplains in catholic houses, but clearly it must have been fairly common. It was one means of ensuring sustenance for the clergy involved who were possibly also engaged in some parochial work and in tutoring children. Waterford and Lismore at this time would have possessed many fairly wealthy catholic families, such indeed as Comerford's own. Some of these families undoubtedly had come into the possession, usually by purchase, of church property. The practice of maintaining a catholic priest as one of the family may well have been a method of compensation to the church for the possession of such property. As regards the number of clergy, a similar and heartening increase is reported around this time by the archbishop of Tuam and the bishop of Elphin.[56]

In all his correspondence with Rome Comerford only mentions the names of a few of the priests of his diocese. Due to the absence of any local parochial records it is not possible to come by a list of the pastors for this period. From chalice inscriptions and other incidental

---

[55] Discussion on population in Ireland may be found in:
Cullen, Louis, 'Economic Trends, 1600-91', N.H.I. vol. iii, 387-407;
---------- 'Population trends in seventeenth century Ireland' *Economic and Social Review*, vi, no. 2 (Jan. 1975) 249-75;
Butlin, R. A., 'Land and People, c. 1600', *N.H.I.*, vol.iii,, 142-167;
McLysaght, *Irish Life in the Seventeenth Century*, 183, 190
[56] 'Relatio Status' of archbishop Malachy O'Queely of Tuam, 1637, 'Miscallanea Vaticano-Hibernica', *Archiv. Hib.*, V (1916), 98
'Relatio Status' of bishop Boethius MacEgan of Elphin, 1637, ibid., 93

references it has been possible to locate about thirty two priests who were at work in the diocese of Waterford and Lismore. The list is contained in Appendix E. These priests are diocesan.

Somewhat surprisingly, Comerford has praise in this report for the regaular clergy who work hard '*in hac vinea excolenda*'.[57]   Happily, he records no clash or controversy with the regulars, a remarkable improvement when contrasted with the manner in which such complaints dominated his early reports. However, in dealing here with the clergy, both regular and secular, he does repeat a complaint which he had previously made in his comments on the *decreta pro recto regimine ecclesiarum Hiberniae* in 1636. It concerns the increasing number of clerics who are returning to Ireland from overseas. He claims that, in the present circumstances, the country cannot afford to support so many ecclesiastics. Unless the Holy Father takes immediate steps to have the numbers reduced the non-catholic powers in the country may take stronger action with the catholic population as a whole. Comerford here seems to have in mind those clerics whom he had referred to before as wandering around the country unattached. His worry is that their ostentatious behaviour may attract the undue attention of the government and so cause trouble for the catholics in general.

In his *relatio* Comerford gives some idea of the amount of organisation and order which he has established in the diocese. In 1631 he considered it an achievement to have gone around the diocese and spoken to the parish priests and to have made five new appointments to parishes in Waterford city. He also in 1631 had little but gloomy reports of the scarcity of priests and of the religious ignorance of the people in the rural areas.[58] Now in the *Relatio Status* he speaks of the diocese as being divided into four deaneries in each one of which is held every two months conferences to deal with '*casus conscientiae*'.[59] These conferences, he states, are of great benefit to the priests. He is pleased also that sermons are preached and Christian doctrine is taught frequently in the city and principal towns. In the rural areas Christian doctrine is being taught more frequently than formerly but the bishop is disappointed that sermons are not being preached sufficiently frequently. However, on the whole, he is happy with the progress the country people are making in the knowledge of the faith. Unfortunately, he has no schools to which students can be admitted openly, as the civil law will not permit such catholic schools. It is a safe assumption that in the diocese at that time there were clandestine schools, conducted in private 'safe' houses where Christian doctrine and probably other subjects were taught by some clergy and also by lay people.

A large section of Comerford's *Relatio Status* deals with the inconveniences suffered by the catholics at the hands of the bishops and clergy of the established church. These inconveniences were to be found mainly in the demand for dues and taxes made by the protestant clergy on the catholic people. This section of the report, in a sense, gives the lie to the *de facto* toleration which Wentworth and his administration extended to catholics. It would

---

[57] 'in the cultivation of this vineyard'
[58] Comerford to Propaganda, 6 July 1630, APF, SOCG, 294, 221R – 222R
[59] 'cases of conscience'

seem from Comerford's account that, at the local level, at the coalface, so to speak, intolerant demands were being made on catholics. This is a problem concerning which Comerford and the other bishops did not specifically complain about in earlier reports to Rome. In his *Relatio Status* to the congregation of the council in 1637 the bishop of Elphin, Boethius Mac Egan, does remark that catholics, on getting married or when having their children baptised, are compelled to pay dues to the protestant ministers, but Comerford alone gives a detailed treatment of the matter.[60] Apparently this practice of the ministers of the established church had become quite widespread. Wentworth, fearing undue disturbance, had let it be known that he did not wish the protestant bishops to be enquiring continually into catholic baptisms and marriages.[61] Comerford lists the different occasions when the ministers of the established church demand money from the catholics and he names the amount that is normally expected. No catholic, he says, is permitted to marry without the express permission of the protestant bishop for which the catholic has to pay thirty julii.,[62] Six and a half julii must be paid to the protestant minister when catholics have their child baptised by a catholic priest. Catholics, to be allowed make their Easter communion, even secretly, have to pay a half julius to the protestant minister. Seven julii must be paid before a catholic may be buried. Frequently, Comerford asserts, the protestant bishop may excommunicate catholics. The absolution from such excommunication involves the payment of a large sum of money and also the humiliating experience of having to beg forgiveness on bended knees before the bishop. Catholics are also compelled to pay for the upkeep of the churches possessed by the protestants and for the purchasing of books of common prayer and vestments and vessels used by the protestants in their services.

The jurisdiction of the protestant bishop is very great, according to Comerford. When he excommunicates a person the civil magistrate, who might himself be a catholic, is compelled to place the excommunicate in prison. For innumerable reasons catholics are summoned to the court of the protestant bishop and there, on one pretext or another, they are fined and the money paid goes to the private use of the bishop. By numerous threats the protestant bishop forbids the catholic parish priest from assisting at the marriage of catholics until he has made sure that the requisite permission has been granted. To close off any possible escape route for all catholics every catholic house is taxed for the support of the protestant clergy. Presumably, the tax to which Comerford here alludes is the gathering of tithes from the catholics by the protestant ministers. The collection of tithes was not easy and was particularly complicated by the law which dealt with it. Above all in the towns the collecting was especially difficult for protestant ministers. There often was physical danger involved when an approach had to be made to surly catholics who refused to co-operate. To avoid such awkward encounters 'tithe-proctors' were

---

[60] 'Relatio Status' of bishop of Elphin, 1637 *Archiv. Hib.* V (1916) 94
[61] Edwards, R. D., 'Church and State in the Ireland of Michél Ó Cléirigh 1626-41', *Measgra I gchuimbre Mhicíl Úi Clérigh*, 13
[62] Comerford is using julius, a Vatican coin, probably to make the dues more understandable to the Roman authorities. At this time one julius was equal to about six pence. The julius was a silver coin struck during the pontificate of pope Julius II (1503-13)

often employed. Theirs indeed was an unenviable employment. Many of the protestant clergy were poor, and pluralism had to be invoked and practiced in order to provide subsistence income for the minister and his family.[63]

The protestant bishop of Waterford and Lismore from 1619-35 was Michael Boyle, a Londoner, whose brother, Richard, was protestant archbishop of Tuam, and whose cousin was Richard Boyle, the first earl of Cork. Boyle complained frequently of his own poverty and that of his clergy. He engaged in continuous disagreement with his cousin, the earl of Cork, concerning the latter's appropriation of much of the church property in the diocese of Waterford and Lismore.[64]

In 1636 Boyle was succeeded as bishop by John Atherton, also an Englishman, from Somerset. He was particularly disliked by the catholics and he clearly is the bishop whom Comerford had in mind in his 1639 *Relatio*. Atherton had many enemies, even from within his own protestant flock. He was accused of many sexual misdemeanours, in particular of the crime of buggery with his steward and tithe proctor, John Childe. They were both tried in Dublin and were found guilty. Atherton was executed in Stephen's Green, Dublin on 5 December 1640. It was a complicated scandal and some felt that Atherton was the victim of malicious rumour and allegation circulated by puritan enemies. In the account of his death, which was said to have been repentant and holy, he admits that the catholics suffered much at his hands but, despite it all, he declares that they did not take part in the accusations against him. His biographer tells us that, as he was on the platform about to be executed, Atherton said he thought he saw the town clerk of Waterford amongst the crowd

> ...if he be, or any other of that Towne, I shall desire them to commend me to my neighbours there, that I have taken notice that none of the Romish Church, though differing from me on points of religion, had a hand in this complaint against me, though they had as much cause as others, for which I conceive I owe them thankes.[65]

It was a significant gesture at an historic moment. Perhaps, it might be assumed that the catholic bishop could have been to the forefront in the mind of the man about to be executed. Comerford was to merit praise in later years for showing respect and consideration to the

---

[63]   A balanced account of the church of Ireland clergy in the seventeenth century is in Barnard, T. C. and Neely, W. E. (eds) *The Clergy of the Church of Ireland 1000-2000, Messengers, Watch and Stewards,* especially 6-43 Empey Adrian, 'Irish clergy in the high and late Middle Ages'
[64]   *Calendar of State Papers Ireland 1633-47,*44 ff.
[65]   Glynn, Marcellus and Martin, F. X. (eds) "The 'Brevis Relatio' of the Irish Discalced Carmelites 1625-1670", <u>Archiv. Hib.</u>, XXV (1962), 138, 140, 141, 153
Barnard, Nicholas, *The Penitent Death of a Woefull Sinner, or, The Penitent Death of John Atherton Executed at Dublin the 5 December 1640*

protestants of his diocese when catholic anger was roused against them during the period of the 1641 rebellion.[66]

Comerford concludes his 1639 report with further references to the protestants in his diocese. He says that there are only about twenty or thirty of the Irish in each of his two dioceses (Waterford and Lismore) who have changed their religion and attended the protestant services. Correspondingly, almost all the English living in the diocese are protestants; about twenty have come over to the catholic church.[67] The protestant clergy are numerous, he states, and, according as the revenue of the established church grows, their number increases. Only one or two Irishmen in the diocese have become ministers of the protestant religion. All the officials of the king, the courts, barons, knights, in the diocese are protestants.

It is of interest that in this special report, not to Propaganda, but to the Congregation of the Council, Comerford dwells so extensively on the protestant situation and the difficulties caused by the protestants to the catholics in his diocese. Unlike the case of Propaganda, perhaps he feels that this is an aspect of the Irish church on which the officials of the Congregation of the Council might need more intensive briefing. Perhaps he wishes to impress, for the record, those officials as to the complexity of the Irish situation and the severe hardships which are suffered by clergy and people in the catholic church in Ireland.

In general, Comerford sums up the position of the catholics in Ireland as unpredictable. At times they are treated harshly and robbed of their possessions, at other times they are accorded reasonable tolerance. It all depends on the mood and interest of the government:

> …nunc expilantur, nunc enim augere rem faliliarem permittuntur; nunc deglubuntur et excoriantur; nunc iterum vires resumere tolerantur ut tandem expilentur[68]

But he thanks God that the Irish are remaining strong in the faith and sincere in their loyalty and obedience to the holy see – nothing can shake this faith and loyalty. It is a source of wonder and ridicule to the heretics:

> et hinc est quod vicinorum regnorum heretici scurriliter loquentes soleant per modum sarcasmi dicere 'Hibernos esse Papistas a natura ingenitos'.[69]

---

[66] This observation, the source for which is not cited, is given in Meehan, C. C., *The Rise and Fall of the Irish Franciscan Monasteries and Memoirs of the Irish Hierarchy in the Seventeenth Century*, 216

[67] By 'Irish' here he obviously includes the 'Old English' as well as the 'Old Irish'. He himself was of Old English stock and that group was very numerous in the diocese. By 'English living in the diocese' he clearly means 'New English'

[68] "at times they are robbed, at other times they are allowed to increase their property, then again they are stripped and mocked, then again they are allowed recover only to be finally pillaged"

[69] "and hence it is that the heretics of the neighbouring kingdoms, speaking jeeringly, are accustomed to say 'the Irish are papists by their very nature'"

Chapter Ten

POLITICAL INVOLVEMENT
(1) Bishop Comerford and the Confederation of Kilkenny

The decade 1630-40 had witnessed considerable progress in the diocese of Waterford and Lismore and generally within the catholic church in Ireland. It was a decade without war and with considerable tolerance in fact, if not in law, of the catholic church throughout the country. The earl of Strafford, Thomas Wentworth, had left his mark and had also left confusion and annoyance. There was welcome economic growth but Wentworth's personal attitude had been tasteless and insensitive. He had offended many people and groups. Old English, New English and Old Irish, each in their own way, had been offended and threatened by his attitude. The established church, it could be said, had done best. Wentworth had gone a fair way towards regularising its finances and he had come down heavily on the planter stock, such as the earl of Cork, to help that church financially. The catholic church continued without legal rights, had no property, and was left with little hope for future progress.

The succeeding decade 1640-50 was to prove dramatically different, although full of complexity. It was, in the main, to be a decade of war, which began with the rising in Ulster on 22 October 1641, when the catholics, especially the Old Irish, still smarting from the flight of the earls in 1607, the Ulster Plantation 1609-13, and the overlordship of the planters who had come largely from Scotland, despaired of airing their grievances to the government in any other way except by force. That war, thus begun, spread throughout most of the rest of Ireland and was to continue in a complex and untidy manner until it was overwhelmed by Cromwellian ferocity at the end of the decade.[1]

It was also to prove a decade of political development, difficulty, and disagreement. Much of the political situation in Ireland was related to and, in many aspects, dictated by the political happenings in England. Charles I was locked in combat with parliament throughout the decade and had also been locked in dispute with Scottish covenanters since the late 1630's. The king desperately, all through the years of the 1640's, needed Irish help and support. He sought to obtain that help through his trusted viceroy James Butler, earl of Ormond, Lord Lieutenant since 1643, and, in a clandestine way through Edward Somerset, earl of Glamorgan in 1645. There was prolonged debate and negotiation between the Irish and the crown's representative as to what help Ireland could give and what help Ireland could get. There were

---

[1] Barnard, Toby, 'Crises of Identify among Irish Protestants, 1641-1685', *Past and Present*, 127 (1990), 39-83

    Clarke, Aidan, 'The 1641 Rebellion and Antipopery in Ireland', Brian MacCuarta (ed.), *Ulster 1641: Aspects of the Rising*, 139-58

    Corish, Patrick, 'The Rising of 1641 and the Catholic Confederacy 1641-45', 'Ormond, Rinuccini and the Confederates, 1645-9' *N.H.I.*, vol. iii, 289-335

peace arrangements concerning which the Irish disagreed seriously amongst themselves and which came to nothing in the end. Parliament was victorious in England and king Charles was put on trial and executed on 30 January 1649. Oliver Cromwell, then effective ruler of England, decided to bring order and subjugation to Scotland and Ireland where there had been much royalist support. He chose Ireland first and he landed at Rathmines with twelve thousand troops on 15 August 1649. In less than a year it could be said the job was done and Cromwell departed from Youghal on 26 May 1650.

It was a decade when aid from abroad was sent to Ireland. The Vatican, which viewed the Irish scene as very much related to the general European counter-reformation struggle, saw its wars and attempts at peace as somewhat similar to what was happening in Portugal, Catalonia, Germany, Bohemia, the Palitanate and other places. The 1640's was the decade when the Thirty Years War, which was a war fuelled by a cocktail of politics and religion came to a relatively harmonious end with the Treaty of Westphalia in 1648. Advised, it is clear, by Luke Wadding, Rome sent to Ireland aid in the form of arms and money several times during the decade. Envoys were sent such as Pier Francesco Scarampi, in 1643, and Dionysio Massari, dean of the archdiocese of Fermo, and, most special of all, GianBattisto Rinuccini, archbishop of Fermo, who arrived at Kenmare on 12 October 1645 and did not leave Ireland for four years when he sailed from Galway on 13 February 1649. The military aspect of the counter-reformation was also expressed by the return to Ireland of Irish military men who had been distinguished in various wars on the continent, such as Owen Roe O'Neill, nephew of the Earl of Tyrone, who arrived back in Ireland in July 1642 and Thomas Preston, brother of the fifth Viscount Gormanstown, who returned in September of the same year.

The main political and constitutional happening, which was initiated really by the catholic church, in this decade was the highly remarkable Confederation of Kilkenny. It was the theatre of much progressive thinking and quite a deal of political disagreement for the seven years of its existence. It had times of glory and times of despair. It was not a parliament; it continuously acknowledged, with strong warmth, the authority of the king, even though it was catholic and he was heretic. It was a very complex institution, drawn from different groupings of Irish society, uneven in its priorities, but honest and hardworking in its efforts. As a general assembly it met nine times in all, eight times in Kilkenny and once in Waterford:

1.	24 October	-	21 November	1642	Kilkenny
2.	20 May	-	19 June	1643	Kilkenny
3.	7 November	-	1 December	1643	Waterford
4.	20 July	-	31 August	1644	Kilkenny
5.	15 May	-	31 August	1645	Kilkenny
6.	7 February	-	4 March	1646	Kilkenny
7.	10 January	-	4 April	1647	Kilkenny
8.	12 November	-	24 December	1647	Kilkenny
9.	4 September '48	-	17 January	1649	Kilkenny

It was an experiment in constitutional democracy, a quite unique development for its time. There were many and deep divisions, some of them connected closely in its later years with the papal nuncio, Rinuccini. Division occurred around special decisions and actions such as the First Ormond Peace in March 1646, the truce with Lord Inchiquin of Munster in June 1648, and the Second Ormond Peace in January 1649.

In this study we will not be dealing in detail with the work of the Confederation but rather with aspects which concerned in a special way, the bishops and, particularly, bishop Comerford of Waterford and Lismore. In recent years historians have written well and coherently on this very complicated period and institution. Perhaps the best narrative account is given by Aidan Clarke and Patrick Corish.[2] Detailed studies on specific aspects have been done by Tadhg Ó hAnnnracháin, Michéal Ó Siochrú, Donal Cregan, John Lowe and other scholars.[3] There are also contemporary works which are printed and are of great value, allowing at times for bias and partisan attitudes.[4]

The Confederation of Kilkenny was a catholic establishment. Right from the beginning the authorities of the catholic church were involved; it might even be said that they were the founding architects of the Confederation. On 2 March 1642 the bishops and vicars of the ecclesiastical province of Armagh met at Kells in county Meath. Their main aim was to give moral judgment and guidance concerning the war that had broken out in 1641.[5] They declared it to be a just war waged primarily against the puritans:

---

[2] Clarke, Aidan,   'Alternative allegiance in early modern Ireland', *Journal of historical sociology*, vol. 5, No. 3 (Sept. 1992), 253-66;

    -------   'Colonial constitutional attitudes in Ireland 1640-1660', *P.R.I.A.* vol. 90, section C, No. 11 (1990), 357-78;

    -------   'Ireland and the general crisis', *Past and Present*, No. 48 (Aug. 1970), 79-99

Corish, Patrick   'The Rising of 1641 and the Catholic Confederacy, 1641-5', *N.H.I.* vol. III, 289-316;

    -------   'Ormond, Rinuccini, and the Confederates, 1645-9' ibid, 317-335;

    --------   'The Cromwellian conquest, 1649-53', ibid., 336-352;

    ---------   'Rinuccini's censures of 27 May 1648', *I.T.Q.*, XVIII, No. 4 (Oct. 1951), 322-37

[3] Ó hAnnracháin, Tadhg, *Catholic Reformation in Ireland The Mission of Rinuccini 1645-1649*

O'Siochrú, Michéal, *Confederate Ireland 1642-1649, A Constitutional and Political Analysis*

Cregan, Donal   'Some Members of the Confederation of Kilkenny', S. O'Brien (ed.), *Measgra I gchuimne Mhíchíl Úi Chléirigh, 23-33*

    ----------   'The Confederation of Kilkenny', Brian Farrell (ed.) *The Irish Parliamentary Tradition*, 102-115

    ----------   'The Social and Cultural Background of a Counter-Reformation Episcopate 1618-60', A. Cosgrave and D. McCartney (eds.) *Studies in Irish History Presented to R. Dudley Edwards*, 85-117

Lowe, John,   The Glamorgan Mission to Ireland 1645-6, *Studia Hibernica*, IV (1964), 155-96

[4] O'Ferrall, Richard and O'Connell, Robert, *Commentarius Rinuccinianus, de sedis Apostolicae Legatione ad foederatos Hiberniae Catholicos per annos 1645-9,* Stanislaus Kavanagh (ed.) 6 vols. I.M.C. (Dublin, 1932-49)

Gilbert, J. T. (ed.), *A contemporary history of affairs in Ireland from a.d. 1641-1652*, 3 vols.

    ---------- (ed.) The history of the Irish Confederation and the war in Ireland (1641-9) 7 vols.

[5] Corish, P., 'The Rising of 1641 and the Confederacy', 1641-5, *N.H.I.*, vol. iii, 297-8

who have always, but especially in recent years, plotted the destruction of the catholics, the destruction of the Irish and the abolition of the king's prerogatives[6]

The meeting, or synod, at Kells went further and declared excommunicate catholics, which included catholics in the Dublin government, who supported the puritans. It also expressed a strong wish that a council of clergy and laity should be set up as a central authority to safeguard the welfare of catholics and to defend the catholics in a military manner, if necessary.

This suggestion of a central authority was to be taken up and receive special attention by meetings in Kilkenny in May and June of 1642, held under the aegis and direction of David Rothe, the highly respected bishop of Ossory. Preparatory work by clergy and invited laity began and the Confederation of Kilkenny met for the first time in October 1642. Two outstanding persons, one an eminent catholic lawyer, Patrick Darcy, the other, a highly respected catholic landowner and lawyer, Sir Nicholas Plunkett, were of crucial importance in the early days of the Confederation.[7] Both were to be intimately involved with the Confederation all through its life. In fact Plunkett was chairman of every session of the General Assembly except one, when he was out of the country. At its preliminary meetings the Confederation stressed that there should be no distinction whatever between the Old Irish and Old English. The Confederation was to be unicameral without distinction, except in honorific matters of precedence between bishops, lay lords and commons. The motto was 'Hiberni unanimes pro Deo, rege et patria'.[8] In essence the Confederation was to be a general assembly consisting of clergy, nobility and lay people (three from every province). The general assembly at each of its sessions would establish a supreme council, consisting of one army general, one bishop, one temporal lord, and eight gentlemen drawn from the different provinces. The supreme council would constitute the executive of the assembly and attend to the business of the Confederation between sessions of the general assembly.[9]

An oath of association was to be taken by every catholic in the country. By this oath one became a member of the Confederation, a confederate catholic. The clergy had charge of the oath and were, through the church's country-wide network, to see that it was administered to catholics. As the oath indicates what the confederation was about it is necessary to quote it verbatim:

---

[6] *Comment. Rinucc.*, 1, 314-19
[7] Plunkett's brother, Patrick, was to become bishop of Ardagh in 1648.
[8] 'Irish united for God, for king, and for fatherland'
[9] Just as Sir Nicholas Plunkett was chairman of practically every session of the general assembley, so Richard Butler, Viscount Mountgarret, was president of every supreme council until the rejection of the First Ormond peace in August 1646. Mountgarret was grand-uncle of the viceroy, James Butler, Marquis of Omond. The secretary of every supreme council until 1646 was Richard Bellings, son-in-law of Mountgarret

I _____ do promise, swear and protest before God, and his saints and angels, during my life to bear true faith and allegiance to my sovereign lord Charles by the grace of God, king of Great Britain, France and Ireland, and to his heirs and lawful successors; and that I will to my power, during life, defend, uphold and maintain all his and their just prerogatives, estates and rights, the power and privilege of this realm, the fundamental laws of Ireland, the free exercise of the Roman Catholic faith and religion throughout this land, and the lives, just liberties, estates and rights of all those that have taken, or shall take this oath, and perform the contents thereof; and that I will obey and satisfy all the orders and decrees made, or to be made, by the supreme council of the confederate catholics of this kingdom, concerning the public cause, and that I will not seek, or receive, directly or indirectly, any pardon or protection, for any act done, or to be done touching this general cause, without the consent of the major part of the said council; and that I will not, directly or indirectly, do any act or acts that shall prejudice the said cause, but will, to the hazard of my life and estate, assist and prosecute and maintain the same. So help me God and his holy gospel.[10]

The Confederation was not a parliament. The king, its sovereign, had his parliaments, however unacceptable, in Dublin and London. But it was a serious coming together, not of Old Irish and Old English as such, but of catholic individuals to safeguard the king's Irish catholic subjects. There were also to be elected provincial councils and county councils under the general assembly at Kilkenny but there is not a great deal of evidence to show how the provincial councils functioned, and almost none at all for the county councils.

In its first session the Confederation drew up schemes for the payment of its supreme council and for the general running costs involved in its work. A beginning was made also for the organisation of provincial armies for military protection. A resolution was made calling for the restoration of the privileges and immunities enjoyed by the catholic church from the reign of Henry III until the reformation. This was a very large demand but it was to remain the primary objective of the clergy who had done so much to bring about the confederate association. This was a crucial issue later on in peace negotiations between Ormond, the viceroy, on behalf of the king and some members of the Confederation.

All the churches and benefices of the protestant clergy in 1641 were 'deemed' the possession of the Roman catholic secular clergy. Church lands and even tithes in catholic ownership were to be kept in the hands of those who joined the confederate cause. As we have noted earlier, much monastic land was held, often in good faith and through purchase, by catholic landowners. High ranking members of the Confederation such as Richard Bellings, secretary of the supreme council and his father-in-law, Viscount Montgarret, president of the

---

[10] Printed in Gilbert, *Ir. Confed.*, ii, 210-11;
      Comment Rinnucc. ii, 511-13

supreme council held such monastic lands. Assembly members informed the clergy that any transfer of land could only be done by act of parliament, and that lay ownership of ecclesiastical property had been legitimised by Cardinal Pole in the mid sixteenth century. At the assembly the provincial of the augustinian eremites, Patrick Comerford's own order, applied to the assembly for the return of the order's property, but his request was greeted with considerable hostility and was turned down.[11]

But there was welcome by the clergy for the decision to return all church buildings to the catholic church. In Waterford and Lismore bishop Comerford fully availed of this decision. Catholic life in Waterford began to flourish. In December 1642 Thomas Strange, guardian of the franciscans in the city, gives the following description of Waterford to Wadding:

> This alone I can say that, though all the realm is in arms, some for and others against us, the city which has most strongly declared for the catholic cause, and which professes it most openly, is this little Rome, where (God be praised) the Catholic religion is openly professed, nor is there a single heretic in all the city. The clergy say masses in the cathedral, and we of all orders preach there on our proper days. I went to our monastery and there said the solemn sung mass on Our Lady's Day in September, and every Sunday we all celebrate there and preach, the people hearing us gladly and joyfully.[12]

One may presume that bishop Comerford had also taken possession of the episcopal residence in place of the protestant bishop, Archibald Adair, who had been appointed in 1641 to succeed John Atherton.

Bishop Comerford was not elected to the supreme council of the Confederation but he seems to have attended all the sessions of the general assembly. He was probably very involved in the organisation of the third session which was held in Waterford from 7 November to 1 December 1643. Two years later in the middle of the fifth session, on 6 July 1645, when there was heated debate concerning negotiations with Ormond with a view to making peace, the general assembly in Kilkenny took time out and proposed that the assembly resume its session a month later. The clergy were fearful lest those supporting the proposed peace with Ormond might enter into an unsatisfactory arrangement with him during the recess. So they delegated two bishops, Patrick Comerford of Waterford and Lismore and Heber McMahon of Clogher, to remain in Kilkenny and to maintain a watch on affairs. They were to have two helpers with them: Walter Lynch (later bishop of Clonfert) and Nicholas French (later bishop of Ferns). If anything prejudicial to the catholic cause should be contemplated by the supreme council

[11] O'Siochrú, Michéal, *Confederate Ireland 1642-1649*, 52
[12] Letter in *Wadding Papers*, F.L.K., D4, ff. 1199R – 1201R

Comerford and McMahon were to protest in the name of the clergy.[13] Comerford was also centrally involved during the two lengthy occasions when the nuncio Rinuccini resided in the city of Waterford: August and September 1646, when the clergy assembled in the city and signed a decree condemning the First Ormond peace; January to April 1648, when discussions were taking place concerning the proposed truce with Lord Inchiquin whose troops were ravaging the province of Munster.

In the early months of the Confederation of Kilkenny a printing press was set up in Waterford operated by a printer, Thomas Bourke, but it was really under the control of the jesuits in the city. It was moved to Kilkenny by the jesuits in 1646.[14] It was the cause of conflict some time later and was commandeered by Richard Bellings, secretary to the supreme council of the Confederation, in order to prevent the nuncio and clergy from printing and distributing their material through it. In its earlier days, while it was still in Waterford, Patrick Comerford had printed by it his book which we referred to earlier. The book contained his aggressive critique of a sermon delivered in Waterford Cathedral by chancellor Robert Daborne in 1617. The book was printed in 1644.[15]

As we have seen from Thomas Strange's letter to Wadding the church in Waterford was knowing happier times when the Confederation of Kilkenny was established. The position of the clergy improved considerably with the return of some church property, especially houses. Some benefices at last began to mean something financial to those who received them. Applications were being made at this time by priests, presumably with the permission of Comerford, to Luke Wadding in Rome to have benefices in the diocese of Waterford and Lismore granted to them. Robert Adams who was parish priest of Cahir, was granted the treasurership of Lismore on 12 October 1644, Richard Butler was granted the rectory of Drumcannon on 26 October 1646, Dermot Carroll was granted the prebendary of Clashmore on 31 January 1645, John Clancy of Dungarvan was granted the treasurership of Lismore on 15 March 1646, Maurice Fleming was granted the 'Anacoretis'[16] of Lismore on 30 December 1646, Paul Keating was granted the chancellorship of Lismore and the church of St. Leonard of Derrygrath on 15 March 1646, George Lea, although a priest of Waterford and Lismore, was granted the church of Knockraffin in the archdiocese of Cashel on 6 January 1645, Donal Leaghy was granted the leprosaria[17] of Lismore on 30 December 1646, Philip Lonergan was

---

[13] *Comment. Rinucc.*, i, 539
[14] O'Siochrú, Mícheál, *Confed. Ireland,* 183-4
[15] Its full title reads: 'The inquisition of a sermon preached in the cathedral church of the city of Waterford, in February 1617, by Robert Daborne Chancellor of the said Cathedrall, written by R.F.P.C. of the Order of S. Augustin and Doctor in Divinity.
Hace est enim gratia, si propter Dei conscientiam sustinet quis tristitias, patiens injuste, I Pet. 2, v.19
For this is thankeworthy, if for conscience towards God, a man sustains sorrowes, suffering unjustly'
[16] 'Anacoretis' refers to lands attached to a hermitage traditionally associated with Lismore. It was possibly Okyle which is located in Camphire in the present parish of Cappoquin. More likely the lands in question are Ballyanchor, the anchorite's homestead.
[17] 'Leprosaria' refers to lands attached to the leper hospital at Lismore, which has been referred to on p.12. Monalour ('The Leper's shrubbery' may be the lands in question, 412 acres)

granted the prebendary of Disert and Kilmoleran on 31 January 1645. Robert Power, parish priest of St. John's parish, Waterford, was granted the deanship of Waterford on 20 November 1643. William Wise was made chancellor of Holy Trinity Church, Waterford, on 26 June 1643.[18]

If Comerford, according to Strange, proved uncharacteristically well disposed to allow the regular clergy preach and officiate 'on their proper days' in the Cathedral, Strange also remarks that Comerford, together with the archbishop of Cashel and the bishop of Cork and Cloyne, objected strongly in the general assembly in Kilkenny to the suggestion that their monastic and other property, which were in the possession of lay landowners, catholic and protestant, should be restored to the regulars.[19] While undoubtedly such a restoration would have caused much dispute and bitterness, it is significant that the strongest opposition to it came from Comerford and Tirry, the two traditional opponents in Munster of the regulars. Their attitude may have been generated as much by their old and, to some extent, unreasonable, anti-regular bias as by consideration of general harmony. As noted earlier, the general assembly, at its first session in 1642, in restoring to the bishops the benefices and churches of their dioceses, did not declare that the monastic property should be restored. The excuse given was that the monasteries and religious houses had been dissolved by act of parliament and the assembly, not being a parliament, had not the power to rescind that act. In fact, however, the regular clergy do seem to have re-occupied quite a number of their churches and houses also which had been taken over from the clergy of the established church.[20]

In the early months of the Confederation bishop Comerford was to appeal to its judicial powers for a decision in respect of a controversy between him and the cistercian order in Waterford over the possession and use of the church of St. John the Evangelist in the city.[21] This was a church which, in pre-reformation times, had been affiliated to the benedictine priory of Bath in England. However, even before the reformation, it had become a parochial church administered by a secular priest. The priest in question, however, was usually presented for appointment by the prior of Bath.[22] Before the expulsion of the protestants in 1641 St. John's continued as a parish church administered, of course, by a protestant vicar. At the same time a secular priest, appointed by the bishop, had been looking after the care of souls in the parish while having no church or property. Dating from a statute of Philip and Mary such a secular priest appointed to ministry in the area of St. John's was always to be presented by the episcopal ordinary for recognition to the lay patron of St. John's who, since the dissolution of the priory, was a member of the Wise family of the city of Waterford. When the church became catholic

---

18 Jennings, B., Ecclesiastical Appointments to Ireland, Aug. 1643-Dec. 1649, *Collectanea Hibernica*, 2 (1960), 24, 144, 49, 32, 38, 40, 57, 21

19 *Wadding Papers*, FLK, D4, ff. 1199R0-1201R

20 Ibid.

21 A lengthy account of this controversy, probably drawn up for the Confederation of Kilkenny, is in *Wadding Papers*, FLK, Di, ff. 357R – 359R

22 Power, P., 'The Priory, Church and Hospital of St. John the Evangelist, Waterford', *Waterford Arch. Soc. Jn.*, II (1896), 83

property again in 1641 the parish priest who had been looking after the care of souls in the area, Robert Power, moved in and occupied the church building.[23] This action was contested by Francis Wise, the lay patron and a catholic, who claimed that bishop Comerford had not, in accordance with law, presented the parish priest to him prior to allowing him occupy the church. Then Wise, having been petitioned by the cistercians, asked the supreme council in Kilkenny to allow the cistercians to say mass and perform other liturgical services in the church of St. John.[24] The council acceded to the request without having heard Comerford's views on the matter. The bishop reacted immediately and sternly. He forbade the cistercians to enter the church until he had placed the case properly before the supreme council. The cistercians ignored his prohibition and proceeded to make their preparations for entry into the church. Comerford reacted by publicly interdicting the church and notifying the supreme council of his action. The cistercians, confident that the decision of the supreme council had made their position legal, again ignored the bishop and offered mass in the church.[25] An order then came from the supreme council suspending its previous ruling until the controversy between the monks and the bishop should be definitely settled. Comerford alleges that he showed this order to the cistercians but they still persisted in celebrating in the church. A second interdict, local and personal, was published by the bishop against them. The cistercians advised the people that the interdict was invalid and so they were not obliged to remain away from mass and devotions in the church. The intransigence of both sides was causing scandal.[26]

The eventual outcome was that both Comerford and the cistercians appeared before the supreme council to argue their case and accept arbitration. The decision handed down by the council favoured the bishop. It declared that in such matters lay patrons were no longer to have any power. The granting of a benefice was judged to be a spiritual matter and no custom or prescription, however old, could make it lawful for a layman to make such a grant. Furthermore, it declared that the benefice of St. John had been a secular one and monks had no right to acquire it. It was finally declared that the cistercians had really no reason to complain as they were well established in the diocese of Waterford and Lismore and did not need an additional church. In this controversy Comerford clearly demonstrated that he had not lost his former intolerance of any encroachment on his rights as bishop by the regular clergy. It was a sad intrusion on what should have been a reasonably happy time for all catholics, lay and clergy, in Waterford city.

---

[23] This was the Robert Power mentioned earlier who was granted the deanship of Waterford in 1643. He very likely ruled the diocese as vicar-apostolic after the death of bishop Comerford and appears to have continued in office until the appointment of bishop John Brenan in 1671.

[24] It has been stated earlier that the cistercians, probably because they possessed a way of life based on the Rule of St. Benedict and so shared a background with the benedictine order, had associations with St. John's Church. Nicholas Fagan was blessed as abbot of Inislounght there and Thomas Madan received the abbatial blessing there from archbishop Fleming in 1626.

[25] Power P., *History of Waterford and Lismore*, 303-04

[26] *Wadding Papers*, FLK, D.I., f.358R

As happened in Dublin, when parliament was in session, convocation of the clergy of the established church also met nearby, so also when the Confederation of Kilkenny was in session as general assembly, convocation of catholic clergy sat at the same time in Kilkenny. Both groups were to meet in Waterford in the month of November 1643. At this convocation of clergy in Waterford the papal envoy, PierFrancesco Scarampi, an oratorian priest, was present. He took advantage of the presence of so many bishops and clergy to propose that once and for all the decrees of the Council of Trent should be properly accepted and promulgated in Ireland. The bishops, including Comerford, agreed and they signed a declaration that the decrees should be formally accepted but, still fearful lest the old conditions of intolerance of catholics might return, they added the well-worn clause that the full observance of the decrees would have to depend on the circumstances of the time.[27] At this time nearby in Waterford the general assembly of the Confederation delegated seven members, headed by viscount Muskerry, to travel to Oxford and present a series of demands to the king.

Through 1644 complicated negotiations were taking place between the confederates and the marquis of Ormond, now created Lord Lieutenant (21 January 1644), with a view to the establishing of a lasting peace. The bishops, in convocation in November 1644, expressed alarm at the lengths to which the members of the Confederation were prepared to go to establish peace with Ormond. A temporary cessation of war had been agreed and was to run until 31 January 1645. The bishops, on 8 November 1644, issued a decree, signed on behalf of the catholic hierarchy by the four archbishops, Hugh O'Reilly of Armagh, Thomas Fleming of Dublin, Thomas Walsh of Cashel, Malachy O'Queely of Tuam, and bishops Patrick Comerford of Waterford and Lismore, John Bourke of Clonfert, David Rothe of Ossory, and other members of the lower clergy. This decree emphasised that the war in which the Irish were engaged since 1641 was just and lawful. Preachers were instructed to stress this point in addressing the people. But, careful to avoid any appearance of division, the decree exhorted all to obey the commands of the supreme council of the Confederation.[28]

While the fifth session of the Confederation was taking place in Kilkenny, May to September 1645, and the convocation of clergy was also meeting in Kilkenny, much heated discussion was taking place concerning the proposed peace with Ormond. One of the major stumbling blocks continued to be the question of restoring to the protestants the churches and benefices taken from them since 1641. The general assembly of the Confederation decided to submit to the convocation of clergy the query whether the oath of the Confederation obliged the members to insist on the possession by the catholics of their churches. Convocation replied in the affirmative and its decision was welcomed by most of the lay deputies in the general assembly. The commissioners of the assembly, who had been appointed by the Confederation to negotiate with Ormond, resented the implication in the decision of the clergy that they had

---

[27] Declaration signed 17 December 1643, *Comment. Rinucc*, i, 434 ff
[28] *Comment. Rinucc.*, i, 499

broken their confederate oath. Strong tension was developing between the convocation of clergy and what might be termed the pro-peace faction in the Confederation. In an effort to soothe the situation the clergy, on 16 June 1645, denied having made any assertion that the commissioners were guilty of perjury. It was the opinion of the clergy that peace could be achieved with a safe conscience, even though a special provision for the retention of the churches might not be inserted in the peace treaty. However, they insisted that, in practice, such retention of churches must be allowed.[29] The clergy, in their letter to the Confederation, counselled a more independent attitude on the part of the commissioners in dealing with Ormond. They had already shown too much leniency in the negotiations.[30] It was at this point (referred to above, p.153) that the general assembly went into recess for a month but the clergy, quite distrustful as to what might happen, deputed bishops Comerford and McMahon to remain on in Kilkenny in case the Ormondist group might cause trouble.

In fact, no new developments seem to have taken place during Comerford's period of vigilance in Kilkenny. When the general assembly reconvened in August 1645 the earl of Glamorgan, Lord Herbert Somerset, a secret envoy of the king and a devout catholic, arrived at Kilkenny ready to negotiate a special treaty, particularly dealing with religious matters, with the confederates. Scarampi was opposed to negotiations with Glamorgan. He questioned both Glamorgan's authority and the offers which he was presenting. Scarampi also felt that nothing substantial should be done until the new papal nuncio, now on his way, should arrive. Despite Scarampi's objections, a secret agreement was entered into and signed with Glamorgan on 25 August 1645. The majority of the bishops, Patrick Comerford amongst them, were in favour of the proposals put forward by Glamorgan, and they voted in their favour.[31] The secret treaty granted free and public exercise of the Roman catholic religion in Ireland. The catholic clergy were to remain in possession of all the churches and benefices occupied by them since October 1641. Catholics were to be exempt from the jurisdiction of the protestant clergy; the catholic clergy were to be allowed free and untroubled jurisdiction over their faithful.[32] In return the Confederation was to send ten thousand men to serve the royal cause in England. They were also to divert two-thirds of the revenue from clerical livings for the maintenance of this force.[33] Copies of this secret treaty were made out for all the bishops. A copy was later found among the possessions of the archbishop of Tuam, Malachy O'Queely, who was killed in a military skirmish near Sligo in October, 1645. O'Queely's copy is said to have contained three signatures: that of Glamorgan, archbishop Walsh of Cashel and bishop Comerford of Waterford and Lismore.[34]

---

[29] O'Siochrú, Micheál, *Condederate Ireland 1642-1649*, 91
[30] Carte, T., *Life of Ormond,* iii, 185 ff
[31] *Comment. Rinucc.,* i, 550, 555-7
[32] O'Siochrú op. cit., 94-5
[33] *Comment. Rinucc,* i, 555-7
[34] Meehan, C.P., *The Confederation of Kilkenny*, 165

Glamorgan's mission to Ireland has puzzled many historians. His secret commission from the king to conclude a treaty with the Irish confederates has been questioned. Did he possess a commission at all? Did he extend and elaborate on a vague commission given to him by the king? One thing is certain: when the Glamorgan treaty eventually became public Charles would not give it the necessary support.[35] It would not be out of character for the king to fail to stand by his own delegate in the moment of crisis. One remembers the fate of Thomas Wentworth; also one does not forget the king's unreliability in respect of the Graces of 1626-28. That king Charles could possibly have granted the liberal concessions contained in the Glamorgan treaty, is really inconceivable. The treaty would seem to have been a desperate effort to obtain help from Ireland without a serious intention on the part of the king of fulfilling the conditions contained in it. But its signing by prominent members of the hierarchy shows how desperate they were to obtain the conditions contained in it. The Glamorgan treaty was to appear again for further discussion when the pope's most impressive and most controversial nuncio, GianBattista Rinuccini, archbishop of Fermo, arrived in Ireland in October 1645.

---

[35] A careful examination and analysis of the Glamorgan treaty and its context is in Lowe, John, 'The Glamorgan Mission to Irland 1645-6', *Studia Hibernica*, No. 4 (1964), 155-96

(2) The Nuncio Rinuccini[36]

GianBattista Rinuccini arrived in Ireland, landing at Kenmare on 21 October 1645. Right from its beginning the Confederation of Kilkenny had sent messengers and messages to continental powers seeking aid and recognition. Agents were appointed to various centres in Europe to keep European powers briefed on the situation in Ireland. The chief representative of the Confederation in Europe was Luke Wadding in Rome, in whom the Confederation placed strong trust. In fact, the hope was that the pope might send him to Ireland as nuncio. A request was sent to Rome that Wadding be made a cardinal but Wadding himself succeeded in ensuring that the request never reached the pope. Priests were very favoured as envoys by the Confederation because of their knowledge of many languages and also because the Irish church network throughout Europe would be available to them. Thus Matthew O'Hartegan, S.J., was in Paris and was succeeded there as envoy by Geoffrey Baron, a layman and nephew of Luke Wadding. The Vatican was generous in response. Pope Urban VIII, through his nephew Cardinal Antonio Barberini, Cardinal Protector of Ireland, arranged that substantial money and arms be sent to Ireland. Cardinal Richelieu of France was contacted by the papal nuncio in that country to arrange aid. Spain too was requested to release Irish military leaders of the calibre of Owen Roe O'Neill and Thomas Preston to lead armies in Ireland in what the Vatican considered, and was encouraged by the Confederation to consider, a religious war.

The Vatican's crowning appointment was Rinuccini, a distinguished curialist and pastoral archbishop, steeped in the reform mentality and spirit of the Council of Trent. Rinuccini was a nobleman of Florence who had a maternal uncle, Cardinal Ottavio Bandini, who was very nearly elected pope in the conclave of 1623 out of which Pope Urban VIII emerged. If Bandini had been elected, Rinuccini would have been an ecclesiastic of the highest possible influence, as cardinal nephew of the pope, and might well have been considered *papabile* himself. He was a deeply religious man of high intellect, kind and urbane in manner, shrewd and perceptive in analyzing problems, people and situations. He was clearly chosen by the sophisticated Romans as admirably suited to deal with a delicate situation. Rinuccini's basic weakness was that he never fully grasped the complexity of the Irish problem, the background

---

[36] There is a great amount of material, manuscript and printed, concerning Rinuccini and his mission to Ireland. Some basic sources are:
Commentarius Rinuccinianus, 6 vols., Gilbert, JJ. *History of the Irish Confederation and the war in Ireland,* 7 vols.
Aiazzi, G., *Nunziatura in Irlanda di Monsignor Gio Baptista Rinuccini Archievescovo di Fermo Negli anni 1645 a 1649*;
Corish, P., 'The Crisis in Ireland in 1648: The Nuncio and the Supreme Council Conclusions' *I.T.Q.,* 22 (1955), 231-57
Hynes, Michael, *The Mission of Rinuccini, Nuncio Extraordinary to Irland, 1645-49*
Ó'hAnnracháin, T., *Catholic Reformation in Ireland The Mission of Rinuccini 1645-49*

out of which the post reformation Ireland had grown, the struggle the hierarchy had to make in order to bring some semblance of tridentine order into the Irish church. Ireland was not Italy.

The instructions which Rinuccini received from Rome are interesting and, in a sense, tell their own story. They are based on reports of Carlo Invernizi, who had been counsellor to PierFrancesco Scarampi in Ireland.[37] Having been briefed on the historical background to the Irish struggle, he was instructed as to the best means of fulfilling his mission well. That mission, it was stressed, was a religious one; the establishment in Ireland of the public and free exercise of the catholic religion. He was to maintain unity amongst the clergy at all costs. The Roman authorities show in the instructions that they suspected something which Rinuccini later found to be true: that some of the senior bishops, such as Patrick Comerford, and other clergy would be content, and might even prefer, the untroubled private exercise of the catholic religion rather than the public exercise of it fully in accordance with the strict discipline of the Council of Trent.[38] As regard the attitude to former church lands, Rome had the same advice to offer the nuncio as it had given in the *Decreta pro Recto Regimine Ecclesiarum Hiberniae* in 1633. The nuncio, it was stated, would probably experience opposition from those catholics who held church lands. He was to try to make some composition with them and to obtain an assurance that all such property as might be recovered in the future from the protestants should be given back to the former ecclesiastical owners or be applied to other religious purposes. Those who held lands which had been secularised by cardinal Pole were not to be disturbed. The religious orders were to be encouraged and properly organised. It is of interest to note that Rinuccini was specifically instructed to obtain for the jesuits a parish church in the city of Waterford. We have seen already that the jesuits and bishop Comerford had been in dispute over the possession of the church of St. Peter in the centre of Waterford city. This item placed in the instructions to the nuncio would seem to be Rome's answer to the appeals from Waterford concerning the matter. As we noted earlier, the jesuits eventually received control of the church.[39] The nuncio was also instructed to beware of Ormond and not to agree to a peace which did not contain a guarantee concerning the public exercise of the catholic religion. He was advised that his most trusted episcopal confidants were to be archbishop Malachy O'Queely of Tuam and bishop Heber McMahon of Clogher.[40]

On 10 November 1645 the nuncio arrived in Kilkenny and was given a solemn reception by bishop David Rothe and the clergy and he met with viscount Mountgarrett and the

---

[37] The instructions are contained in *Comment. Rinucc.*, i, 601-20; also in Aiazzi, *Nunziatura*, XXXV-LII. This work has been translated into English, rather unsatisfactorily, by Annie Hutton, *The Embassy in Ireland*

[38] Report of Rinuccini to Rome, after his departure from Ireland, Aiazzi, *Nunziatura*, 397

[39] cf. Supra, 78-82

[40] A few days after the nuncio's arrival in Ireland, archbishop O'Queely was killed in a military skirmish near Sligo. Bishop McMahon was appointed commander of the Ulster army after the death of Owen Roe O'Neill in 1650. Shortly afterwards he too was killed in battle at Scarrifhollis, Co. Donegal, in June 1650

supreme council of the Confederation. He declared afterwards that he detected a certain tension in his meeting with the council and he felt that Mountgarrett was not enthusiastic about his presence in Kilkenny.[41] Reception formalities over, the supreme council briefed the nuncio on the progress which was being made in the peace negotiations with Ormond. They were anxious to secure his support for the proposed peace. They insisted that the Glamorgan treaty, which the nuncio examined, though valid, would have to remain secret for the present lest it compromise the king who was in a very difficult position in England.

Glamorgan himself hastened back from Dublin to Kilkenny in order to meet with the nuncio and to present him with a letter of recommendation from king Charles.[42] Rinuccini, having become conversant with the facts on all sides, declared against those who were anxious to sign a peace with Ormond. He could not agree that the confederates could observe their oath of association while publishing only the political articles of a peace and keeping the religious ones, drawn up with Glamorgan, a secret. The struggle had begun between Rinuccini and what might be termed the Ormondist or peace party in the Confederation. It was a struggle that was to grow and was not to end as long as the nuncio remained in Ireland and as long as the Confederation of Kilkenny remained in being.

Rinuccini, to emphasise his opposition to the making of peace with Ormond brought together, on 20 December 1645, the archbishops of Dublin and Cashel and the bishops of Waterford and Lismore, Ossory, Cork and Cloyne, Clogher, Clonfert and Ferns. They all signed a protest against any possible treaty that would not contain sufficient guarantees for the freedom of public worship.[43] But, not withstanding this protest, the supreme council continued its negotiations with Ormond and eventually on 28 March 1646, the peace with Ormond, subsequently referred to as The First Ormond Peace, was signed.[44] It was a long rambling document. Religious matters were not really included but were rather consigned to a reference to 'his majesty's gracious favour and further concession'. Rinuccini, in Limerick at the time, heard that the peace had been signed and he left Limerick for Waterford where it had already been arranged to hold a national synod of the clergy which he was due to address. On 30 July 1646, while Rinuccini was on his journey to Waterford, Ormond made public the articles of his peace with the Confederation of Kilkenny. On 3 August it was published by the supreme council in Kilkenny and heralds were sent to officially and publicly announce it in the larger towns.

Rinuccini was in combative mood especially since June 1646, when his close friend and ally, Owen Roe O'Neill, had won a significant victory over the parliamentarian party at the battle of Benburb (5 June 1646). The nuncio's morale was further boosted by the welcome he received on his way from Limerick to Waterford. The Commentarius Rinuccinianus describes

---

[41]   Aiazzi, cf. cit., 71-3
[42]   *Comment. Rinucci*, ii, 77-70
[43]   Ibid., ii, 72-89
[44]   Gilbert, *I.r. Confed.*, V, 286-308

with admiration the reception he was given in two of the largest towns in the diocese of Waterford and Lismore: Clonmel and Carrick-on-Suir, (which in fact was Ormond's own native town). It describes his arrival in Waterford city where he was met by the magistrates and was accompanied to the cathedral where bishop Comerford received him with splendid ceremonial and conducted him into the cathedral under a baldachino borne by the city magistrates. The enthusiasm of Waterford city and the town of Clonmel for the nuncio and for his stand against the Ormondist party in the Confederation was also demonstrated by the forcible ejection from both places of the herald sent from Kilkenny to proclaim the Ormond peace.[45]

The convocation of clergy at Waterford examined and discussed the terms of the peace and issued a solemn declaration on it on 12 August 1646. This declaration, signed by the nuncio, the archbishops of Dublin and Cashel, the bishops of Waterford and Lismore, and nine other bishops, Elphin, Killaloe, Clonfert, Leighlin, Ardfert, Killala, Limerick, Clogher, Ferns, condemned the peace. It stated that the clergy, having heard the views of theologians, were unanimously agreed that all catholic confederates who adhered to the peace or who agree with those who favour it are to be considered absolute perjurers. The reason is that in the articles of the peace no mention is made of the catholic religion or of its security, nor is attention paid to the preservation of the privileges of the nation as was promised in the oath of association. Instead everything is referred to the will of the king from whom in the present state of affairs nothing certain can be expected. The declaration by the clergy ends by saying that the question of whether those who favour the peace should be excommunicated or not is being left over to another session of the convocation of the clergy.[46]

Heated letters were exchanged between Kilkenny and Waterford, between Richard Bellings, secretary of the supreme council and the clergy. Representatives were sent by the supreme council to Waterford in an effort to win over the clergy, but to no avail. On 16 August the convocation of clergy dissolved, but on the previous day eight men had been delegated to assist the nuncio in Waterford in the determination of church policy in this delicate situation. Patrick Comerford was one of those chosen, the others being the archbishop of Dublin, the bishops of Clonfert, Clogher, Ferns, and Robert Barry, vicar apostolic of Ross, and Robert Nugent, prefect of the apostolic mission of jesuits in Ireland. This group issued on 17 August the most fateful declaration yet made throughout the whole controversy. The group, acting for all the clergy, solemnly declared excommunicate the commissioners who negotiated the Ormond peace and also all those instrumental in enforcing it. All cities and towns which permitted the proclamation of the peace were interdicted.[47] Clerics who supported the peace and confessors who attempted to absolve those who adhered to it were to be suspended. Catholics were forbidden under pain of excommunication to pay taxes to agents of the supreme

---

[45] *Comment. Rinucc.*, ii, 284
[46] *Comment. Rinucc.*, ii, 340 ff
[47] Placing a place under interdict was a solemn declaration that ecclesiastical functions and ceremonies could not take place in it

council. The clergy were to withhold church revenue. On the same day bishop Comerford and some of the clergy signed a letter to be brought to cardinal Pamphili, Secretary of State in Rome, by Dionysio Massari, dean of Fermo and assistant to Rinuccini in Ireland, in which the nuncio was highly praised and his calumniators denounced.[48]

The publication from Waterford of the ecclesiastical censures against the adherents of the Ormond peace proved a great blow to the supreme council of the Confederation. One could say that real reconciliation became impossible afterwards between the clergy and the Old Irish on the one side and the largely Old English pro-Ormond faction on the other. Ormond, at the request of the supreme council, marched to Kilkenny in an attempt to subdue the opponents of the peace. But the clergy had carried most of the country to the support of the nuncio and the lord lieutenant received no co-operation from most of the provincial towns: Clonmel and Ormond's own Carrick-on-Suir refused to side with him. He had to hasten back to Dublin with his troops in case he would be cut off by the advancing army of Owen Roe O'Neill.[49]

On 10 September 1646 the nuncio and the clergy who were still assembled in Waterford replied to an Ormondist assertion that the clergy wished to sever the connection between Ireland and the crown. They published a declaration of their fidelity to God and to the king. They pointed out that for three years they had sought to come to an agreement with the king. They have contributed over £100,000 to Ormond for the king to help him in his troubles in England. They declared that they would defend to the end the rights of the catholic church and were prepared to lay down their lives for the king, provided he guaranteed their religious liberties. They called on their people to forget their unreal distinction of Old Irish and Old English and unite in the defence of their rights.[50]

For most of August and September 1646 Rincuccini was at Waterford and received hospitality and welcome from the civil and religious leaders of the city. He appears to have stayed at the home of Robert Wadding, a relative of Luke, and, for his protection, the magistrates of the city appointed a guard to remain on watch at all times outside the house.[51] The *Commentarius Rinuccinianus* records that in September 1646 news reached Waterford that Rinuccini's mother had died. She was Virginia Bandini, sister of Cardinal Ottavio Bandini. The nuncio, assisted by the archbishops of Cashel and Dublin and the bishops of Waterford and Lismore and Ferns celebrated solemn office and requiem mass for her soul in Christchurch Cathedral.[52]

In the same month of September Owen Roe O'Neill and his army were near Kilkenny and had declared themselves supporters of the clergy against the supreme council. Strengthened by this good news, Rinuccini and a great number of clergy, assembled at Waterford, decided to

---

[48] *Comment. Rinucc.* ii, 873
[49] Ibid., ii, 356-8
[50] Ibid., ii, 383-6
[51] Meehan, C. P., *Confederation of Kilkenny*, 194, *Comment. Rinucc.*, ii, 385
[52] *Comment. Rinucci.*, ii, 387

proceed solemnly to Kilkenny and assume control of the Confederation. They did so on 18 September 1646. This was a major development and was little short of a clerical coup d'état. It marks the climax of the nuncio's power in Ireland. The supreme council members were imprisoned and a temporary government was appointed with the nuncio at its head. Those appointed to assist the nuncio from the hierarchy were the same bishops as had been delegated to assist him the previous August with the exception of Patrick Comerford. It is not possible to draw any definite conclusion from Comerford's non-appointment. Perhaps, one can only surmise, he may have felt that the clergy had gone too far, particularly in the excommunication and the imprisonment. Most of those imprisoned were of Old English stock like himself. One asks the question at this juncture because in later years, at least, he showed a reluctance to give full support to an open break with the Old English section of the Confederation and he seemed to disagree with the overly robust tactic of the nuncio.

Rinuccini's intention now was to organise a march on Dublin and gain full control of the country for a thoroughly catholic Confederation. Thomas Preston, a colonel in the service of Spain, who had returned to Ireland to provide military help in 1642 and who was not on good terms with his fellow military-man, Owen Roe O'Neill, had been given charge by the Confederation of the army of Leinster. The nuncio now requested him to join with Owen Roe O'Neill and his Ulster army to march on Dublin.

For many reasons, not least the ill feeling between Preston and O'Neill, the march on Dublin was a failure. This failure was a major set-back for the nuncio and his party. In a real sense the prestige of Rinuccini was to decline in the two years left to him in Ireland. An immediate consequence of the failure to take Dublin was that the nuncio felt obliged to have released the members of the Ormondist faction who were in prison.[53]

It is simplistic and somewhat facile to view Rinuccini as the motivation of all that the clergy did in the convocation at Waterford and at other times also. A specialist historian on Rinuccini and on his years in Ireland has written well and skilfully on the role of the Irish clergy and their relationship with Rinuccini.[54] He discusses the Irish hierarchy before the arrival of the nuncio at all, and their capacity for real leadership in the decade 1630-40 as well as their strong and authoritative leadership in the setting up of the Confederation of Kilkenny. During the 1640's, whenever the bishops united around an issue, this was generally accepted by both clergy and laity as the official position of the church. The nuncio undoubtedly received the obedience of many, not all, of the Irish bishops, but they clearly had a mind of their own as was exemplified in the detailed discussion in Waterford concerning the First Ormond peace and their unwillingness to support the nuncio fully in some of the later actions which he took. A certain reluctance seemed to possess Patrick Comerford concerning the Ormond peace and especially

---

[53] Hynes *The Mission of Rinuccini*, 128

[54] O'hAnnracháin Tadhg, 'Lost in Rinuccini's shadow: the Irish clergy 1645-9', Mícheál Ó Siochrú (ed.) *Kingdoms in Crisis, Ireland in the 1640's*, 176-191

over the excommunication and interdict imposed by the nuncio after the Inchiquin truce in 1648. Comerford was one of the signatories of the Second Ormond peace in August 1649.

The year 1647 was a varied one for the Confederation of Kilkenny. A new general assembly (the seventh) met in January. It was a very divided group, but on 18 January all united in order to declare Ireland dedicated to the Blessed Virgin Mary.[55] Quickly, debate resumed, particularly as to the correctness or otherwise of engaging again with the Lord Lieutenant in negotiations leading to another peace. There was much fear that Ormond would make good the threats he had recently been uttering of surrendering Dublin to the parliamentarian forces which were steadily coming over from England. If this were to happen it was generally believed that nothing would save either the royal or the catholic cause. In fact, on 19 June 1647, Ormond did surrender Dublin to the parliamentarians and left the country. It would be well over a year before Ireland would see him again.[56]

1647 had seen not only political set-backs for the Confederation of Kilkenny but also military failure. Preston's army was severely routed in August at Dungan's Hill near Trim by Colonel Michael Jones, the chief parliamentary commander and new master of Dublin. Owen Roe O'Neill had failed to lure Jones into giving battle. Murrogh O'Brien, baron Inchiquin and earl of Thomond, who vacillitated several times in allegiance between parliament and king, was, at this stage, a supporter of the former and was raging through Munster destroying towns and pillaging the countryside.

A major controversy was to develop later concerning Inchiquin and his war of pillage. Side by side with the developing debates concerning a new peace with the absent Ormond there was a frenzy, on the part of the supreme council in Kilkenny, to create a truce with Inchiquin who was destroying Munster and might shortly take Kilkenny itself. A new general assembly (the eighth) gathered in Kilkenny on 12 November 1647. It met for the first session just as fresh news arrived that Inchiquin had literally destroyed the confederate army of Munster, under viscount Taaffe, at Knocknanuss, near Mallow, on 13 November 1647. Waterford county, the main area of the diocese of Waterford and Lismore, had suffered grievously from the scourge of Inchiquin during 1647. In May he had taken Dromana, Cappoquin and Dungarvan. In the autumn he had devastated the historic town of Cashel in county Tipperary. The new supreme council of the Confederation, on which the Old Irish representatives were few, had to deal urgently with the menace of Inchiquin when it met in November. The council was divided between the Old English and the clergy. It decided that negotiations would have to be opened with Inchiquin in a desperate bid to keep him from taking Waterford city and Kilkenny. On 15 April 1648 the council summoned the provincial assemblies of Munster and Leinster to Kilkenny to endorse a truce with Inchiquin. Rinuccini was also invited but he refused to come, strongly declaring his opposition to any weak surrender to such a heretic who had treated the

---

[55] *Comment. Rinucc.*, ii, 506
[56] Rinuccini's report of and expression of indignation at this act of Ormond is contained in a letter to the nuncio in France, 14 August 1647, Aiazzi, *Nunziatura*, 237 ff

Irish catholics so wickedly.[57] The supreme council however went ahead. Envoys were sent to Dungarvan to negotiate a truce with Inchiquin. The council was not in the mood to give prolonged consideration to the protests of the nuncio. As they viewed the situation, Munster would be so much safer if there was a cessation of fighting.

From late January until early April Rinuccini was in residence in Waterford once again, and it was from here that his negotiations with the supreme council in Kilkenny were taking place. He was becoming fearful, possibly even for his life, as his relationship with the Confederation deteriorated. Perhaps he felt more secure in Waterford because of its nearness to Duncannon, one of the finest and best defended sea fortresses in the country. Should it be necessary for him to leave Ireland quickly, Duncannon would be one of the best points of departure. He felt strengthened in Waterford when, in March 1648, the dean of Fermo, Massari, arrived back from Rome with money and some arms for the confederate cause. He also brought with him papal bulls authorising the consecration of nine bishops to vacant sees. Massari also had with him a controversial gift: the sword of Hugh O'Neill, earl of Tyrone, who had died in Rome in 1616. The pope sent the sword to Ireland as a gift for Owen Roe O'Neill, nephew of the earl. It seems certain that it was Luke Wadding who proposed this solemn gesture of support to the pope. The gesture caused much disquiet with the Confederation of Kilkenny. Rome was leaving no doubt where its loyalty lay.[58] As regards the nine new bishops they had all been recommended by Rinuccini. The supreme council had claimed that it should have been allowed exercise its right to have a veto in respect of candidates proposed for Irish bishopricks. Rinuccini refused to consult the council and claimed that Rome alone had the right to appoint bishops. The nine bishops were: Patrick Plunkett for Ardagh, Anthony MacGeoghegan for Clonmacnois, Arthur Magennis for Down and Connor, Oliver Darcy for Dromore, Terence O'Brien for Emly, Boethius Egan for Ross, Walter Lynch for Clonfert, Robert Barry for Cork and Cloyne, Hugo de Burgo for Kilmacduagh. On the 19 March 1648 the majority of these were consecrated in Waterford cathedral by the nuncio assisted by bishop Comerford and other bishops. It must indeed have been an impressive ceremony in a building which some years previously had belonged to the established church. Around this time also the nuncio baptised in the Cathedral, Waterford, four Mahommedans, who probably were traders or seamen.[59]

Reluctantly in late March or early April 1648 Rinuccini, accompanied by many of the bishops, left Waterford and went to Kilkenny where the supreme council was pressing ahead with the arrangement of a truce with Inchiquin. There, on 27 April, the nuncio, the four archbishops and ten bishops, including Patrick Comerford, signed a declaration condemning the proposed truce. The matter of the Inchiquin truce was very serious for Comerford because, according to the proposed articles of the truce, there was to be little safeguard for the catholics

[57]   *Comment. Rinucc.*, iii, 97
[58]   Corish, P., 'Ormond, Rinuccini and the Confederates 1645-9', *N,H.I.*, vol. iii, 328
        Comment. Rinucc, iii, 59-61
[59]   Ibid., iv, 53, 56

and their religion in any areas to be placed under the control of Inchiquin. In the negotiations at Dungarvan, Inchiquin had demanded that Waterford county, much of which he had previously ravaged, should be included in the areas placed under his control if he were to agree to a cessation of the war. Comerford was strong in his condemnation of this proposed clause because most of his diocese of Waterford and Lismore would lose back to the protestants the churches and other property which the catholics had repossessed after the 1641 rising.

On 20 May 1648 the supreme council signed the truce with Inchiquin on terms mainly of his own choosing. Waterford county was included in the areas under his control. By this time, when the truce was signed, the nuncio had left Kilkenny and was at Maryborough with Owen Roe O'Neill, probably for his own protection. Rinuccini received the news that the truce had been signed with Inchiquin. His reaction to the news was very controversial and most would say it was disproportionate. The reasons for this reaction are very complex and have been given detailed attention by scholars of repute in modern times.[60] The complexities are not for this study. The fact is that Rinuccini panicked and called on four other bishops who were with him in Maryborough, Egan of Ross, Magennis of Down and Connor, Barry of Cork and Cloyne, McMahon of Clogher to pronounce excommunication against all who should support the truce with Inchiquin. This pronouncement in the name of all the bishops of Ireland was made at Ferbane on 30 May 1648. The notice concerning the excommunication was posted in Kilkenny and other towns. Within days of hearing this news, the supreme council decided to appeal to Rome against the censure of the nuncio. Rinuccini did not oppose the appeal but he declared that the censure had immediate effect and was to remain in force until Rome had decided on the appeal. From this point on, the nuncio and the Confederation or, at least the supreme council, were in open conflict.

The Irish bishops were in great difficulty, caught between the nuncio and the supreme council. Rinuccini forbade them from attending the general assembly in Kilkenny called for September 1648. It was to be the ninth meeting and, as things turned out, the last of all the meetings of the Confederation of Kilkenny. Despite Rinuccini's opposition eight bishops attended: Tuam, Kilfenora, Killala, Dromore, Ardagh, Meath, Ossory, Limerick. When the session was well under way the archbishop of Cashel, Thomas Walsh, and bishop Patrick Comerford of Waterford and Lismore, arrived in Kilkenny and took part in discussions concerning a proposed Second Ormond peace with the lord lieutenant, who had arrived back in Ireland on 30 September 1648. In general, Rinuccini's supporters did not attend this final general assembly; in particular, the Old Irish bishops stayed away and were henceforth recognised, in a formal way, as supporters of the nuncio against the confederate assembly.

---

[60] Corish P., 'Rinuccini's censure of 27 May 1648', *I.T.Q.* XVIII, No. 4 (Oct. 1951), 322-37;
     --------- 'The Crisis in Ireland in 1648: the Nuncio and the Supreme Council – conclusions', *I.T.Q.*
        XXII, No. 3 (July 1955), 231-57
  O'hAnnracáin, T. op. cit., 199-206
  O'Siochrú, M., op. cit., 172-4, 177-84

The nuncio had attached to the censure of excommunication an interdict on all persons and places which had supported the Inchiquin truce. The bishops were in a very difficult quandary. It was obvious that many of them felt that Rinuccini had embarked on a course of action which would never bring harmony to the country. Five bishops, Dublin, Meath, Ossory, Ardagh and Dromore, wrote to the nuncio, who had now moved to Galway, asking him to adopt a more moderate attitude. His reply was very negative.[61]

Bishop Comerford supported the nuncio in this crisis arising from the Inchiquin truce but it seems that he did so, less out of conviction that the imposition of such censures, such as excommunication and interdict, were prudent, but out of loyalty to the representative of the holy see. In subsequent letters he always insisted on his loyalty to Rinuccini.[62] When the decree of excommunication was announced by the nuncio, Comerford was in Kilkenny. We have no evidence that he had any direct involvement in the negotiations associated with the Inchiquin truce but he must have followed them with interest. He was in a position to observe and judge that, while the nuncio could not but denounce the truce which caused so much hardship to catholics and their church, there were understandably urgent reasons compelling the supreme council to come to some agreement quickly with Inchiquin and halt his murderous campaign. David Rothe, the bishop of Ossory, who at first had been inclined to accept the decree of excommunication, was later convinced, mainly by his jesuit advisers, who were a force in Kilkenny, that the censures were invalid. Thereupon Rothe refused to impose the interdict on the churches in Kilkenny.[63] Comerford, susceptible as ever to Rothe's influence, was inclined to agree with him. He was influenced especially by the consideration that, once an appeal to Rome had been made, the censures should be suspended until the holy see had made a decision. Probably he was prepared to grasp at any legitimate means to save the country and the people from the deadly effects of excommunication and interdict. His subsequent behaviour indicates that he was not enthusiastic for the nuncio's action and that he obeyed out of loyalty to the holy see. On his return to the diocese from Kilkenny he consulted his clergy and came to the conclusion that, in fact, the validity of the censures seemed certain and hence they would have to be obeyed. Consequently, he enforced strictly the interdict in Waterford and wherever in his diocese the cessation was being observed.[64] On 12 June 1648 the supreme council wrote to Comerford deploring the fact that he had closed all the churches and had forbidden the people to attend mass. The council expressed amazement that he should so easily wish to inflict such hardships on the people and forget so quickly the zeal with which they had stood by him in times of persecution. As the diocese of Ossory deserved well from its bishop so surely did Waterford from Comerford. The council considered that his attitude was all the more surprising

[61] Hynes, op. cit., 206
[62] Comerford to Rinuccini, 14 June 1648, *Comment. Rinucc.* iii, 322 ff
[63] Aiazzi, op, cit., 320 ff
[64] Hynes, op. cit., 212
       Letter of Supreme Council to Comerford, 12 June 1648, *Comment. Rinucc.* iii, 320 ff

because, together with the archbishop of Cashel, he had been invited to hear all the facts. The council says that he seemed to have departed from Kilkenny content with the course that had been adopted. He had given as his opinion that the council's appeal to Rome had a devolutive effect so that the excommunication and interdict were suspended pending Rome's decision. The council expressed the hope that he would allow the faithful to use their churches; otherwise the council might be compelled, by virtue of their oath, to confiscate his public property.[65]

Two days later the bishop replied to the supreme council.[66] He declared that, on his return to Waterford from Kilkenny, he had assembled the most learned of the regular and secular clergy in his diocese to discuss the question of the excommunication and interdict. It was their unanimous judgement that the interdict was valid and should be enforced. In acting thus, the bishop states, they were following the rule of obedience and were in no way anxious to cause disturbance or division. He agrees that he did say in Kilkenny that a legitimate appeal would suspend the censures. He gave good consideration to the example of the bishop of Ossory, but the equally important example of other bishops, not inferior in learning and charity, had also to be taken into account. While conscious of his own shortcomings, he accepts responsibility for what had been done in Waterford. He affirms that he alone has full authority over his diocese. Ironically he remarks that the threat to confiscate his possessions cannot have much avail because the enemy (Inchiquin) already had taken possession of the greater part of them. Comerford concludes by telling the supreme council that, even if they deprive him of all that is left because of his simple act of obedience to the sanctions of the church, he will continue to pray that they will govern well and successfully.

The moderate, almost apologetic, tone of this letter would indicate that Comerford sympathised with the anguish of the supreme council in the dilemma caused by the nuncio's strong action. In the letter he makes no attempt to defend the necessity or prudence of the nuncio's action. He deals merely with the validity of the censures and with his own obligation to observe them. It does seem likely that his own personal opinion was that the censures had been imprudently levied. On the same day that he replied to the supreme council he also wrote to Rinuccini who was in Galway[67] He professes his complete obedience to the nuncio but does not comment on the prudence or otherwise of the excommunication and interdict. He remarks that the imposition of the interdict had been very difficult in Waterford. It is, however, being observed in all the churches of the city, although some members of the regular clergy, claiming privileges, do not hesitate to declare the interdict suspended and they proceed to conduct worship in some private houses. He reminds the nuncio strongly of the intense strife caused by the imposition of the censures, and he stresses the discredit that is being heaped on the bishops

---

[65] *Comment. Rinucc.*, iii, 320 ff
[66] Ibid., iii, 321
Moran, *Spicil. Ossor.*, i, 308
De Burgo, Thomas, *Hibernia Dominica,* 898
[67] *Comment. Rinucc.* iii, 322

at the present time. There is no-one to protect the bishops. He refers to the possibility of the supreme council proceeding against him by force. As a consolation and favour he asks the nuncio to allow himself the privilege of celebrating mass secretly in his private oratory with the assistance of a server, and of confessing his sins to an approved confessor. He says, with that pessimism that was characteristic of him, that there are many in Waterford who are pleased at the prospect of the bishop being deprived of his possessions.

As in Waterford, so also in Clonmel were the churches closed and the interdict, by and large, observed. In fact, of all the Munster dioceses the interdict seems to have been most rigidly enforced in Waterford and Lismore. In the archdiocese of Cashel its observance was almost impossible because the supreme council had strong control there. In Limerick, while many of the clergy obeyed, the bishop, Edmund O'Dwyer, opposed the censures. The bishop of Kilfenora, Walter Lynch, adhered to the council party against the nuncio. The remaining bishops of the province, while obedient to the nuncio, could do little or nothing to enforce his will. Inchiquin during his campaign had occupied the cathedral of Cloyne, and protestant services had already resumed in it. The bishop of Cork and Cloyne, Robert Barry, was constantly with the nuncio in the west of Ireland so could not personally exercise much jurisdiction in his distant diocese in the South.[68]

From Galway Rinuccini replied to Comerford's letter on 6 July 1648.[69] He expresses high praise for the obedience and loyalty of Waterford and its bishop. He tells Comerford that he has arranged with the franciscan provincial to remedy the matter of the regular clergy who claim privilege to release them from observing the censures. The nuncio is very happy to allow the bishop celebrate mass. The same privilege can be given to the regulars who are obedient; they may have one mass each day in their house. Similarly, the secular clergy, provided the mass is celebrated behind closed doors and that it has been made known that permission to so celebrate has been obtained. Rinuccini asks Comerford to help him convene a full assembly of clergy in order to discuss the censures.

Comerford wrote to Rinuccini again on 17 July 1648 regretting that it would be impossible for him to leave Waterford and attend such a meeting. This letter is depressing. The enemy cavalry, he states, surround him on all sides; he is sure that he would meet his death if he should fall into their hands. He says that, because of his stand with the nuncio in the crisis, not only the heretics but his own catholic subjects are against him:

> Non solum haeretici sed et catholici frendent in me dentibus suis, et malevolentiam suam celari nescientes illam apertis verbis produnt.[70]

---

[68] Hynes, op. cit., 212-14
[69] *Comment. Rinucc.*, iii, 431
[70] "Not only the heretics but also the catholics gnash their teeth against me, and, not knowing how to hide their malevolence, they attack with open words"

Because of his precarious position, he tells the nuncio, his clergy and friends dissuade him from making the journey to meet Rinuccini. His health too, he says, is poor. He concludes his letter by asking the nuncio to grant relief to them all who groan under the penalty of the interdict.[71] While still loyal to the nuncio, Comerford here appears to be deliberatly painting an excessively depressing picture of his plight in order to avoid further aggravation of his position by having to attach himself to the nuncio as an adviser. He clearly is not anxious to be so removed from his diocese as was his neighbour bishop Robert Barry of Cork and Cloyne.

As he remarked in his two letters to Rinuccini in the summer of 1648, Comerford was very perturbed by the damage that was being done in his diocese by the imposition of the interdict. In November 1648 he and his dean, Robert Power, together with the leading members of the regular clergy in the diocese, wrote to the nuncio and openly asked that the interdict be lifted.[72] This letter reads as a pathetic plea from well meaning priests who, having done much to build up the church in recent years, now see most of their efforts being negatived by the imposition of the interdict. They point to the fact that they have been six months groaning under the rigid observance of the censures, which are not being observed at all, or at least not so strictly, in neighbouring towns and cities. They ask for a relaxation for the following reasons: each day they sadly witness the decline in the devotion of the people who hitherto had been good and pious catholics. There are infinite dangers to souls arising from the deprivation of the sacraments and the mass. It is being threatened that the heretics will occupy the churches which the catholics have vacated, and all the good results of the rising of 1641 will have been lost.. The catholic clergy are still largely dependent on the charity of the people and there is no guarantee that the people will continue in their generous disposition when they are being denied continually the spiritual services of the priests. Finally the Waterford group feel that they, being innocent, are bearing unduly heavy penalties for the guilty. At the same time the clergy of Clonmel sent a similar plea to the nuncio to have the interdict lifted.[73] Similar pleas had also come to the nuncio from other towns such as Galway, Wexford, Limerick and he had agreed to the lifting of the interdict. We have no formal or written information that he behaved similarly towards Waterford and Clonmel but it is surely reasonable for us to assume that he did.[74]

A keen theological and canon law debate was taking place, and was to continue for decades to come, concerning the validity of Rinuccini's censures. The nuncio got his own personal canon lawyer, Walter Enos, to draw up a defence of the censures. The result was a

---

[71] *Comment. Rinucc.*, iii, 432 ff
[72] Ibid. iii, 566. The letter is signed by bishop Comerford; Fr. Peter Strange, prior of the dominicans, Fr. Joseph Everard, guardian of the franciscans, Fr. John Hartery, cistercian, Fr. Michael Hackett, precentor of the cathedral, Fr. Edward Clare, jesuit rector, Fr. Robert Power, dean of Waterford.
[73] Ibid., iii, 556 ff.: signed by Thomas White, vicar of Clonmel, Edmond Bray, guardian of the franciscans, Thomas Prendergast (doctor of theology), John Goghe (sic) rector of Jesuits.
[74] Hynes, op. cit., 233

'Vindication of the Clergy'.[75] This document denounced the supreme council and showed that Rinuccini had the necessary authority to inflect such penalties. The supreme council got its own expert advice. It requested bishop David Rothe of Ossory to obtain the opinions of theologians in Kilkenny on a list of queries concerning the censures and the appeal against them to Rome. Peter Walsh, a franciscan, who in later years was to receive notoriety for his royal remonstrance of 1662, produced the answers to the queries submitted. His work was signed by bishop Rothe and a number of theologians. The jesuits were particularly prominent in opposing the nuncio on the validity of the censures, at least as to their binding force while an appeal had been sent to Rome.[76]

From the controversy eight bishops are clearly seen as opponents of the nuncio's action. These bishops refused to accept the censures. The bishops were: province of Munster: Edmund O'Dwyer of Limerick, Walter Lynch of Kilfenora; province of Leinster: David Rothe of Ossory; province of Ulster, Thomas Dease of Meath, Oliver Darcy of Dromore, Patrick Plunkett of Ardagh; province of Connaught: Archbishop John Bourke of Tuam, Francis Kirwan of Killala. The nuncio was unmoved by pleas made to him from some of these bishops to take a more moderate attitude to the Inchiquin truce. The eight bishops attended the ninth and final general assembly of the Confederation of Kilkenny, beginning on 4 September 1648, and they joined in the declaration against Rinuccini.

On 30 September 1648 Ormond, the lord lieutenant returned to Ireland. He met with Inchiquin and was assured of his loyalty. Inchiquin had left the parliamentary cause and now was a loyalist once again. Then Ormond moved to his own seat or residence of Carrick-on-Suir and began to negotiate with representatives of the Confederation in relation to the Second Ormond peace. At Carrick-on-Suir he was met and welcomed by the archbishop of Tuam, John Bourke. At Kilkenny he received the welcome of seven of the bishops who had declared against the nuncio. On 18 October the general assembly of the Confederation of Kilkenny appointed commissioners to conclude a peace with Ormond. This was done despite the fact that, in a real sense, Ormond was by now almost a man of straw. The king, whose representative he was, was about to be arrested and put on trial for his life. In fact the Second Ormond peace was signed within just two weeks of the execution of king Charles which took place at Whitehall on 30 January 1649.

---

[75] *Comment. Rinucc.*, iii, 299-305
The *Vindication of the Clergy*, 15 June 1648, is signed by the bishops of Clogher, Cork and Cloyne, Ross and Down and Connor.

[76] Corish, P., 'The Crisis in Ireland in 1648: the Nuncio and the Supreme Council: conclusions', *I.T.Q.* xxiii, No. 3 (July 1955), 231-7
The jesuits' part in the controversy was the subject of a complaint by Rinuccini to Rome, letter to cardinal Pamphili, 16 June 1648, Aiazzi, op. cit., 320 ff. The jesuit general in Rome sent a special visitator, Verdier, to enquire into the matter. Those bishops and members of the supreme council who did not favour the nuncio, praised the jesuits highly: cf. letter of archbishop of Tuam and bishops of Ossory, Meath, Killala, Limerick, Kilfenora, Dromore, to Verdier, 20 January 1648, jesuit general archives, Rome, *Anglia* 29, f. 25.
Similar letter from same to same, APF, SOCG, 298, f. 45R. There is also a letter from the supreme council to Verdier, 29 January 1648, jesuit general archives, Rome, *Anglia*, 29, f. 25

On the same day that Ormond had landed in Cork, 30 September 1648, two special envoys from Rome landed at Waterford: bishop Nicholas French of Ferns and Sir Nicholas Plunkett, brother of the bishop of Ardagh and chairman of the confederate general assembly. They had been sent to Rome to support the appeal of the supreme council against the nuncio's censures. They did not return empty-handed. They brought a letter from pope Innocent X to the bishops of Ireland approving their efforts to secure the rights of the church and insisting on the necessity of harmony and unanimous action. They also brought a letter from Cardinal Roma, addressed to Rinuccini, declaring that there were divided views in Rome concerning the prudence of his actions in imposing the censures.[77] French and Plunkett disclosed the contents of both letters to the general assembly in Kilkenny and, in a genuine effort to reconcile the opposing sections in the Confederation, they gave a more benign account of Rome's views on the whole matter than was the case. The nuncio, almost under siege in Galway, felt that his standing and influence was eroded by the two envoys. He was convinced, quite correctly, that Luke Wadding in Rome was mainly responsible for the two letters. Later, when the nuncio returned to Rome, he refused to associate with Wadding.[78]

These letters and the encouraging speeches of bishop French and sir Nicolas Plunkett gave some hope to the supreme council and to the eight dissenting bishops who had opposed the nuncio. These bishops now invited the rest of the hierarchy to come to Kilkenny for discussions in November 1648. From Galway Rinuccini forbade the bishops to accept the invitation, but the archbishop of Cashel and the bishop of Waterford and Lismore and the bishop of Emly had already answered the invitation. Before he had reached Kilkenny the bishop of Emly, Terence O'Brien, heard of the nuncio's prohibition and he returned home. But archbishop Walsh and Comerford had arrived at Kilkenny and stayed there. Later Rinuccini asserted that these two bishops had not openly disobeyed his prohibition but had been deceived and, having arrived in Kilkenny, were prevented from leaving it again.[79] Their presence was important in order to make up the number without which the subsequent peace with Ormond could not have been signed. While it is possible, and even likely, that Walsh and Comerford may not have been aware of the nuncio's prohibition when they went to Kilkenny, Rinuccini is probably exaggerating in his implication that they were almost forcibly detained there. In the case of Comerford, at least, it would appear that he had been most anxious to achieve harmony at all costs and anxious to undo the deadly damage caused by the censures. He never, in the few subsequent letters of his which survive, protests that he was coerced in any way to take part in what occurred at Kilkenny. In fact, the authors of the *Commentarius Rinuccinianus* seem aware

---

[77] *Comment. Rinucc.* iii, 668
Carinal Giulio Roma, archbishop of Porto and Santo Rufino was a member of the congregation for Irish affairs in Rome.
[78] For a treatment of this question cf. Canice Mooney, 'Was Wadding a Patriotic Irishman?', *Fr. Luke Wadding Commenorative Volume,* 15-92
cf. also Corish, P., 'Bishop Nicholas French and the Second Ormond Peace 1648-9' *Irish Historical Studies,* 6 (1948), 83-100
[79] Aiazzi, op. cit., 372

of this fact. While they are of the opinion that Walsh and Comerford were in a different category from the rest of the dissenting bishops, they do not consider them free from blame for acting as they did in Kilkenny.[80] It would seem that, just as Comerford originally stood by the nuncio in his imposition of the interdict because of his loyalty to the holy see, so now he was only too relieved to avail of the alleged condonation by the holy see of the activity of the dissenting eight bishops and to join them in their efforts to obtain a second peace with Ormond.

On 17 January 1649 the second peace with Ormond was agreed. Comerford signed the agreement.[81] The Old Irish bishops had not come to Kilkenny. The eleven bishops who signed were all of Old English stock. The impression was created, wrongly in fact, that the split in the Confederation of Kilkenny was between the nuncio and the Old Irish bishops on the one side and the Old English bishops on the other.

The Second Ormond peace was a peace which, even in theory, marked little advance on the First Ormond peace of 1646. In fact, it offered the catholics little or nothing because the articles in it for the toleration of the catholic religion were to be left to the good will of the king to grant. It was indeed very unlikely that the king would ever be in a position again to grant any concessions to the Irish. In fact the king was dead within two weeks of the signing of the peace. The catholics, according to the terms of the peace, were not granted their churches or benefices. All that was declared was that the present possession should not be disturbed until a parliament of the king should impose a final solution. In actual fact Inchiquin, who was now once again on the side of Ormond and the king, interpreted the article on church property as entitling him to all church property in the dioceses of Ardfert, Cork and Cloyne, Ross, Waterford and Lismore. Comerford, in agreeing to the peace, had really surrendered the possessions of the church in his diocese.[82] A consequence of this peace was that the Confederation of Kilkenny was dissolved and a commission of trust was set up to co-operate with Ormond in administering the catholic quarters of the country. The bishops who had signed the peace also sent a circular letter around the country declaring that, despite appearances, the rights of the catholics were safeguarded.[83] In fact the signing of the Second Ormond peace was the formal undoing of all that had been achieved by the Irish catholics, Old Irish and Old English, since arms were first taken up in 1641. The only real justification for the action of those who signed it was that they believed, as indeed was only too true, that their greatest enemy, the English parliament, would soon put into effect its intention of completely subduing Ireland. What was needed above all, they felt, was unity. They had failed to find unity amongst themselves or under Rinuccini. Perhaps they would find it under Ormond. In fact, their efforts were in vain. The Irish cause was lost at this stage, even if the peace with Ormond had never been signed. The Confederation of Kilkenny

---

[80] *Comment. Rinucc.*, IV, 39-41, 106
[81] Ibid., IV, 204
[82] Hynes, op. cit., 246
[83] *Comment. Rinucc.* IV, 38

had burned itself out in dissension and bitterness. Soon the Cromwellian armies would deliver the *coup de grace*.

The signing of the Second Ormond peace marked the end for Rinuccini. The signing, followed immediately by the execution of the king, made firm the nuncio's resolve to leave Ireland. On 23 February 1649 he sailed form Galway.[84] His mission, at the beginning so full of hope, had ended in failure. This failure must partly be laid at the feet of his own inflexibility and intransigence.[85] It is too facile to hold against him that he did not understand the situation in Ireland. His massive correspondence reveals a remarkable grasp of the divisions and complications in the country. For an Italian, who knew very little English, his zeal and energy in acquainting himself with the state of affairs was very commendable. Rinuccini's mission could probably never have succeeded. One wonders, as might have happened in a more benign and ecumenical time, if the two central players in the Irish scene in the 1640's, Rinuccini and Ormond, had met and discussed matters in a constructive and tolerant manner, would the outcome have been different? Probably not. They never met and they never wanted to meet. The tragedy of Rinuccini, perhaps, was that his behaviour, prompted primarily by zeal for the catholic cause, in the end served only to increase further the division between the different groups in Ireland, and even extended that division deep into the ranks of the catholic hierarchy. Reconciliation was difficult afterwards and for more than thirty years division was to continue amongst the Irish clergy, at home and on the continent of Europe, concerning the validity of the censures of 1648 and the necessity, or not, of obtaining absolution in relation to them from Rome. The division between the Old Irish and the Old English had been in Ireland for centuries before Rinuccini and it was still sufficiently strong in the seventeenth century to make the success of the confederate experiment very difficult indeed. More than any other figure the lord lieutenant, Ormond, could be said to have caused the ruin of the Irish cause. His control over the Old English had been very strong. He spared no effort to divide the Confederation and to discredit the nuncio. He succeeded in both.

In a precise and profound way Patrick Corish sums up the failure of Rinuccini in the conclusion of the relevant chapter in the New History of Ireland vol. 111[86]

> Inevitably, he was to be accused of dividing the Irish catholics by his intransigence, but if he left them divided he also found them divided, and divided on an intractable issue with no precedents to point to its solution, mainly the legal basis for the existence of the Catholic Church under a Protestant ruler. Shortly after his arrival he faced a crisis in which he could not follow his instructions to secure the position of the church while at the same time keeping himself clear of political issues. He decided not to allow the essential interests of religion, as he saw them, to be put at risk, and it

---

[84] Hynes, op. cit., 252
[85] Corish, P., 'The Crisis in Ireland in 1648', *I.T.G.* XXII No.. 3 (July 1955), 234-7
[86] Corish, P., 'Ormond, Rinuccini and the Confederates', 1645-9' *N.H.I.* vol. iii, 334-5

is hard to see how he could have decided otherwise. He might be criticised for not having a clearer or more flexible view of what was really essential, but in the last resort this is to fault him for not being greatly in advance of his time, for not having found the answer to a problem to which there was no contemporary solution. He might perhaps with more reason be faulted for the inflexibility of his tactics, especially in the excommunication of 1648, but excommunication had been successful in 1646, and, if at that time he had not taken the course he did, would he have had any alternative to leaving the country and confessing his mission a failure as he had to do three years later in 1649?

Bishop Comerford emerges from the whole affair in a rather ambiguous light. From the beginning he had taken his stand with the other bishops in helping to organise the Confederation of Kilkenny. He set his face against the tendency to make too hasty a peace with Ormond in 1646. He seems to have gained a considerable prominence in being chosen with bishop McMahon of Clogher to check the tendencies of the Ormondists in the Confederation in July 1645. Later, in August 1646, he was chosen again to help the nuncio in preventing the signing of the First Ormond peace. His loyalty to and respect for Rinuccini were unquestionable. The nuncio spoke highly of his treatment in Waterford. In his report to Rome at the end of 1649 he refers in glowing terms to that city's loyalty:

> Inter quas omnes urbes referi nullas sedis apostolicae reverentiores Waterfordia in Logenia et Galvia in Conacia.[87]

For two long spells Comerford must have been in very close contact with the nuncio while the latter resided in Waterford: 21 July – 18 September 1646, when the great clergy convocation was held which condemned the First Ormond peace; the second was in the early months of 1648 when Rinuccini was negotiating with the supreme council on the proposed Inchiquin truce. He showed special support for the nuncio in his imposition of the interdict in 1648, despite the misery and unpopularity which resulted. However, eventually he seems to have become weary of the endless argument and division. In his letters, written later from exile in France, he repeatedly deplores the fact that it was such division which ruined the Irish cause.[88] Like many of the other bishops he probably felt that Rinuccini had gone too far in his reaction to the Inchiquin truce. It was no longer 1646 when the confederate position had been so strong that it had seemed insane to give in to Ormond. In those circumstances he himself had been in full

---

[87] *Comment. Rinucc.*, V, 464. The nuncio errs in placing Waterford in the province of Leinster (Lagenia): 'Of all the cities I recall none were more reverent towards the Apostolic See than Waterford in Leinster and Galway in Connaught' cf. also Aizzi, op. cit., 418

[88] Comerford to Cardinal Pamphili Secretary of State, St. Malo, 3 March 1651 *Spicil. Ossor.*, I, 363 ff. Same to Rinuccini, 23 March 1651, *Comment. Rinucc.*, V, 80-82

agreement with the nuncio's excommunication. But a truce with Inchiquin, even on terms that were not too satisfactory, surely, to some extent, could be understood and excused. No-one knew better than Comerford, from the havoc caused in his diocese, the need there was for a respite of some kind. It is likely that, while he did not agree with the aspect of the truce which might have the effect of placing much of the church property in his own diocese under Inchiquin's control, he may not have considered the signing of the truce and the immediate relief that might flow from it, so unpardonable as to merit the heavy sanction imposed by Rinuccini. Comerford, like Luke Wadding and so many other catholic clergy, was a member of the Old English class and it cannot have been easy for him throughout this whole period to go against his racial loyalty and place himself without qualification in the camp of the nuncio and the Old Irish. He must naturally have had sympathy with the strong loyalty to the king and the anxiety of many of his kinsmen concerning the possession of their property. It would, one is compelled to argue, be unfair to judge him severely for his final defection from the nuncio and for his part in the signing of the Second Ormond peace in January 1649. It was the imposition of the interdict that drove him, as it did so many other bishops, priests and laity, to desperation. It was heart-breaking for many of them to have to declare their own kinsmen excommunicate and to shut against them the doors of the churches which those same kinsmen had done so much to re-open.

Chapter Eleven

FALL OF WATERFORD: BISHOP COMERFORD'S EXILE AND DEATH

1649 was indeed an eventful year. The Second Ormond peace was signed on 19 January; the Confederation of Kilkenny ceased on that day; the king was executed on 30 January, nuncio Rinuccini sailed from Galway for Brittany and thence to Rome on 23 February; Oliver Cromwell arrived in Ireland on 15 August. By the end of the year he had subdued much of the country. It was a year when the landscape of Ireland changed with much pillage and death, when the ecclesiastical landscape was sweepingly altered; perhaps most serious of all it was a year when plague swept through the land, beginning, it is thought, in Galway and reaching every town and countryside. The plague was to last for several years.

After the execution of the king and the establishment of the commonwealth, Cromwell and parliament felt the need to protect the new English state from outside dangers such as royalist forces from Ireland and Scotland. Ireland was the first to be dealt with and, indeed, was to be taught a stern lesson. The memories and vivid accounts of the massacres of 1641, particularly in Ulster, added a severe edge of vengeance to the Cromwellian campaign.

The Cromwellian conquest has been well researched and described.[1] Here we just hint at the general picture. By the end of 1649 Cromwell's forces controlled the country east of a line from Derry through Newry, Dundalk, Drogheda, Trim, Dublin, New Ross, Wexford, Dungarvan, Cappoquin, Youghal, Cork, Bandon, Kinsale and Mallow. By May 1650, when Cromwell left for England, this line had been pushed well westward to include Carlow, Kilkenny, Thomastown, Fethard, Clonmel, Macroom. By the end of 1650 Waterford and Duncannon had fallen and the only large towns left unconquered were Limerick which surrendered in November 1651 and Galway which surrendered in May 1652.

Cromwelliam forces had overrun the entire diocese of Waterford and Lismore; castles were attacked and taken: Kilmacthomas, Kilmeaden, Dunhill, Dromana. All the main towns were taken, some by force, some surrendered: Waterford city, Dungarvan, Carrick-on-Suir, Clonmel, Cahir, Cappoquin. Bishop Comerford was confined to a plague-stricken city of Waterford. In little more than one year all had changed.

Our information on Comerford's final days in his diocese comes mainly from two letters written by him to Rome from France. In them he describes the horror of the last months before Waterford was compelled to surrender to Cromwell's general and son-in-law, Henry

---

[1]   Corish, Patrick, 'The Cromwellian Conquest, 1649-53', *N.H.I.*, vol. iii, 336-52
      ----------   'The Cromwellian Regine, 1650-60', op. cit. 353-86
      Barnard, T.C., *Cromwellian Ireland: English Government and Reform in Ireland, 1640-1660*
      Murphy, Denis, *Cromwell in Ireland*
      Fraser, Antonia, *Cromwell Oor Chief of Men*

Ireton, on 10 August 1650.[2] He says that the city was besieged for eight months and no help or reinforcements were received from outside. The greatest enemy of all was the plague which was sweeping through Ireland at the time, but which attacked Waterford with particular ferocity. The casualties, between citizens and soldiers, numbered about five thousand. Other contemporary accounts corroborate the truth of the bishop's report concerning the plague.[3] At last when there was practically no ammunition left he (Comerford) advised the city commissioners to surrender. They did so. The only condition they could get for their bishop was that he should leave Ireland within three months. A contemporary account has survived which depicts the bishop being turned out of his house on the Mall and general Ireton lodged in his place. The cathedral was inhabited by the parliamentary soldiers and mock sermons were delivered from the pulpit.[4] Comerford himself later recalls that the churches and altars were profaned and transformed into sleeping quarters and stables. No longer was mass celebrated or sermons given or sacraments administered. What priests were spared from the plague were expelled by the enemy.[5] A jesuit report to which reference was made in an earlier chapter corroborates this statement by the bishop. The report states that Waterford, after its fall to Ireton, was desolate; the life of the church was completely suspended and all the hard work of Comerford's twenty years' episcopacy seemed undone.[6]

Shortly after the fall of Waterford bishop Comerford left Waterford for the continent. He sailed from Duncannon. After a hazardous journey he found his way to St. Malo on the coast of Brittany. Most of the other bishops in Ireland were also forced into exile by the Cromwellian administration. St. Malo was a noted seaport where many Waterford merchants traded and some of them had settled there. Families with the name of Hayes, Wall, Fitzgerald, Gough in the town, had strong Waterford connections. Comerford may have resided in St. Malo with relatives and friends of his own.[7] He spent some months in St. Malo where his health appears to have been poor. He wrote from there to the cardinal protector of Ireland, Pamphili, saying that he intended to remain there until he should be aware of the outcome of the war in Ireland. If things improved he would return to his diocese as quickly as possible. Otherwise he did not know what he would do.[8] In fact, probably seeing that the Irish cause was hopelessly lost, he soon afterwards left St. Malo and settled in the city of Nantes. Nantes was a well known haven of refuge for Irish ecclesiastics at this time. Even more so than at St. Malo, there

[2] Comerford to Carinal Pamphili, St. Malo, 3 March 1651, *Spicil. Ossor.*, I, 363-5
     Same to Rinuccini, 23 March, 1650, *Comment. Rinucc.* V, 80-82
[3] Letter of John Fodder to Lady Percival, 16 Aug 1650, *Report on the Manuscripts of the Earl of Egmont*, i, 496
[4] 'Ireton in Waterford'.*Waterford Arch. Soc. Jn.*, 191-2
[5] Comerford to Cardinal Pamphili, op. cit., 363
[6] Report in jesuit general archives, Rome, *Anglia 41, Hiberniae Historia, 1599-1692* ff. 336V – 342V
[7] O'Connor, Thomas and Lyons, Mary Ann (eds.), *Irish communities in early modern Europe*; Lyons, Mary Ann, 'The emergence of an Irish community in Saint-Malo 1550-1710', O'Connor, T., (ed.) *The Irish in Europe*, 107-26
[8] Fr. Patrick Hackett, O.P., in a letter to Rinuccini, 21 April 1651, tells him that Comerford is still in St. Malo;
     cf. also Comerford to Pamphili, 3 March 1651, Moran, op. cit., i, 364

were many traders and merchants. Several Irish bishops found their way to Nantes during the Cromwellian period, such as Robert Barry of Cork and Cloyne and Patrick Plunkett of Ardagh.[9]

Comerford's health continued to deteriorate after his arrival in Nantes but the capuchins there befriended him and treated him, we are told by the Commentarius Rinuccinianus, with the dignity befitting a bishop.[10] His last days were spent in the capuchin convent of La Fosse, situated on a hill above the city and commanding a splendid view of the river Loire. Here he died on Sunday 10 March 1652 at the age of sixty-six. Notice of his death and the celebration of its octave are to be found in the municipal archives of the city of Nantes.[11]

He was solemnly buried in the Cathedral of S. Pierre, Nantes, in a crypt newly created for the interment of the bishops of Nantes. Ten years later on 7 July 1662 bishop Robert Barry of Cork and Cloyne died in Nantes where he had spent his last ten years of exile acting as auxiliary bishop.[12] Bishop Barry was interred in the episcopal crypt where Comerford had been buried. In life they worked as neighbours in Ireland; in death their mortal remains lie side by side in Nantes. John Lynch records a folk memory that, at the burial of Barry, Comerford's body was found to be incorrupt.[13] Unfortunately, alterations to the choir of the cathedral in the eighteenth century caused the filling in of the crypt, where the tombs of the bishops lay; so the tomb of Patrick Comerford and Robert Barry can no longer be seen. A plaque erected by the Chapter of Nantes in his memory reads:

> "Ici repose très Révérend Père en Dieu Patrice de Comerford, évêque de Waterford et de Lismore en Irlande. Persécuté dans son pays par les factieux d'Angleterre, il se retira en France, ou il trouva sûreté et protection. Plein de confiance dans les Bontés de l'Eternel, il vecut avec patience et supporta les malheurs de cette vie avec resignation. Il mourut l'an de Seigneur 1652"[14]

As we pause at the tomb of Patrick Comerford in Nantes, having attempted to tell his story and mark his involvement in Ireland and in the church of Waterford and Lismore, a few

---

[9] APF, SOCG, 298, f. 47 RV

[10] Comment. Rinucc, V, 82

[11] Archives communales de la ville de Nantes anterieures a 1790. Registres des Paroisses: serie GG, sepultures 210: registeres de la paroisse de St. Nicholas – Sepultures - 1645-1655, f. 171R
"Le quatorzième jour de Mars mil six cent cinquante deux a esté commencé une octave á haute voix pour defunct Monseigneur L'Illustrissime et Reverendissime Père en Dieu Messire Patrice Comerford, vivant evesque di Waterford et de Lismore en Hybernie, frère religieux de l'Ordre de Eremites de Saint Augustin. Lequel décedé en la communion de Notre Mère Sant Eglise le Dimanche mixiesme des dicts mois et an, et le Mardy ensuivant son corps fut solennellement inhume en l'Eglise Cathedrale de Sant Pierre du Nicts Nantes"
"Le vingt et uniesme jours de Mars mil six cent cinquante deux a été faict le service d'octave de defunct Messire Patrice Comerfort, vivant evesque de Waterford et de Lismore"

[12] Bolster, Evelyn, A History of the Diocese of Cork from the Reformation to the Penal Era, 239

[13] Lynch, J., De Praesulibus Hiberniae, ii, 18;
Hurley, P., 'Memoir of Dr. Patrick Comerford, O.S.A., Bishop of Waterford and Lismore, 1629-52', I.E.R. VIII (1887), 1092 quoting from a Ms. History, 'L'Historie Lapidaire de Nantes'

[14] Lynch, J., op. cit., ii, 118

lines pointing ahead at the state of Ireland after his death are in order. A quotation from Benignus Millett O.F.M. sums up, I believe, in a pithy manner what lay ahead:

> The year 1650 saw the noon day splendour of the catholic revival in Ireland rapidly receding before the lengthening shades of pillage and oppression. Religious reorganisation faltered and gradually collapsed in the face of persecution. In the opening decade of the second half of the seventeenth century the Puritans made an all-out, ruthlessly systematic attempt to exterminate Catholicism in Ireland. Their efforts did not succeed, but the Cromwellian settlement put a strong and wealthy protestant ascendancy in control and established a social system that remained unchanged for two and a half centuries. On the return of Charles II the work of reorganising and revitalising the church in Ireland, so successfully directed in the years 1622-49 by the newly-founded congregation *de Propaganda Fide*, was begun again. It continued, with varying degrees of success, for the next thirty years.[15]

During the early 1650's churches, chapels, oratories and religious houses were plundered and desecrated all over Ireland. Three bishops were killed: Boethius Egan of Ross was hanged near Carrigadrohid in May 1650 by order of lord Broghill, son of the earl of Cork; Heber MacMahon of Clogher was killed and his head displayed on the tower of Enniskillen in September 1650; Terence O'Brien of Emly was publicly hanged in October 1651 after the surrender of Limerick. At least one thousand, perhaps nearer two thousand priests, secular and regular, had to leave the country under very real and serious danger of execution. The flow of ecclesiastics to the continent of Europe reached its peak in 1653. We read that there were sixty Irish priests in the city of Nantes in July 1653.[16] There were many more in the cities and towns of Flanders, France, Italy, Spain and Portugal. The priests who remained behind in Ireland led a hunted life in a very furtive church where even the mass-rock was an unsafe altar. 1650-60 was probably the most difficult and cruel decade that the Irish catholic church has ever endured. From mid 1654 till almost the end of 1659 there was only one bishop in the country: Eugene MacSweeney of Kilmore, who was allowed remain because of sickness and old age.

It is generally accepted that by 1656 priests and religious were beginning to return from the continent but it was a matter really of being smuggled into the country. The period of savage persecution was short but its results were to last a long time.

Waterford and Lismore was not to have a bishop again for nineteen years when John Brennan of the diocese of Ossory, was appointed in 1671. Rome was slow in appointing

---

15   Millett, B., 'Survival and Reorganisation 1650-95', Corish (ed.) *A History of Irish Catholicism*, iii, No. 7, 1.
16   Millett, B., op. cit. 5
Mathorez, 'Notes sur les Prêtres Irlandais réfugiés a, Nantes aux XVIIᵉ siècle', *Revue d'histoire de l'eglise de France*, 3, 165-8

bishops because of the dangers to all catholics in the country. In March 1657 Rome sanctioned, as it had done in the early years of the seventeenth century, the appointment, not of bishops but of vicars apostolic to Dublin, Ross, Ossory, Limerick, Emly, Cashel, Clogher, Down and Connor, Killaloe, Ardfert, Waterford and Lismore. The vicars for Waterford and Lismore were former Dean Robert Power who had laboured with bishop Comerford in his last years and who was to continue until the arrival of bishop John Brennan in 1671. Around 1660 there appears to have been a second vicar apostolic, mainly operating in the western part of the diocese, Thomas White, who was a very old man.[17] Rome's next major move in the reorganisation of the Irish church took place in 1669 when Oliver Plunkett was appointed archbishop of Armagh, and archbishops were also appointed to the other provinces, Peter Talbot to Dublin, William Burgat to Cashel, James Lynch to Tuam. Two years later in 1671 bishops were appointed to Waterford and Lismore, Down and Connor, Clogher, Killaloe, Clonfert, Elphin. Times were improving and Rome was becoming confident that the tridentine hierarchical system, which had begun in the time of Patrick Comerford, could be revived. There were troubles still ahead and the infamous penal laws were soon to begin. But the system had withstood and outlived the onslaught of Cromwell and was readying itself to meet new challenges. As the seventeenth century drew to a close it was to be proved that the efforts and achievements of people like Patrick Comerford had not been in vain.

---

[17] Power, P., *Waterford & Lismore, a Compendious History of the United Dioceses*, 15

Appendix A

DECRETA PRO RECTO REGIMINE ECCLESIARUM HIBERNIAE
APF, ACTA, 8, ff.3337R—344V

The decrees here given are those contained in the minutes of the General Congregation of Propaganda for 16 December 1633. Under this date is given the fullest list of the decrees available. As was remarked in the text the first three sections were not sent to the Irish bishops for comment. From bishop Comerford's comments it would seem that the sections 'circa regulares Hiberniae' and 'utrique clero' were not received by him exactly as given here but in the more concise, though substantially unchanged, form in which they are given in the minutes of the meeting on 19 January 1635 (APF, ACTA, 10, 176r—177v)

DECRETA PRO EMINENTISSIMO DOMINO CARDINALI
PROTECTORE HIBERNIAE

Circa promotionem episcoporum in Hibernia ad commendationem magnatum, propter quas plerumque dignos exclude ac indignos vel saltem inutiles ad ecclesias metropolitanas ac cathedrales promoveri contingit, sacra congregatio probavit sententiam eminentissimi cardinalis protectoris, qui dixit se habiturum peculiarem rationem ne propter praedictas commendationes fiant huiusmodi provisiones; ut de caetero digniores ad episcopatus Hiberniae promoveri possint, iussit a rectoribus seminariorum pro ipsa Hibernia erectorum, et a superioribus religionum, procurari notitiam alumnorum et religiosorum Hibernorum qui scientia et moribus idonei fuerint, ac magis in ipsius Hiberniae ecclesiis laboraverint.

De non promovendis subiectis unius provinciae ad episcopatum alterius, ob diversitatem morum et consuetudinem quae in regni praedicti provinciis existit, sacra congregatio censuit ita fieri posse, cum etiam iure communi id sancitum reperiatur; quibus autem committenda sit executio decretorum quae fiunt in curia Romana pro Hibernia, sacra congregatio censuit archiepiscopis et episcopis de quorum dioecesibus erit negotium super quo decretum emanaverit.

De bonis ecclesiasticis occupatis a laicis in Hibernia sacra congregatio censuit nihil hoc tempore rescribendum circa litteras cardinalis Poli eiusque dispensationem, sed concede posse

Circa promotionem regularium ad ecclesias Hiberniae metropolitanas, vel cathedrales, quae plerumque dissidia pariunt, dum episcopi regulares suis faventes religionibus, aliis praeiudicant, sacra congregatio censuit saltem in quatuor metropolitanis saeculares sacerdotes esse promovendos, huiusmodi resolutionem non esse propalandam sed tantum in praxi servandam.

facultatem recuperandi bona ecclesiastica ab haereticis occupata, tam ecclesiasticis quam laicis, addita clausula obligationis ea restituendi veris dominis, restituto pretio a recuperatoribus soluto, ac refectis melioramentis ab eisdem factis.

DECRETA PRO SANCTO OFFICIO, ET CONGREGATIONE PARTICULARI CIRCA REFORMATIONEM FACULTATUM MISSIONARIORUM

De facultatum a sede apostolica episcopis Hiberniae concessarum abusu extra proprias dioecesis, eo quia in illis habetur clausula quod praefati episcopi illis uti possint in tribus regnis Magnae Britanniae regi subiectis, sacra congregatio dixit posse commoneri assessorem Sancti Offitii ut curet per Sanctitatem suam facultates episcoporum restringi ad eorum dioeceses tantum.

De libris contra episcopos et cleros saeculares Hiberniae, et in specie de illo sub nomine Edmundi Ursulani inscripto Examen Iuridicum etc., et de concionibus circa hierarchiam ecclesiasticam, quod scilicet regulares fuerunt ante clerum, sacra congregatio dixit si per Sanctum Offitium non fuerint provisum, esse quam primum providendum, mediantibus generalibus religionum, ac nuntio apostolicae sedis, et in speciali libros quamprimum supprimendos, quia ut scribit archiepiscopus Cassalensis, nisi quantocius supprimatur dictus liber Edmundi, schisma fiet grave, et propositiones in dicto libro contentas quis audeat scribere, aut aliquid edere, quia intellexit multos ex saecularibus iam paratos esse ad scriptionem et editionem librorum de illis.

Relata deinde censura dicti libri Edmundi Ursulani facta a quatuor episcopis Hiberniae, et ab uno vicario apostolico provinciae Casselensis, sacra congregatio iussit copiam dictae censurae remitti ad Sanctum Offitium, cum instantia dictorum episcoporum pro illius prohibitione, ne multiplicantur libri, et schisma fiat inter clerum saecularem et regularem.

Insuper iussit de praedicto libro Edmundi agi cum reverendissimo Bocabella, ut circa illum illa provisio fiat quae de similibus libris fuit facta pro Anglia, Scotia et Gallia.

Circa denique facultates administrandi sacramenta parrochialia, quae missionariis concedantur, quia in Hibernia sunt episcopi et parochi, patres censuerunt in congregatione particulari pro reformatione facultatum a sanctissimo Domino nostro instituta, habendam esse peculiarem rationem ne huiusmodi facultates concedantur in praeiudicium episcoporum et parochorum.

DECRETA PRO REVERENDISSIMO DOMINO DATARIO

De frequentibus dispensationibus quae Romae conceduntur filiis presbyterorum Hibernorum, ut possint promoveri ad ordines, et de brevibus quae circa ordinationes Hibernorum extra tempora, sine dimisoriis et testimonialibus propriorum ordinariorum, expediuntur, et denique de collationibus beneficiorum quae Romae fiunt sine eorundem ordinariorum approbatione Hibernorum, cum scandalo populorum, et contentionibus et litibus plurimis, sacra congregatio dixit his abusibus provideri posse si Sanctissimus Datario et secretario brevium significare dignetur ne huiusmodi expeditiones amplius faciunt inconsulta sacra congregatione de propaganda fide.

Insuper patres censuerunt, si Sanctissimo placuerit, collationes dignitatum, etiam primarum post pontificales, et beneficiorum quorumque hactenus per archiepiscopos et episcopos factas generaliter esse confirmandas, exceptis illis de quibus sedes apostolica iam providit. De vacantibus vero, praelatos praedictos commonendos esse ut eorum notitiam, cum nominibus illorum qui suo iudicio de his provideri possunt, ad sacram congregationem mittant, quae apud sanctissimum Dominum nostrum officis sua interponat, ut ab iisdem praelatis commendati provideantur per viam secretam, et sine impensa.

DECRETA CIRCA ARCHIEPISCOPOS ET EPISCOPOS

De superfluo episcoporum Hiberniae numero, ob quem nimis populi gravantur, et ob necessariae subventionis defectum dignitati episcopali plurimum detrahitur, sacra congregatio censuit huiusmodi corrigi posse per moderationem numeri episcoporum, quae fieri poterit altero ex duobus modi, videlicet, instituendo tres episcopos cum archiepiscopo in singulis provinciis minoribus, et in maioribus quatuor, et assignando episcopatus vacantes institutis episcopis in administrationem, prout eis commodius fuerint, vel instituendo quidem episcopos, ut supra, eisque assignando in administrationem vacantes ecclesias, et per vices et turnum, ita ut ecclesiae quae una vice fuerint in administratione dentur in titulum, et e contra, hancque provisionem significandam esse cleris et populis Hiberniae, ut modus quem illi probaverint, durante schismate tantum et non ulterius ac retineri facilius posit.

De multitudine episcoporum in una provincia, et eorum paucitate in alia, sacra congregatio dixit per ea quae circa excessivum numerum episcoporum dicta sunt satis dispositionem provisum esse, vel per translationem episcoporum nunc posse provinciae accomodari.

De visitatione liminum apostolorum sacra congregatio censuit, attenta paupertate episcoporum Hiberniae, et necessitate residentiae eorum, sanctissimum Dominum nostrum posse cum eis dispensare, sicut dispensavit cum multis episcopis in partibus infidelium, ut scilicet limina praedicta visitare possint per procuratorem etiam non dioecesanum existentem in curia, hancque dispensationem restrigendam esse ad 25 annos proximos futuros.

De visitationibus diocesum et provinciarum Hiberniae, sacra congregatio quoad illas dioeceses, ne nimis populi gravantur, censuit monendos esse episcopos ut sacri concilii Tridentini ordinationem diligenter observant, et gravando eorum conscientias, illis praecipiendum ut moderate se gerant, habitis ratione locorum, personarum, ac negotiorum in visitatione expediendorum.

Quo vero ad visitationem provinciarum, sacra congregatio censuit observandam dispositionem sacri concilii Tridentini ubi concilia provincialia celebrari possunt; ubi vero non poterunt, archiepiscopos debere ad sedem apostolicam recurrere pro obtinendo facultate suas visitandi provincias, signifactis causis ob quas necessaria sit eorum visitatio.

De appelationibus quas episcopi cum praeiudicio suo archiepiscopos nimis facile admittere conqueruntur, congregatio dixit praecipiendum esse praedictis archiepiscopis, ut diligenter observant decretum sacrae congregationis episcoporum de mandato felicis recordationis Clementis 8 die 16 Octobris 1600 edito, quod reperitur impressum epud Quarantum, in summa bullarii, in verbo archiepiscopalis authoritas, 18, authoritas.

De receptione sacri concilii Tridentini in tota Hibernia, sacra congregatio dixit id omnino fieri debere, si potest. Quod attinet ad exemptionem regularium, quia in Hibernia sunt episcopi, sacra congregatio censuit servandas dispositiones sacri concilii Tridentini et constitutionis Gregorii XV de exemptis.

DECRETUM CIRCA VICARIOS APOSTOLICOS HIBERNIAE

Si quae dicta sunt circa superfluum episcoporum numerum ab archiepiscopis et episcopis et clericis Hiberniae fuerint probata, vicarii apostolici cessabunt, quia episcopi in ecclesiis vacantibus, quarum administrationem suscipiunt, suos poterunt constituere vicarios.

DECRETA CIRCA REGULARES HIBERNIAE

De importunis exactionibus eleemosinarum quae fiunt per regulares, sacra congregatio dixit commonendos esse generales, ut abusui omnino provideant, alias provisionis episcoporum demandabitur.

De regularibus qui dum sunt in parochiis vel illis praeficiuntur a suis superioribus, nolunt se subjicere episcopis in pertinentibus ad curam animarum, iuxta sacri Tridentini decreta, et felicis recordationis Gregorii XV constitutionem, sacra congregatio dixit distinguendos esse tres casus. Primus est quando regulares ob defectum sacerdotum ab ipsis episcopis parocchiis praeficiuntur, 2dus, quando a suis superioribus in parochiis unitis vel annexis eorum monasteriis et conventibus deputantur; et in his duabus casibus regulares debere episcopis subjici in pertinentibus ad curam animarum, iuxta praedictum sacrum concilium et constitutionem. 3tius est quando regulares habent missionem ab Urbe, et facultates quae expediuntur a Sancto Offitio, et hoc casu sacra congregatio censuit addenda esse verba quae iura episcopalia et parochialia praeservant circa curam animarum et administrationem sacramentorum.

De religiosis qui divitibus in spiritualibus inserviunt et pauperes deserunt, sacra congregatio dixit monendos superiores regularium illarum religionum quae sunt in Hibernia, ut provideant ne religiosi eis subjecti pauperes necessitatem operariorum habentes in materia tam gravi, animarum scilicet salutem concernente, deserant, sed eis sicut divitibus haec charitatis officia libenter exhibeant.

De clausura quae violator a regularibus ubi servari potest, de eorum vagationibus cum vestibus et equis eorum professioni indecentibus, sacra congregatio censuit superiores reliogionum commonendos esse ut his abusibus omnino provideant.

De novitiatibus qui fiunt in Hibernia sine clausura, et aliis observationibus in novitiis instituendis, ita ut multi dubitent de suis professionibus, sacra congregatio dixit generales super hoc articulo audiendos esse.

Re regularibus in concionibus de ordinariis obloquentibus, sacra congregatio extare Clementinum Dudum de sepultura, de cuius observatione debent regulares a suis superioribus commoneri.

De reliquiis sanctorum quae ob quaestum circumferuntur a cisterciensibus, sacra congregatio respondit id prohibendum esse iuxta formulam a sacra congregatione concilii quaestoribus eleemosinarum praescriptam, cuius tenor est ut sequitur: Delecti ad quaerendas eleemosinas continent se intra limites, et non sint dictarum eleemosinarum participes, istoque munere pie et modeste, sine ullo dolo ullave fraude fungantur, quaestorum nomen nullo modo gerant, non secum ferant ulla privilegia, non reliquias, non minis aut imprecationibus inducant fideles ad eleemosinam praestandam, non petant tanquam debitum aut solitum, neque ulla arte etiam praetextu dicendi cuiusvis Sancti orationem, pecunias vel alia bona extorqueant, sed tanquam a sponte dantibus eleemosinas recipient in usum etc.

Praeterea, nullo pacto praedicent nisi in singulis dioecesibus a locorum ordinariis saltem fuerint semel ad id approbati.

DECRETA UTRIQUE CLERO, ET SAECULARI ET REGULARI, HIBERNIAE

De abusibus tam in clero saeculari et regulari introductis, ut non nisi pecunia aut muneribus acceptis ministrant sacramenta, sacra congregatio iussit moneri archiepiscopos et episcopos, ac regularium superiores, ut current huiusmodi abusus omnino tolli.

De presbyteris saecularibus qui cauponas frequentare dicuntur, cum mulieribus, atque etiam cum haereticis, iussit similiter archiepiscopos et episcopos moneri ut huiusmodi abusus tollant.

De conviviis, tam a clero saeculari quam regulari, etiam cum mulieribus, et haereticis, sacra congregatio dixit idem quod proxime supra.

De sepulturis, sacra congregatio in primis quoad praecedentiam parochum saecularium censuit servandas esse pontificias constitutiones, secundum quas clerus saecularis praecedere debet regularem. 2o. Quoad praesidentiam in officio, dixit servandam esse declarationem eminentissimorum dominorum cardinalium concilii Tridentini interpretum, cuius tenor est: Sacra congregatio concilii saepius censuit, quoties cadavers defunctorum ad ecclesiam fratrum mendicantium deferantur, officia mortuorum et reliqua quae in huiusmodi ministerio adhiberi solent, non a canonicis atque a clero saculari, sed a fratribus obiri et peragi debere.

3o. Circa promissiones etiam bonorum aeternorum fiunt a regularibus, ut ad eligendam sepulturam in eorum ecclesias moribundos inducant, sacra congregatio dixit extare prohibitionem Clementinam Religiosi, quae ab iisdem regularibus servari omnino debet sub poenis in eis contentis.

4o. Quoad quartam canonicam, dixit servandam esse dispositionem sacri concilii Tridentini, sessione 25, capite 13, De Regularibus.

5o. et postremo, quoad eleemosinas quae fiunt in campo pro defunctis aliquot dies ab eorum sepultura, sacra congregatio dixit audiendos esse superiores regularium.

Appendix B

COMMENTS OF BISHOP COMERFORD ON THE DECRETA PRO RECTO
REGIMINE ECCLESIARUM HIBERNIAE: 20 January 1636, APF, SOCG, 140,
ff.43RV & 46R

Fratris patricii episcopi Waterfordiensis et Lismorensis annotationes in decreta transmissa a
Sacra Congregatione de propaganda fide ad commodum ecclesiae regimen in Hibernia
stabiliendum.

Ut iussus proferam quod censeo, dicam brevius, quae res tanta diu desiderat: quamvis
quid certi statuere perdifficile sit in tanta rerum vicissitudine, et persecutionem tempestate, qua
non minus quam marinis fluctibus, haec insula alternis annis undequaque concutitur.

AD DECRETA CIRCA ARCHIEPISCOPOS ET EPISCOPOS HIBERNIAE

Ad 1. Censeo, durante schismate sufficere in provincia Casselensi quatuor episcopos cum
archiepiscopo, nempe Corcagiensem, Limericensem, Waterfordensem et   Laonensem:,
Imilicensem vero dioecesim et Finiborensem, cum vacaverint, in administrationem posse
concede, illam Casselensi, hanc Limiricensi: Ardfertensem autem et Rossensem dioeceses
regendas esse per vicarious generales apostolicos. Plurimum etiam expedire, ut suffragia cleri
dioecesani, et vicinorum episcoporum in provisionibus, quae posthac fient, audiantur: et
quantum fieri potest, eligantur episcopi, et vicarii apostolici de gremio loci.

Ad 2 dico, in provincia Tuamensi, quae indigere videtur episcopis, posse institui unum,
vel alterum episcopum cum iam constitutis, ac proinde translationem episcoporum neque
requiri, neque expedire.

His addiderim, rationi et iuri consonum esse, ut sine commendatitiis ordinariorum, non
dentur in curia tituli dignitatum, aut beneficiorum in his partibus: quia, ex contrario usu
nascuntur quotidie lites et dissidia inter ecclesiasticos, qui advertentes vanissimos titulos sine
discrimine conferri cuilibet petenti, plurimum scandalizantur: indigne etiam ferunt laici catholici
sacerdotes benemeritos, et sibi gratissimos, a parochiis, quibus diu et laudabiliter servierunt,
amoveri per nominales hos beneficiarios, quorum beneficia, fructus, et redditus usurpantur a
ministris protestantibus: reliquum vero sit sacerdotibus, qui invigilant parochiis parochianorum
catholicorum eleemosinis, et libera beneficentia ali, quod genus spontaneae benevolentiae, seu
gratificationis acerrime contendunt laici se impensuros in sacerdotes de gremio loci, vel in
sacerdotes quorum consuetudine, et pastorali solicitudine per plures annos fructuose usi sunt,
non vero in sacerdotes, ut plurimum juvenes, sibi incognitos, et minus dignos, qui sine

commendatitiis ordinariorum istos meros beneficiorum titulos, a curia romana suffirari (?) videntur.

Ad 3. De visitatione liminum apostolorum, assero provide quidem, et merito Sacram Congregationem censuisse: et contrarium quodam modo impossibile esse, durante schismate.

Ad 4. Sancte et prudenter statuitur modus visitandi dioeceses et provinciae.

Ad 5. Pernecessarium esse, ut hoc decretum de appelationibus in integrum observetur.

Ad 6. De receptione decretorum Sacri Concilii Tridentini, utilem et necessarium esse censeo illam constitutionem, quantum tempora ferunt: similiter, et dispositiones Sacri Concilii Tridentini, et consitutiones Gregorii XV de exemptis.

AD DECRETA CIRCA REGULARES HIBERNIAE

Censeo singula salubriter, et iuste ordinate esse: des vix, et ne vix quidem adduci possum, ut credam, quod superiores regularium dignum statuant modum importunes eleemosinarum exactionibus, aut praecipiant suis abstinere a receptione novitiorum, qui (proh dolor) vix ullam aut pietatem aut mortificationem, aut monasticam disciplinam addiscunt in praetensis suis novitiatibus, arbitrantes se omnibus numeris absolutos religiosos esse, suo muneri cumulatissime satisfecisse, si aliquot in anno diebus habitum religionis gestent, et saepius per vicos, et pagos cursitando eleemosinas conquirant. Ad quem abusum penitus tollendum, sicut dignum et necesse est, quod interveniat immediata Summi pontificis prohibitio, sic etiam ad vetandum morem quendam romanae datariae concedendi scholaribus Hibernis indulta, ut extra tempora promoveantur ad sacros ordines, ad titulum missionis, (in qua omnino supervacanei sunt) etiam sine dimissoriis suorum ordinariorum. Nisi itaque severior aliquis obex quantocius isti abusui statuatur, certe tot sacerdotes plerumque indocti, et immorigeri, turmatim repatriantes facient sibi invicem angustias, populum catholicum nimis gravabunt, clerum in vilipendium, et vituperium adducent, ac vagis suis et frequentibus discursibus de dioecesi in dioecesim, de parochia in parochiam, innumerata scandala parient.

AD DECRETA UTRIQUE CLERO COMMUNIA

Ad 1. Quod sciam, non exiguntur apud nos munera, aut pecuniae pro sacramentorum administratione , contra sacrorum canonum, et pontificiarum constitutionum dispositionem, nisi calumniae delatores vitio vertere velint conciliis provincialibus, quod summulam quondam pecuniae satis tenuem statuerint solvendam parochis intuitu laboris in administratione sacramentorum, cum alia media non suppetant, quibus alantur. Parochi praeterea in mandatis habent, ut nunquam, ob non solutionem, pauperes a sacramentorum perceptione reiciant.

Ad 2. Utiliter quidem, et sancte provisum est contra frequentantes tabernas, et sumptuosa convivia celebrantes in festis patronorum, qua de re in nostris synodis provincialibus; et dioecesanis poenalia statuta sunt condita: viderint regularium superiores suis subditis. Praedictis addere liceat, dignum sane esse, quod Summus Pontifex suferat lapidem offensionis, qui cum maximo scandalo adhuc volvitur inter parochos, et regulares circa praecedentiam, et praesidentiam in officiis, quae fiunt pro defunctis in domibus laicorum, qui eligunt sepulturam, vel sunt sepulti in monasteriis: regulares enim contendunt sibi praecedentiam et praesidentiam deberi, si fieret officium in monasterio, similiter etiam in domo laica, quam sibi, propter iniquam temporum conditiones, oratorium constituent, et nominant: asserentes talia oratoria gaudere privilegiis monasteriorum: parochi vero pro suo iure adducunt, quod domus illa, quam regulares sibi constituent, vel nominant oratorium est intra fines parochiae, est mere laica, est conducta ad tempus, subest iurisdictioni ordinarii, ac proinde non gaudere privilegiis et exemptionibus monasteriorum, in grande praeiudicium parochorum.

Omnia ecclesiae et eius sub Christo capiti, qua debeo reverentia, submitto.

Datum e loco nostri refugii in Hibernia hac die 20 Januarii 1636.

Fr. Patricius episcopus Waterfordensis et Lismorensis.

Appendix C

LETTER OF BISHOP COMERFORD CONCERNING THE DECRETA PRO RECTO REGIMINE ECCLESIARUM HIBERNIAE: 25 January 1636, APF, SOCG, 140, ff. 44R-45R

llustrissime Domine.

Quam singulari ecclesiam Hiberniae beneficio devinxeris luculenter testatum est in assidua sollicitudine, et plusquam paterna cura qua optimo ecclesiae regimini in Hibernia abunde prospicis. Et quia non alium laborum tuorum scopum tibi constituis, quam summam Dei gloriam, fidei incrementum, et animarum salutem, augurari tibi, non est quod formidem, foelicem et optatum exitum piisimorum tuorum conatuum; si quid autem in me est virium, si quid meriti, totum id sane tibi, vir ornatissime, puriter et humanissime, voveo. Exemplar decretorum ad me misit metropolitanus minus habens, quem alia, quae mihi contigit vidisse exemplaria: singula decreta spirant prudentiam, scientiam, pietatem, et optimum charitatis odorem: ad quae, pro meo captu, adieci braviusculas annotationes, quas Sacrae Congregationi praesentari rogo. Hactenus autem distuli censum meum de his decretis proferre, ratus, quod sicut in litteris tuis commonuisti, singuli archiepiscopi convocarent suae provinciae suffraganeos, et superiores regularium, et cum eis conferrent, qua ratione, communi pace et concordia memorata decreta executioni demandari possent: sed ut nuper accepi, quatuor metropolitani convenientes clam in unum locum, de singulis decretis iudicium suum tulerunt: arbitrantes forte periculosum, nimis laboriosum, et supervacaneum fore, in turbato hoc rerum statu suffraganeos suos, et superiores regularium in unum adnicere locum. Reliquum igitur est singulis suffraganeis, ut seorsim sententiam suam dicant, pro quorum pietate, zelo, eruditione et prudentia spondere non dubito.

    Quid ego censeam de numero episcoporum in hac provincia Cassalensi breviter dixi, et nunc adiicio, quod sicut ob superfluum episcoporum numerum, et institutionem in dioecesibus quibusdam minutis, augustioribus, et minus commodis, populi aliqualiter gravantur, et ob necessariae subventionis defectu dignitati episcopali nonnihil detrahitur, ita quorundam episcoporum provisiones, in singulis provinciis non vulgarem utilitatem, splendorem, munimen, incrementum, solatium et progressum ecclesiae catholicae in Hibernia adferunt: episcoporum vigilantia, et authoritate clerus tam regularis tum saecularis magis in officio continetur: ecclesiae romanae canones, et concilia vires acquirunt: et innumeris malis obviam itur. Qui vero inter nos avent plurium dioecesium administrationem certe populorum commodo, aut utilitati non prospiciunt, qui in singulis dioecesibus per proprios suos episcopos, vel vicarios generales apostolicos rectius gubernentur; certe maximam et periculosissimam, cui impares sunt, curam improvidi cupiunt: et onus angelicis humeris formidandum sustinent, et satis superque ponderis ferunt: si singuli singulis suis dioecesibus, quibus praesunt, debita sollicitudine invigilent: denique dum amplissima territorii exoptant, nihil aliud, quam longas et latas excursiones, et onerosas, nimisque molestas circuitiones meditantur: quibus episcopali dignitati plus detrahitur, quam necessariae subventionis defectu. Non negaverim tamen dignum esse, ut augustae quaedam et minus commodae dioecesis aut uniantur, aut in administratione concedantur.

Et quia in mentionem incidi de necessariae subventionis defectu, quo nunc laborant episcopi in Hibernia, libet raptim innuere unam ex praecipuis huius indigentiae causis. Oborto schismate Henrici octavi magna pars (ut notissimum est) bonorum ecclesiasticorum a laicis usurpari coepit: et hinc est, quod plures catholicae in Hibernia, vel dono Regis, vel aliquali pecunia enumerata obtinuerint haec bona: alii vero catholici praetio soluto emerunt decimas, et alios redditus ecclesiasticos a protestantibus: alii denique ab iisdem quotannis emunt. Moris autem erat apud hos catholicos occupantes, vel ementes bona ecclesiastica, iuxta monitum cardinalis Poli in sua dispositione, seu potius ad praesciptum iuris divini, naturalis et ecclesiastici, nec non constitutionum nationalium, et provincialium huius regni, in congruam sustentationem operariorum ecclesiasticorum quotannis certam aliquam summulam pecuniae clam elargiri. Sed ecce temporum iniquitatem. Postquam Dei et Sedis Apostolicae providentia, episcopi, vel vicarii apostolici in singulis dioecesibus, et inferiores pastores in parochiis instituti sunt, qui gregi sedulo invigilant, qui sacramenta strenue administrant, qui pondus diei et aestus ferunt, catholici isti laici occupantes vel ementes decimas, obventiones, et alia ecclesiastica bona, clancularibus quibusdam praestigiis perverse obstinante tuentur se non obligari ad quidpiam solvendum catholicis episcopis, vel parochis, et praetendunt hanc esse resolutionem quorundam doctorum virorum anonymorum, qui occultari caute cupiunt, dum mercedem pastoribus debitam ipsi, pro utili data opinione, recipiunt. Operae pretium ergo foret, si Summus Pontifex dignaretur declarare praefatam resolutionem istorum praetensorum sapientum esse erroneum et noxam; et pariter laicos istos occupantes, vel ementes bona ecclesiastica teneri in conscientia censi aliquid annue contribuere episcopis, et parochis ad eorum congruam sustentationem.

Prudenter sane, et pie significasti in novissimis tuis litteris, plures lites, et controversias amicabili compositione hic inter nos terminari posse; nam est valde indecens minutissimas quasque querelas amore vindicate (ut plurimul fit) deferre ad sublimissimam illam curiam, quae tot gravissimorum negociorum undis in dies exercetur. Dedecet etiam viros primarios, et ecclesiae principes tanto odio et ira obcaecari, ut non vereantur sese conviciis et opprobriis lacessere, donec ex parva scintilla magnum tandem excitant incendium; exasperate autem quidpiam in malam partem interpretanter. Non ferunt haec tempora in quolibet summum ius prosequi, aut animositatem exercere, aut aculeos figere: avertat Deus scandala; et donet Eminentissimis Dominis Cardinalibus gratiam discernendi, ubi maior culpa insit, et adhibendi tantis malis opportune remedia.

Pervenit forte ad aures tuas difficultates quae nuper oborta est inter suffraganeos et metropolitanum nostrum de loco celebrandi concilium provinciale: dum metropolitanus locum posceret nunc in extremis et longe dissitis dioecesibus totius provinciae, quarum vix est angulus, in quo non habitant plures haeretici, ex quibus alii sunt magnates, alii equites, alii justiciarii, alii praesidiarii milites, alii ministri regii, et turba multa cleri protestantis et colonorum, in quorum viciniis celebrare concilium provinciale, non solum esset periculosum ipsis praelatis convenientibus, verum etiam laicis catholicis, qui in suis terris, vel aedibus admitterent tam celebrem praelatorum conventum. Suffraganei vero asserunt consonum esse sacris caonibus, quod in congregationibus conciliorum habeatur ratio, ut qui vocentur ad concilium, non fatigentur propter discrimina itinerum; proinde huiusmodi congregationes et conventus debere fieri in loco non multo remoto, imo proportionate respectu eorum, qui debent venire; debere etiam haberi rationem temporis, ut non in hyeme fiant concilia, cum isto tempore, ut plurimum periculosa sit itineratio. Ulterius dicunt dioecesul ipsam metropolitani, et alias duas dioeceses, quae iacent in medio provinciae, e se loca multo commodiora, et habere minora impedimenta, et minus ab haereticis incoli, et aliis commoditatibus magis abundare: ac proinde hanc difficultatem facile componi posse, nisi quis velit nedum in scirpo quaerere, aut supervacuas querelas, et lites exuscitare.

Nisi vererer Eminentissimum Dominum Protectorem saepius arduis districtum negotiis audacter interpellare, liniolas aliquas ad eum missisem; sed ne officio meo omnino deesse videar, quaeso te meo nomine illi plurimam salutem impartiri, et immortales agere gratias pro innumeris, iisque maximis, quibus Hiberniae ecclesiam beneficiis affecerit: pro qua paterna solicitudine, et singulari benevolentia me, meosque apud Deum habebit simper deprecatores.
D. Fernensis (ut mihi significavit D. Ossoriensis) diro calculi cruciatu nuper laboravit: sed, laus Deo, convaluit, et ut diu valeat, nostra omnium in hoc regno plurimum interest, quippe qui nulla in parte egregium non agit praesulem. Sed iam timeo ne epistola haec longius, quam par est, producta, te defatigaverit, et serioribus implicatum negotiis interturbaverit. Vale igitur in seros annos, humanissime vir, et quam hactenus in posterum etiam hanc ecclesiam benevolentia tua prosequi ne graveris, meque solatio gratissimarum tuarum litterarum diu carere non permittas: quamvis difficillimum sit litteras tuto in hac (proh dolor) bellorum tempestate, qua maxima, et praecipua Europae pars saevius iactatur.

Datum Waterfordiae 25 Januarii 1636.

Illustrissimae Dominationis Vestrae addictissimus.

Fr. Patricius Waterfordensis et Lismorensis m.pr.

Appendix D

COMMENTS OF THE FOUR ARCHBISHOPS ON THE DECRETA PRO RECTO REGIMINE ECCLESIARUM HIBERNIAE, 28 NOVEMBER 1635, APF, SOCG, 140, F.33R.

Circa decreta a Sacra Congregatione de propaganda fide ad bonum ecclesiarum Hiberniae regimen et transmissa ad nos, ut quae regno commode incommodave sint significemus ita sentimus.

Circa primum decretum de superfluo episcoporum numero censemus in provinciis maioribus sufficere tres institui episcopos, ut in minoribus duos episcopos cum metropolitanis, et reliquos episcopatus debere in administrationem assignari iuxta tenorem decreta vicinioribus episcopus sicut metropolitano et suffraganeis suis melius videbitur expedire. Unde sentimus nullos deinceps vicarios apostolicos instituendos; institutos vero vicarios apostolicos continuandos dum scilicet bene gesserint, ita tamen ut in omnibus subiiciantur metropolitanis; unum autem institutum vicarium apostolicum dominum Mathaeum Rochaeum in Laglenensi dioecesi amovendum propter varias cleri et populi eclamationes opinamur, et praeterea quod nullus etiam authoritate apostolica suffultus eum audeat visitare. De translatione episcoporum agemus in proximis conciliis provincialibus, et quod nobis visum fuerit, significabimus.

Ad tertium decretum quod est de visitatione liminum apostolorum dispensationem in hac visitatione nobis concede sicut aliis episcopis est concessa ut constat ex decreto.

Quartum decretum quod est de visitationibus provinciarum et dioecesum censemus debere in integrum observari.

Septimum decretum de receptione Concilii Tridentini in hoc regno Hiberniae libenti animo complectimur, iis enim nostrum qui illud non receperunt in animis est et semper erat concillium recipere opportune tempore. Quoad aliam partem huius decreta de exemptione scilicet regularium censemus expedire ut ad litteram observatur.

AD DECRETA CIRCA REGULARES

Ad primum dicimus debere observari inviolabiliter in duobus primis casibus. Canones enim sunt. Quoad tertium casum eiusdem decreta de religiosis missionariis sentimus horum facultatibus necessario inserendam esse clausulam illam (quae iura episcopalia et parochialia praeservent) et ut inseratur imposterum, et moneantur utentes facultatibus antea obtentis ut eiusdem clausulae tenorem observant instanter petimus.

Quoad tertium decretum de novitiatibus regularium optamus ut a Sacra Congregatione definitive resolvamur. Quartum de circumgestatione reliquiarum per quaestorem eleemosinarum censemus pium, regno commodum er per illud praedictis quaestoribus tam in ordine ad salutem animae quam ad famae conservationem bene provisum.

AD DECRETA COMMUNIA UTRIQUE CLERO

Ad primum, nulla sacramenta intuitu lucri aut munerum contra canones praescripta nos non latentia administrantur apud nos: verum in dictarum provinciarum conciliis provincialibus est taxata pro parochis intuitu laboris gravis in administratione sacramentorum necessario subeundi ob locorum distantiam quaedam summula pecuniae solvenda per eos quibus sacramenta administrantur in sustentationem parochorum quibus alia media sufficientia non suppetunt, non enim habent proventus aliquos ex decimus aut redditibus sed solis talibus eleemosinis vivunt quae satis tenues sunt frigescente iam charitate et impediente adversario eleemosinarum largitionem.

Secundum decretum est ad pedem litterae observandum praescribentibus illud canonibus et nostris statutis provincialibus et synodalibus, poenis illius transgressoribus ordinantibus. In his tamen sicut in aliis nos Sanctae Romanae Curiae nos submittimus.

Datum ex loco nostrii refugii in Hibernia die 28 Novembris 1635.

Hugo Archiepiscopus Ardmachanus totius Hiberniae primas.

Fr. Thomas Fleming archiepiscopus Dublinensis, Hiberniae primas.

Thomas Archiepiscopus Cassilensis.

Malachias Archiepiscopus Tuamensis.

Appendix E

A LIST OF SECULAR (DIOCESAN) PRIESTS SERVING IN THE DIOCESE OF WATERFORD AND LISMORE DURING THE EPISCOPATE OF PATRICK COMERFORD.

It is not always clear whether those who were listed as students for Waterford and Lismore in Salamanca and Bordeaux were, in fact, ordained priests or did return to Ireland.

Adams Robert	Received the treasurership of Lismore on 12 October 1644[1]. Seems to have been parish priest of Cahir and to have died c. 1649[2]
Browne, Thomas	Student in Salamanca 1603[3]
Barron, John	Student in Salamanca 1603[4]
Butler (Bootler), Richard	Received Drumcannon rectory, 26 October 1646[5]
Cantwell, Simon	Reported as having died before 1648; held the monastery of Cahir[6]
Carroll, Dermot	Received the prebendary of Clashmore (Mora) on 32 January 1645[7]
Clancy, John	Dungarvan priest; received the treasurership of Lismore 15 March 1646[8]; killed during the sack of Dungarvan 1642[9]
Comerton (Comerford), John	Student in Salamanca 1606[10]
Comerford, Thomas	Student in Salamanca 1602[11]
Comerford, Nicholas	Cousin of bishop Comerford; chanter of Waterford cathedral; probably became dean of the cathedral and prior of St. John's Waterford[12]
Coppinger, John	Student in Bordeaux

---

[1] B. Jennings, O.F.M. (ed.) 'Ecclesiastical appointments to Ireland, Aug. 1643 – Dec. 1649', *Collectanea Hibernica* 2 (1060) 24
[2] *Waterford Arch. Soc. Jn.* X (1907), 260 ff
[3] Students of the Irish College, Salamanca (1595-1619), *Archiv. Hib., II (1913)* 12. Although included in this list are students of continental colleges, it is not certain that they persevered and became priests or that they returned to their native diocese; it is likely that some of them, like Patrick Comerford, joined religious orders
[4] Ibid., 16 ff.
[5] *Collect. Hib.*, 2, 144
[6] Ibid., 49
[7] Ibid., 32
[8] Ibid., 38
[9] G. Giblin, O.F.M. (ed.) 'Vatican Library: Mss. Barberini Latini', *Archiv. Hib.* XVIII (1955) 95
[10] Salamanca Students, *Archiv. Hib.* II (1913) 19
[11] Ibid., 10
[12] *Wadding Papers*, 336, 346

Cantwell, Michael	An ex jesuit who was appointed agent of several of the bishops in Rome. This appointment was regretted because he was involved in Paris in the matter of the Sorbonne Propositions
Cormingus (Cormac?)	Student in Salamanca (1609)[13]
Daly, William	Student in Salamanca (1909)[14]
Dempsey, Terence	Inscription on a chalice in Waterford cathedral carries his name and date 1646[15]
English William	From a Will dated 1669, it is stated he is parish priest of Tubrid[16]
Fleming, Maurice	Received the 'anacoretis' of Lismore, 30 December 1646[17]
Grant, Francis	Student in Salamanca 1605[18]
Hai (Hay? Hayes?) Richard	Student at Louvain[19]
Hackett, Michael	Nephew of bishop Comerford; although a priest of the archdiocese of Cashel, his uncle sought the monastery of Cahir for him[20]
Hackett, Patrick	Nephew of bishop Comerford; composed a literary epitaph on the death of the bishop. Was proposed as vicar apostolic of Waterford and Lismore after Comerford's death[21]
Hoare, Edmund	Dungarvan priest. Educated at Bordeaux. Killed during the sack of Dungarvan in 1642[22]
Holane, James	Parish priest of Templetenny (part of modern Ballyporeen parish); said to have died in 1703 aged ninety years[23]
Keating, Geoffrey (Céitinn, Seathrún)	Born in Nicholastown near Cahir c. 1570. Studied on the Continent; was in Bordeaux, probably after ordination. A scholar of great distinction; wrote many outstanding works in Irish, most famous being 'Forus Feasa ar Éirinn'. Died before 1644. Buried in Tubrid[24]
Keating, Paul	Received the chancellorship of Lismore and the church of St. Leonard of Derrygrath (in present Ardfinnan parish) 15 March 1646[25]
Lea, Laurence	Vicar general of Waterford and Lismore. Died shortly after the appointment of bishop Comerford[26]

[13] 'Salamanca Students' *Archiv. Hib.*, II (1913) 25
[14] O'Boyle, James, op. cit., 52
[15] Power, *Waterford and Lismore*, 280
[16] Ibid., 83
[17] *Collect. Hib.* 2, 40
[18] 'Salamanca Students' *Archiv. Hib.*, II (1913) 14
[19] *Waterford Arch. Soc. Jn.*, X (1907) 161
[20] *Wadding Papers*, 405 ff
[21] *Comment. Rinucc.*, V, 81 ff. Ibid., 503; APF, SOCG, 298, f. 44R
[22] Vatican Library: Mss. Barberini Latini, *Archiv. Hib.* XVIII (1955), 95
[23] *Waterford Arch. Soc. Jn.*, II (1896), 248
[24] Power, op. cit., 22-24
[25] *Collect. Hibern.*, 2, 38

Lea George	Although a priest of Waterford and Lismore, he received the church of Knockraffin in the archdiocese of Cashel, 6 January 1645[27]
Leaghy, Donal	Received the leprosaria of Lismore, 30 December 1646[28]
Lombard, John	Student in Salamanca 1602[29]
Lonergan, Philip	Received the prebendary of Disert and Kilmoleran, 31 January 1645[30]
Lonergan, Bernard	Student in Bordeaux[31]
Madden, John	Student in Bordeaux[32]
Mernin, John	Student in Bordeaux[33]
Mulcahy, Nicholas	Parish priest of Ardfinnan; was hanged by Cromwelliam troops in front of his house[34]
Murty, John	Student in Bordeaux[35]
O'Brien, Thadaeus	Dungarvan priest. May have been dean of Lismore[36]
O'Casey, William	Parish priest of St. Mary's Clonmel. A learned man[37]
O'Donnell (Daniell), Constantine	In 1649 bishop Comerford was requested by a wealthy family named Matthews to appoint O'Donnell as parish priest of Cahir[38]
O'Neill, Peter	Student in Bordeaux[39]
O'Riordan, William	Student in Bordeaux[40]
Power, Robert	A bequest in the Will of William English, parish priest of Tubrid, was made to him. He was parish priest of St. John's parish, Waterford. On 20 November 1643 he received the deanship of Waterford; he seems to have ruled the diocese as vicar apostolic until the appointment of bishop John Brennan in 1671[41]
Power, Thomas	Student in Bordeaux [42]
Power, William	Student in Bordeaux[43]

---

[26] *Wadding Papers,* 23, 25, 62, 88, 230, 346
[27] *Collect. Hibern.,* 2, 57
[28] Ibid., 40
[29] 'Salamanca Students' *Archiv. Hib.,* II (1913) 15
[30] *Collect Hibern.,* 2, 35
[31] O'Boyle, op. cit., 52
[32] Ibid.
[33] O'Boyle, op. cit., 52
[34] Power, op. cit., 67
[35] O'Boyle, op. cit., 51
[36] APF, SOCG, 298, f. 812R
[37] Power, op. cit., 94
[38] *Waterford Arch. Soc. Jn., X (1907) 260*
[39] O'Boyle, op. cit., 52
[40] Ibid.
[41] Power, op. cit., pp. 306, 315; Collect. Hib., 2, 21
[42] O'Boyle, op, cit., 52
[43] O'Boyle, op, cit., 5

Purcell, Patrick	From a chalice inscription we learn that he was parish priest of Kilsheelan and Kileash in 1631[44]
Quinlan, Dermot	Described as a *'Sacerdos Lismorensis'* on two chalices found at Kilworth, Co. Cork dated 1608 and 1644[45]
Sherlock, John	Student at Salamanca 1604[46]
Strang, John	Student at Bordeaux[47]
Strang, Richard	Student at Salamanca 1605[48]
Sweeney, Daniel	Lismore priest whose name is found on a chalice dated 1640[49]
Travers, Walter	Parish priest of Baptistgrange involved in controversy with Edmund Everard[50]
Wadding, Thomas	Student at Salamanca 1609[51]
Walsh, Patrick	Priest of the city of Waterford; was accused of having encouraged the spoliation of protestant graveyards in 1641[52]
Walsh, Robert	Student at Salamanca 1609[53]
Watson, John	Received the prebendaries of Clonea, Holycross, Stradbally and Kilrossanty by apostolic letter of Urban VIII in 1632[54]
White, John	Student at Salamanca 1602[55]
White, Thomas	Parish priest, St. Mary's, Clonmel. Was forced to go into hiding on the surrender of Clonmel to Cromwell. A chalice in Clonmel bears his name and date 1638[56]
White, William	Student at Salamanca 1602[57]
Wise, William	Received the chancellorship of Holy Trinity Cathedral, Waterford, 26 June 1643[58]

---

[44] Power, op. cit., 209
[45] Ibid., 222
[46] 'Salamanca Students' *Archiv. Hib.*, II (1913) 17
[47] O'Boyle, op. cit., 52
[48] 'Salamanca Students' *Archiv. Hib.*, II (1913) 18
[49] Power, op. cit., 222
[50] *Wadding Papers,* 294, 325
[51] 'Salamanca Students' *Archiv. Hib.*, II (1913) 23
[52] Thomas Fitzpatrick, *'Waterford during the Civil War 1641-1653'* Waterford 1912, 15
[53] 'Salamanca Students' *Archiv. Hib.*, II (1913) 24
[54] R. Dodd, O.P., (ed.) 'Vatican Archives, Instrumenta Miscellanea', *Archiv. Hib.*, XIX (1956) 138
[55] 'Salamanca Students' *Archiv. Hib.*, II (1913) 15
[56] Power, op. cit., 145
[57] 'Salamanca Students' *Archiv. Hib.*, II (1913) 14
[58] *Collect. Hib.*, 2 (1960) 21

Appendix F

Processus Datariae, vol. 8, ff. 21r-39r

1629, WATERFORD, PATRICK COMERFORD

DECLARATION BY NOTARY. 15 January 1629. Cardinal Francesco Barberini, at the command of Pope Urban VIII and in accordance with the commission signed by Joannes Antonius Thomasius, notary of the Inquisition, having decided to set up a process of enquiry into the life and good morals of Patrick Comerford, Augustinian, who is to be promoted to the diocese of Waterford vacant by the death of its last bishop, and into the state of that diocese, has cited the following witnesses, and ordered them to be examined by Domenico Cecchini, and has commissioned me, the notary, to draw up the process in legal form.

WITNESSES. (1) Anthony Hickey, Franciscan. (2) Eugene Callanan, priest of the diocese of Killaloe.

FIRST WITNESS. Anthony Hickey, Franciscan, aged about forty years, deposed on 16 January 1629 at the residence of Domenico Cecchini, that he had known Comerford for the past ten years in Flanders and at Rome, and that he was born in the city of Waterford in lawful wedlock of catholic parents. Comerford would be about forty-five years of age, and was a priest when Hickey first came to know him. He is a master in theology, having graduated at Florence nine years ago, and he has preached frequently in Spain and in Ireland, and has converted many to the faith. Many offices were held by him in the Augustinian order, such as visitator, and prior in the Irish province. He has had the cure of souls in Ireland. Because of his learning and sanctity of life Hickey considers him worthy to be promoted to the see of Waterford.

The city of Waterford is in Munster, and is the second most important city in the country; the population would be about 30,000, and except for the ministers, all the people are catholics. The cathedral there is an ancient building of fine structure, and is dedicated to the Holy Saviour, but the non-catholics hold their services in it at present and have possession of all the revenues. The vicar general and the chapter and others deputed by the vicar general look after the needs of the faithful. The residence of the bishop is in the hands of the non-catholics. To the diocese of Waterford is united that of

Lismore. Lismore Cathedral is almost in ruins. The combined dioceses are vacant for many years by the death of the last bishop. Hickey says he knows these things because he has been in Waterford city.

SECOND WITNESS. Eugene Callanan, priest of the diocese of Killaloe, son of the late John Callanan, and rector of the Irish seminary at Rome, aged about twenty-eight years, declares he has known Comerford for ten years, first in Flanders, and afterwards at Rome; when Callanan was a student at the college in Flanders, Comerford came there, and thus they first became acquainted with each other. Comerford was born in the city of Waterford, and would be about forty-four years of age; he has been a priest since Callanan first got to know him. He has made many converts by his preaching. Many years ago he took the master's degree in theology at Florence; he has preached often in Ireland, and has held the offices of vicar general and of prior of the Canons Regular of St. Augustine.

Waterford city is in Munster and subject to the king of England, but in olden times it was under the jurisdiction of the Holy See and paid tribute to the pope, every house paying a certain amount. The episcopal residence in Waterford is near the cathedral. The rest of Callanan's deposition is almost the same as that given above by Hickey. At the end Callanan adds that he knows the things mentioned by him because he was in the towns of Waterford and of Lismore, and according to what he has heard, no bishop has been in charge of these dioceses since bishop Walsh, the last occupant of the see, died fifty years ago.

ATTESTATION BY HIERONYMUS DE GHETTIS. Hieronymus de Ghettis, prior general of the hermits of St. Augustine, attests at Rome on 17 January 1629, that Comerford was born in the city of Waterford of noble and catholic parents. He received the Augustinian habit in Portugal, and did his philosophical and theological studies in that country. From Portugal he was sent to Flanders, and from there, at the request of his superiors, he went to the general chapter held at Rome in 1620, for the purpose of promoting the interests of the catholic faith in Ireland. At the academy in Florence he received the master's degree in theology; then he went to Ireland, and preached there for a good many years, and converted many to the faith. Having been appointed prior of the monastery of the canons regular of St. Augustine at Kells by the apostolic see, he carried out his duties with great success. Besides, he replenished the Augustinian order in Ireland with so many priests that it now contains the number required to set up a province, and during his stay conducted himself in a most exemplary way in the Curia and in the priory of St. Augustine. The writer recommends that he be appointed bishop.

ATTESTATION OF THOMAS WALSH. Thomas Walsh, archbishop of Cashel, makes his attestation at Madrid on 28 February 1627. he wishes to make it known that the bearer of this document, Patrick Comerford, of the Hermits of St. Augustine, doctor in theology, and prior of the monastery of Kells, who is on his way to Rome, is worthy of all commendation because of the integrity of his life and doctrine, and the nobility of his parents; he considers him worthy to be promoted to any diocese, as he has laboured for many years amidst the persecution in Ireland, administered the monastery of Kells with great success, and converted some heretics and schismatics. His parents are among the leading citizens of Waterford, and to their house during time of persecution the clergy were wont to fly for refuge and asylum. Because of all his good qualities, Walsh recommends that a bishopric be given him.

PROFESSION OF FAITH. This is in print, and is signed by Comerford. Immediately following it is a statement, dated 15 January 1629, saying Comerford made the profession of faith and took the oath before Cardinal Francesco Barberini, and in the presence of Eugene Callanan, and Matthew O'Queely, Irish priests.

STATEMENT CONCERNING PROGRESS. On Thursday, 4 January 1629, at a general meeting of the Holy Roman Inquisition held in the presence of the pope and cardinals, Urban VIII chose Comerford to fill the see of Waterford, and ordered that a process of enquiry concerning the see and the nominee be instituted, and that Comerford be proposed and preconized in consistory before His Holiness by Cardinal Francesco Barberini. The statement is signed by Joannes Antonius Thomasius, notary of the Inquisition.

(The above is a translation and some comment by Fr. Cathaldus Giblin, O.F.M. in 'The processus Datariae and the appointment of Irish Bishops in the seventeenth century' *Father Luke Wadding Commemorative Volume, 551 – 554).*

Bibliography

1. SOURCES

A. UNPUBLISHED

1. ROME:

    i.   Archivio della sacra Congregazione di Propaganda Fide

        a) ACTA Vols. 1 – 21 (1622-52)

        b) Scritture Riferite nei Congressi, Irlanda Vol. I (1622-68)

        c) Scritture Originali Riferite nelle Congregazioni Generali

            Vols. 14 (1635), 77 (1635), 89 (1644), 100 (1631), 102 (1628), 105 (1635), 106 (1637), 129 (1627), 130 (1628), 131 (1629), 132 (1630), 133 (1633), 134 (1634), 135 (1636), 136 (1637), 137 (1638), 138 (1639), 139 (1640), 140 (1640), 141 (1642), 145 (1645), 150 (1632), 289 (1652-56), 294 (1636), 295 (1648), 298 (1648)

            Volumes 14, 140, 294, 298 contain exclusively Irish material.

        d) Lettere della Sacra Congregazione

            Vols. 1-30 (1622-54)

        e) Missioni Miscellanee

            Vol. 10

    ii   Archives of Augustinian Generalate,via del S. Uffizio, Rome

        Regestum Rmi Hieronymi de Ghettis ab anno 1627 ad an. 1629. This was the only unpublished volume which contained material concerning Patrick Comerford.

    iii   Archives of Jesuit Generalate, Borgo S. Spirito, Rome, Anglia 41, Hiberniae Historiae, 1599-1692. Contains reports from the Irish Jesuit Mission.

        Hiberniae Catalogi Antiqui, 1611-44. Contains faculty grants for the Irish Mission.

iv   Archives of Irish College, Via Ss. Quattro, Rome. Contains original document concerning Rules of the College, signed by Luke Wadding and Patrick Comerford, entitled: *Institutiones Domus Hibernorum de Urbe al Illmo. et Rmo. Cardle Ludovisio S.R.E. Vice Cancellarius ac Protectore Fundata primo die anni 1628.* Contains also the original petition of the jesuits for the granting of St. Peter's Church, Waterford.

1. NANTES:

Archives Communales de la ville de Nantes Anterieures a 1790. Registres des Paroisses: serie GG, Sepultures 210: Registre de la Paroisse de St. Nicholas – Sepultures 1644-55

Contains funeral notices of bishop Comerford

3. DUBLIN:

Franciscan Archives, Killiney:

D.I. – D.X. A collection of seventeenth century letters and papers, including the correspondence of Luke Wadding, that after 1638 being yet unpublished.

D.I. contains an account of the controversy between bishop Comerford and the cistercians in regard to the occupation of the priory of St. John the Evangelist, Waterford

4. MOUNT MELLERAY ABBEY

Burke Papers: Mss of the late Canon William Burke. Contains interesting references to Waterford of the late sixteenth and early seventeenth century.

Power Papers: Some Mss. of the late Canon Power dealing mainly with the cistercian order

B. PUBLISHED

Aiazzi, G. (ed.)   *Nunziatura in Irlanda di Monsignor Gio. Baptista Rinuccini Archievescovo di Fermo negli anni 1645 a 1649* (Florence, 1844)

———   (Annie Hutton, trans.) *The Embassy in Ireland of Monsignor G. B. Rinuccini, archbishop of Fermo, in the years 1645-1649* (Dublin, 1873)

Brady, Maziere (ed.)   *State Papers concerning the Irish Church in the time of Queen Elizabeth* (London, 1868)

Calendar of State Papers, Domestic Series

     1640   (London, 1880)

     1641- 3   (London, 1887)

     1644- 5   (London, 1890)

     1645- 7   (London, 1891)

     1648– 9   (London 1893)

Calendar of State Papers relating to Ireland

     1601- 3   (London, 1870)

     1606- 8   (London, 1874)

     1615-25   (London, 1880)

     1625-32   (London, 1900)

     1633-47   (London, 1901)

Comerford, Patrick   *The Inquisition of a Sermon preached in the Cathedral Church of the City of Waterford, in February 1617, by Robert Daborne, Chancellor of the said Cathedrall & C. written by the R.F.P.C. of the Order of S. Augustin, Doctor in Divinity, Waterford, 1644*

Conway, Dominic (ed.)   'Guide to Documents of Irish and British interest in Fondo Borghese, Series I', *Archivium Hibernicum,* XXIII (1960), 1-147

____ (ed.) 'Guide to Documents of Irish and British interest in Fondo Borghese, Series II-IV', *Archivium Hibernicum,* XXIV (1961), 31-102

Corish, Patrick (ed.) 'Two Reports on the Catholic church in Ireland in the early seventeenth century' *Archivium Hibernicum,* XXII (1959), 140-62

Coronatae Virtuti Reverendiss
D. Patritii Quemerfordi ex Sacro Eremit. D. Augustini Ordini Episcopi Waterfordiensis & Lismorensis inaugurati plausque seminarii Hibernorum de Urbe (Roma, 1629)

'Documents Illustrating the History of Waterford',
Waterford Arch. Soc. Jn. VIII (1902/3) 103-15

Dodd, Romuald (ed.) 'Vatican Archives: Instrumenta Hiscellanea', *Archivium Hibernicum* XIX (1956), 135-40

Dunlop, Robert *Ireland under the Commonwealth, Being a selection of documents relating to the Government of Ireland from 1651 to 1659 with Historical Introduction and Notes,* (Manchester, 1913)

Giblin, Cathaldus 'The Processus Datariae and the Appointment of Irish Bishops in the Seventeenth Century', *Father Luke Wadding Commemorative Volume* (Dublin – London, 1957)

____ (ed.) 'Catalogue of Material of Irish Interest in the Collection Nunziatura di Fiandra, Vatican Archives: Part I, vol. 1-50' *Collectanea Hibernica I (1958)*

Gilbert, S. T. (ed.) *An Aphorismical Discovery of Treasonable Faction, or a Contemporary History of Affairs in Ireland from 1641-52 with an Appendix of Original Letters and Documents,* 3 vols. (Dublin 1877-80)

____ (ed.) *History of the Irish Confederation and the War in Ireland* 7 vols. (Dublin, 1882-91)

Glynn, Marcellus and Martin, F.X. (eds.)
          "The 'Brevis Relatio' of the Irish Discalced Carmelites 1625-1670" by Father Paul Browne, O.D..C., *Archiv. Hib.* XXV (1962), 136-163

Hagan, J. (ed.)
          'Miscellanea Vaticano – Hibernica, Relationes Status' *Archivium Hibernicum* V (1916), 74-156

Hogan, Edmond (ed.)
          Ibernia Ignatiana: Sen Ibernorum Societatis Jesu Patrum Monumenta Collecta vol. I (1540-1607), (Dublin, 1880)

Hogan, James
          Letters and Papers relating to the Irish Rebellion between 1642-46 (Dublin 1935)

Harris, Paul
          Arktomastix – Sive Edmondus Ursulanus propter usurpatum judicium de tribunali dejectus, et propter libellum famosum in judicium vocatus (Dublin, 1633)

____
          The excommunication by the L. Archbishop of Dublin, Thomas Fleming, alias Barnwell, friar of the order of St. Francis, against the inhabitants of the diocese of Dublin, for hearing the Masses of Peter Caddell d. of divinity and Paul Harris priest (2nd edition enlarged, Dublin, 1633)

____
          Frates Sobrii Estote 1 Pet. 5:8 or an admonition to the fryars of the kingdom of Ireland to abandon such hereticall doctrines as they daylie publish to the corruption of our holy faith the ruine of souls and their owne damnation which sleepeth not by Paul Harris, pr. (Dublin, 1634)

____
          Exile exiled occasioned by a mandate from Rome procured by Thomas Fleming alias Barnwell archbishop of Dublin and friar of the Order of St. Francis, from the Congregation of Cardinals de Propaganda Fide for the banishment of Paul Harris out of the diocese of Dublin. (Dublin, 1635)

Historical Manuscripts Commission
          Calendar of the Manuscripts of the Marquis of Ormonde, preserved at Kilkenny Castle ,vol. II (London, 1903)

   ——   *Report on the Manuscripts of the Earl of Egmont*, vol. i
            (London, 1905)

   ——   *Report on Franciscan Manuscripts preserved at the
            Convent, Merchant's Quay, Dublin* (Dublin, 1906)

Jennings, Brendan   'Ecclesiastical Appointments to Ireland Aug. 1643 –
            Dec. 1649' , *Collectanea Hibernica* 2 (1960) 18-64

   ——   (ed.) *The Wadding Papers 1614-1638*, (Dublin 1953)

   ——   (ed.) 'Miscellaneous Documents I, 1588-1634' *Archivium
            Hibenicum* XII (1946), 70-200

   ——   (ed.) 'Miscellaneous Documents II, 1625-40', *Archivum
            Hibernicum* XIV (1949), 1-29

   ——   (ed.) 'Acta Sacrae Congregationis de Propaganda Fide 1622-50',
            Archivium Hibernicum, XXII (1959), 28-139

Jesuit Memorials of the Irish Province S.J.,
            Printed privately between 1899 and 1914

Lombard, Peter   *De Regno Hiberniae Commentarius*, (Louvain, 1632), ed. P.
            F. Moran (Dublin, 1868)

Lynch, John   *De Praesulibus Hiberniae Potissimis Catholicae Religionis
            in Hibernia Serendae, Propagandae, et Conservandae
            Authoribus,* ed. John F. O'Doherty (2 vols. Dublin, 1944)

Martin, F. X. and De Meijer, A (eds.)
            'Irish Material in the Augustinian General Archives, Rome,
            1354-1624' *Archivium Hibernicum* XIX (1956), 61-134

Millett, Benignus (ed.) 'Calendar of Scritture Riferite Nei Congressi, Irlanda
            Propaganda Archives', vol. I (1625-68) *Collectanea
            Hibernica*, 6 and 7 (1963-4), 18-211

   ——   (ed.) 'Correspondence of Irish Interest in the Lettere in
            Propaganda Archives, vol. 27-34 (1649-64)' *Collectanea
            Hibernica*, XXX (1988), 7-25

Moran, Patrick Francis   *Spicilegium Ossoriense: being a collection of original letters and papers, illustrative of the history of the Irish Church from the Reformation to the year 1800*, 3 vols. (Dublin, 1874-84)

O'Ferrall, R., and O'Connell, R

Commentarius Rinuccinianus de sedis Apostolicae Legatione ad foederatos Hiberniae Catholicos per annos 1645-1649. Florentia opus susceprunt atque obsolverunt per annos 1661-1666 Fr. Peter Richarius (Barnabas O'Ferall) Longfordensis, Fr. Peter Robertus (Daniel O'Connell) Desmondensis uterque e provincia Hibernica Ordinis Min. Capuccinorum, ed. Stanislaus Kavanagh, O.F.M. Cap., 6 vols I.M.C. (Dublin, 1932-49)

Olden, Michael   'Episcopal Comments on the Decreta pro recto regimine Ecclesiarum Hiberniae', *Archivium Hibernicum*, XXVI (1964), 1-12

The Statutes at large passed in the parliaments held in Ireland…

vols i-iii (1310 – 1698), (Dublin, 1786)

O'Donnell, T. J. (ed.)   *Selections of the Zoilomastix of Philip O'Sullivan Beare.* (Dublin, 1960)

O'Doherty, D. J. (ed.)   'Students of the Irish College, Salamanca' *Archivium Hibernicum* ii (1913) 1-36; iii (1914), 87-112

Ursulanus, Edmundus (pseud.) Francis O'Mahony or Matthews,

Examen luridicum censurae facultatis theologiae Parisiensis; et eiusdem civitatis Archiepiscopi latae circa quasdam propositiones Regularibus Regni Hiberniae falso impositas (Frankfurt, 1631)

Wadding, Luke   *Annales Minorum* 32 vols., 3rd ed. (Rome, 1931-64)

White, Newport B.,   *Extents of Irish Monastic Possessions 1540-41,* I.M.C. (Dublin 1943)

_____   *Irish Monastic and Episcopal Deeds* (Dublin, 1936)

2. SECONDARY WORKS

Bagwell, Richard   *Ireland under the Tudors, with a succinct account of the earlier history* 3 vols., (London, 1885-90; reprint 1973)

____   *Ireland under the Stuarts and during the Interregnum,* 3 vols. (London, 1909-16)

Barnard, Nicholas   *The Penitent Death of a woefull sinner. Or the Penitent Death of John Atherton executed at Dublin the 5 of December 1640)* (London, 1641)

Barmard, Toby   *Cromwellian Ireland, English Government and Reform in Ireland* (Oxford, 1975)

____   '1641: A bibliographical essay', Brian MacCuarta (ed.) *Ulster 1641: Aspects of the Rising* (Belfast, 1993)

Barmard, T. L. and Neely, W.G. (eds.)
     The Clergy of the Church of Ireland 1000-2000 (Dublin, 2006)

Beckett, J. C.   *The making of Modern Ireland, (1603-1923)* (London, 1966; reprint 1969)

Bolster Evelyn   *A history of the Diocese of Cork from the Reformation to the Penal era* (Cork, 1982)

Bossy, John   'The Counter-Reformation and the people of Catholic Europe' *Past and Present*, 47 (1970), 51-70

____   'The Counter-Reformation and the people of Catholic Ireland', *Historical Studies*, 8 (1974), 153-70

____   *The English Catholic Community, 1557-1850* (London, 1976)

Boyle, P.   'The Irish College at Bordeaux, 1603-1794' *Irish Ecclesiastical Record*, (1907), 127-45

Bradshaw, Brendan and Keogh, Daire (eds.)

    Christianity in Ireland: Revisiting the story (Dublin, 2002)

Brady, Ciarán and Gillespie Raymond (eds.)

    Natives and Newcomers: Essays on the making of Irish Colonial Society, 1534-1641 (Dublin, 1986)

Brady, John   'The Irish Colleges on the Continent', *Ir. Cath. Hist. Comm. Proc.* (1957)

Brady, W. M.   *The Episcopal Succession in England, Scotland and Ireland A.D. 1400-1875,* 2 vols. (Rome, 1876-7)

_____   *Essays on the English State Church in Ireland* (London, 1869)

Breathnach, Edel, McMahon, Joseph O.F.M., John McCafferty (eds.)

    The Irish Franciscans 1534-1900 (Dublin, 2009)

Browne, J.   'Kilkenny College', *Proceedings of the Kilkenny Archaeological Society*, vol. I, (1849-51), 221-3

Burke, W. P.   *Irish Priests in Penal Times, 1660-1760* (Waterford, 1914)

_____   *The History of Clonmel* (Waterford, 1907)

Byrne, M. J. (ed.)   'The Irish War of Defence 1598-1600' extract from the *De Hibernia Insula Commentarius* of Peter Lombard (Cork, 1930)

Byrne, Niall   *The Irish Crusade, a History of the Knights Hospitaller, the Knights Templar, and the Knights of Malta in the South-East of Ireland* (Dublin 2008)

Burton, Edwin H.   The Life and Times of Bishop Challoner (1691-1781), vol. i (London, 1909)

Canny, Nicholas   'The Formation of the Irish Mind: Religion, Politics and Gaelic Irish Literature, 1580-1750' *Past and Present,* 95 (1982), 91-116

	The Upstart Earl: A Study of the Social and Mental World of Richard Boyle, first Earl of Cork, 1566-1643 (Cambridge, 1982)
——	*From Reformation to Restoration: Ireland, 1534-1640* (Dublin, 1987)
——	*Kingdom and Colony: Ireland in the Atlantic World, 1560-1800* (Baltimore, 1988)
——	'The Attempted Anglicisation of Ireland in the Seventeenth Century: An exemplar of "British History"', J. F. Merritt (ed.) *The Political World of Thomas Wentworth, Earl of Strafford, 1621-41* (Cambridge, 1995)
——	'What really happened in 1641', Jane Ohlmeyer (ed.) *Ireland: From Independence to Occupation* (Cambridge, 1995)
Carrigan. W.	*The History and Antiquities of the Diocese of Ossory*, vol. IV (Dublin, 1905)
Carte, Thomas	*History of the Life of James, Duke of Ormonde; containing an account of the most remarkable affairs of his time, and particularly of Ireland under his government; with an Appendix and a Collection of Letters,* second edition, 6 vols. (Oxford, 1851)
Clarke, Aidan	*The Old English in Ireland, 1625-42* (London, 1966)
——	*The Graces, 1625-41*, Irish Historical Series, 8 (Dundalk, 1968)
——	'Pacification, Plantation and the Catholic Question', 'Selling Royal Favours', 'The Government of Wentworth', 'The Breakdown of Authority', T. W. Moody, F. X. Martin, F. J. Byrne (eds.) *A New History of Ireland, iii, Early Modern Ireland, 1534-1691* (Oxford, 1976), 187-288
——	The Atherton File, *Decies*, xi (1070), 45-55

— 'The Colonization of Ulster and the Rebellion of 1641, 1603-60', T. W. Moody and F. X. Martin (eds.), *The Course of Irish History* (Cork, 1978), 189-203

— 'The 1641 Depositions', P. Fox (ed.) *Treasures of the Library, Trinity College Dublin*, (Dublin, 1986), 111-122

— 'Alternative allegiance in early modern Ireland', *Journal of Historical Sociology* vol. 5, No. 3 (Sept. 1992), 253-266

— 'Colonial constitutional attitudes in Ireland 1640-1660', *P.R.I.A.* vol. 90, section C, no. 11 (1990), 357-375

— 'Ireland and the General Crisis', *Past and Present*, no. 48 (Aug. 1970), 79-99

— 'The 1641 rebellion and anti-popery in Ireland', Brian MacCuarta (ed.) *Ulster 1641: Aspects of the Rising* (Belfast, 1993), 139-158

Clarke, Howard B. (ed.)   *Irish Cities* (Cork, 1995)

Cleary, G. O.F.M.   *Father Luke Wadding and St. Isidore's College Rome* (Rome, 1925)

Coleman, J.   'The Earl of Cork's appropriation of the revenues of the See of Lismore and St. Mary's Collegiate Church, Youghal', *Waterford Arch. Soc. Jn.* XI (1908) 230 ff

Corboy, J.   'Father James Archer S.J., 1550-1625', *Studies* xxxiii (1944), 99–107

Corish Patrick   'Bishop Nicholas French and the Second Ormond Peace, 1648-9', *I.H.S.*, 6 (1948), 83-100

— 'Rinuccini's Censure of 27 May 1648', *I.T.Q.*, 18 (1951), 322-37

— 'Two Contemporary Historians of the Confederation of Kilkenny: John Lynch and Richard O'Ferrall, *I.H.S.*, 8 (1952-3), 217-36

—— 'The Crisis in Ireland in 1648: the Nuncio and the Supreme Council, Conclusions, *I.T.Q.*, 22 (1953), 231-57

—— 'Father Luke Wadding and the Irish Nation', *I.E.R.*, 88 (1957), 377-95

—— 'The Reorganization of the Irish Church, 1603-41' *Ir. Cath. Hist. Comm. Proc.*, iii (1957), 1-14

—— 'An Irish Counter-Reformation Bishop: John Roche', *I.T.Q.* 25 (1958), 14-32, 102-23; 26 (1959), 101-16, 313-30

—— 'The Rising of 1641 and the Catholic Confederacy, 1641-45', 'Ormond, Rinuccini and the Confederates, 1645-9', 'The Cromwellian Conquest, 1649-53', 'The Cromwillian Regime, 1650-60', T. W. Moody, F. X. Martin and F. J. Byrne (eds.), *A New History of Ireland, iii, Early Modern Ireland, 1534-1691* (Oxford, 1976), 289-386

—— *The Catholic Community in the Seventeenth and Eighteenth Centuries* (Dublin, 1981)

—— *The Irish Catholic Experience* (Dublin 1985)

—— (ed.) Radicals, Rebels and the Establishments, *Hist. Studies,* 15 (Belfast, 1985*)*

Cox, Richard   *Hibernia Anglicana*, 2 parts, 2 vols. (London, 1689-90)

Cregan, Donal F.   'Some Members of the Confederation of Kilkenny', S. O'Brien (ed.) *Measgra i gcuimhne Mhicíl Úi Chléirigh* (Dublin, 1944), 34-44

—— 'The Confederation of Kilkenny', Brian Farrell (ed.), *The Irish Parliamentary Tradition* (Dublin, 1973), 102-15

—— 'The Social and Cultural Background of a Counter-Reformation Episcopate, 1618-60', A. Cosgrove and D. McCartney (eds.), *Studies in Irish History Presented to R. Dudley Edwards* (Dublin, 1979), 85-117

Cunningham, Bernadette *The World of Geoffrey Keating: History, Myth and Religion in Seventeenth-Century Ireland* (Dublin, 2000)

de Burgo, Thomas *Hibernia Dominicana* (Cologne, 1762)

Dickens, A. G., *The English Reformation* (London, 1972)

Downey, Edmund *The Story of Waterford* (Waterford, 1914)

Dunlop, Robert Ireland from the Plantation of Ulster to the Cromwellian Settlement (1611-59), *Camb. Mod. Hist.,* iv (1906), ch. XVIII, 513-38

Edwards, R. Dudley *Church and State in Tudor Ireland. A History of the Penal Laws against Irish Catholics 1534-1603* (London, 1935)

_____ 'Church and State in the Ireland of Michél O Cléirigh, 1626-41', S. O'Brien (ed.) *Measgra in gcuimhne Michil Úi Cléirigh* (Dublin, 1944), 1-20

_____ '*Ireland, Elizabeth I, and the Counter-Reformation*', Elizabethan government and society: essays presented to Sir John Neale, ed. S. T. Bindoff, Joel Hurstfield and C. H. Williams (London, 1961), 315-39

Egan, F. W. History, Guide and Directory of Waterford (Kilkenny 1893)

Fitzpatrick, Brendan *Seventeenth-Century Ireland: The War of Religions* (Dublin, 1988)

Fitzpatrick, Elizabeth and Gillespie, Raymond (eds.)
 The parish in medieval and early modern Ireland (Dublin, 2006)

Fitzpatrick, Thomas *Waterford during the Civil War (1641-53),* (Waterford, 1912)

Flynn, Thomas, O.P. *The Irish Dominicans (1936-1641),* (Dublin, 1993)

Ford, Alan *The Protestant Reformation in Ireland, 1590-1641* (Frankfurt, 1985)

217

Forrestal, Alison   *Catholic Synods in Ireland, 1600-1690* (Dublin, 1998)

Foster, R. F.   *Modern Ireland, 1600-1972* (London, 1988)

Franciscan Fathers   *Father Luke Wadding: Commemorative Volume*
                          (Dublin, 1957)

Gams, Pius Bonifacius, O.S.R.
                          Series Episcoporum Ecclesiae Catholicae (Ratisbon, 1873)

Gauchat, Patritius, O.M. Conv.
                          Hierarchia Catholica, Medii et recentioris Aevi, IV
                          (Munich, 1935)

Gillespie, Raymond   'Harvest crises in early seventeenth century Ireland,'
                          Irish Economic and Social History 2 (1984), 5-18

____   *Devoted People: Belief and Religion in Early Modern
                          Ireland* (Manchester, 1997)

____   *Seventeenth Century Ireland* (Dublin, 2006)

Gwynn, A and Hadcock, N.
                          Medieval Religious Houses Ireland (Dublin, 1970)

Hansard, Joseph   *The History of the County and City of Waterford*
                          (Dungarvan, 1870)

Henchy, Monica   'The Irish College of Salamanca', *Studies,* LXX (1981),
                          220-7

Hill, Christopher   'Seventeenth-century English radicals and Ireland',
                          P. J. Corish (ed.), *Radicals, Rebels and Establishments*
                          (Hist. Studies, XV, Belfast, 1985), 33-49

Hughes, P.   *The Reformation in England* 3 vols. (London, 1952-54)

____   *Rome and the Counter-Reformation in England*
                          (London, 1942)

Hurley, Patrick	'Memoir of Dr. Patrick Comerford O.S.A., Bishop of Waterford and Lismore, 1629-1652, *I.E.R.* VIII (1887), 1082-1093
Hynes, Michael, I.	*The Mission of Rinuccini, Nuncio Extraordinary to Ireland 1645-1649* (Dublin, 1932)
____	'The Irish Republic in the Seventeenth Century', *Catholic Historical Review*, 23 (1937), 293-311
Irwin, Liam	'The role of the presidency in the economic development of Munster', *Journal of the Cork Historical and Archaeological Society*, LXXXII (1977), 102-114
'Ireton in Waterford'	*Waterford Arch. Soc. Jn.* 1 (1894-5), 191-192
Jones, F. M., C.SS.R.	'Canonical Faculties on the Irish Mission in the reign of Queen Elizabeth 1558-1603', *I.T.Q.* XX (1953) 152-171
____	'The Counter-Reformation', Corish (ed.), *Ir. Catholicism*, iii, ch. 3 (1967), 152-172
____	*Mountjoy, 1563-1606, the last Elizabethan Deputy* (Dublin and London, 1958)
Kearney, Hugh F.	'Ecclesiastical Politics and the Counter-Reformation in Ireland 1618-48', *Journal of Ecclesiastical History* ii (1960), 202-12
____	*Strafford in Ireland, 1633-41: A Study in Absolutism*, 2nd ed., (Cambridge, 1989)
Knowler, William (ed.)	*The Earl of Strafford's letters and despatches*, 2 vols. (London, 1799)
Knox, R. Buick	*James Ussher, Archbishop of Armagh* (Cardiff, 1967)
Lenihan, Pádraig	*Confederate Catholics at War 1641-9* (Cork, 2001)
Lennon, Colm	'Richard Stanihurst (1547-1618) and Old English Identity', *I.H.S.*, XXI, no. 82 (Sept. 1978), 121-43

—   *Richard Stanihurst; the Dubliner*, 1547-1618
                           (Dublin, 1981)

—   'The Counter-Reformation in Ireland 1542-1641',
                           Ciaran Brady and Raymond Gillespie (eds.), *Natives and*
                           Newcomers: essays on the making of Irish Colonial Society,
                           1534-1641 (Dublin, 1986), 75-92

—   *Sixteenth-Century Ireland: The Incomplete Conquest*
                           (Dublin, 1994)

Lowe, John   'The Glamorgan Mission to Ireland 1645-6',
                           Studia Hibernica, no. 4 (1964), 155-96

Lynch, John   *The life and death of the most Reverend Francis Kirwan,*
                           bishop of Killala, translated by C. P. Meehan
                           (Dublin, 1884)

McCarthy, J.   'The Reformatory Decrees of the Council of Trent', *I.E.R.*,
                           LXVIII (1946), 165-177

McClintock, Aileen   'The Earls of Ormond and Tipperary's role in the governing
                           of Ireland 1603-1641', *Tipperary Hist. Jn.* (1988), 159-72

MacCuarta, Brian (ed.)   *Ulster 1641: Aspects of the Rising* (Belfast, 1993)

McDowell, R. B. and Webb, D.A.
                           Trinity College Dublin, 1592-1952: an academic history
                           (Cambridge, 1982)

MacLysaght, Edward   *Irish Life in the Seventeenth Century* (Cork, 1950)

McRedmond, Louis   *To the Greater Glory: a History of the Irish Jesuits*
                           (Dublin, 1991)

Mant, R.   *History of the Church of Ireland from the Reformation to*
                           the Revolution (London, 1840)

Martin, F. X.   *Friar Nugent: A Study of Francis Lavalin Nugent*
                           1569-1635, Agent of the Counter-Reformation (Rome and
                           London, 1962)

Meehan, C. P.,	*The Rise and Fall of the Irish Franciscan Monasteries and Memoirs of the Irish Hierarchy in the Seventeenth Century* (Dublin, 1877)
⎯⎯	*The Confederation of Kilkenny* (Dublin, 1905)
Millett, Benignus	'Irish Literature in Latin', T. W. Moody, F. X. Martin, F. J. Byrne (eds.), *A New History of Ireland*, iii *Early Modern Ireland, 1534-1691 (Oxford, 1977), 566-82*
⎯⎯	*The Irish Franciscans, 1651-1655* (Rome, 1964)
⎯⎯	'Survival and Reorganization, 1650-1695', Corish (ed.) *A History of Irish Catholicism*, iii, pt. 7 (Dublin, 1968)
Mockler, J.	'The City of Waterford in the Seventeenth Century' *Waterford Arch. Soc. Jn.*, vi (1900), 18-31
Moody, T. W., Martin, F.X., Byrne, F. J. (eds.)	*A New History of Ireland*, iii, *Early Modern Ireland, 1534-1691* (Oxford, 1976)
Mooney, Canice	'Donagh O'Daly O.F.M. c.1600-64 – a forgotten Irish figure of the Counter-Reformation in Austria and Bohemia, *Studia Hibernica*, XIX (1979), 7-25
⎯⎯	'Was Wadding a Patriotic Irishman?', *Father Luke Wadding Commemorative Volume* (Dublin, 1957), 15-92
Moran, Patrick Francis	*A History of the Catholic Archbishops of Dublin, Vol. I* (Volume II not published) (Dublin ,1864)
⎯⎯	*Historical Sketch of the Persecutions suffered by the Catholics of Ireland under the Rule of Cromwell and the Puritans* (Dublin, 1884)
Morrissey, Thomas	*James Archer of Kilkenny* (Dublin, 1979)
⎯⎯	'The Irish student diaspora in the sixteenth century and the early years of the Irish College at Salamanca', *Recusant History,* XIV, no. 4 (1978), 242-60

Moryson, Fynes   *An itinerary containing his ten yeares travel through*
          ....Germany, Bohmerland, Switzerland, Netherland,
          Denmark, Poland, Italy, Turkey, France, England, Scotland
          and Ireland 3 parts. London, 1617, new ed. in 4 vols,
          Glasgow, 1907-08

Murphy, D.   *Cromwell in Ireland* (Dublin, 1883)

Murphy, John A.   'The Politics of the Munster Protestants, 1641-9' *Journal of*
          the Cork Historical and Archaeological Society, 76 (1971),
          1-20

Nash, R. C.   'Irish Atlantic trade in the seventeenth and eighteenth
          centuries', *William & Mary Quarterly*, XLII, no. 3 (1985),
          329-56

Nolan, William and Power, Thomas P
          Waterford: History and Society (Dublin, 1992)

Nicolson, Adam   *Power and Glory, Jacobean England and the making of the*
          King James Bible (London, 2003)

O'Boyle, James   *The Irish Colleges on the Continent* (Dublin, 1935)

O'Cahan, T. S.,   *Owen Roe O'Neill* (London, 1968)

O'Conbhuidhe, Colmcille *The Cistercian Abbeys of Tipperary* (Dublin, 1999)

O'Connor, Thomas and Lyons, Mary Ann (eds.)
          Irish Communities in Early-Modern Europe (Dublin, 2006)

O'Connor, Thomas *Irish Jansenists 1600-1700 (Dublin, 2008)*

O'Fiaich, Tomás   'Republicanism and Separation in the Seventeenth
          Century', *Léachtaí Cholm Cille*, 2 (1971), 74-87

————   'Edmond O'Reilly, Archbishop of Armagh, 1657-1669',
          Father Luke Wadding, 171-228

Ó hAnnracháin, Tadgh *Catholic Reformation in Ireland. The mission of Rinuccini*
          1645-1649 (Oxford, 2002)

___	'Lost in Rinuccini's shadow; the Irish clergy 1645-9', Micheál O'Siochrú (ed.) *Kingdoms in Crisis – Ireland in 1640's* (Dublin, 2001)
Ohlmeyer, Jane (ed.)	*Ireland from Independence to Occupation, 1641-60* (Cambridge, 1993)
___	*Political Thought in Seventeenth-Century Ireland: Kingdom or Colony* (Cambridge, 2000)
Olden, Michael	'Counter-Reformation Problems: Munster' *Ir. Cath. Hist. Comm. Proc.* (Dublin, 1967), 21-32
___	'Kinsale to Benburb – a Valuable Breathing Space in Irish History', *Léactaí Cholm Cille* 2 (Maynooth, 1971)
O'Mórdha, Séamus	'Hugh O'Reilly (1581-1653), a Reforming Primate', *Breifne*, 4 (1970), 345-69
___	'Heber McMahon, Soldier Bishop of the Confederation of Kilkenny', *Clogher Record Album, a Diocesan History* (Monaghan, 1975)
O'Riordan, S.	'Rinuccini in Galway, 1647-49', *Journal of the Galway Archaeological and Historical Society*, 23 (1948), 19-51
Ó'Siochrú, Micheál	*Confederate Ireland, 1642-1649: A Constitutional and Political Analysis* (Dublin, 1999)
___ (ed.)	*Kingdoms in Crisis: Ireland in the 1640s* (Dublin, 2001)
Parker, Geoffrey	*The Thirty Years' War* (London, 1984)
Perceval-Maxwell, Michael	
	'The Ulster Rising of 1641 and the Depositions', *Irish Historical Society,* 21 (1978-9), 144-67
Power, Patrick,	'The Priory, Church and Hospital of St. John the Evangelist, Waterford', *Waterford Arch. Soc. Jn.* II (1896), 81-97

— 'Sundrie Priests and Friars', *Waterford Arch. Soc. Jn., XVI* (1913), 122-8

— 'Parva Roma – Waterford of the early Seventeenth Century', *The Catholic Record of Waterford and Lismore*, II (Oct. 1914) 428-30, III (March 1915 – Feb. 1916), 22-24, 44-46

— *Waterford and Lismore, a Compendious History of the United Diocese* (Cork, 1937)

— *Place Names of the Decies* 2nd edition (Cork, 1952)

— *History of the Irish Cistercians* (unpublished: in library of Mount Melleray Abbey)

Power, Thomas   'Richard Boyle's ironworks in County Waterford', *Decies* (1977), 26-30

Ranger, T. O.   'Strafford in Ireland: a Revaluation, Aston, Trevor (ed.) *Crisis in Europe 1560-1660 (*London, 1965)

Renehan, Laurence   *Collections on Irish Church History*, ed. Daniel McCarthy 2 vols. (Dublin, 1861-1874)

Rennison, William   *Succession List of the Bishops, Cathedral and Parochial Clergy of the Dioceses of Waterford and Lismore* (Waterford, 1920). This work deals only with the clergy of the Church of Ireland.

Rice, G.   'Thomas Dease, Bishop of Meath, and some questions concerned with the Rights to Ecclesiastical Property alienated at the Reformation' *Ríocht na Midhe,* 6/1 (1975), 69-89

Ronan, M. V.   *The Reformation in Dublin 1536-1558* (London, 1926)

— *The Reformation in Ireland under Elizabeth, 1558-1580* (London, 1930)

Russell, Conrad | *The Fall of the British Monarchies 1637-1642* (Oxford, 1991)

Russon, J. R., | 'Les Sepultures Episcopales dans le Cathedrale de Nantes' *Societate Archaeologique et Historique de Nantes et de la Loire-Inferieure* LXXV (1935), 151-171

Ryan, Conor | 'Religion and State in Seventeenth-Century Ireland', *Archivium Hibernicum* xxxiii (1975), 122-23

Ryland, R. H. | *History, Topography and Antiquities of Waterford* (London, 1824), (republished Kilkenny, 1982)

Sesions, W. K. | *The first printers in Waterford, Cork and Kilkenny pre-1700* (York, 1990)

Sheehan, A. J. | 'The Recusancy Revolt of 1603: A Reinterpretation', *Archivium Hibernicum*, XXXVIII (1983), 3-13

Sheehan, R. P. | 'An Irish Diocese in the Seventeenth Century', *I.E.R.* 1 (1897), 1-20

Silke, J. J. | 'Primate Lombard and James I', *I.T.Q.* 22 (1955), 124-50

____ | 'Primate Peter Lombard and Hugh O'Neill', *I.T.Q.*, 26 (1959), 15-30

____ | 'The Irish Abroad, 1534-1691' *A New History of Ireland*, iii, *Early Modern Ireland, 1534-1691* (Oxford, 1976) 582-633

Smith, Charles | *The Ancient and Present State of the County and City of Waterford* (Dublin, 1746)

Smith, David | 'Peter Lombard (1554-1625) Prelate, Politician, Pragmatist', *Decies* no. 56 (2000), 35-53

Stanihurst, Richard | A treatise containing a plain and perfect description of Ireland...... Raphael Holinshed, *Chronicles* (1577 ed.)

Spelman, Joseph | 'The Irish in Belgium' *I.E.R.* (1886)

Stradling, R. A.   *The Spanish Monarchy and Irish Mercenaries: The Wild Geese in Spain 1618-68* (Dublin, 1994)

Townshend, D   *The Life and Letters of the Great Earl of Cork* (London, 1904)

Trevor-Roper, Hugh   *Catholics, Anglicans and Puritans. Seventeenth-Century Essays.* (Chicago, 1988)

Wall, Thomas   'Irish Enterprise in the University of Paris (1651-1653)', *I.E.R.*, 5/64 (1944), 94-106, 159-72

___   'Parnassus in Waterford', *I.E.R.* 8/64 (1947), 730-749

Walsh, T. J.   'The Irish College at Bordeaux'. *Journal of the Cork Historical and Archaeological Society* Lii (1947), 10-25

Walton, Julian   *The Royal Charters of Waterford* (Waterford, 1992)

Wedgwood, C. V.   *The King's Peace 1637-1641* (London, 1966)

Index

Durante, Bishop Gonsalvo, 39

Edmundus Ursulanus (Frances Matthew),
  88, 89, 93, 132
Enniskillen, Tower of, 182
Enos, Walter, Priest, Canon Lawyer, 172
Everard, Edmond, 76, 77, 78
Everard, Joseph O.F.M. Waterford, 172
Fagan, Nicholas, O. Cist., 35-36
Faithlegg, 12
Falkland, Lord Deputy, 55, 57
Ferbane, Pronouncement of
  Excommunication, 30 May 1648, 168
Fitzgerald Family, 4, 48
Fitzharris, Laurence, O. Cist., 72
Flaghey (Flahy, Flaghy), John, Teacher, 16,
  17, 40, 52
Fleming, Maurice, Priest, 'Anacoretis',
  Lismore, 154
Fleming, Thomas O.F.M., Archbishop of
  Dublin, 46, 53, 65, 107, 131
Flight of the Earls 1607, 126, 148
Florence, 30
'Forus Feasa ar Éirinn', 27
La Fosse, Capuchin Convent in Nantes,
  Franciscans, 10
'Frates Cruciferi' Crutched Friars, 77
French, Bishop Nicholas, Ferns, 47, 163,
  174

Glamorgan, Earl of, 158-159
Goghe, John, S. J., Clonmel, 172
Greyfriars Abbey O.F.M., 10

Hackett, Michael, Priest, Precentor of
  Waterford Cathedral, 172
Hackett, Patrick Priest, 4
Hamilton, Archbishop Malcolm, Cashel, 54
Harris, Paul, 85, 87, 93, 94
Hartery, John, O. Cist., Waterford, 172
Hayes Family, 180
Henrietta Maria, Queen, wife of King
  Charles I, 54
Hickey, Anthony, O.F.M., Rome, 202, 203
Holy Ghost Hospital, Waterford, 13
Holy Office, 74, 128, 132
Hospices, 12
Hospitals, 12
Howlin, John, S.J., 27

St. Ignatius of Loyola, 78
Inchiquin Truce, May 1648, 167-169
Ingoli, Francesco, 74, 105
Inishlounaght (de Surio), Abbey, 9, 72
'Inquisition of a Sermon', 32-34
Invernizi, Carlo, 161
Ireton, General Henry, 179, 180
Isabella, Archduchess, Spain, 41
St. Isidore's College, Rome, 38, 130
'Ius Sepulturae', 56, 108, 109, 110, 111,
  136-137

Jesuits, 49-50, 78-82
St. John's Church (Within), 9
St. John's Church (Without), 9
St. John of Jerusalem, Order of, 76, 77, 78
Jones, Colonel Michael, Commander,
  Parliamentary Forces, Dublin, 166
Julius II, Pope, 145

Kearney, Archbishop, David, Cashel, 46
Keating, Paul, Priest, Chancellor of
  Lismore, 154
Kells Abbey, Kilkenny, 29, 30, 32-34
Kells, Co. Meath, 150, 151
Kenmare, 160
Kilbarry, 12
Kilcash, 48
Kilgobinet, 51
Kill, 9
Killea, 9
Killure, 12
Kilmacthomas, 179
Kilmeaden, 179
Kilmolash, 12
Kilmolleran, 155
Kilrossanty, 51
Kiltegan, 51
Kirwan, Bishop Francis, Killala, 47, 168,
  173
Knights Hospitallers, 12
Knights Templars, 12
Knocknanuss, Mallow, Battle of, 13 Nov.
  1647, 166
Knockraffin, 154

Lainich, Nicholas, S. J., 80
Lancaster, Bishop John, Waterford and
  Lismore, 51
La Fosse, Capuchin, Convent, Nantes, 181

St. Peter's Church, Waterford, 9, 80-82
Philadelphus, 86
Philalethes, 86
Plague in Waterford, 179, 180
Plantation of Connaught, 140
Plunkett, Sir Nicholas, Chairman of
  General Assembly, 151
Plunkett, Bishop Patrick O. Cist., Ardagh,
  47, 167, 168
Plunkett Thomas, 86
Pole, Cardinal Reginald, 42, 102, 104, 105
Power, Patrick, 15-16, 49, 72, 155
Power, Robert, Dean of Waterford, 155,
  172
Prendergast, Thomas D.D., Clonmel, 172
Preston, Colonel Thomas, 160, 165, 166

'Quarta Canonica' 137
'Quarta Funeraria' 109

Rafter, Thomas, S. J., 80
Ragged, Paul, O. Cist., 74
Raleigh, Sir Walter, 48
Rathgormack, 71
Relatio Status, 138-147 passim
Rennison, William, 51
Richelieu, Cardinal, 160
Rinuccini, Archbishop, 160-178 passim
Roche, John, Bishop Ferns, 47, 68, 69, 77,
  107, 129, 136
Roma, Cardinal Guilio, Member of
  Congregation of Irish Affairs, Rome, 174
'Romerunners', 8
Rothe, David, Bishop Ossory, 46, 53, 63,
  91, 119, 120, 127, 173

Salamanca, 26
Sall, Andrew, S. J., 80, 82
Salmeron, Alfonso, S. J., 78
St. Malo, 180
Santiago, 26
St. Saviour's Priory, Waterford, 10
Scarampi, Pier Francesco, 149, 157, 161
Scarrifhollis, Battle of, June 1650, 161
Secretariat of Briefs, Rome, 74, 107, 131
Seville, 26
Shanrahan, 51
Sherlock Family, 2
Sherlock, Patrick, S. J., Compostella, 40
St. Silvestro al Quirinale, 38-39

Smith, Richard, Bishop of Chalcedon, 61,
  88
Sorbonne Propositions, 83-94 passim
St. Stephen's Church, Waterford, 9, 12
Stanihurst, Richard, 4, 18
Strange, Peter, O.P., Waterford, 172
Strange, Pierse, S. J., 80
Strange, Richard, O.S.A., 28, 90
Strange, Thomas, O.F.M., 40, 75, 83, 84,
  85, 86, 120, 153, 155
Suarez, Francesco, 29
Swords Parish, Dublin, 85
Synods, 53, 127

Taaffe, Theobold, Earl of Carlingford, 166
St. Thomas of Acon, Order of, 12
Tirry, Bishop William, Cork and Cloyne,
  46, 119-120
Tobin, James, Spy, 27
Torniellus, Curial Official, Rome, 130
Travers, Walter, Priest, 76-77
Trent, Council of, 24-25, 43-45, 63, 116-
  118
Trinitarian Order, 34
Tullaghorton, 51

Urban VIII, Pope, (1623-48), 59
Urbs Intacta, 6
Ussher, Archbishop James, Armagh, 54
Vais, Bishop Benedicto, 39
Verdier, Mercure, S. J., Visitor sent to
  Ireland 1648, 173
Vicars Apostolic, 35, 46, 66, 187, 190
'Vindication of the Clergy', June 1648,
  172-173
'Viri Docti', 103
Vitelleschi, Mario S.J., 49

Wadding, Ambrose, S.J., Dilingen, 5
Wadding, Luke, O.F.M., Rome, 15, 17, 26,
  37, 38, 40, 41, 57, 58, 60, 72, 73, 74, 75,
  76, 77, 83, 84, 85, 87, 90, 91, 92, 99,
  102, 103, 113, 114, 116, 120, 130, 135,
  136, 153, 154, 155, 160, 167, 176
Wadding, Luke, S.J., Compostella,
  Valladolid and Dilingen, 40
Wadding (Godinez), Michael S.J., Mexico,
  5
Wadding, Peter, S.J., Louvain, Prague, 5
Wadding, Richard, O.S.A., Coimbra, 28

231

Wadding, Robert, Waterford, 164
Wall Family, 180
Walsh, James, S.J., 82
Walsh, John, Priest, Spain, 40
Walsh, Martin, Priest, Naples and Rome,
    40
Walsh, Nicholas, Bishop of Ossory, 42
Walsh, Patrick, Bishop of Waterford and
    Lismore, 35, 42, 50
Walsh, Peter, O.F.M., Kilkenny, 173
Walsh, Thomas, Vicar Apostolic,
    Waterford, (1613-1626), 36, 46, 47
    Archbishop of Cashel, (1626-1652),
    112-124 passim
Weatherhead (Whalley), Bishop Thomas,
    Waterford and Lismore, 51
Wentworth (later Earl of Strafford),
    Thomas, Lord Deputy, 139-142
Wexford, 1, 2, 4, 21, 27, 180, 186
White, James, Vicar Apostolic, Waterford
    and Lismore (1600-1613), 19-23, 35
White, John, Vicar Apostolic, Waterford
    and Lismore (1568-1600), 35
White, Peter, Dean, Teacher, 18-19
White, Stephen, S.J., Spain and Ireland, 4
White, Thomas, S.J., Salamanca, Seville,
    Santiago, 4, 26
White, Thomas, Vicar of Clonmel, 172
Wolfe, David, S.J., 25, 79-80
Woodlock Family, 40
Woodlock, James, Mayor of Waterford, 55
Wise, Francis, 156
Wise, William, Chancellor of Waterford
    Cathedral, 155
Wiseman, Cardinal Nicholas, Westminster,
    46
Wyse, Andrew, 40
Wyse, William, 9

Youghal, 179